the DOLLHOUSE family

the DOLLHOUSE family

M.R. CAREY WRITER

PETER GROSS LAYOUTS

VINCE LOCKE FINISHES

CRIS PETER COLORIST **TODD KLEIN** LETTERER

JESSICA DALVA COLLECTION COVER ARTIST

THE DOLLHOUSE FAMILY CREATED BY
M.R. CAREY AND **PETER GROSS**

CURATED FOR **HILL HOUSE COMICS** BY **JOE HILL**

THE DOLLHOUSE FAMILY

DC COMICS, 2900 WEST ALAMEDA AVE., BURBANK, CA 91505

PRINTED BY TRANSCONTINENTAL INTERGLOBE, BEAUCEVILLE, QC, CANADA. 9/4/20. FIRST PRINTING.

ISBN: 978-1-77950-464-7

LIBRARY OF CONGRESS CATALOGING-IN-PUBLICATION DATA IS AVAILABLE.

PEFC Certified

This product is from sustainably managed forests and controlled sources

PEFC/01-31-106   www.pefc.org

CHRIS CONROY EDITOR – ORIGINAL SERIES
MAGGIE HOWELL ASSISTANT EDITOR – ORIGINAL SERIES
JEB WOODARD GROUP EDITOR – COLLECTED EDITIONS
ERIKA ROTHBERG EDITOR – COLLECTED EDITION
STEVE COOK DESIGN DIRECTOR – BOOKS
AMIE BROCKWAY-METCALF PUBLICATION DESIGN
SUZANNAH ROWNTREE PUBLICATION PRODUCTION

BOB HARRAS SENIOR VP – EDITOR-IN-CHIEF, DC COMICS

JIM LEE PUBLISHER & CHIEF CREATIVE OFFICER
BOBBIE CHASE VP – GLOBAL PUBLISHING INITIATIVES & DIGITAL STRATEGY
DON FALLETTI VP – MANUFACTURING OPERATIONS & WORKFLOW MANAGEMENT
LAWRENCE GANEM VP – TALENT SERVICES
ALISON GILL SENIOR VP – MANUFACTURING & OPERATIONS
HANK KANALZ SENIOR VP – PUBLISHING STRATEGY & SUPPORT SERVICES
DAN MIRON VP – PUBLISHING OPERATIONS
NICK J. NAPOLITANO VP – MANUFACTURING ADMINISTRATION & DESIGN
NANCY SPEARS VP – SALES
JONAH WEILAND VP – MARKETING & CREATIVE SERVICES
MICHELE R. WELLS VP & EXECUTIVE EDITOR, YOUNG READER

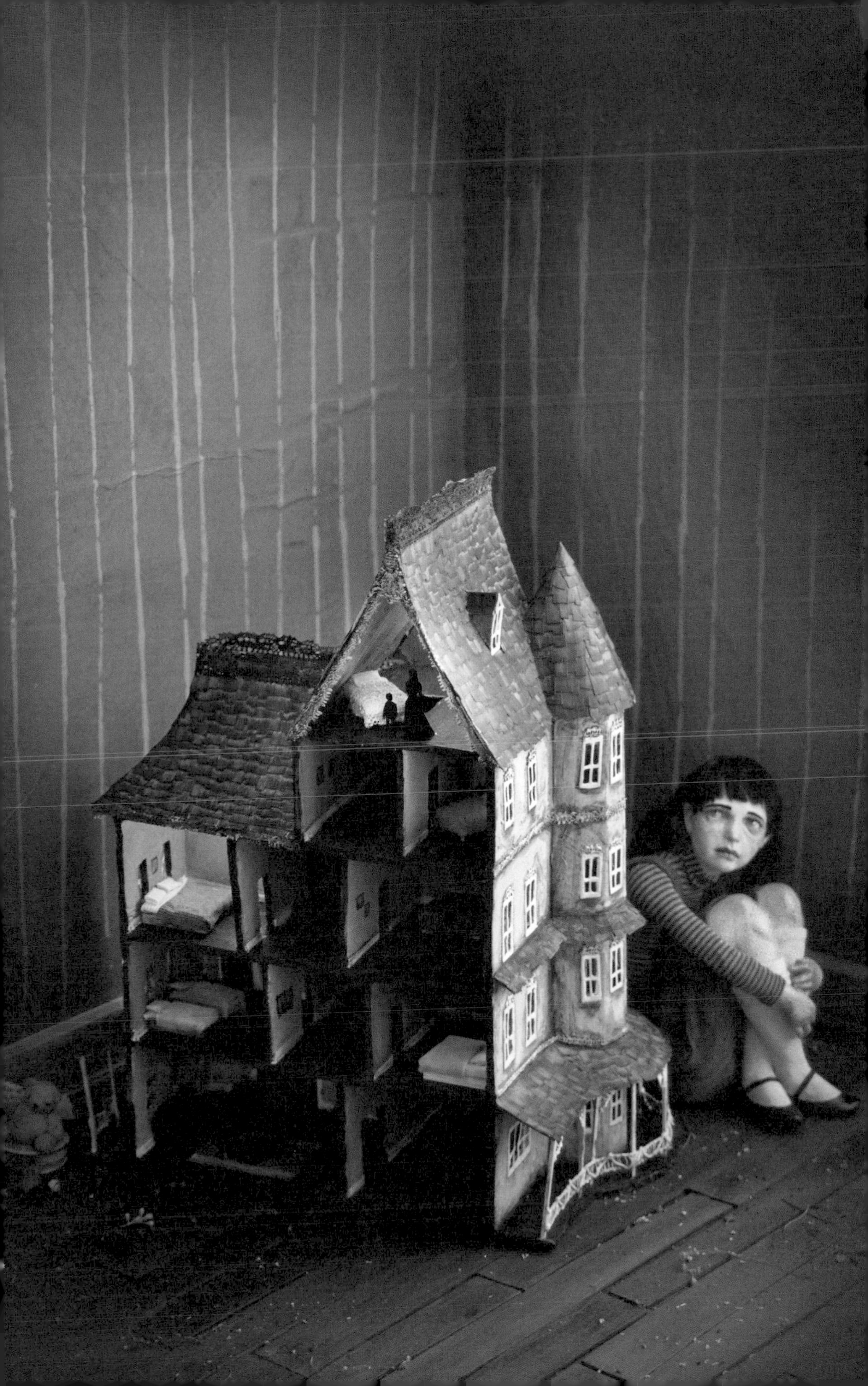

ONE BY ONE
GO DOWN

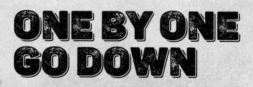

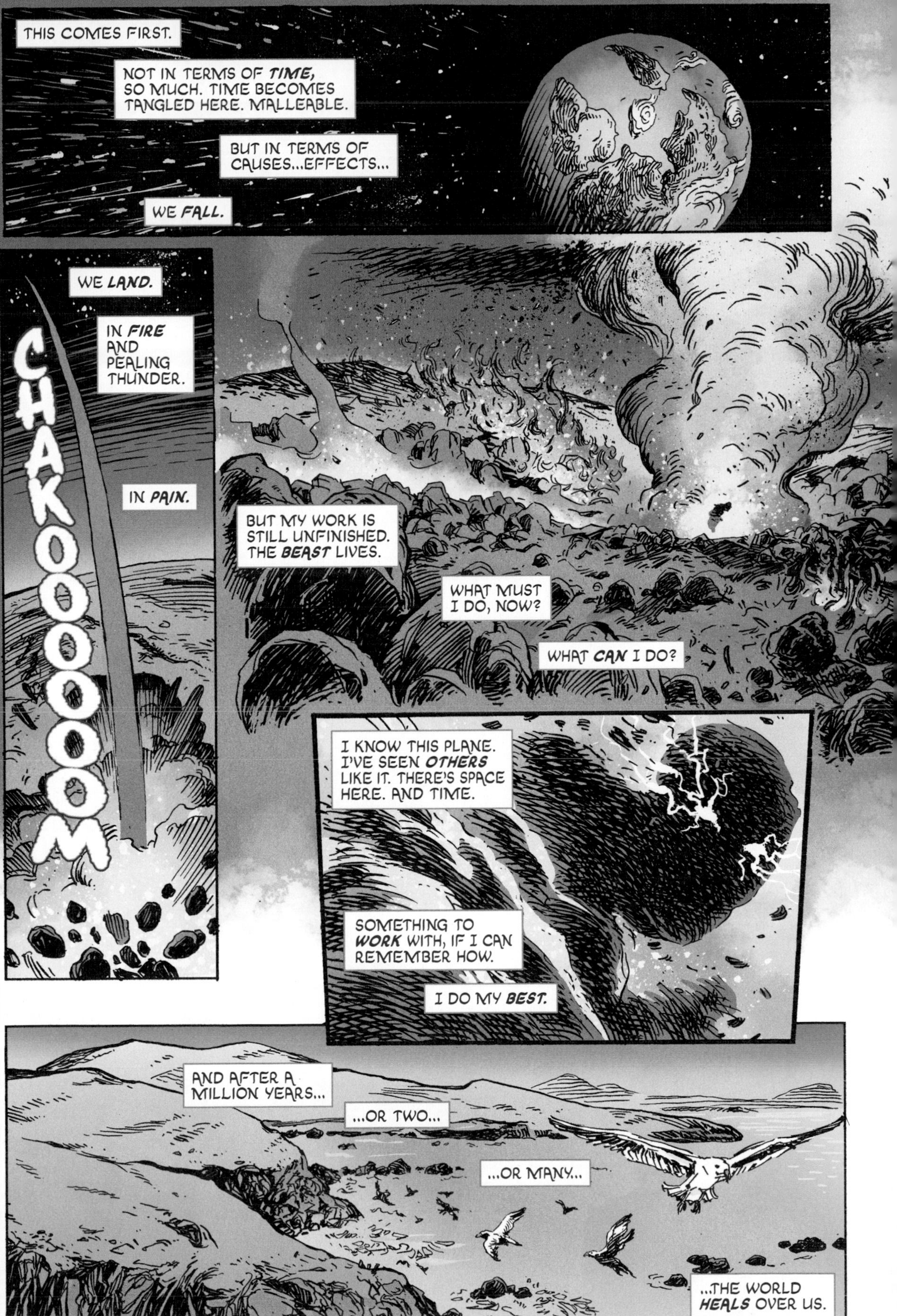
THIS COMES FIRST.
NOT IN TERMS OF *TIME*, SO MUCH. TIME BECOMES TANGLED HERE. MALLEABLE.
BUT IN TERMS OF CAUSES...EFFECTS...
WE *FALL*.
WE *LAND*.
IN *FIRE* AND PEALING THUNDER.
CHAKOOOOOOM
IN *PAIN*.
BUT MY WORK IS STILL UNFINISHED. THE *BEAST* LIVES.
WHAT MUST I DO, NOW?
WHAT *CAN* I DO?
I KNOW THIS PLANE. I'VE SEEN *OTHERS* LIKE IT. THERE'S SPACE HERE. AND TIME.
SOMETHING TO *WORK* WITH, IF I CAN REMEMBER HOW.
I DO MY *BEST*.
AND AFTER A MILLION YEARS...
...OR TWO...
...OR MANY...
...THE WORLD *HEALS* OVER US.

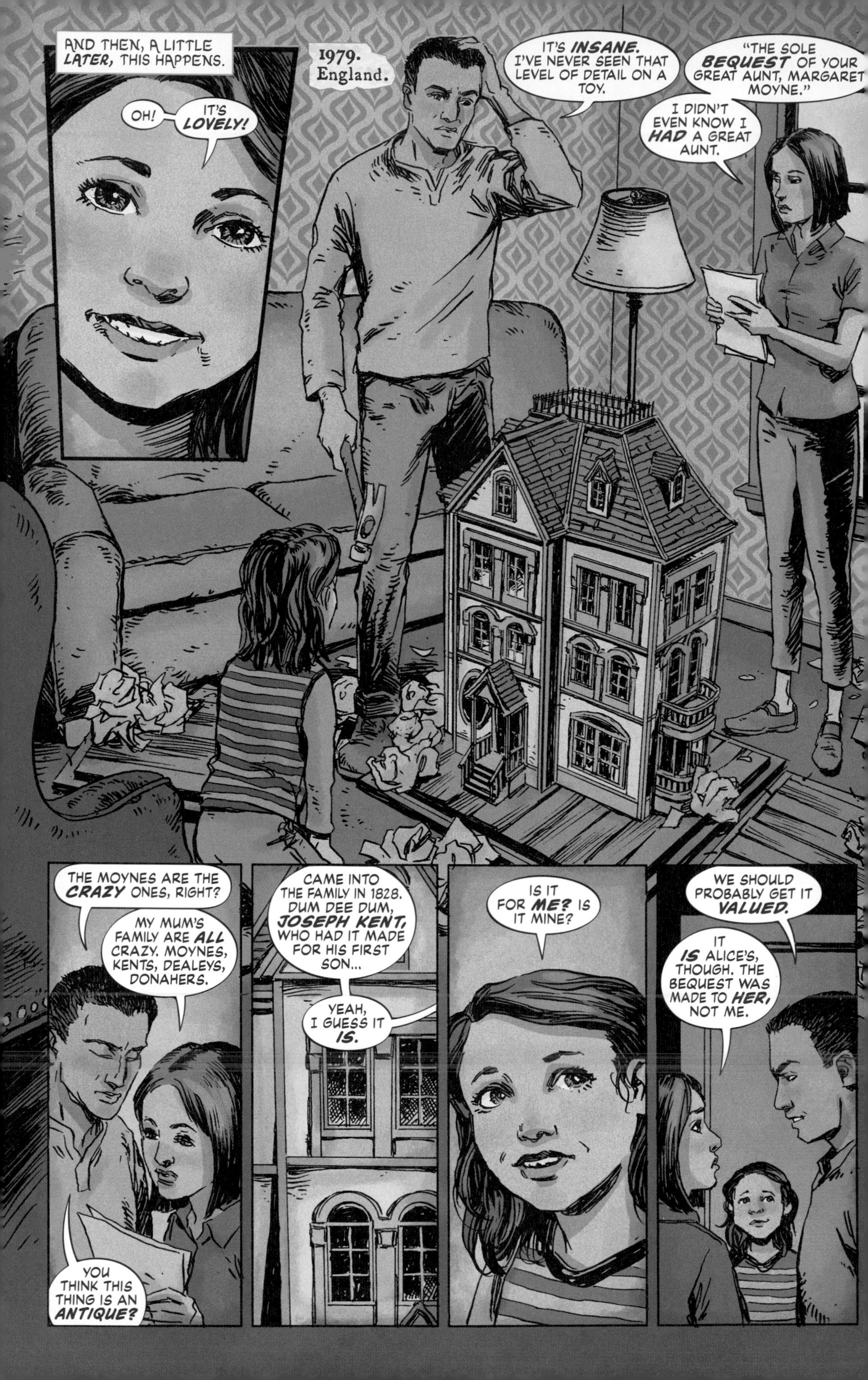
AND THEN, A LITTLE LATER, THIS HAPPENS.
OH!
IT'S LOVELY!
1979. England.
IT'S INSANE. I'VE NEVER SEEN THAT LEVEL OF DETAIL ON A TOY.
"THE SOLE BEQUEST OF YOUR GREAT AUNT, MARGARET MOYNE."
I DIDN'T EVEN KNOW I HAD A GREAT AUNT.
THE MOYNES ARE THE CRAZY ONES, RIGHT?
MY MUM'S FAMILY ARE ALL CRAZY. MOYNES, KENTS, DEALEYS, DONAHERS.
YOU THINK THIS THING IS AN ANTIQUE?
CAME INTO THE FAMILY IN 1828. DUM DEE DUM, JOSEPH KENT, WHO HAD IT MADE FOR HIS FIRST SON...
YEAH, I GUESS IT IS.
IS IT FOR ME? IS IT MINE?
WE SHOULD PROBABLY GET IT VALUED.
IT IS ALICE'S, THOUGH. THE BEQUEST WAS MADE TO HER, NOT ME.

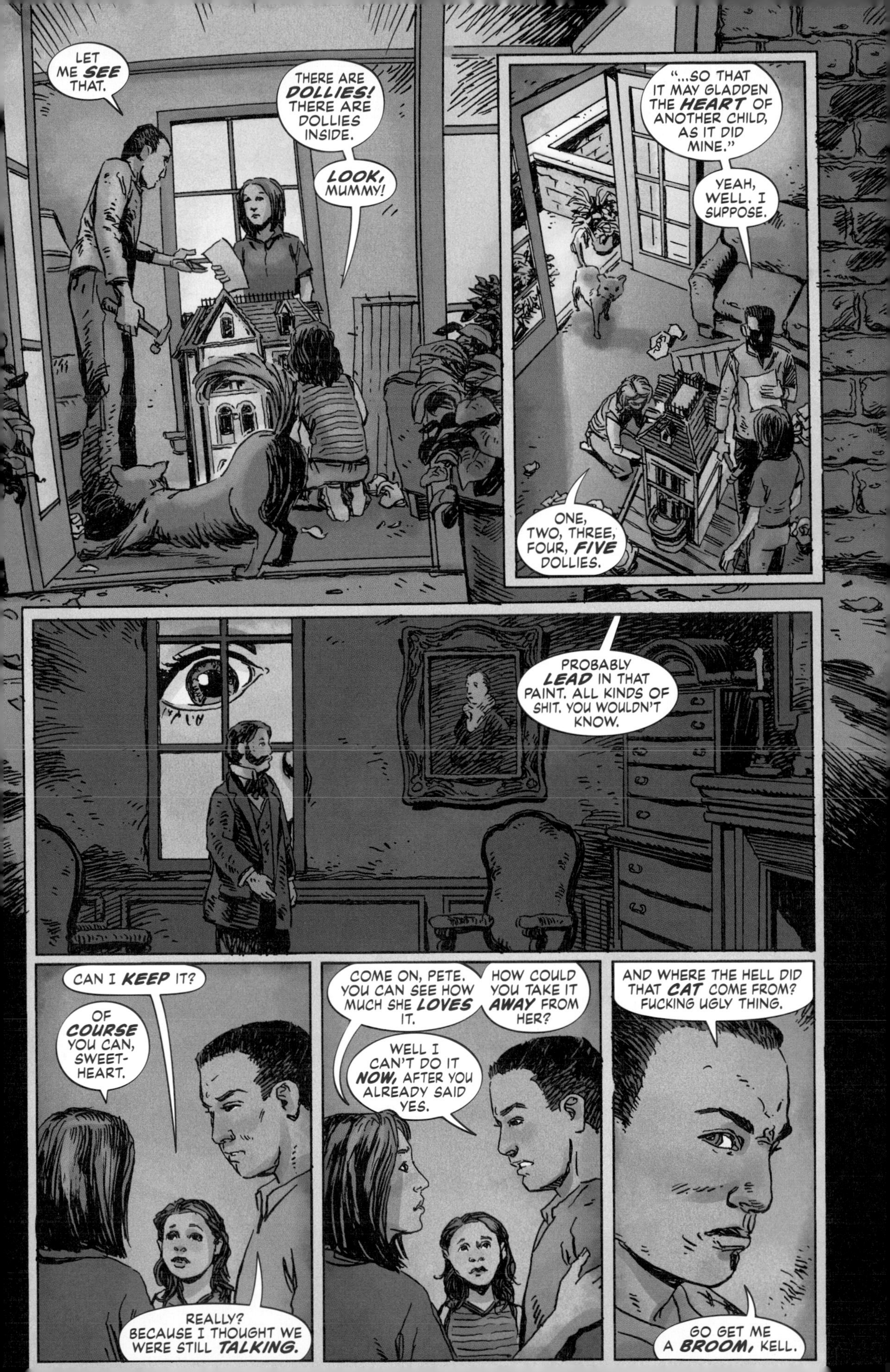
LET ME **SEE** THAT.
THERE ARE **DOLLIES!** THERE ARE DOLLIES INSIDE.
LOOK, MUMMY!
"...SO THAT IT MAY GLADDEN THE **HEART** OF ANOTHER CHILD, AS IT DID MINE."
YEAH, WELL. I SUPPOSE.
ONE, TWO, THREE, FOUR, **FIVE** DOLLIES.
PROBABLY **LEAD** IN THAT PAINT. ALL KINDS OF SHIT. YOU WOULDN'T KNOW.
CAN I **KEEP** IT?
OF **COURSE** YOU CAN, SWEET-HEART.
REALLY? BECAUSE I THOUGHT WE WERE STILL **TALKING.**
COME ON, PETE. YOU CAN SEE HOW MUCH SHE **LOVES** IT.
HOW COULD YOU TAKE IT **AWAY** FROM HER?
WELL I CAN'T DO IT **NOW,** AFTER YOU ALREADY SAID YES.
AND WHERE THE HELL DID THAT **CAT** COME FROM? FUCKING UGLY THING.
GO GET ME A **BROOM,** KELL.

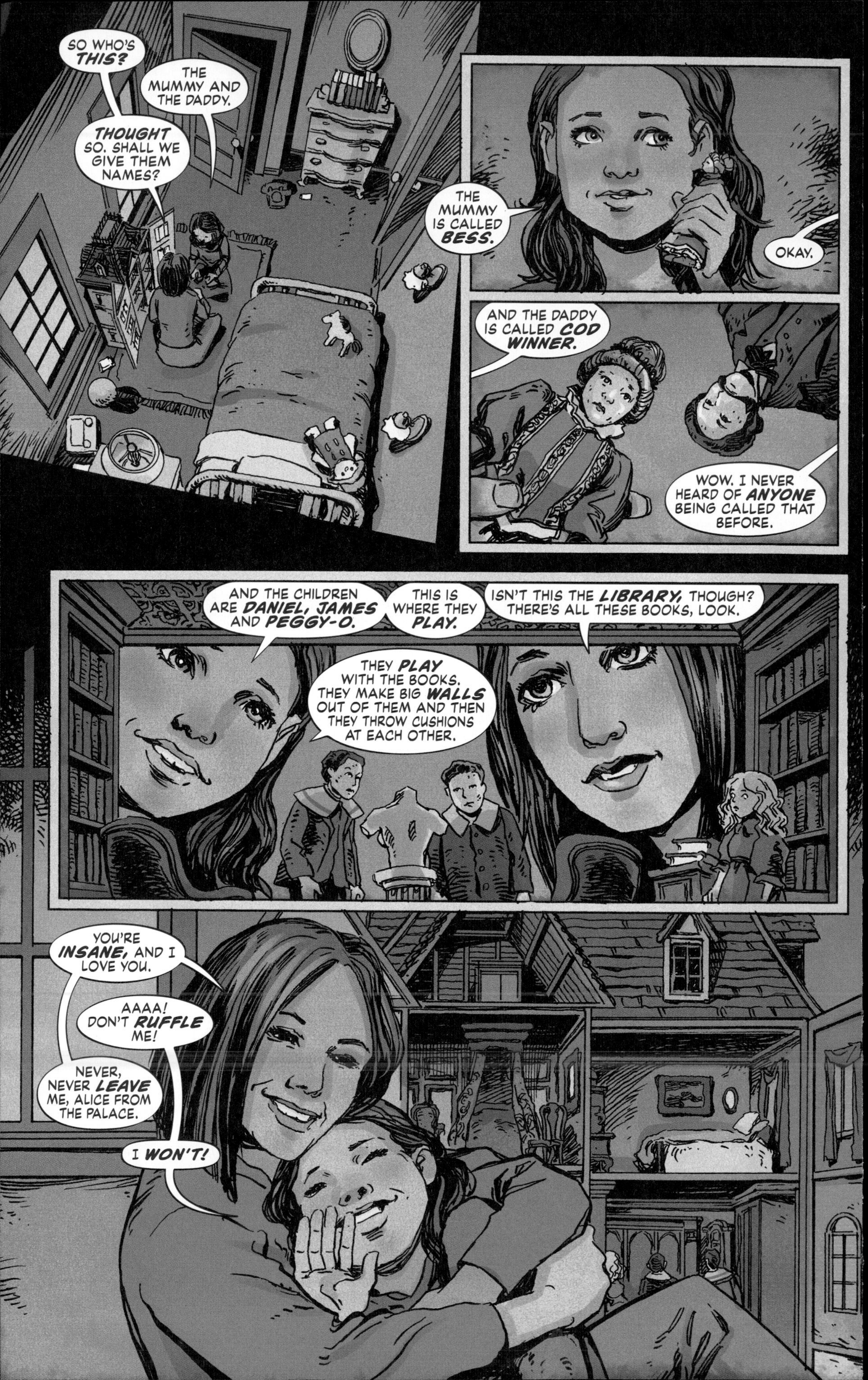
SO WHO'S THIS?
THE MUMMY AND THE DADDY.
THOUGHT SO. SHALL WE GIVE THEM NAMES?
THE MUMMY IS CALLED BESS.
OKAY.
AND THE DADDY IS CALLED COD WINNER.
WOW. I NEVER HEARD OF ANYONE BEING CALLED THAT BEFORE.
AND THE CHILDREN ARE DANIEL, JAMES AND PEGGY-O.
THIS IS WHERE THEY PLAY.
ISN'T THIS THE LIBRARY, THOUGH? THERE'S ALL THESE BOOKS, LOOK.
THEY PLAY WITH THE BOOKS. THEY MAKE BIG WALLS OUT OF THEM AND THEN THEY THROW CUSHIONS AT EACH OTHER.
YOU'RE INSANE, AND I LOVE YOU.
AAAA! DON'T RUFFLE ME!
NEVER, NEVER LEAVE ME, ALICE FROM THE PALACE.
I WON'T!

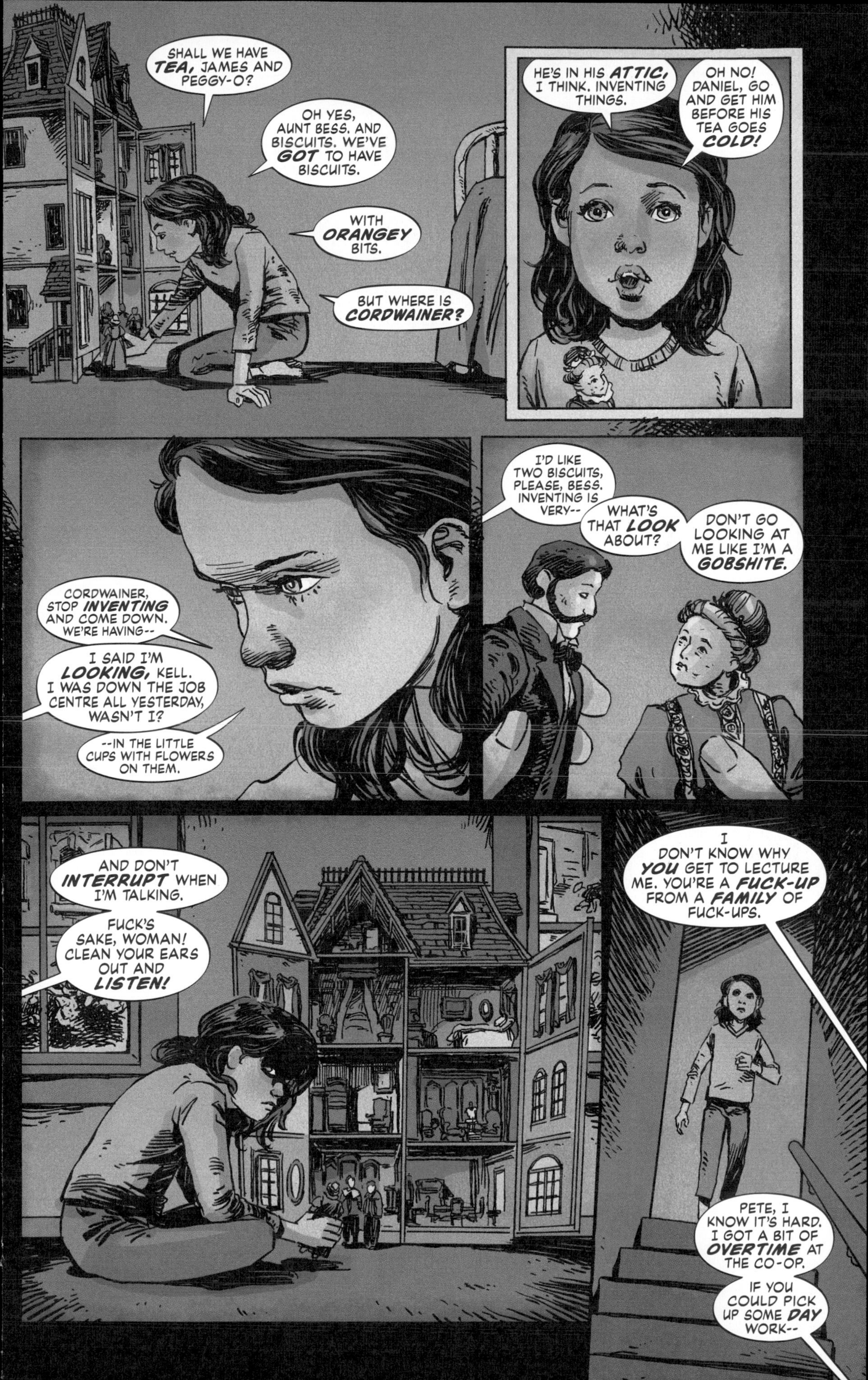
SHALL WE HAVE TEA, JAMES AND PEGGY-O?
OH YES, AUNT BESS. AND BISCUITS. WE'VE GOT TO HAVE BISCUITS.
WITH ORANGEY BITS.
BUT WHERE IS CORDWAINER?
HE'S IN HIS ATTIC, I THINK. INVENTING THINGS.
OH NO! DANIEL, GO AND GET HIM BEFORE HIS TEA GOES COLD!
CORDWAINER, STOP INVENTING AND COME DOWN. WE'RE HAVING--
I SAID I'M LOOKING, KELL. I WAS DOWN THE JOB CENTRE ALL YESTERDAY, WASN'T I?
--IN THE LITTLE CUPS WITH FLOWERS ON THEM.
I'D LIKE TWO BISCUITS, PLEASE, BESS. INVENTING IS VERY--
WHAT'S THAT LOOK ABOUT?
DON'T GO LOOKING AT ME LIKE I'M A GOBSHITE.
AND DON'T INTERRUPT WHEN I'M TALKING.
FUCK'S SAKE, WOMAN! CLEAN YOUR EARS OUT AND LISTEN!
I DON'T KNOW WHY YOU GET TO LECTURE ME. YOU'RE A FUCK-UP FROM A FAMILY OF FUCK-UPS.
PETE, I KNOW IT'S HARD. I GOT A BIT OF OVERTIME AT THE CO-OP.
IF YOU COULD PICK UP SOME DAY WORK--

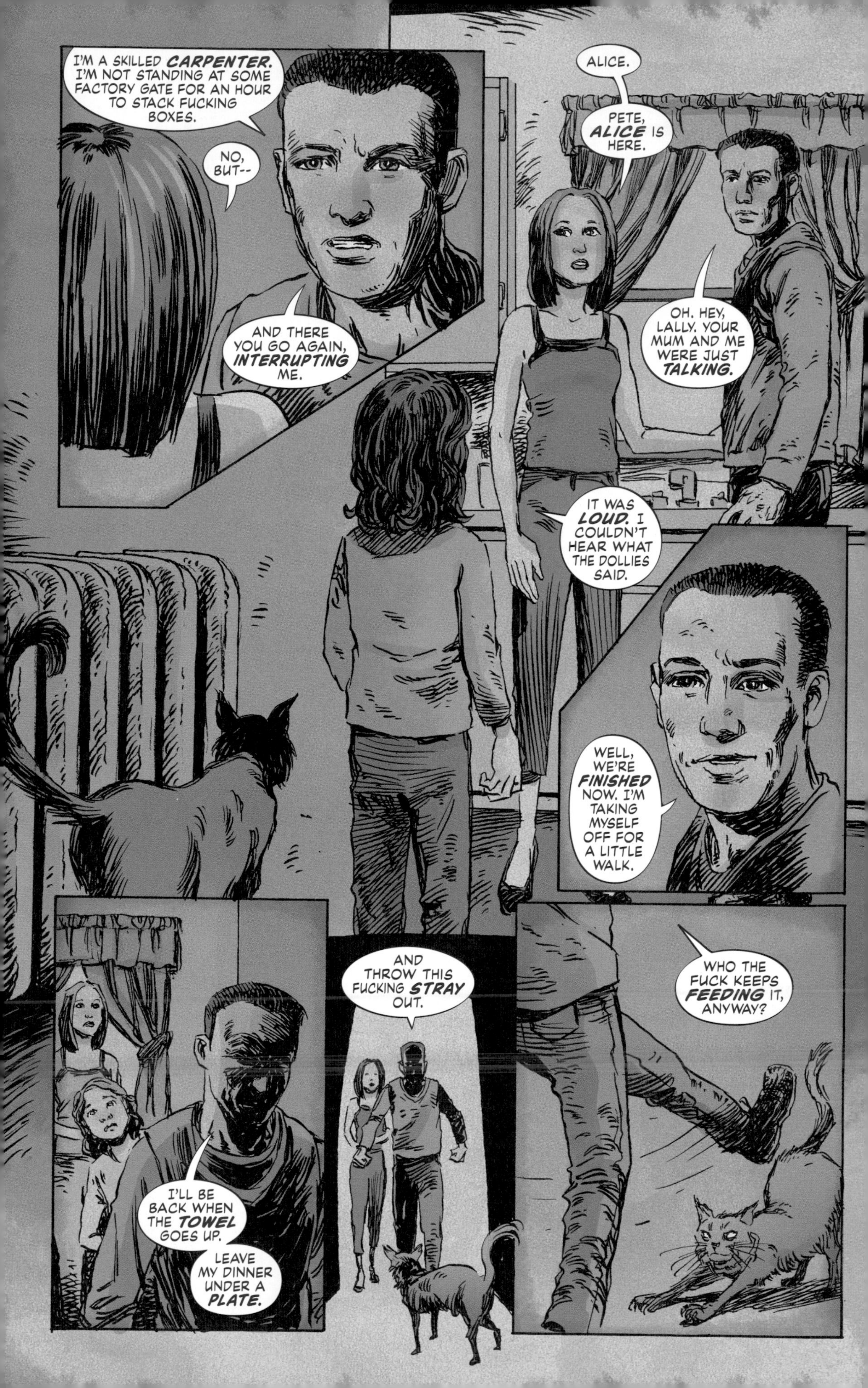
I'M A SKILLED CARPENTER. I'M NOT STANDING AT SOME FACTORY GATE FOR AN HOUR TO STACK FUCKING BOXES.
NO, BUT--
AND THERE YOU GO AGAIN, INTERRUPTING ME.
ALICE.
PETE, ALICE IS HERE.
OH. HEY, LALLY. YOUR MUM AND ME WERE JUST TALKING.
IT WAS LOUD. I COULDN'T HEAR WHAT THE DOLLIES SAID.
WELL, WE'RE FINISHED NOW. I'M TAKING MYSELF OFF FOR A LITTLE WALK.
I'LL BE BACK WHEN THE TOWEL GOES UP.
LEAVE MY DINNER UNDER A PLATE.
AND THROW THIS FUCKING STRAY OUT.
WHO THE FUCK KEEPS FEEDING IT, ANYWAY?

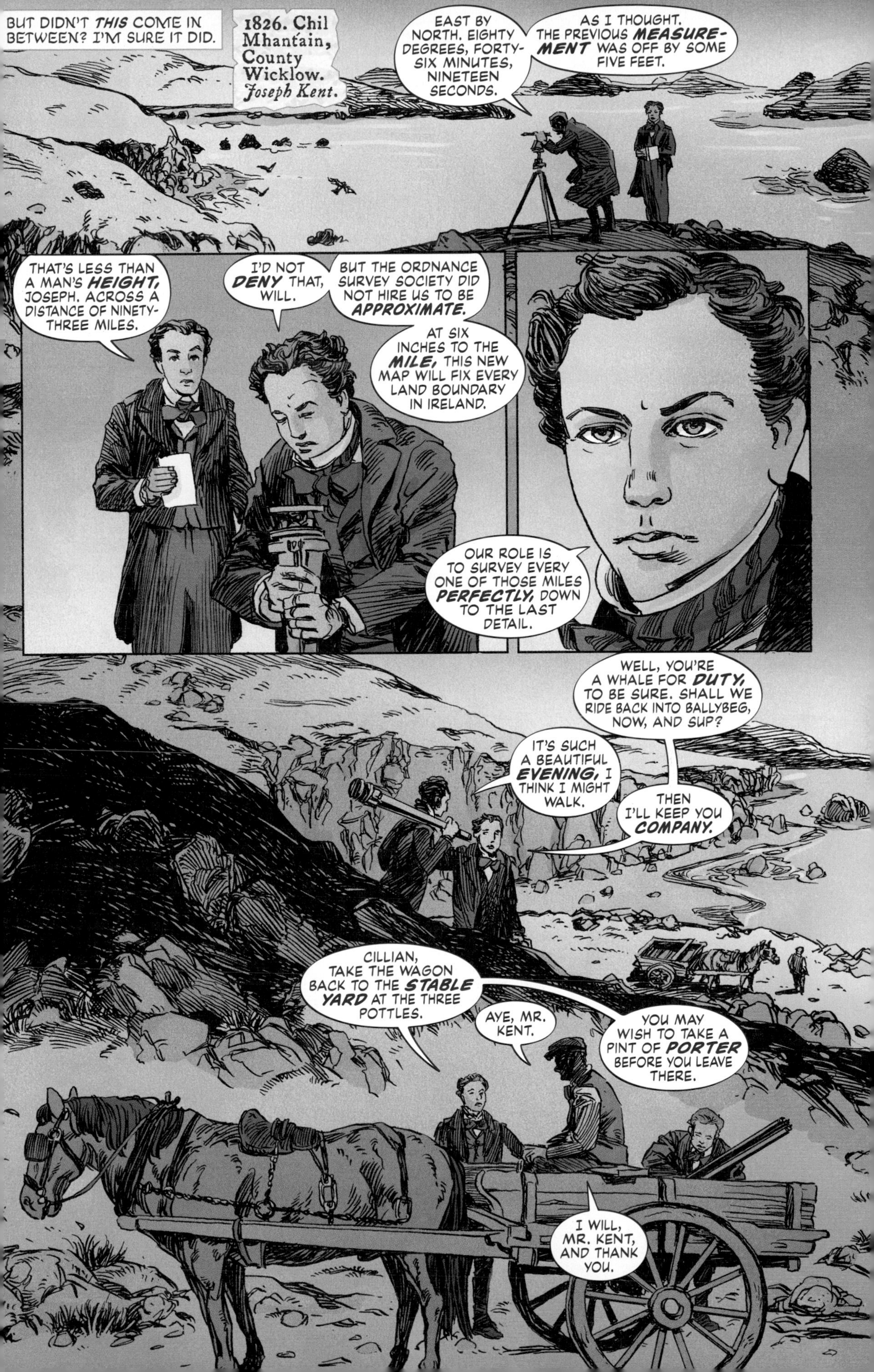

BUT DIDN'T THIS COME IN BETWEEN? I'M SURE IT DID.
1826. Chil Mhantáin, County Wicklow. Joseph Kent.
EAST BY NORTH. EIGHTY DEGREES, FORTY-SIX MINUTES, NINETEEN SECONDS.
AS I THOUGHT. THE PREVIOUS MEASUREMENT WAS OFF BY SOME FIVE FEET.
THAT'S LESS THAN A MAN'S HEIGHT, JOSEPH. ACROSS A DISTANCE OF NINETY-THREE MILES.
I'D NOT DENY THAT, WILL.
BUT THE ORDNANCE SURVEY SOCIETY DID NOT HIRE US TO BE APPROXIMATE.
AT SIX INCHES TO THE MILE, THIS NEW MAP WILL FIX EVERY LAND BOUNDARY IN IRELAND.
OUR ROLE IS TO SURVEY EVERY ONE OF THOSE MILES PERFECTLY, DOWN TO THE LAST DETAIL.
WELL, YOU'RE A WHALE FOR DUTY, TO BE SURE. SHALL WE RIDE BACK INTO BALLYBEG, NOW, AND SUP?
IT'S SUCH A BEAUTIFUL EVENING, I THINK I MIGHT WALK.
THEN I'LL KEEP YOU COMPANY.
CILLIAN, TAKE THE WAGON BACK TO THE STABLE YARD AT THE THREE POTTLES.
AYE, MR. KENT.
YOU MAY WISH TO TAKE A PINT OF PORTER BEFORE YOU LEAVE THERE.
I WILL, MR. KENT, AND THANK YOU.

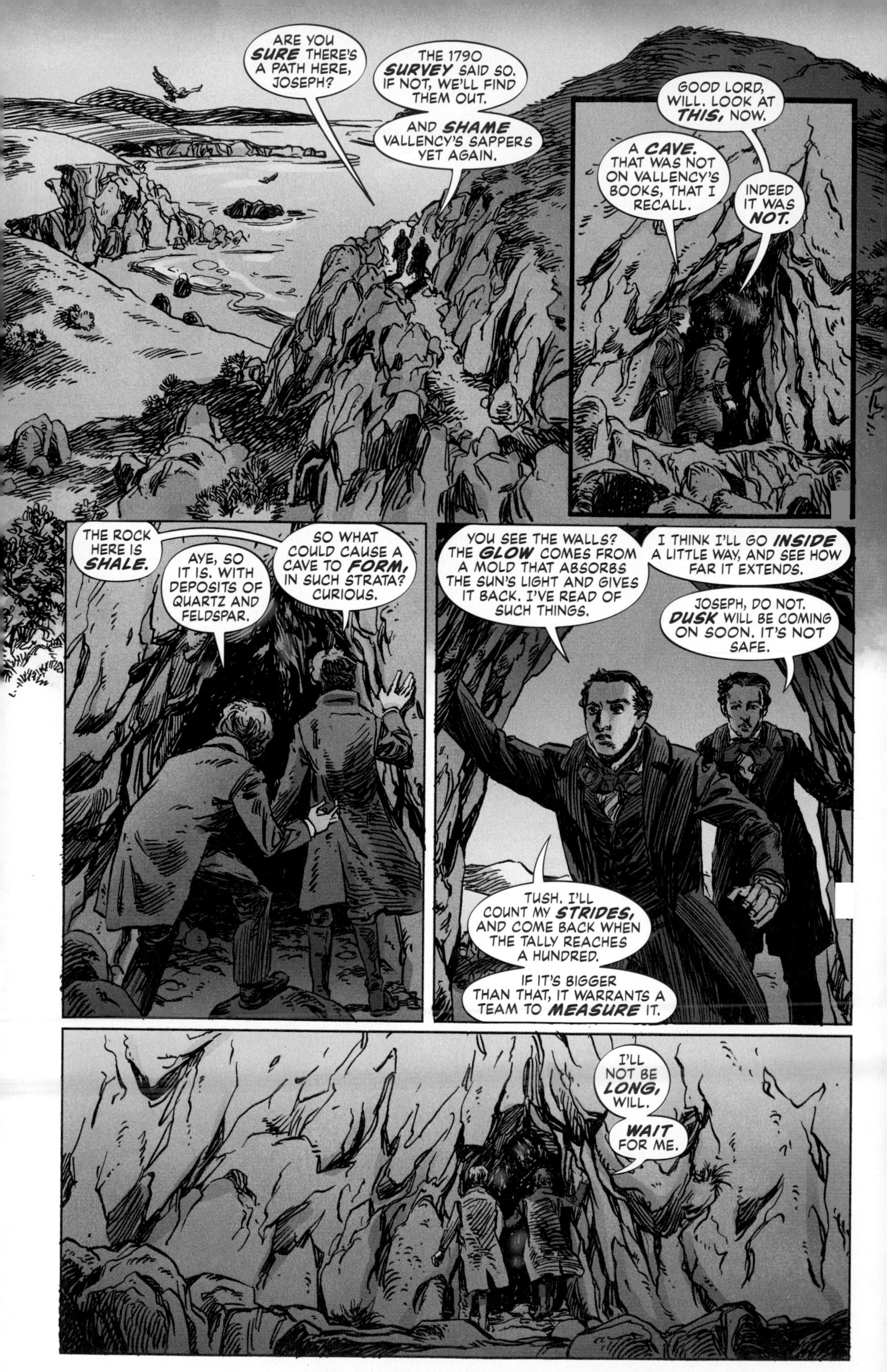
ARE YOU SURE THERE'S A PATH HERE, JOSEPH?
THE 1790 SURVEY SAID SO. IF NOT, WE'LL FIND THEM OUT.
AND SHAME VALLENCY'S SAPPERS YET AGAIN.
GOOD LORD, WILL. LOOK AT THIS, NOW.
A CAVE. THAT WAS NOT ON VALLENCY'S BOOKS, THAT I RECALL.
INDEED IT WAS NOT.
THE ROCK HERE IS SHALE.
AYE, SO IT IS. WITH DEPOSITS OF QUARTZ AND FELDSPAR.
SO WHAT COULD CAUSE A CAVE TO FORM, IN SUCH STRATA? CURIOUS.
YOU SEE THE WALLS? THE GLOW COMES FROM A MOLD THAT ABSORBS THE SUN'S LIGHT AND GIVES IT BACK. I'VE READ OF SUCH THINGS.
I THINK I'LL GO INSIDE A LITTLE WAY, AND SEE HOW FAR IT EXTENDS.
JOSEPH, DO NOT. DUSK WILL BE COMING ON SOON. IT'S NOT SAFE.
TUSH. I'LL COUNT MY STRIDES, AND COME BACK WHEN THE TALLY REACHES A HUNDRED.
IF IT'S BIGGER THAN THAT, IT WARRANTS A TEAM TO MEASURE IT.
I'LL NOT BE LONG, WILL.
WAIT FOR ME.

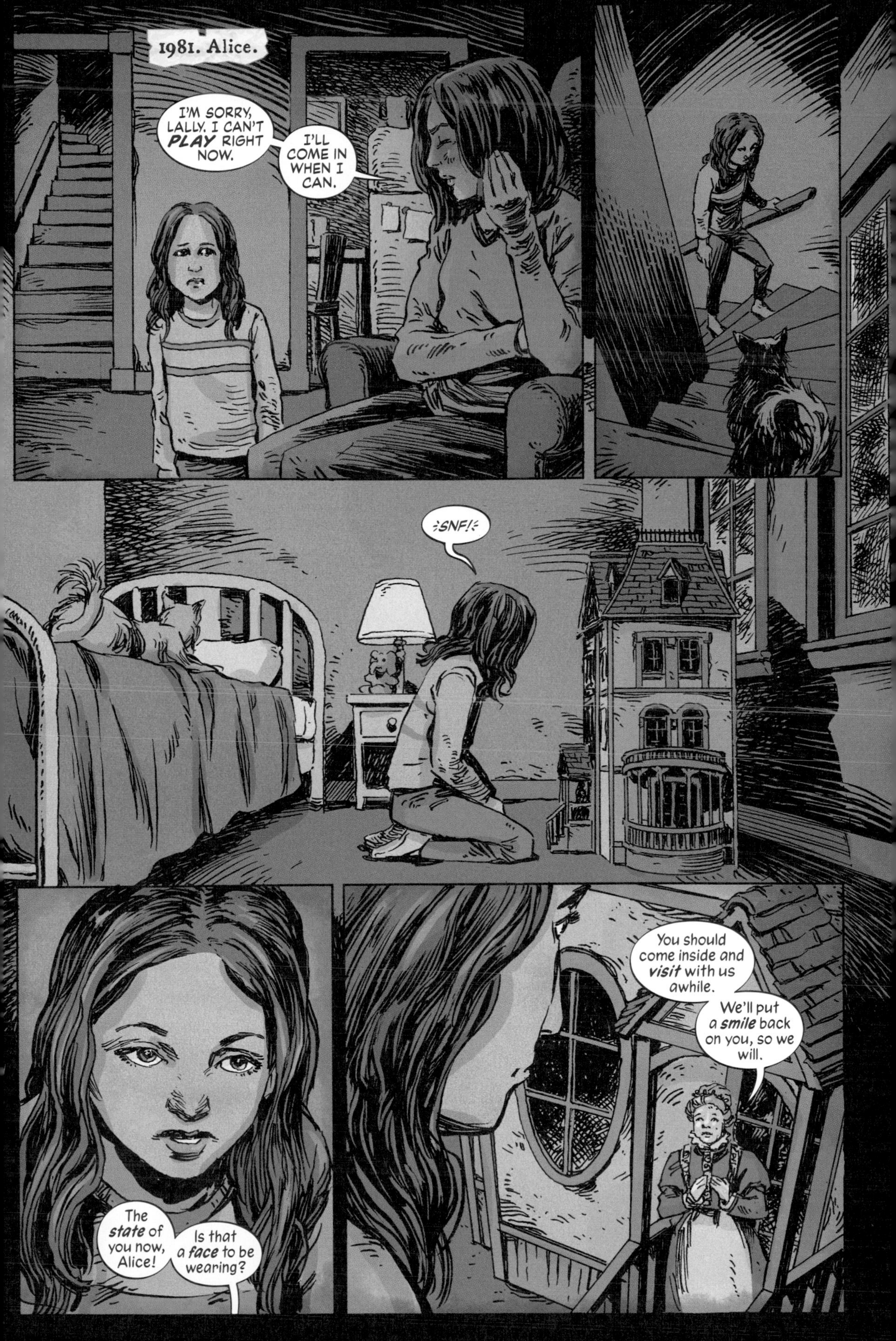
1981. Alice.
I'M SORRY, LALLY. I CAN'T PLAY RIGHT NOW.
I'LL COME IN WHEN I CAN.
SNF!
The state of you now, Alice!
Is that a face to be wearing?
You should come inside and visit with us awhile.
We'll put a smile back on you, so we will.

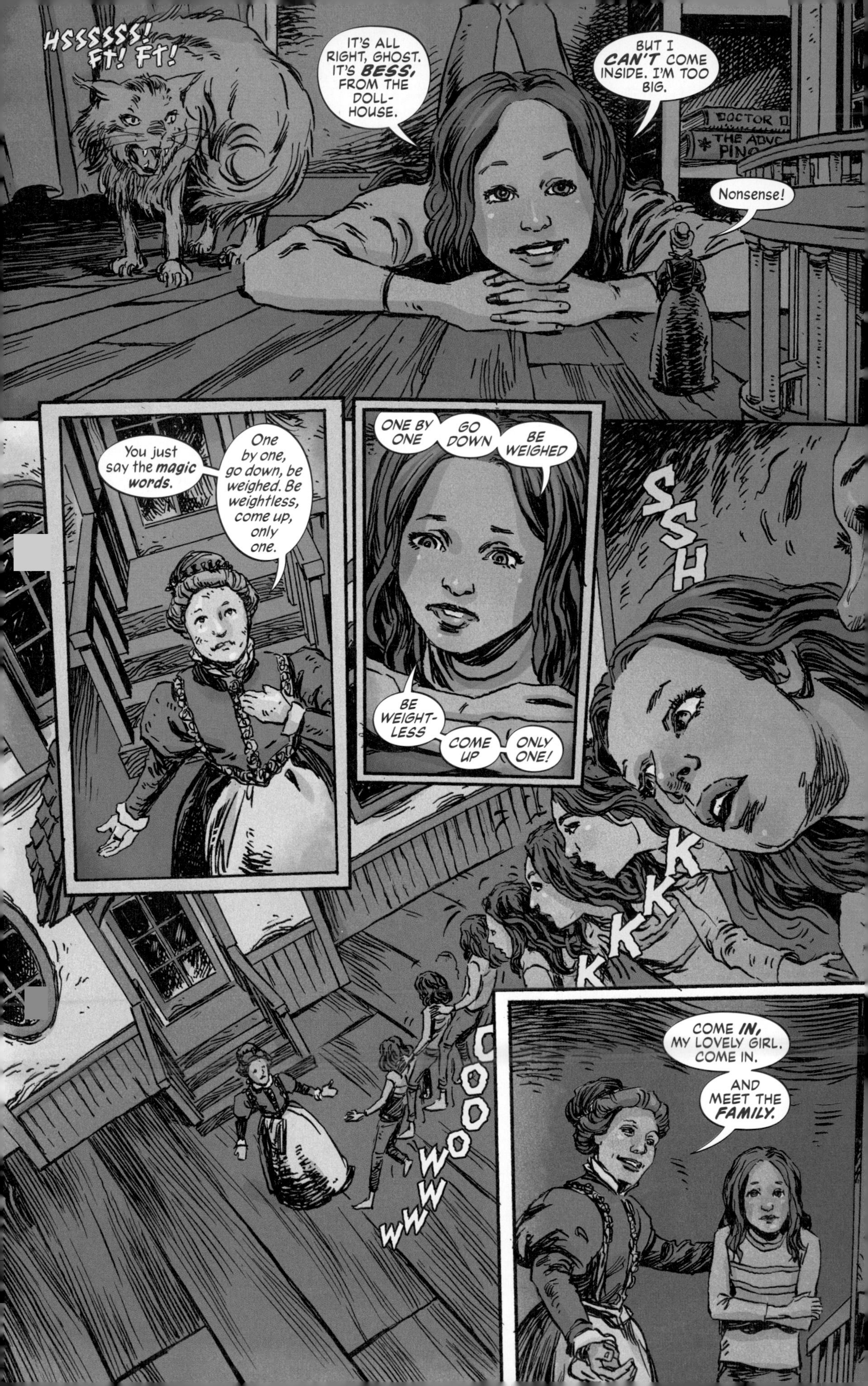
HSSSSSS! FT! FT!
IT'S ALL RIGHT, GHOST. IT'S **BESS,** FROM THE DOLL-HOUSE.
BUT I **CAN'T** COME INSIDE. I'M TOO BIG.
Nonsense!
You just say the **magic words**.
One by one, go down, be weighed. Be weightless, come up, only one.
ONE BY ONE
GO DOWN
BE WEIGHED
BE WEIGHT-LESS
COME UP
ONLY ONE!
SSH
KKKKK
WWWWOOOOO
COME **IN,** MY LOVELY GIRL. COME IN.
AND MEET THE **FAMILY.**

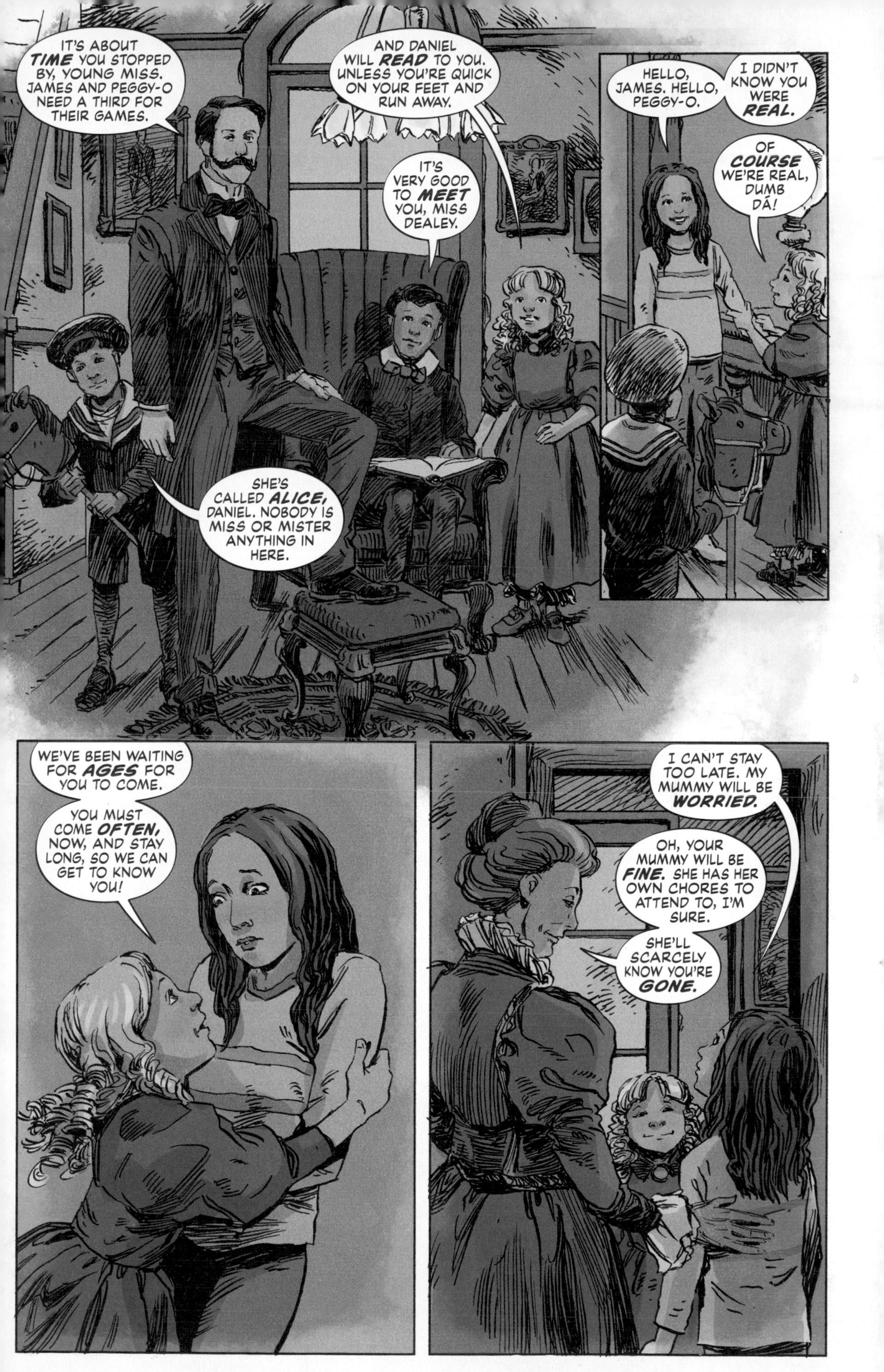
IT'S ABOUT TIME YOU STOPPED BY, YOUNG MISS. JAMES AND PEGGY-O NEED A THIRD FOR THEIR GAMES.
AND DANIEL WILL READ TO YOU. UNLESS YOU'RE QUICK ON YOUR FEET AND RUN AWAY.
IT'S VERY GOOD TO MEET YOU, MISS DEALEY.
SHE'S CALLED ALICE, DANIEL. NOBODY IS MISS OR MISTER ANYTHING IN HERE.
HELLO, JAMES. HELLO, PEGGY-O.
I DIDN'T KNOW YOU WERE REAL.
OF COURSE WE'RE REAL, DUMB DÁ!
WE'VE BEEN WAITING FOR AGES FOR YOU TO COME.
YOU MUST COME OFTEN, NOW, AND STAY LONG, SO WE CAN GET TO KNOW YOU!
I CAN'T STAY TOO LATE. MY MUMMY WILL BE WORRIED.
OH, YOUR MUMMY WILL BE FINE. SHE HAS HER OWN CHORES TO ATTEND TO, I'M SURE.
SHE'LL SCARCELY KNOW YOU'RE GONE.

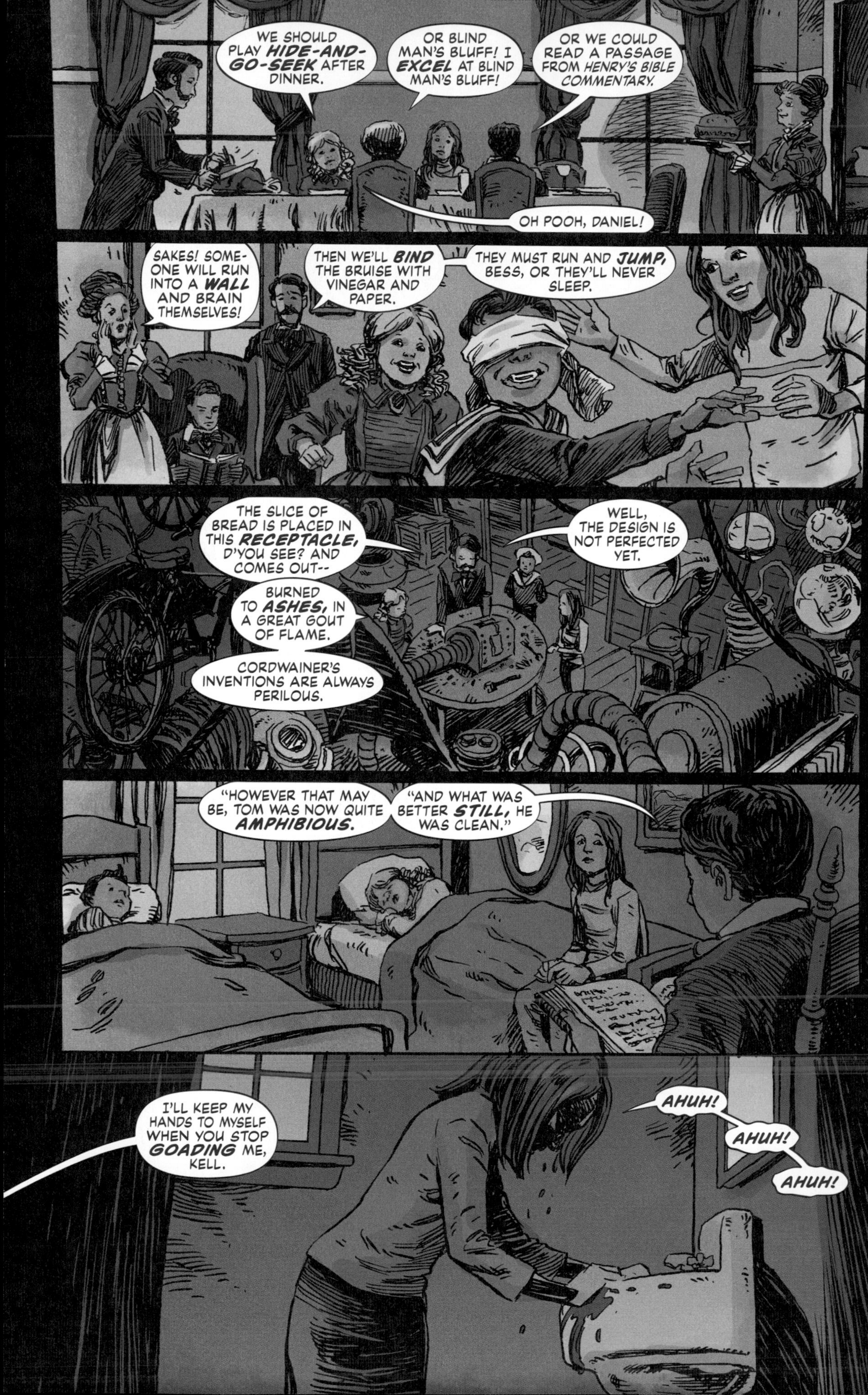
WE SHOULD PLAY HIDE-AND-GO-SEEK AFTER DINNER.
OR BLIND MAN'S BLUFF! I EXCEL AT BLIND MAN'S BLUFF!
OR WE COULD READ A PASSAGE FROM HENRY'S BIBLE COMMENTARY.
OH POOH, DANIEL!
SAKES! SOME-ONE WILL RUN INTO A WALL AND BRAIN THEMSELVES!
THEN WE'LL BIND THE BRUISE WITH VINEGAR AND PAPER.
THEY MUST RUN AND JUMP, BESS, OR THEY'LL NEVER SLEEP.
THE SLICE OF BREAD IS PLACED IN THIS RECEPTACLE, D'YOU SEE? AND COMES OUT--
BURNED TO ASHES, IN A GREAT GOUT OF FLAME.
CORDWAINER'S INVENTIONS ARE ALWAYS PERILOUS.
WELL, THE DESIGN IS NOT PERFECTED YET.
"HOWEVER THAT MAY BE, TOM WAS NOW QUITE AMPHIBIOUS.
"AND WHAT WAS BETTER STILL, HE WAS CLEAN."
I'LL KEEP MY HANDS TO MYSELF WHEN YOU STOP GOADING ME, KELL.
AHUH!
AHUH!
AHUH!

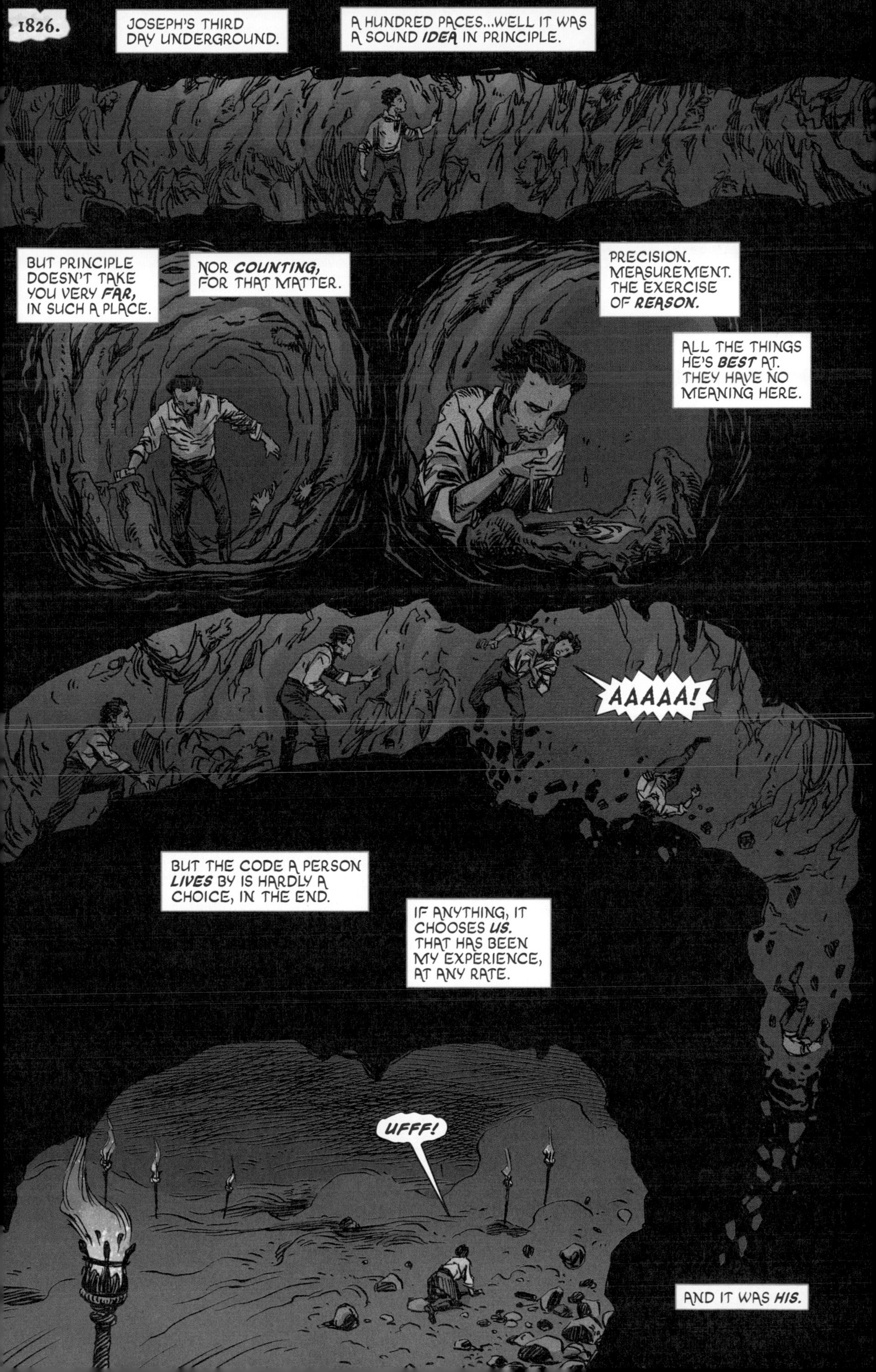
1826.
JOSEPH'S THIRD DAY UNDERGROUND.
A HUNDRED PACES...WELL IT WAS A SOUND IDEA IN PRINCIPLE.
BUT PRINCIPLE DOESN'T TAKE YOU VERY FAR, IN SUCH A PLACE.
NOR COUNTING, FOR THAT MATTER.
PRECISION. MEASUREMENT. THE EXERCISE OF REASON.
ALL THE THINGS HE'S BEST AT. THEY HAVE NO MEANING HERE.
AAAAA!
BUT THE CODE A PERSON LIVES BY IS HARDLY A CHOICE, IN THE END.
IF ANYTHING, IT CHOOSES US. THAT HAS BEEN MY EXPERIENCE, AT ANY RATE.
UFFF!
AND IT WAS HIS.

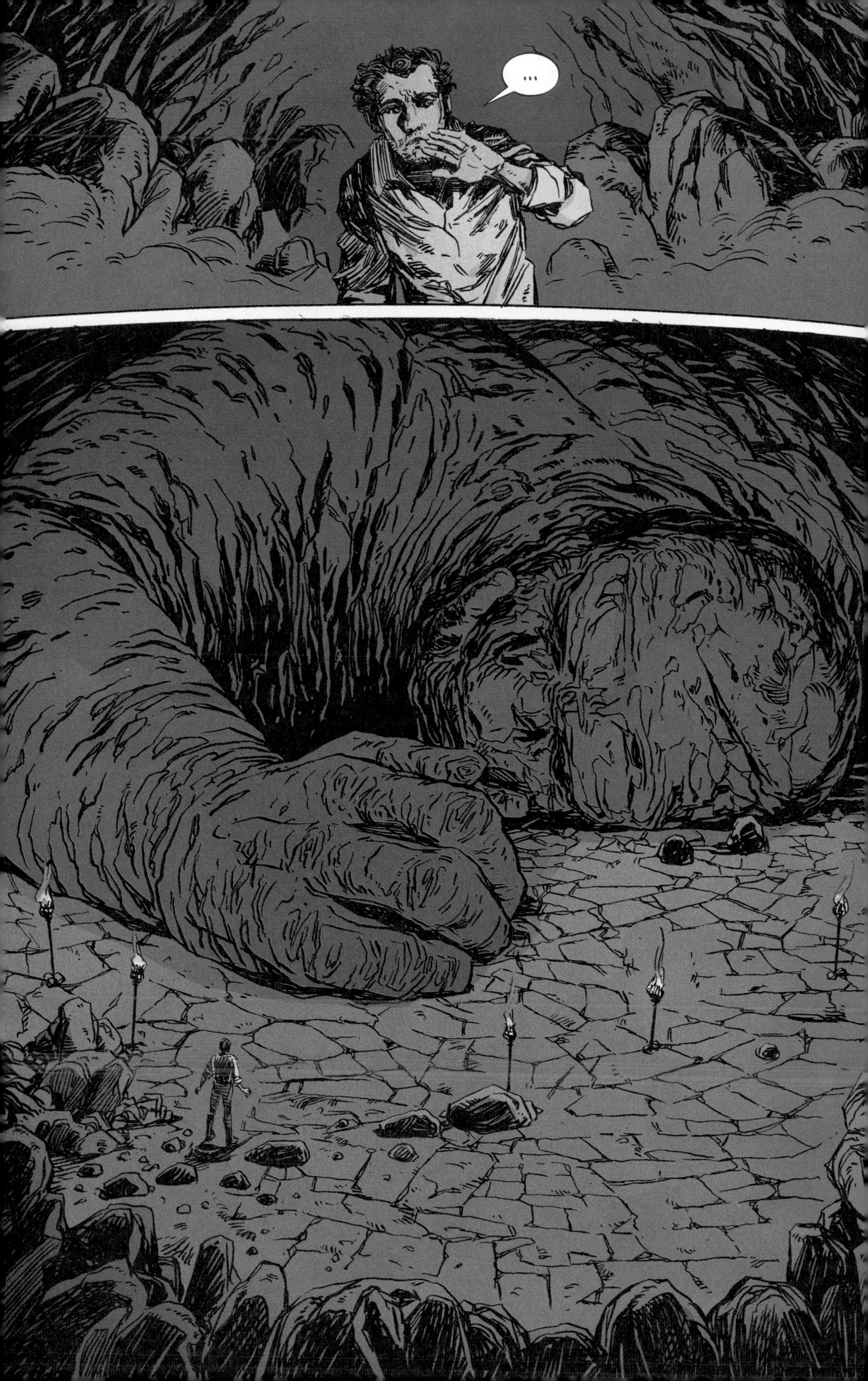
...

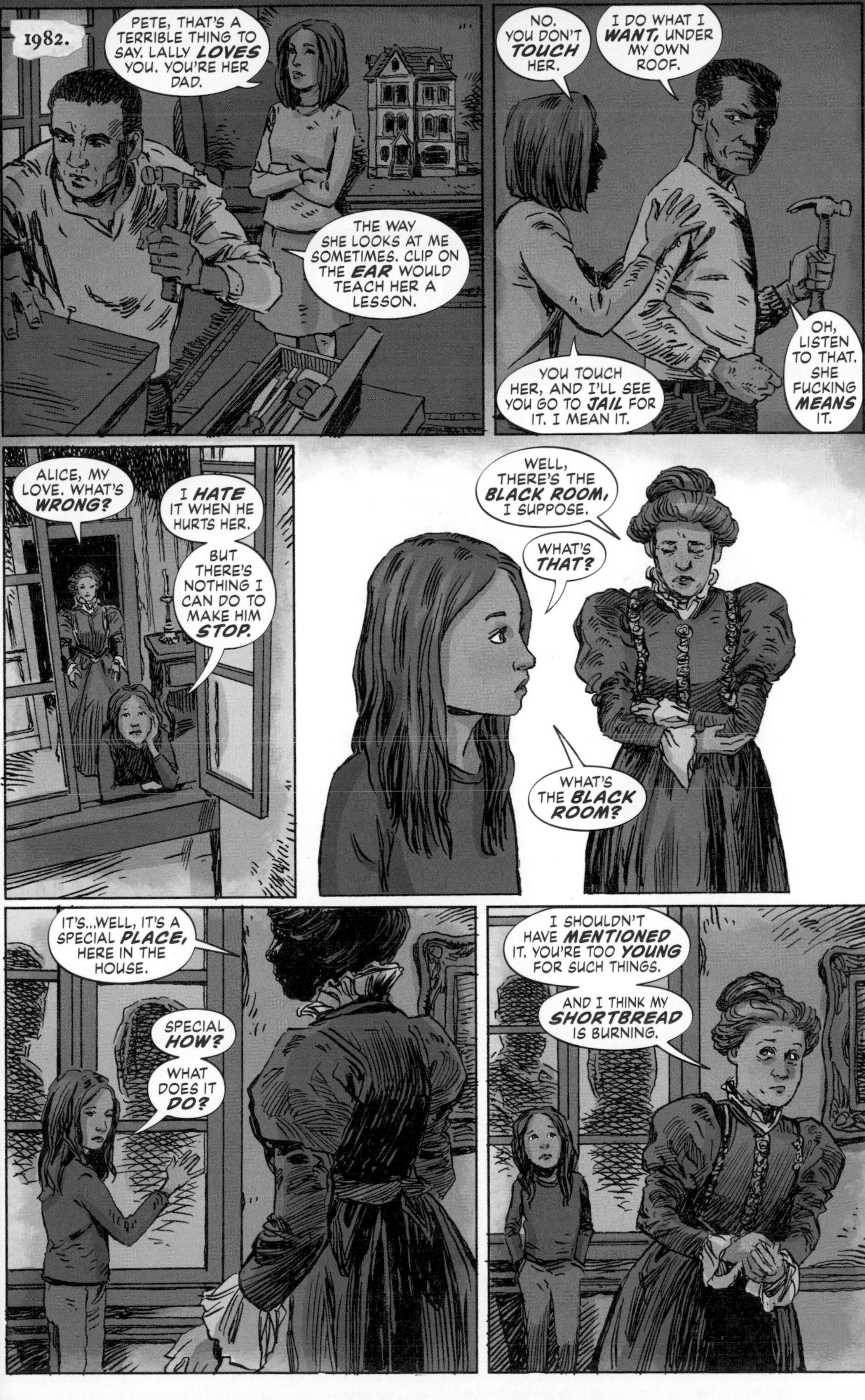
1982.
PETE, THAT'S A TERRIBLE THING TO SAY. LALLY LOVES YOU. YOU'RE HER DAD.
THE WAY SHE LOOKS AT ME SOMETIMES. CLIP ON THE EAR WOULD TEACH HER A LESSON.
NO. YOU DON'T TOUCH HER.
I DO WHAT I WANT, UNDER MY OWN ROOF.
YOU TOUCH HER, AND I'LL SEE YOU GO TO JAIL FOR IT. I MEAN IT.
OH, LISTEN TO THAT. SHE FUCKING MEANS IT.
ALICE, MY LOVE. WHAT'S WRONG?
I HATE IT WHEN HE HURTS HER.
BUT THERE'S NOTHING I CAN DO TO MAKE HIM STOP.
WELL, THERE'S THE BLACK ROOM, I SUPPOSE.
WHAT'S THAT?
WHAT'S THE BLACK ROOM?
IT'S...WELL, IT'S A SPECIAL PLACE, HERE IN THE HOUSE.
SPECIAL HOW?
WHAT DOES IT DO?
I SHOULDN'T HAVE MENTIONED IT. YOU'RE TOO YOUNG FOR SUCH THINGS.
AND I THINK MY SHORTBREAD IS BURNING.

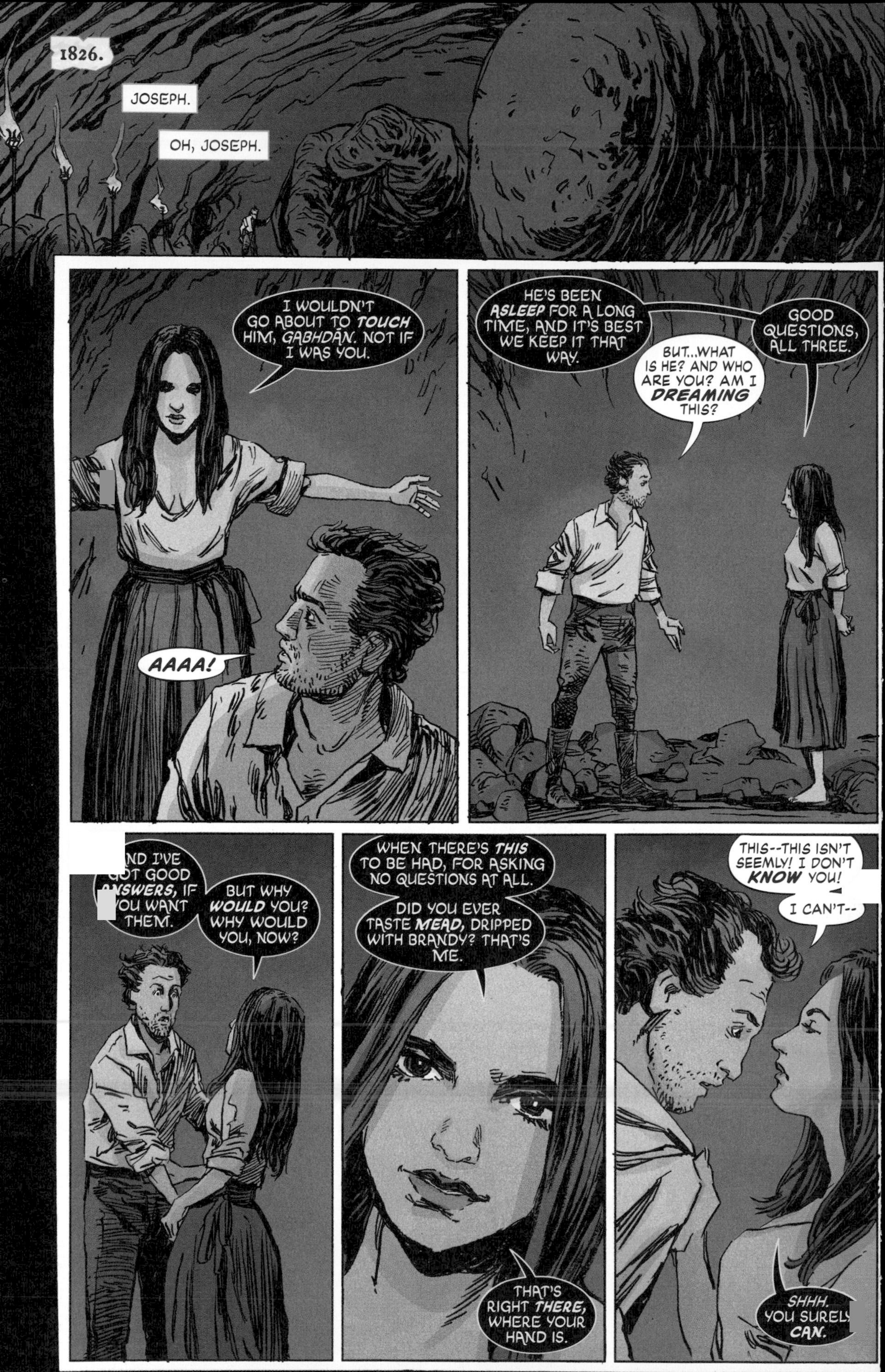
1826.
JOSEPH.
OH, JOSEPH.
I WOULDN'T GO ABOUT TO TOUCH HIM, GABHDÁN. NOT IF I WAS YOU.
AAAA!
HE'S BEEN ASLEEP FOR A LONG TIME, AND IT'S BEST WE KEEP IT THAT WAY.
BUT...WHAT IS HE? AND WHO ARE YOU? AM I DREAMING THIS?
GOOD QUESTIONS, ALL THREE.
ND I'VE OT GOOD NSWERS, IF OU WANT THEM.
BUT WHY WOULD YOU? WHY WOULD YOU, NOW?
WHEN THERE'S THIS TO BE HAD, FOR ASKING NO QUESTIONS AT ALL.
DID YOU EVER TASTE MEAD, DRIPPED WITH BRANDY? THAT'S ME.
THAT'S RIGHT THERE, WHERE YOUR HAND IS.
THIS--THIS ISN'T SEEMLY! I DON'T KNOW YOU!
I CAN'T--
SHHH. YOU SURELY CAN.

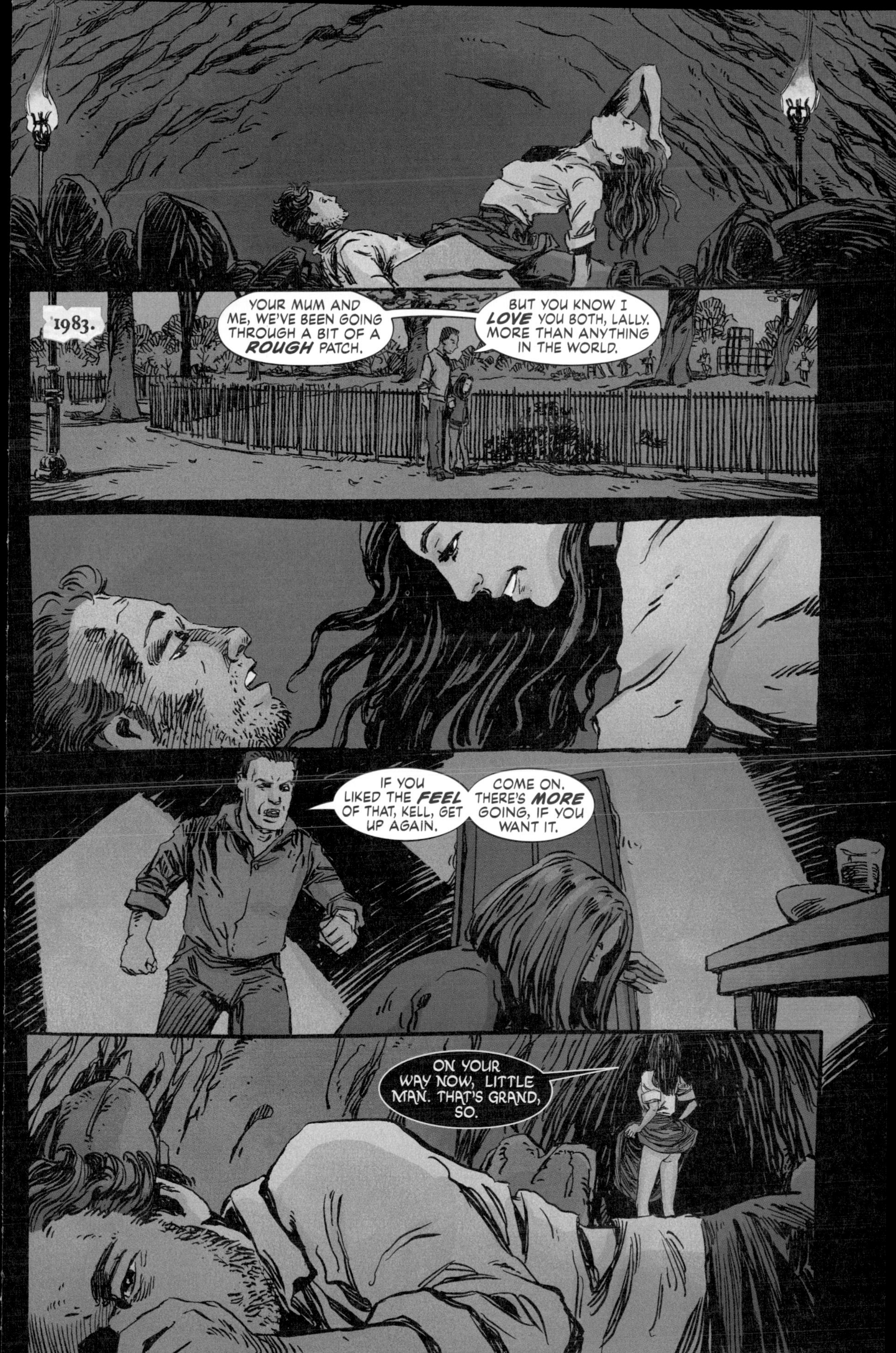
1983.
YOUR MUM AND ME, WE'VE BEEN GOING THROUGH A BIT OF A ROUGH PATCH.
BUT YOU KNOW I LOVE YOU BOTH, LALLY. MORE THAN ANYTHING IN THE WORLD.
IF YOU LIKED THE FEEL OF THAT, KELL, GET UP AGAIN.
COME ON. THERE'S MORE GOING, IF YOU WANT IT.
ON YOUR WAY NOW, LITTLE MAN. THAT'S GRAND, SO.

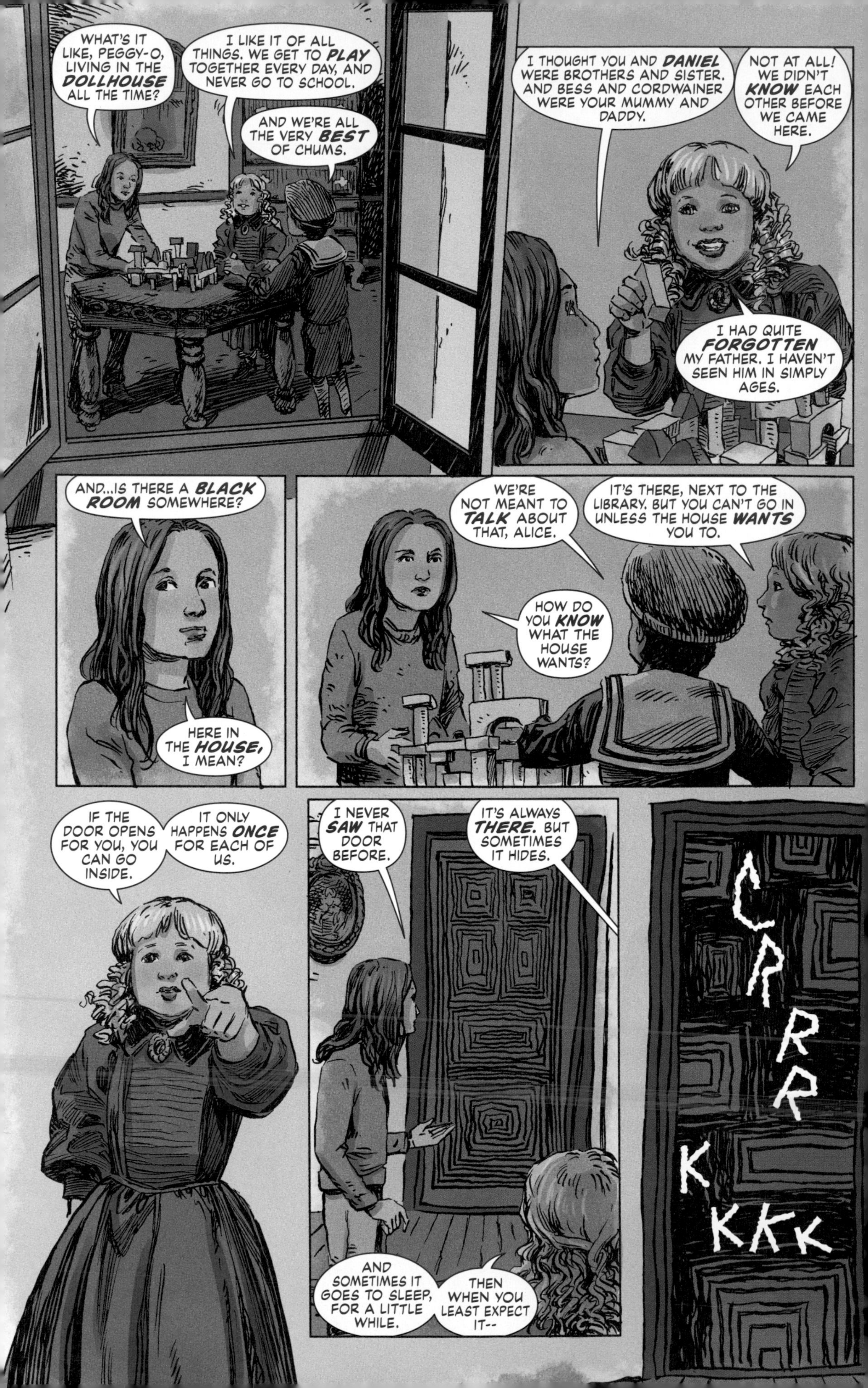
WHAT'S IT LIKE, PEGGY-O, LIVING IN THE DOLLHOUSE ALL THE TIME?
I LIKE IT OF ALL THINGS. WE GET TO PLAY TOGETHER EVERY DAY, AND NEVER GO TO SCHOOL.
AND WE'RE ALL THE VERY BEST OF CHUMS.
I THOUGHT YOU AND DANIEL WERE BROTHERS AND SISTER. AND BESS AND CORDWAINER WERE YOUR MUMMY AND DADDY.
NOT AT ALL! WE DIDN'T KNOW EACH OTHER BEFORE WE CAME HERE.
I HAD QUITE FORGOTTEN MY FATHER. I HAVEN'T SEEN HIM IN SIMPLY AGES.
AND...IS THERE A BLACK ROOM SOMEWHERE?
HERE IN THE HOUSE, I MEAN?
WE'RE NOT MEANT TO TALK ABOUT THAT, ALICE.
IT'S THERE, NEXT TO THE LIBRARY. BUT YOU CAN'T GO IN UNLESS THE HOUSE WANTS YOU TO.
HOW DO YOU KNOW WHAT THE HOUSE WANTS?
IF THE DOOR OPENS FOR YOU, YOU CAN GO INSIDE.
IT ONLY HAPPENS ONCE FOR EACH OF US.
I NEVER SAW THAT DOOR BEFORE.
IT'S ALWAYS THERE. BUT SOMETIMES IT HIDES.
AND SOMETIMES IT GOES TO SLEEP, FOR A LITTLE WHILE.
THEN WHEN YOU LEAST EXPECT IT--
CRRRKKKK

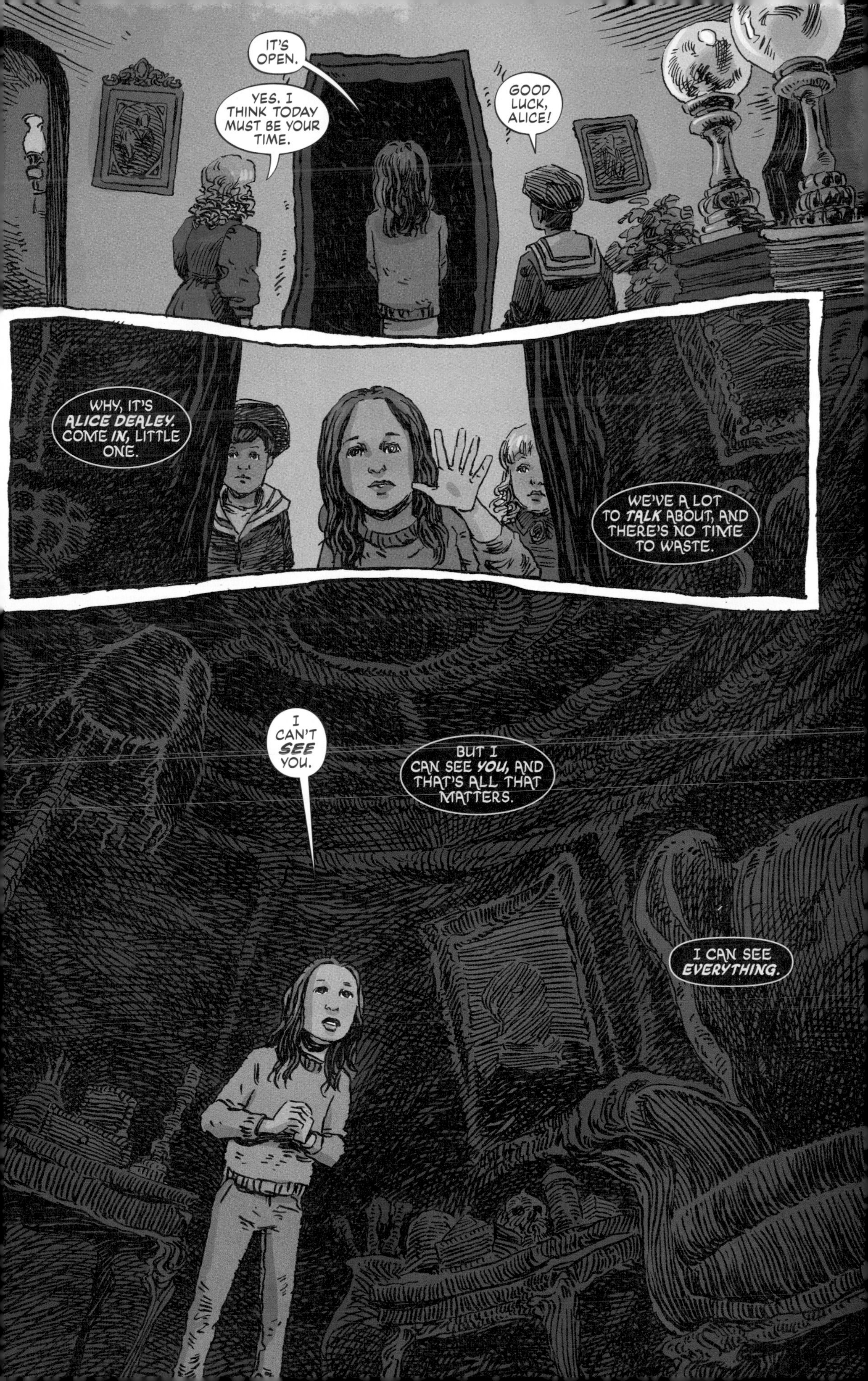
IT'S OPEN.
YES. I THINK TODAY MUST BE YOUR TIME.
GOOD LUCK, ALICE!
WHY, IT'S ALICE DEALEY. COME IN, LITTLE ONE.
WE'VE A LOT TO TALK ABOUT, AND THERE'S NO TIME TO WASTE.
I CAN'T SEE YOU.
BUT I CAN SEE YOU, AND THAT'S ALL THAT MATTERS.
I CAN SEE EVERYTHING.

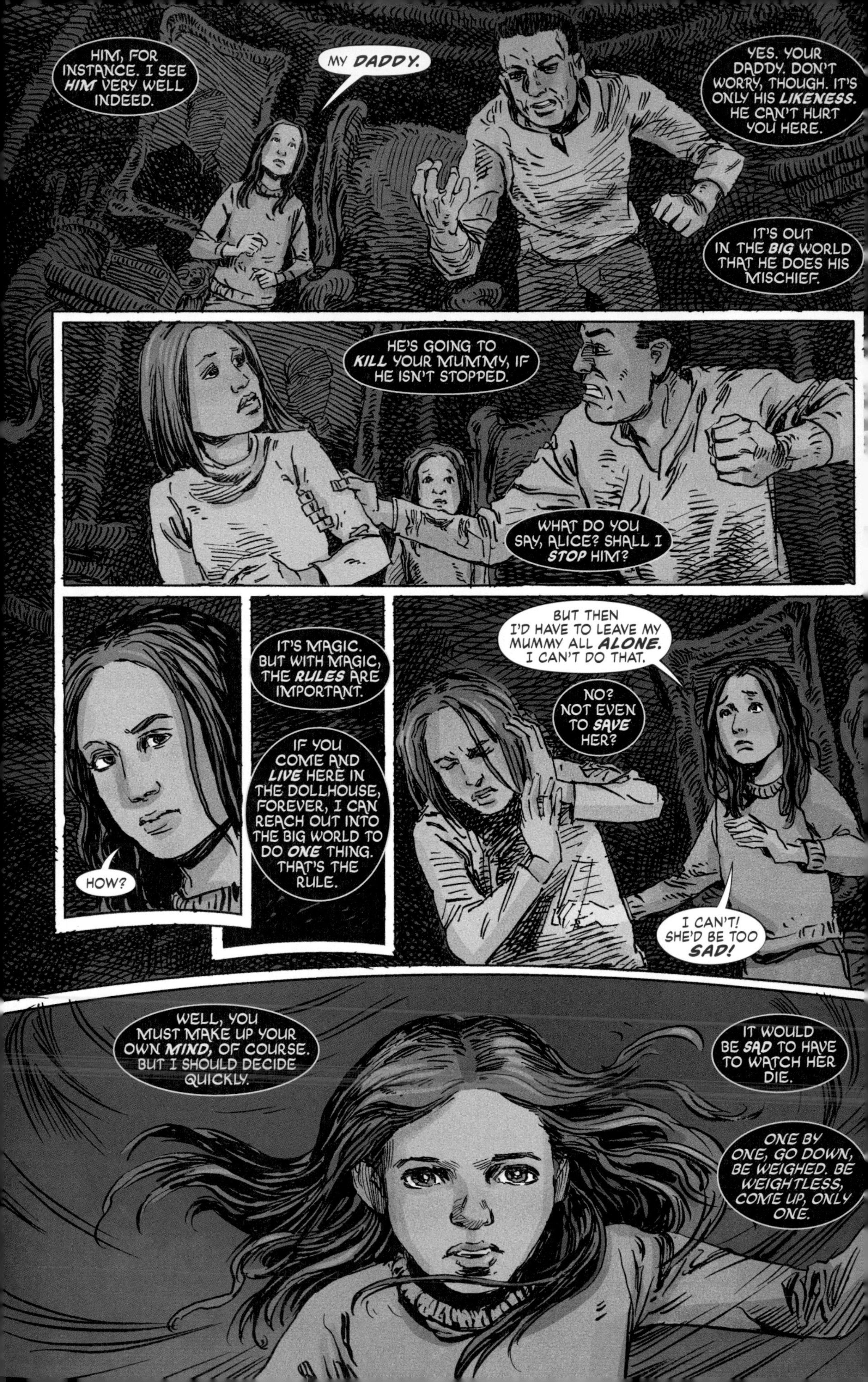
HIM, FOR INSTANCE. I SEE HIM VERY WELL INDEED.
MY DADDY.
YES. YOUR DADDY. DON'T WORRY, THOUGH. IT'S ONLY HIS LIKENESS. HE CAN'T HURT YOU HERE.
IT'S OUT IN THE BIG WORLD THAT HE DOES HIS MISCHIEF.
HE'S GOING TO KILL YOUR MUMMY, IF HE ISN'T STOPPED.
WHAT DO YOU SAY, ALICE? SHALL I STOP HIM?
HOW?
IT'S MAGIC. BUT WITH MAGIC, THE RULES ARE IMPORTANT.
IF YOU COME AND LIVE HERE IN THE DOLLHOUSE, FOREVER, I CAN REACH OUT INTO THE BIG WORLD TO DO ONE THING. THAT'S THE RULE.
BUT THEN I'D HAVE TO LEAVE MY MUMMY ALL ALONE. I CAN'T DO THAT.
NO? NOT EVEN TO SAVE HER?
I CAN'T! SHE'D BE TOO SAD!
WELL, YOU MUST MAKE UP YOUR OWN MIND, OF COURSE. BUT I SHOULD DECIDE QUICKLY.
IT WOULD BE SAD TO HAVE TO WATCH HER DIE.
ONE BY ONE, GO DOWN, BE WEIGHED. BE WEIGHTLESS, COME UP, ONLY ONE.

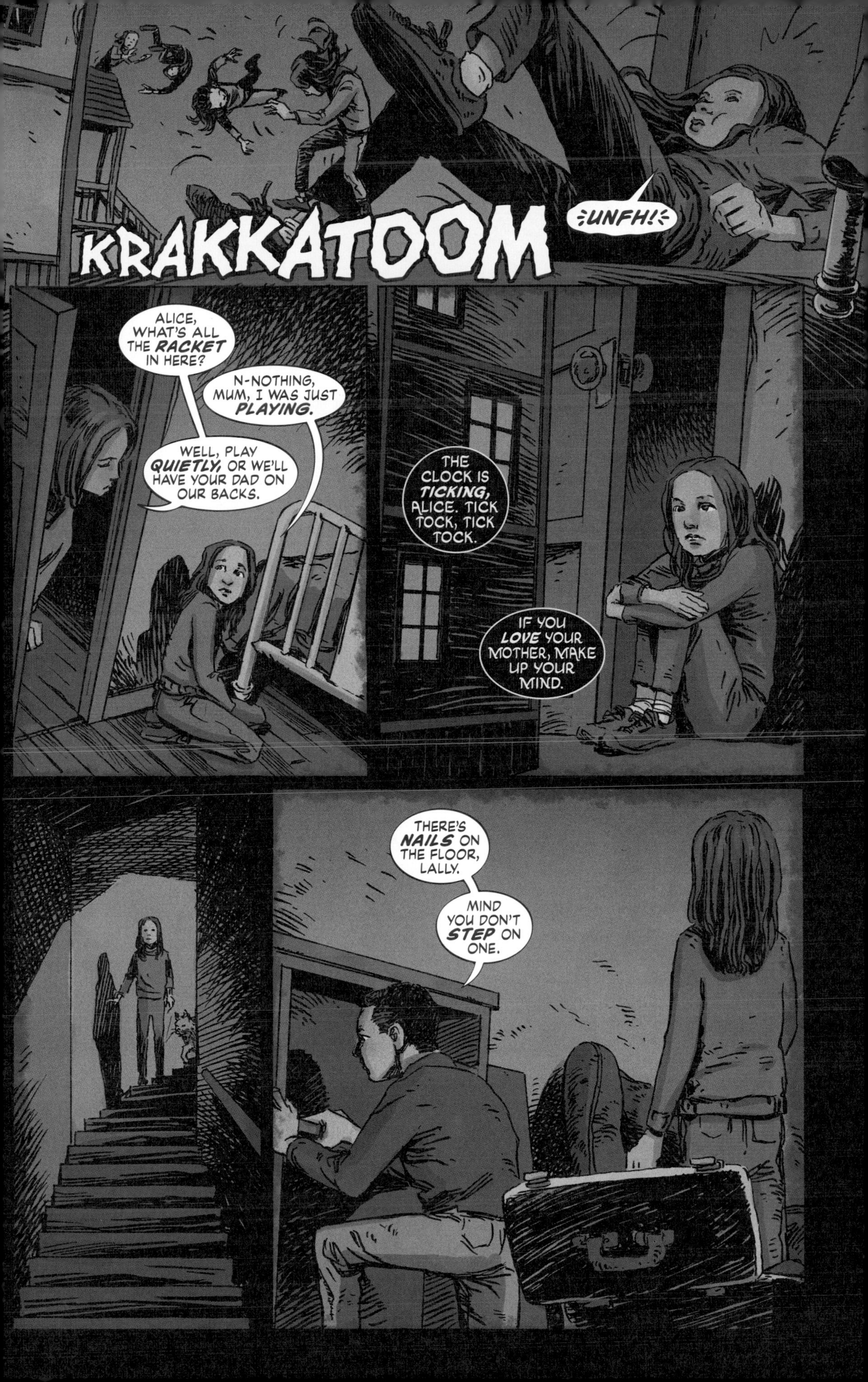

KRAKKATOOM
UNFH!
ALICE, WHAT'S ALL THE RACKET IN HERE?
N-NOTHING, MUM, I WAS JUST PLAYING.
WELL, PLAY QUIETLY, OR WE'LL HAVE YOUR DAD ON OUR BACKS.
THE CLOCK IS TICKING, ALICE. TICK TOCK, TICK TOCK.
IF YOU LOVE YOUR MOTHER, MAKE UP YOUR MIND.
THERE'S NAILS ON THE FLOOR, LALLY.
MIND YOU DON'T STEP ON ONE.

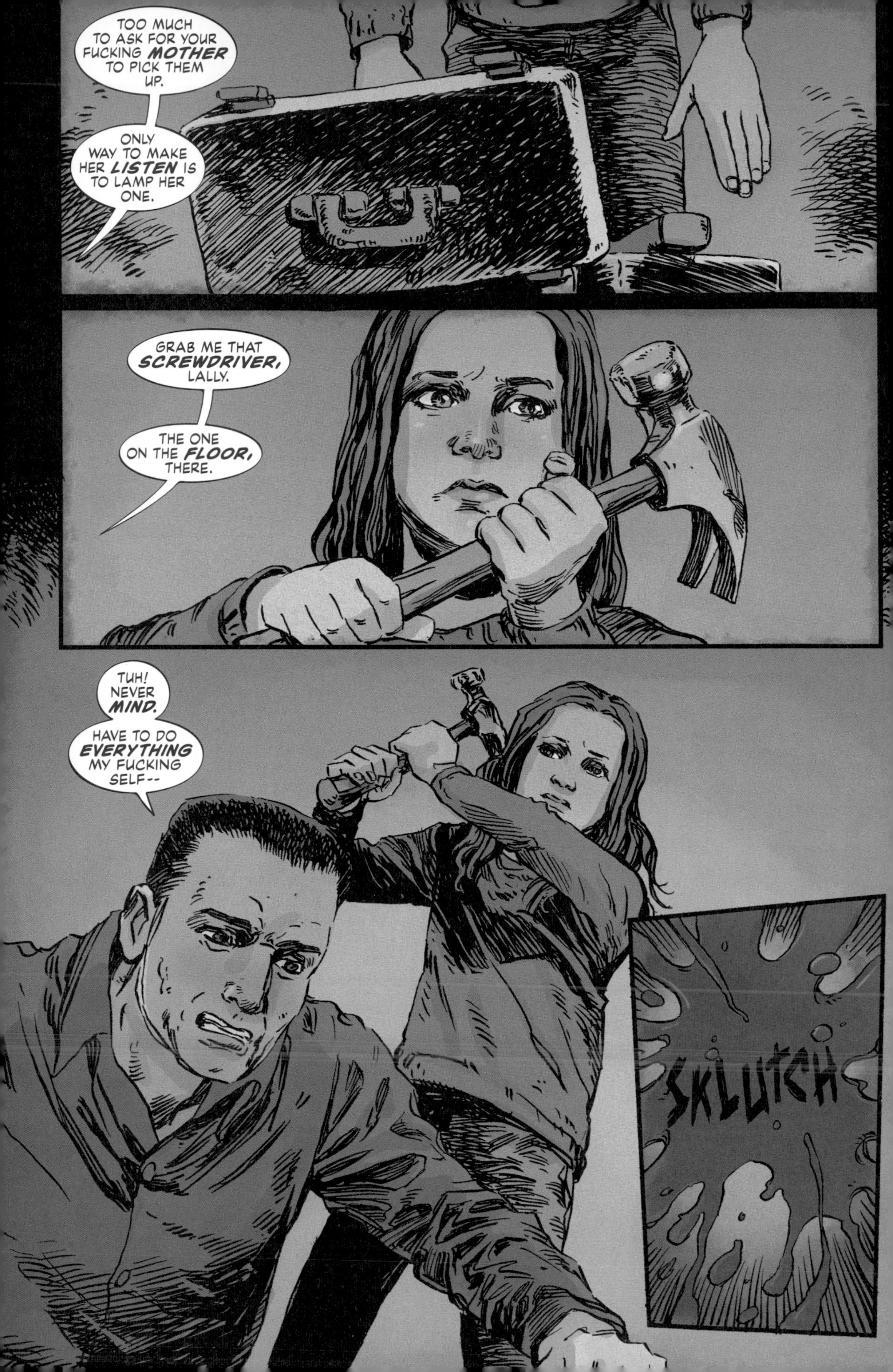
TOO MUCH TO ASK FOR YOUR FUCKING MOTHER TO PICK THEM UP.
ONLY WAY TO MAKE HER LISTEN IS TO LAMP HER ONE.
GRAB ME THAT SCREWDRIVER, LALLY.
THE ONE ON THE FLOOR, THERE.
TUH! NEVER MIND.
HAVE TO DO EVERYTHING MY FUCKING SELF--
SKLUTCH

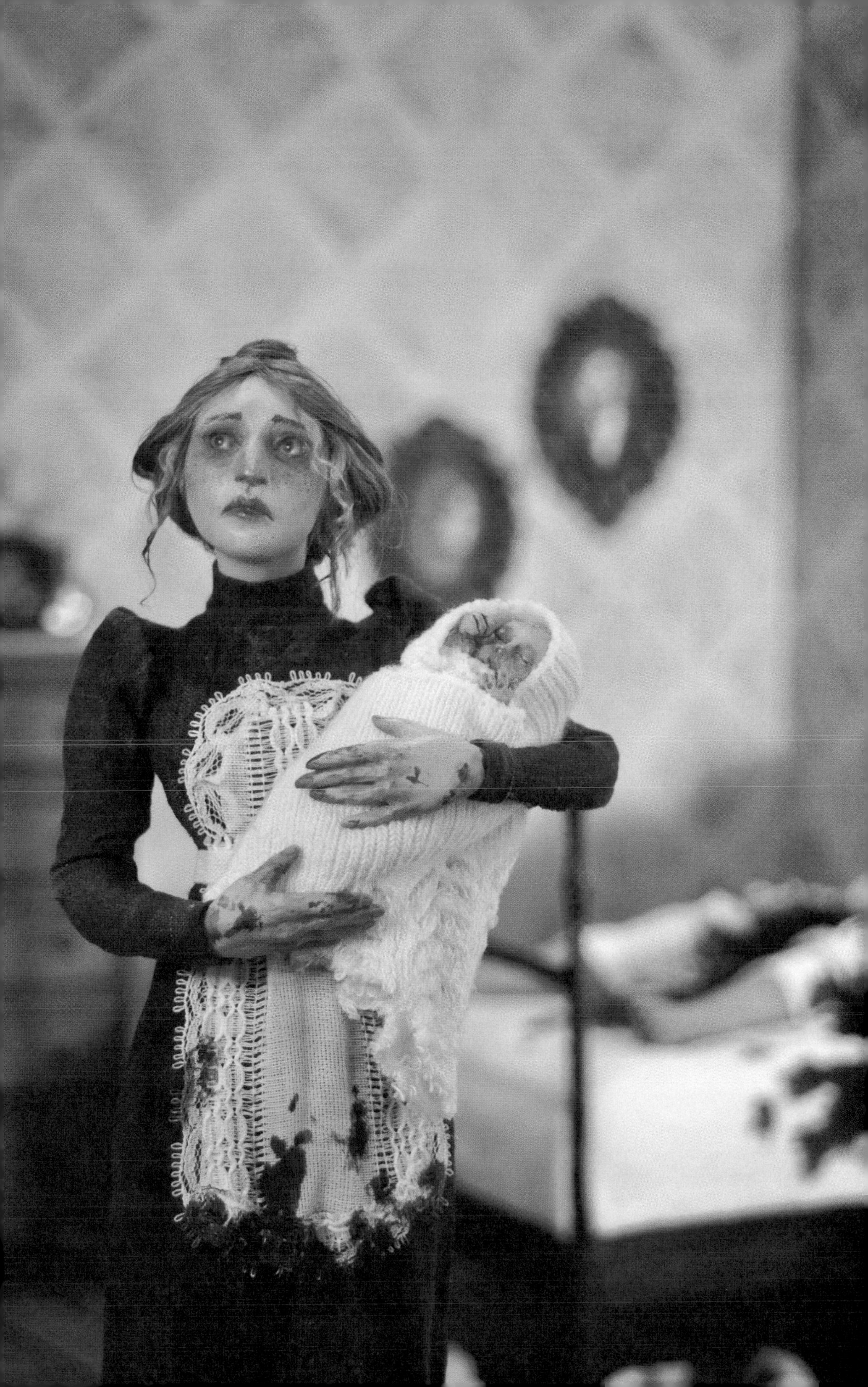

BE WEIGHED

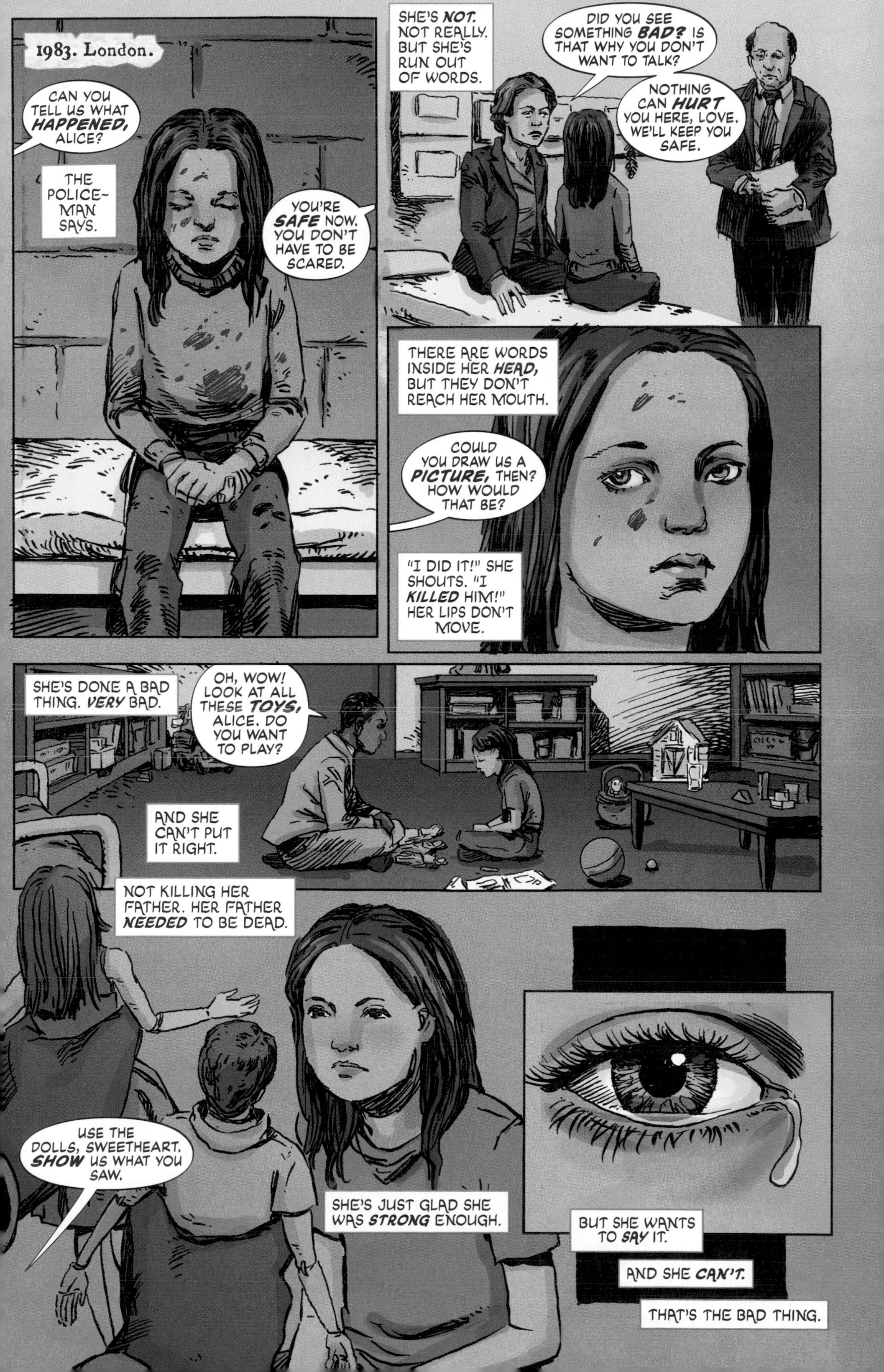
1983. London.
CAN YOU TELL US WHAT HAPPENED, ALICE?
THE POLICEMAN SAYS.
YOU'RE SAFE NOW. YOU DON'T HAVE TO BE SCARED.
SHE'S NOT. NOT REALLY. BUT SHE'S RUN OUT OF WORDS.
DID YOU SEE SOMETHING BAD? IS THAT WHY YOU DON'T WANT TO TALK?
NOTHING CAN HURT YOU HERE, LOVE. WE'LL KEEP YOU SAFE.
THERE ARE WORDS INSIDE HER HEAD, BUT THEY DON'T REACH HER MOUTH.
COULD YOU DRAW US A PICTURE, THEN? HOW WOULD THAT BE?
"I DID IT!" SHE SHOUTS. "I KILLED HIM!" HER LIPS DON'T MOVE.
SHE'S DONE A BAD THING. VERY BAD.
OH, WOW! LOOK AT ALL THESE TOYS, ALICE. DO YOU WANT TO PLAY?
AND SHE CAN'T PUT IT RIGHT.
NOT KILLING HER FATHER. HER FATHER NEEDED TO BE DEAD.
USE THE DOLLS, SWEETHEART. SHOW US WHAT YOU SAW.
SHE'S JUST GLAD SHE WAS STRONG ENOUGH.
BUT SHE WANTS TO SAY IT.
AND SHE CAN'T.
THAT'S THE BAD THING.

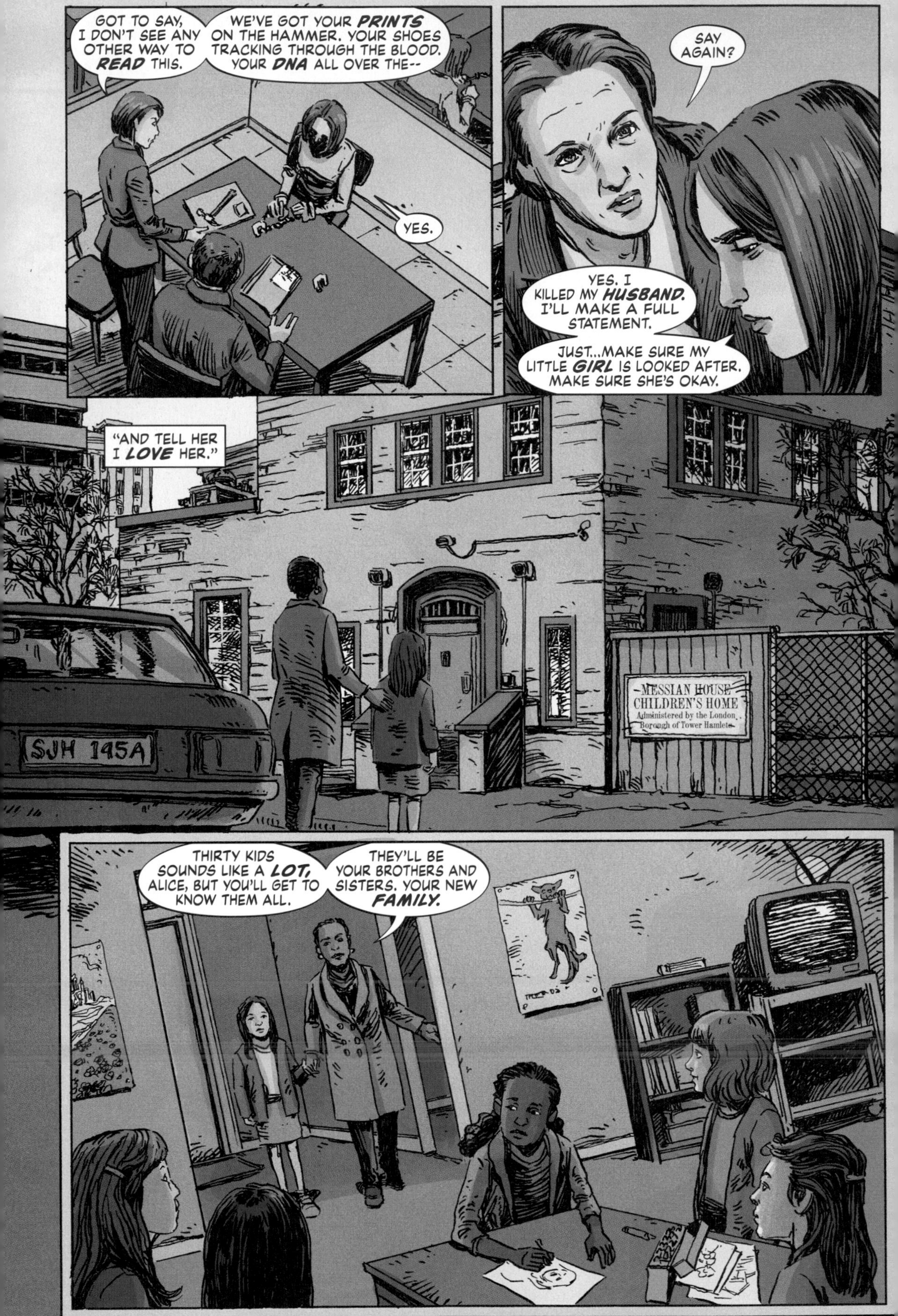

GOT TO SAY, I DON'T SEE ANY OTHER WAY TO READ THIS.
WE'VE GOT YOUR PRINTS ON THE HAMMER. YOUR SHOES TRACKING THROUGH THE BLOOD. YOUR DNA ALL OVER THE--
YES.
SAY AGAIN?
YES. I KILLED MY HUSBAND. I'LL MAKE A FULL STATEMENT.
JUST...MAKE SURE MY LITTLE GIRL IS LOOKED AFTER. MAKE SURE SHE'S OKAY.
"AND TELL HER I LOVE HER."
SJH 145A
MESSIAN HOUSE CHILDREN'S HOME
Administered by the London Borough of Tower Hamlets
THIRTY KIDS SOUNDS LIKE A LOT, ALICE, BUT YOU'LL GET TO KNOW THEM ALL.
THEY'LL BE YOUR BROTHERS AND SISTERS. YOUR NEW FAMILY.

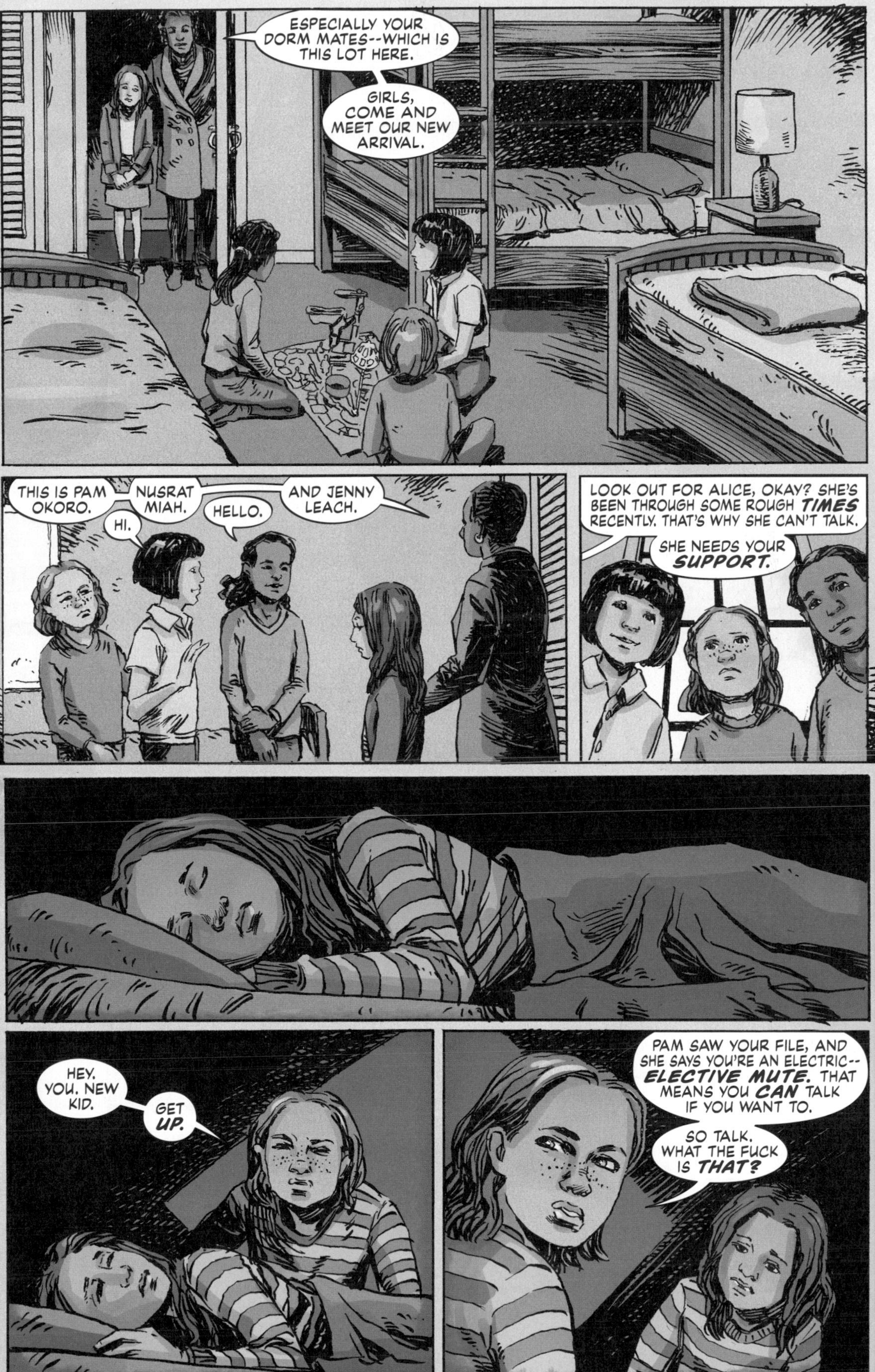
ESPECIALLY YOUR DORM MATES--WHICH IS THIS LOT HERE.
GIRLS, COME AND MEET OUR NEW ARRIVAL.
THIS IS PAM OKORO.
HI.
NUSRAT MIAH.
HELLO.
AND JENNY LEACH.
LOOK OUT FOR ALICE, OKAY? SHE'S BEEN THROUGH SOME ROUGH *TIMES* RECENTLY. THAT'S WHY SHE CAN'T TALK.
SHE NEEDS YOUR *SUPPORT.*
HEY. YOU. NEW KID.
GET *UP.*
PAM SAW YOUR FILE, AND SHE SAYS YOU'RE AN ELECTRIC-- *ELECTIVE MUTE.* THAT MEANS YOU *CAN* TALK IF YOU WANT TO.
SO TALK. WHAT THE FUCK IS *THAT?*

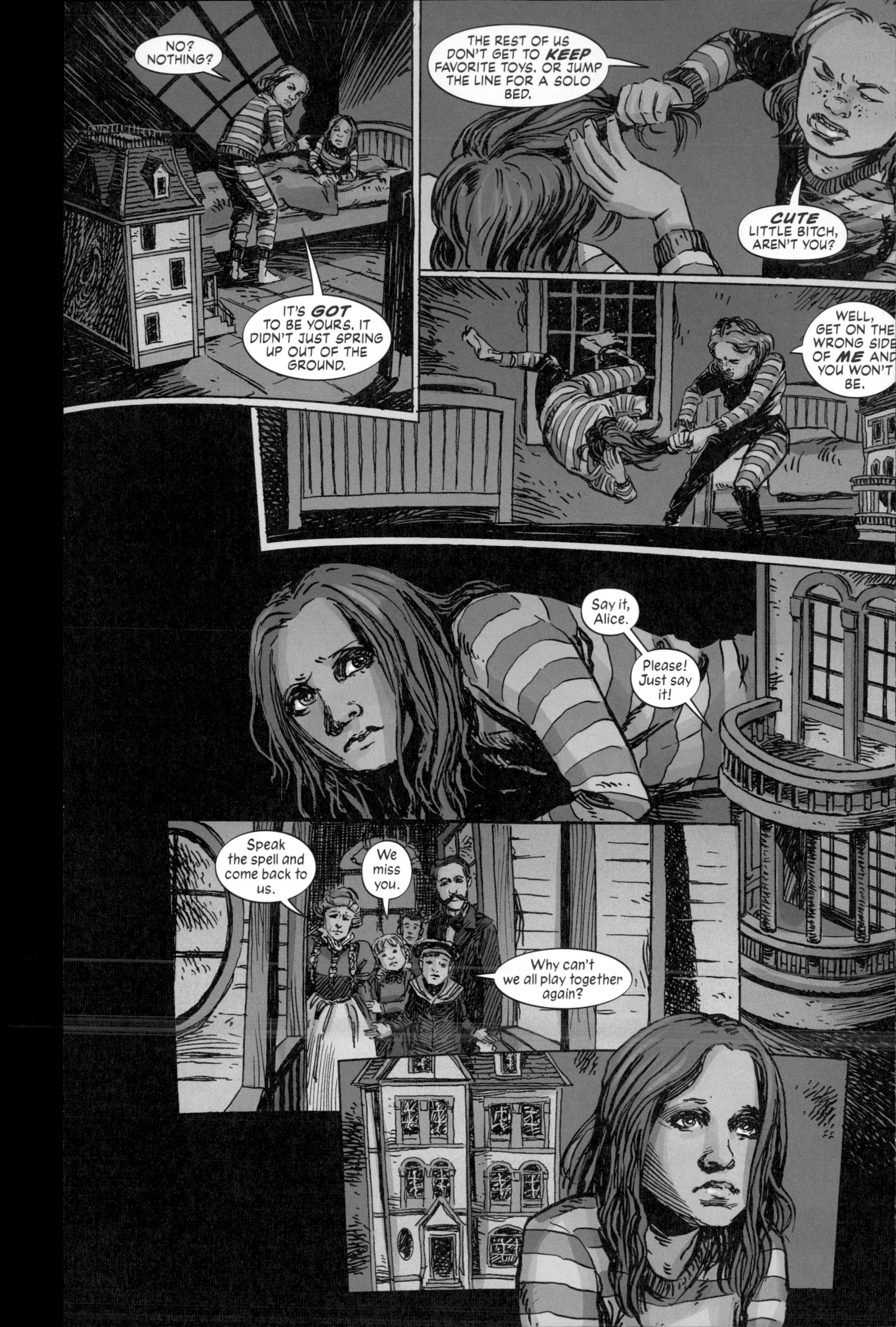
NO? NOTHING?
IT'S GOT TO BE YOURS. IT DIDN'T JUST SPRING UP OUT OF THE GROUND.
THE REST OF US DON'T GET TO KEEP FAVORITE TOYS. OR JUMP THE LINE FOR A SOLO BED.
CUTE LITTLE BITCH, AREN'T YOU?
WELL, GET ON THE WRONG SIDE OF ME AND YOU WON'T BE.
Say it, Alice.
Please! Just say it!
Speak the spell and come back to us.
We miss you.
Why can't we all play together again?

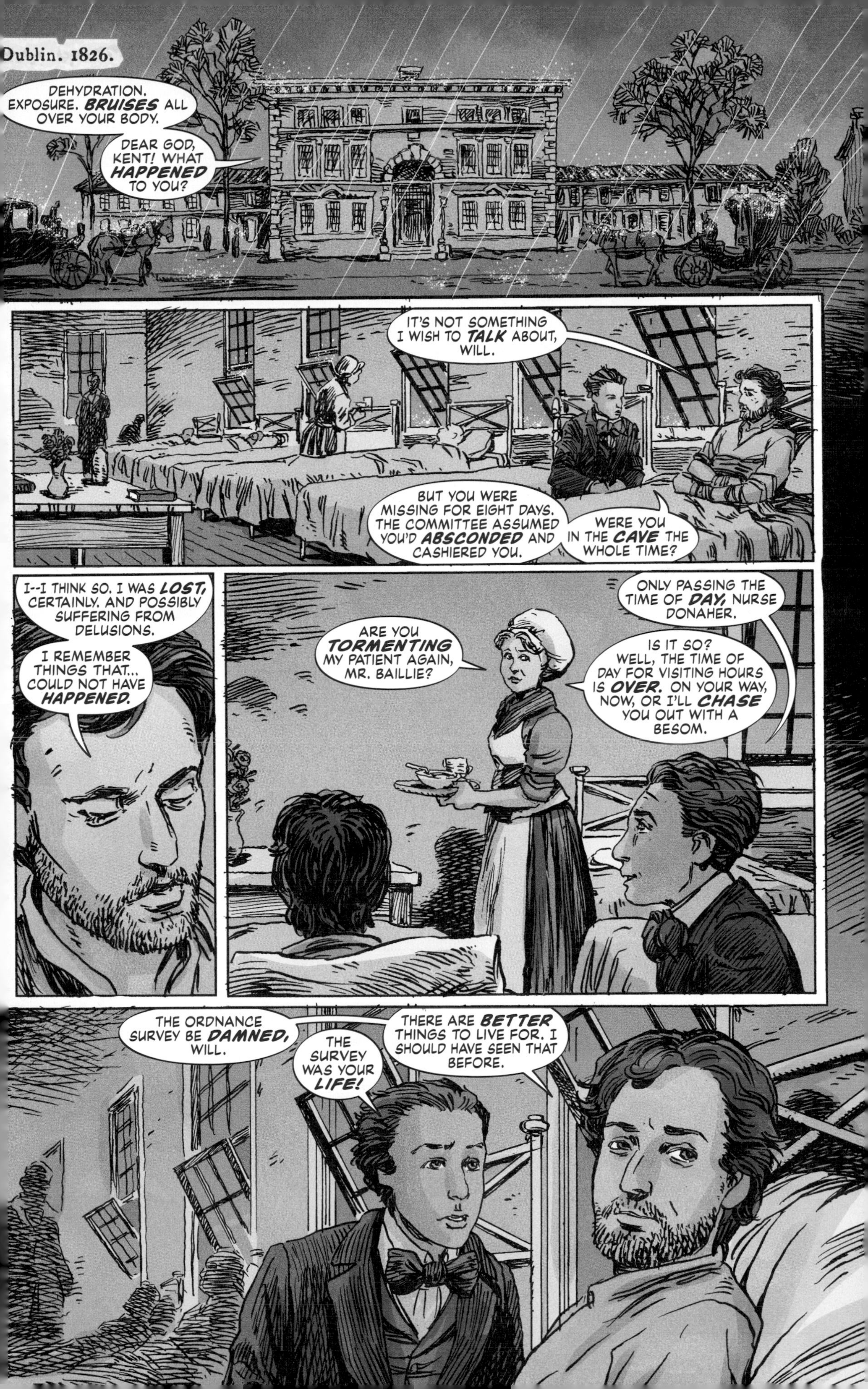
Dublin. 1826.
DEHYDRATION. EXPOSURE. BRUISES ALL OVER YOUR BODY.
DEAR GOD, KENT! WHAT HAPPENED TO YOU?
IT'S NOT SOMETHING I WISH TO TALK ABOUT, WILL.
BUT YOU WERE MISSING FOR EIGHT DAYS. THE COMMITTEE ASSUMED YOU'D ABSCONDED AND CASHIERED YOU.
WERE YOU IN THE CAVE THE WHOLE TIME?
I--I THINK SO. I WAS LOST, CERTAINLY. AND POSSIBLY SUFFERING FROM DELUSIONS.
I REMEMBER THINGS THAT... COULD NOT HAVE HAPPENED.
ARE YOU TORMENTING MY PATIENT AGAIN, MR. BAILLIE?
ONLY PASSING THE TIME OF DAY, NURSE DONAHER.
IS IT SO? WELL, THE TIME OF DAY FOR VISITING HOURS IS OVER. ON YOUR WAY, NOW, OR I'LL CHASE YOU OUT WITH A BESOM.
THE ORDNANCE SURVEY BE DAMNED, WILL.
THE SURVEY WAS YOUR LIFE!
THERE ARE BETTER THINGS TO LIVE FOR. I SHOULD HAVE SEEN THAT BEFORE.

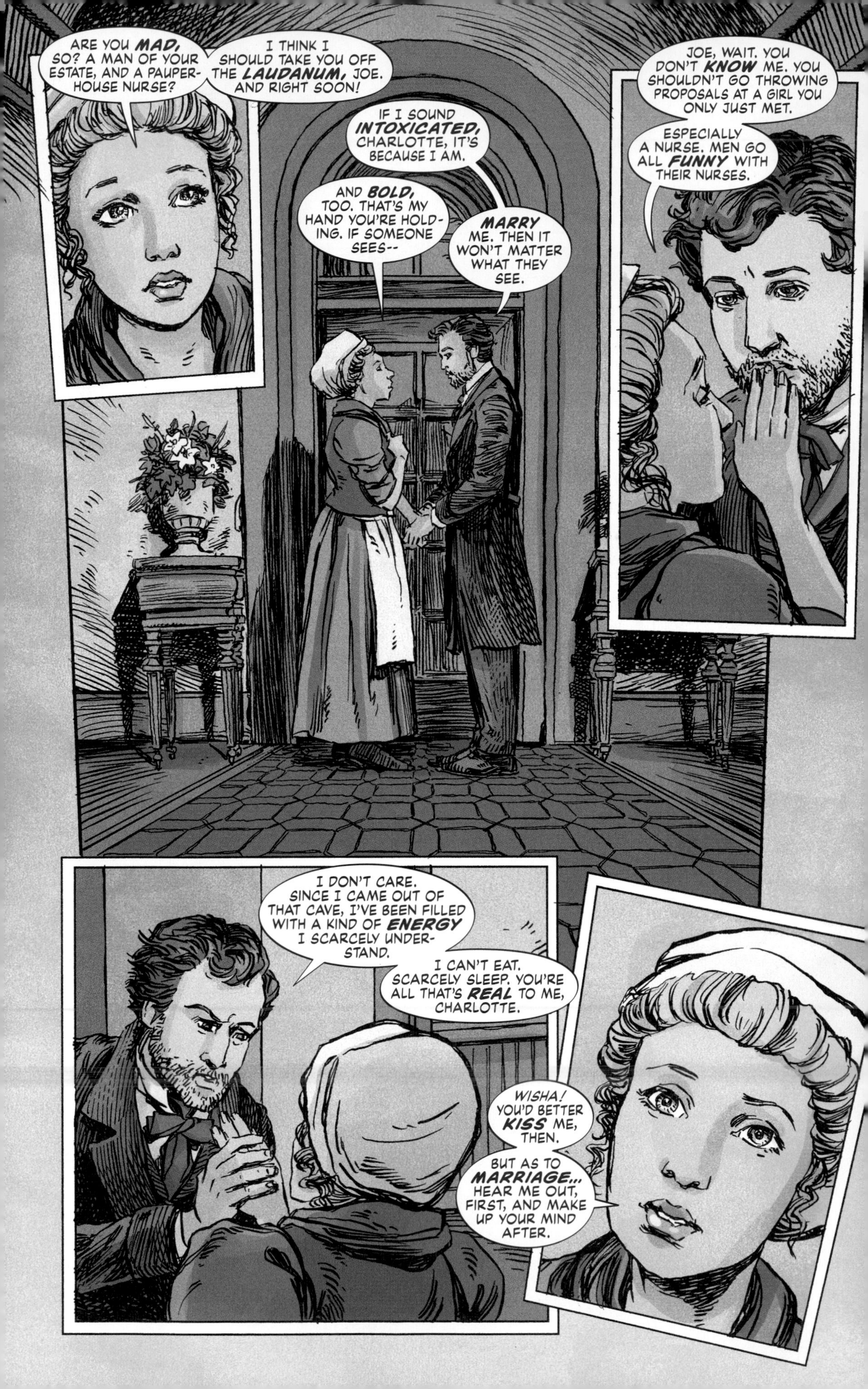

ARE YOU MAD, SO? A MAN OF YOUR ESTATE, AND A PAUPER-HOUSE NURSE?
I THINK I SHOULD TAKE YOU OFF THE LAUDANUM, JOE. AND RIGHT SOON!
IF I SOUND INTOXICATED, CHARLOTTE, IT'S BECAUSE I AM.
AND BOLD, TOO. THAT'S MY HAND YOU'RE HOLDING. IF SOMEONE SEES--
MARRY ME. THEN IT WON'T MATTER WHAT THEY SEE.
JOE, WAIT. YOU DON'T KNOW ME. YOU SHOULDN'T GO THROWING PROPOSALS AT A GIRL YOU ONLY JUST MET.
ESPECIALLY A NURSE. MEN GO ALL FUNNY WITH THEIR NURSES.
I DON'T CARE. SINCE I CAME OUT OF THAT CAVE, I'VE BEEN FILLED WITH A KIND OF ENERGY I SCARCELY UNDERSTAND.
I CAN'T EAT. SCARCELY SLEEP. YOU'RE ALL THAT'S REAL TO ME, CHARLOTTE.
WISHA! YOU'D BETTER KISS ME, THEN.
BUT AS TO MARRIAGE... HEAR ME OUT, FIRST, AND MAKE UP YOUR MIND AFTER.

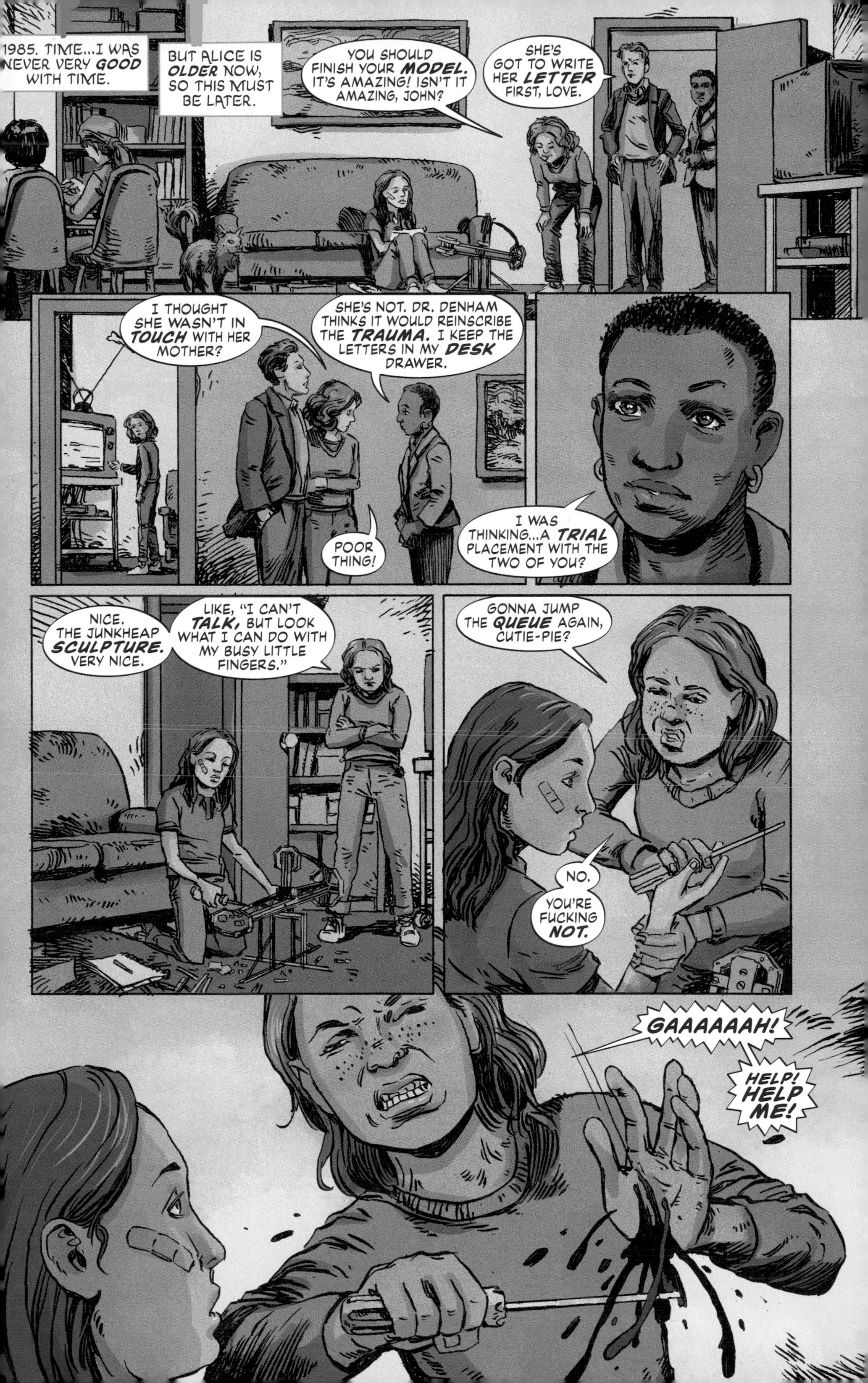

1985. TIME...I WAS NEVER VERY GOOD WITH TIME.
BUT ALICE IS OLDER NOW, SO THIS MUST BE LATER.
YOU SHOULD FINISH YOUR MODEL. IT'S AMAZING! ISN'T IT AMAZING, JOHN?
SHE'S GOT TO WRITE HER LETTER FIRST, LOVE.
I THOUGHT SHE WASN'T IN TOUCH WITH HER MOTHER?
SHE'S NOT. DR. DENHAM THINKS IT WOULD REINSCRIBE THE TRAUMA. I KEEP THE LETTERS IN MY DESK DRAWER.
POOR THING!
I WAS THINKING...A TRIAL PLACEMENT WITH THE TWO OF YOU?
NICE. THE JUNKHEAP SCULPTURE. VERY NICE.
LIKE, "I CAN'T TALK, BUT LOOK WHAT I CAN DO WITH MY BUSY LITTLE FINGERS."
GONNA JUMP THE QUEUE AGAIN, CUTIE-PIE?
NO.
YOU'RE FUCKING NOT.
GAAAAAAH!
HELP! HELP ME!

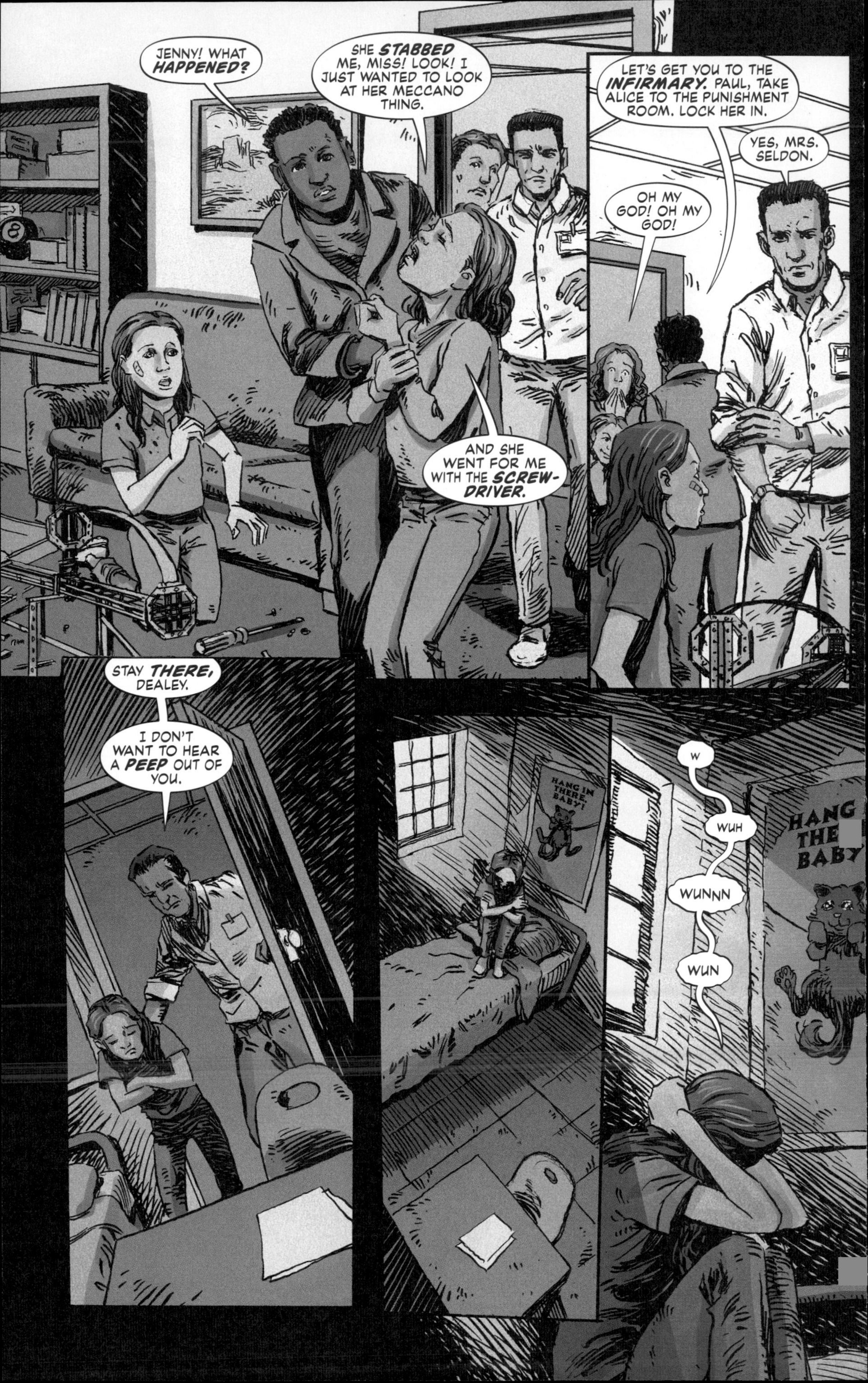
JENNY! WHAT *HAPPENED?*
SHE *STABBED* ME, MISS! LOOK! I JUST WANTED TO LOOK AT HER MECCANO THING.
AND SHE WENT FOR ME WITH THE *SCREW-DRIVER.*
LET'S GET YOU TO THE *INFIRMARY.* PAUL, TAKE ALICE TO THE PUNISHMENT ROOM. LOCK HER IN.
YES, MRS. SELDON.
OH MY GOD! OH MY GOD!
STAY *THERE,* DEALEY.
I DON'T WANT TO HEAR A *PEEP* OUT OF YOU.
HANG IN THERE, BABY!
W
WUH
WUNNN
WUN

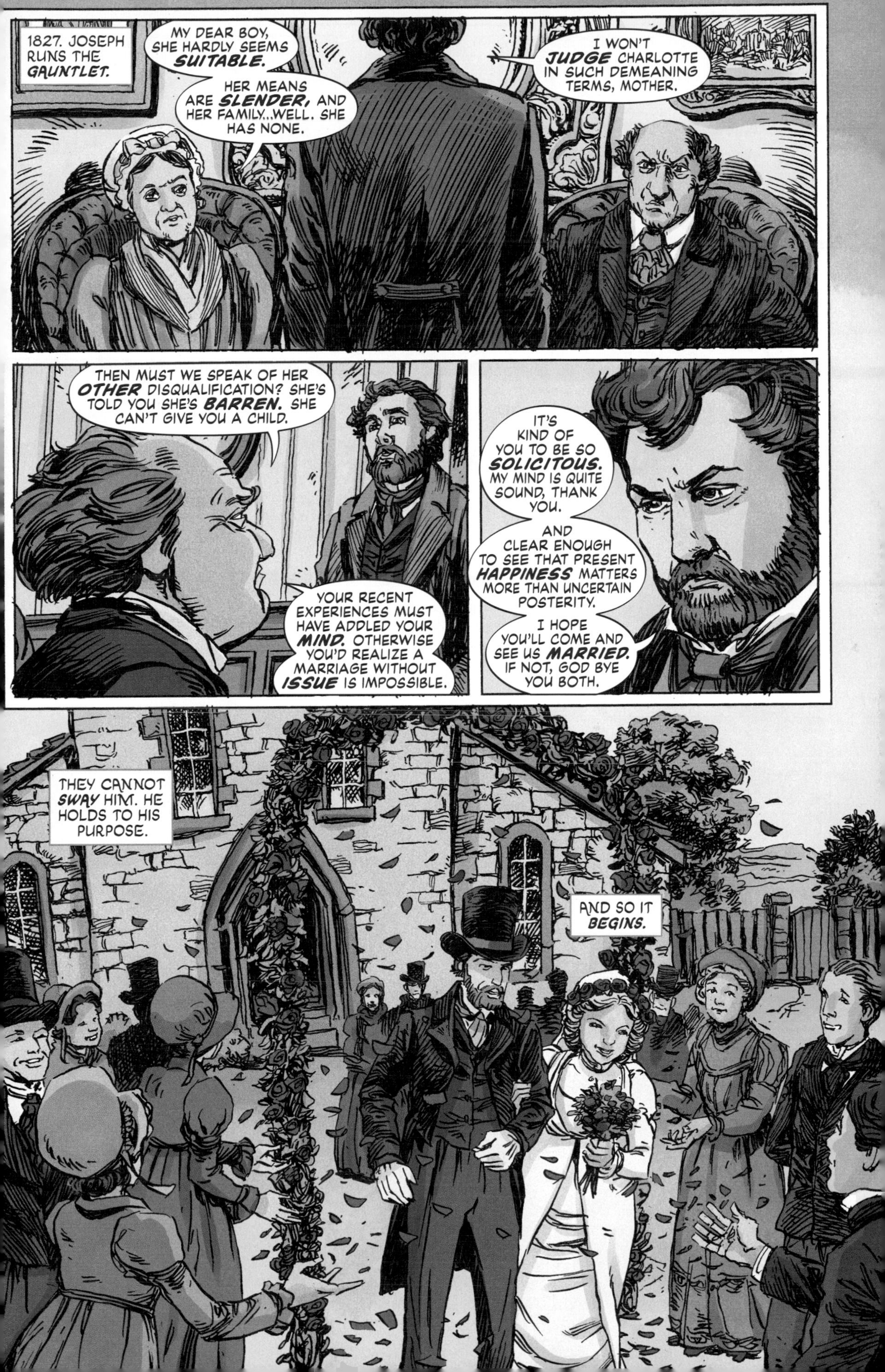
1827. JOSEPH RUNS THE GAUNTLET.
MY DEAR BOY, SHE HARDLY SEEMS SUITABLE.
HER MEANS ARE SLENDER, AND HER FAMILY...WELL. SHE HAS NONE.
I WON'T JUDGE CHARLOTTE IN SUCH DEMEANING TERMS, MOTHER.
THEN MUST WE SPEAK OF HER OTHER DISQUALIFICATION? SHE'S TOLD YOU SHE'S BARREN. SHE CAN'T GIVE YOU A CHILD.
YOUR RECENT EXPERIENCES MUST HAVE ADDLED YOUR MIND. OTHERWISE YOU'D REALIZE A MARRIAGE WITHOUT ISSUE IS IMPOSSIBLE.
IT'S KIND OF YOU TO BE SO SOLICITOUS. MY MIND IS QUITE SOUND, THANK YOU.
AND CLEAR ENOUGH TO SEE THAT PRESENT HAPPINESS MATTERS MORE THAN UNCERTAIN POSTERITY.
I HOPE YOU'LL COME AND SEE US MARRIED. IF NOT, GOD BYE YOU BOTH.
THEY CANNOT SWAY HIM. HE HOLDS TO HIS PURPOSE.
AND SO IT BEGINS.

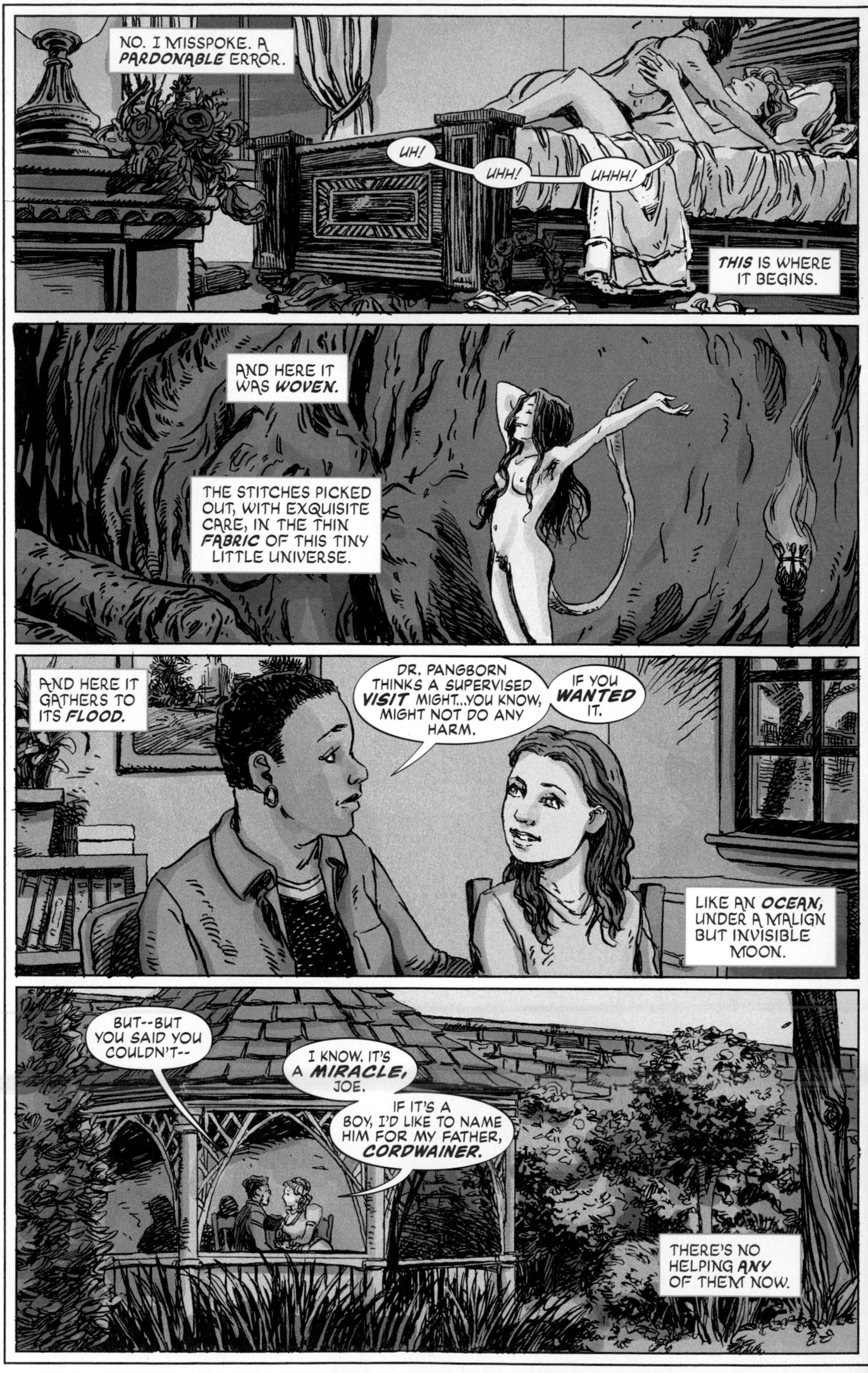
NO. I MISSPOKE. A PARDONABLE ERROR.
UH!
UHH!
UHHH!
THIS IS WHERE IT BEGINS.
AND HERE IT WAS WOVEN.
THE STITCHES PICKED OUT, WITH EXQUISITE CARE, IN THE THIN FABRIC OF THIS TINY LITTLE UNIVERSE.
AND HERE IT GATHERS TO ITS FLOOD.
DR. PANGBORN THINKS A SUPERVISED VISIT MIGHT...YOU KNOW, MIGHT NOT DO ANY HARM.
IF YOU WANTED IT.
LIKE AN OCEAN, UNDER A MALIGN BUT INVISIBLE MOON.
BUT--BUT YOU SAID YOU COULDN'T--
I KNOW. IT'S A MIRACLE, JOE.
IF IT'S A BOY, I'D LIKE TO NAME HIM FOR MY FATHER, CORDWAINER.
THERE'S NO HELPING ANY OF THEM NOW.

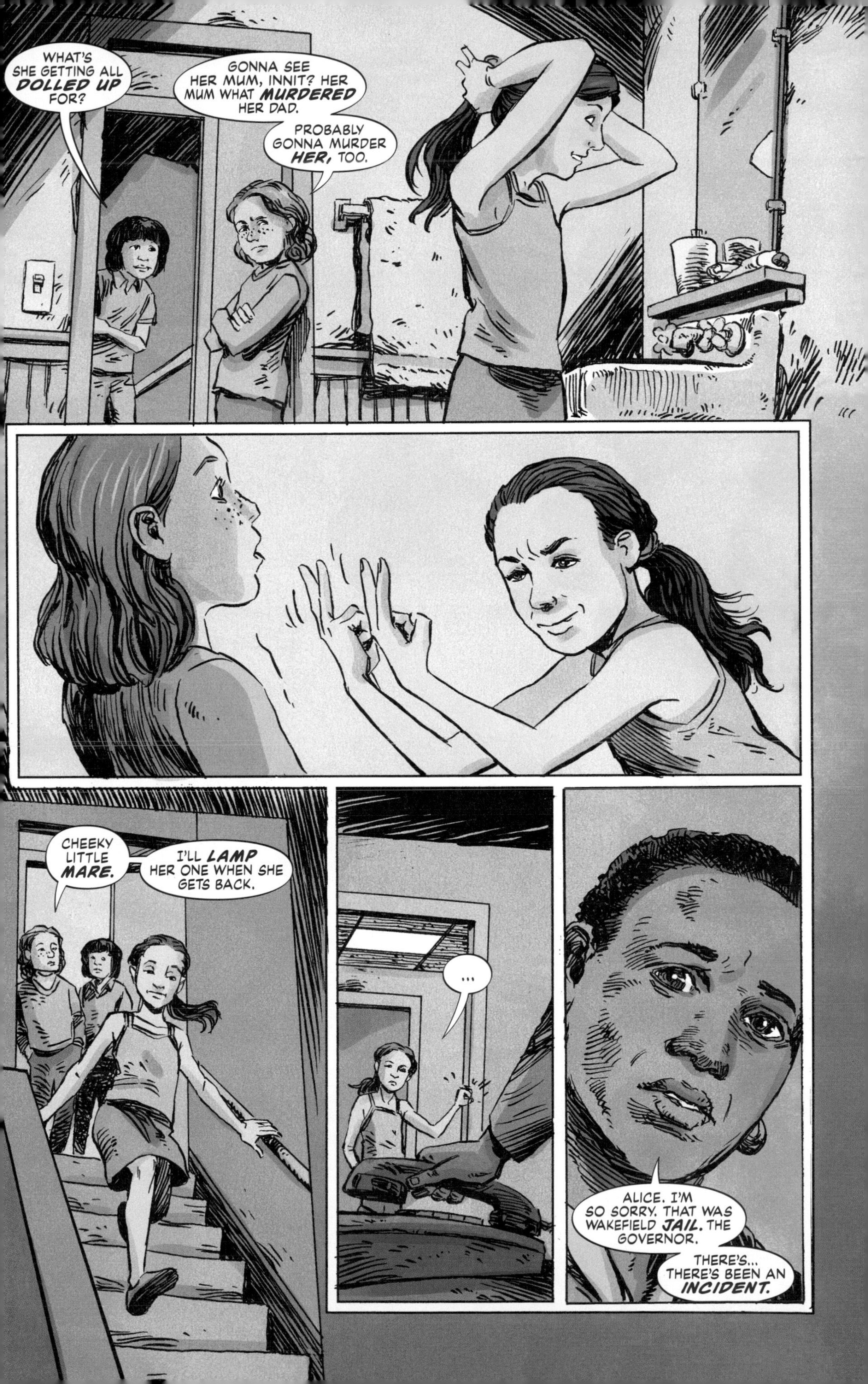
WHAT'S SHE GETTING ALL DOLLED UP FOR?
GONNA SEE HER MUM, INNIT? HER MUM WHAT MURDERED HER DAD.
PROBABLY GONNA MURDER HER, TOO.
CHEEKY LITTLE MARE.
I'LL LAMP HER ONE WHEN SHE GETS BACK.
...
ALICE. I'M SO SORRY. THAT WAS WAKEFIELD JAIL. THE GOVERNOR.
THERE'S... THERE'S BEEN AN INCIDENT.

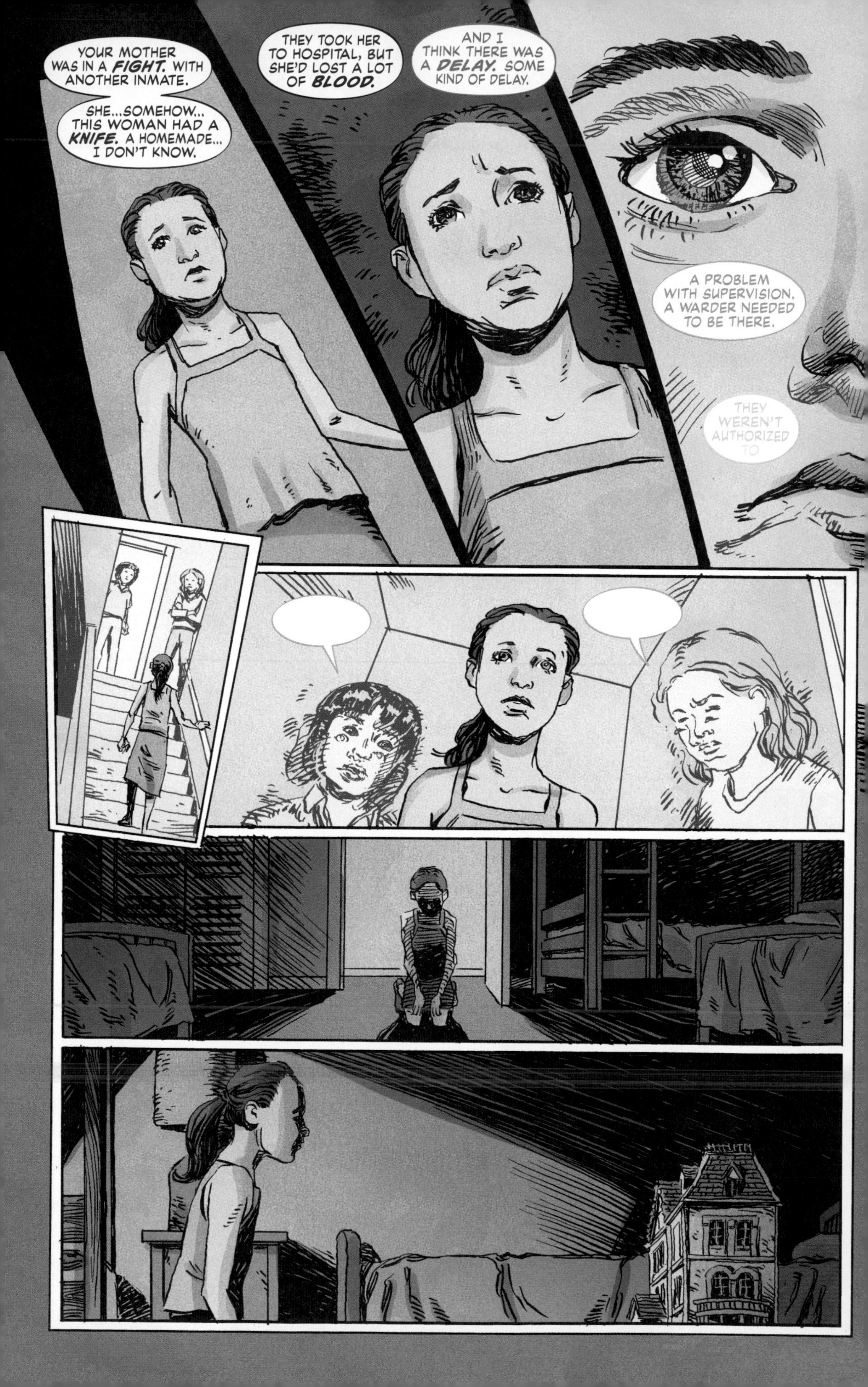
YOUR MOTHER WAS IN A FIGHT. WITH ANOTHER INMATE.
SHE...SOMEHOW... THIS WOMAN HAD A KNIFE. A HOMEMADE... I DON'T KNOW.
THEY TOOK HER TO HOSPITAL, BUT SHE'D LOST A LOT OF BLOOD.
AND I THINK THERE WAS A DELAY. SOME KIND OF DELAY.
A PROBLEM WITH SUPERVISION. A WARDER NEEDED TO BE THERE.
THEY WEREN'T AUTHORIZED TO

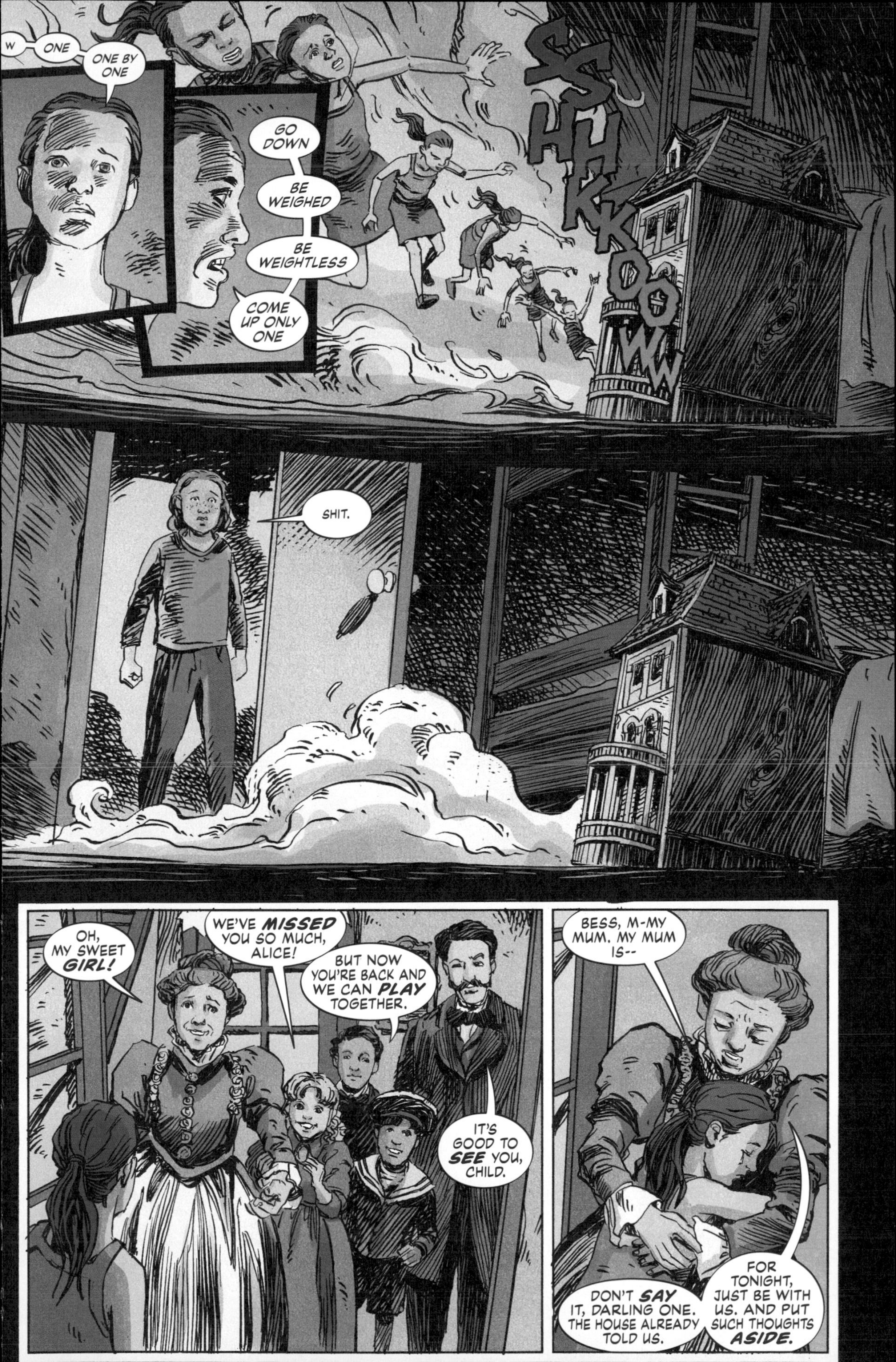
W
ONE
ONE BY ONE
GO DOWN
BE WEIGHED
BE WEIGHTLESS
COME UP ONLY ONE
SSHHKKOOWW
SHIT.
OH, MY SWEET GIRL!
WE'VE MISSED YOU SO MUCH, ALICE!
BUT NOW YOU'RE BACK AND WE CAN PLAY TOGETHER.
IT'S GOOD TO SEE YOU, CHILD.
BESS, M-MY MUM. MY MUM IS--
DON'T SAY IT, DARLING ONE. THE HOUSE ALREADY TOLD US.
FOR TONIGHT, JUST BE WITH US. AND PUT SUCH THOUGHTS ASIDE.

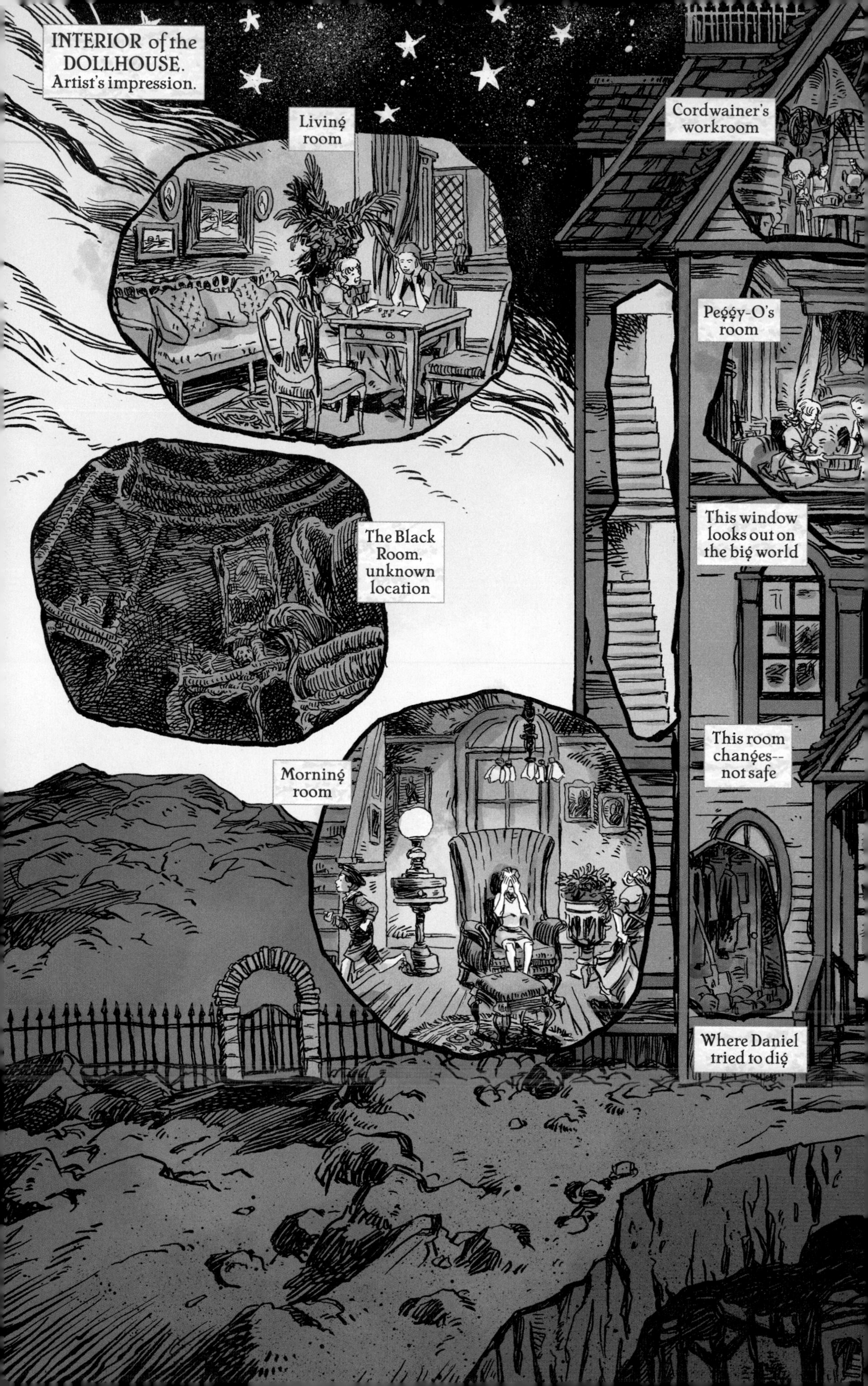
INTERIOR of the DOLLHOUSE. Artist's impression.
Living room
Cordwainer's workroom
Peggy-O's room
The Black Room, unknown location
This window looks out on the big world
This room changes-- not safe
Morning room
Where Daniel tried to dig

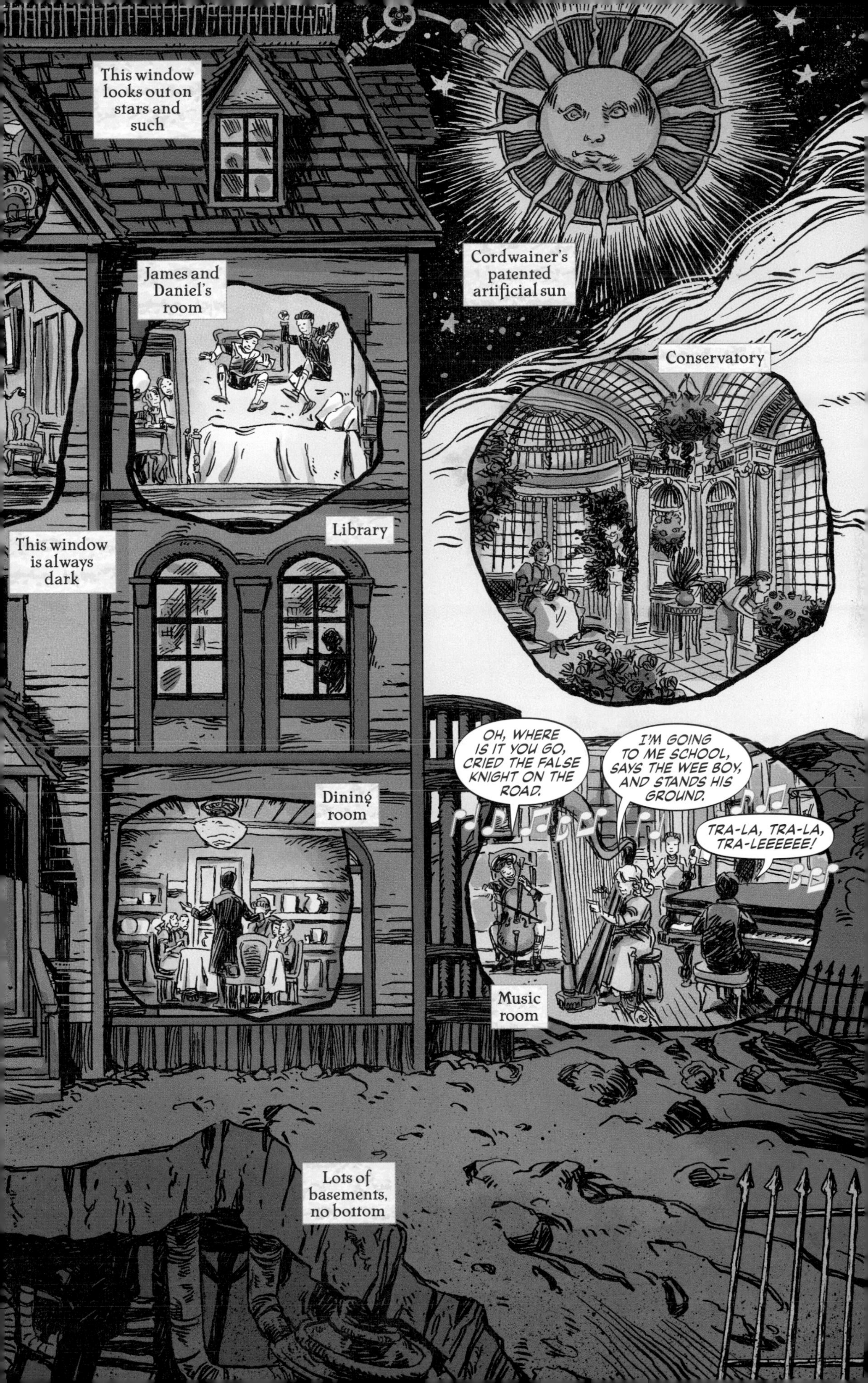
This window looks out on stars and such
Cordwainer's patented artificial sun
James and Daniel's room
Conservatory
This window is always dark
Library
Dining room
OH, WHERE IS IT YOU GO, CRIED THE FALSE KNIGHT ON THE ROAD.
I'M GOING TO ME SCHOOL, SAYS THE WEE BOY, AND STANDS HIS GROUND.
TRA-LA, TRA-LA, TRA-LEEEEEE!
Music room
Lots of basements, no bottom

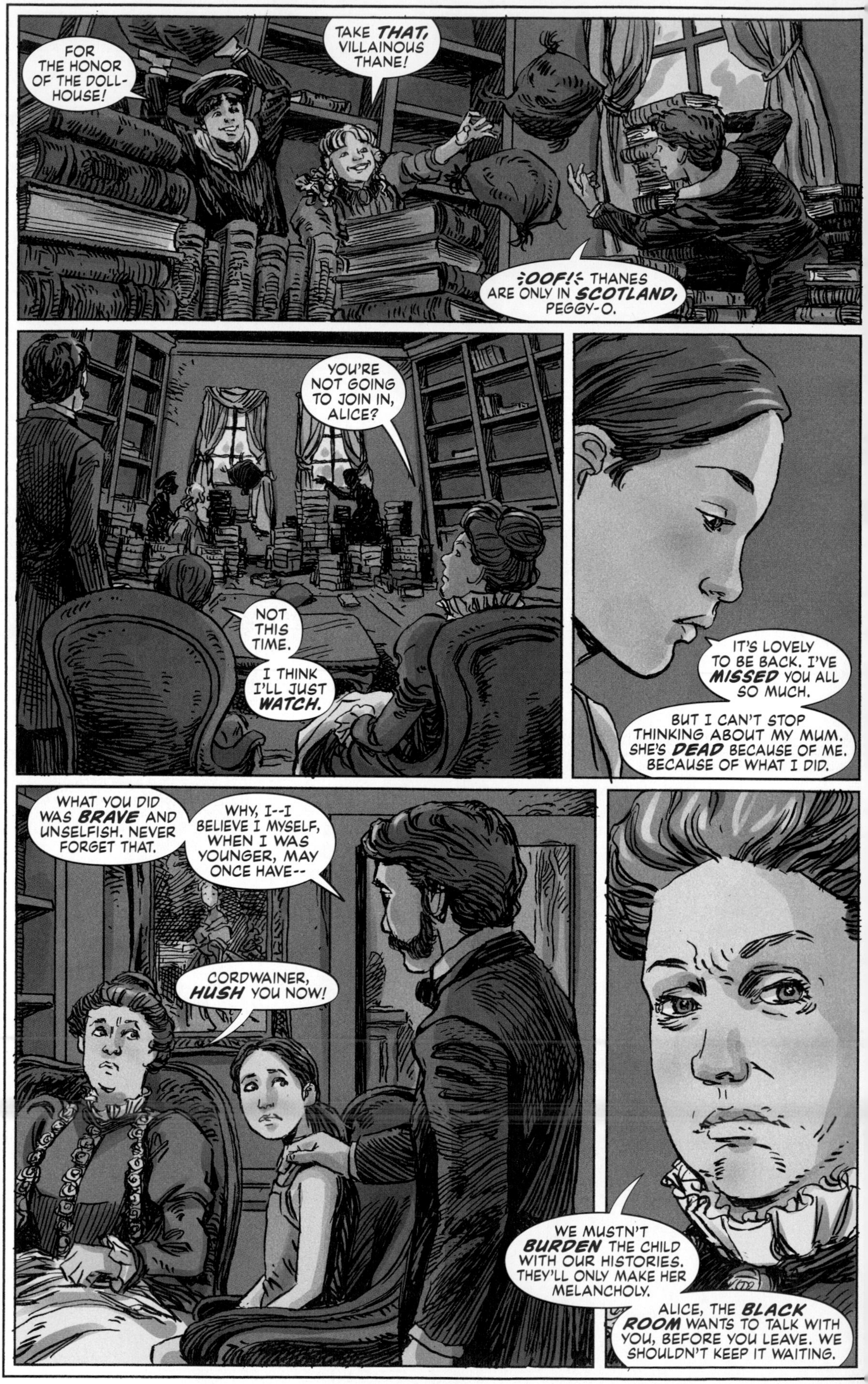
FOR THE HONOR OF THE DOLL-HOUSE!
TAKE THAT, VILLAINOUS THANE!
OOF! THANES ARE ONLY IN SCOTLAND, PEGGY-O.
YOU'RE NOT GOING TO JOIN IN, ALICE?
NOT THIS TIME.
I THINK I'LL JUST WATCH.
IT'S LOVELY TO BE BACK. I'VE MISSED YOU ALL SO MUCH.
BUT I CAN'T STOP THINKING ABOUT MY MUM. SHE'S DEAD BECAUSE OF ME. BECAUSE OF WHAT I DID.
WHAT YOU DID WAS BRAVE AND UNSELFISH. NEVER FORGET THAT.
WHY, I--I BELIEVE I MYSELF, WHEN I WAS YOUNGER, MAY ONCE HAVE--
CORDWAINER, HUSH YOU NOW!
WE MUSTN'T BURDEN THE CHILD WITH OUR HISTORIES. THEY'LL ONLY MAKE HER MELANCHOLY.
ALICE, THE BLACK ROOM WANTS TO TALK WITH YOU, BEFORE YOU LEAVE. WE SHOULDN'T KEEP IT WAITING.

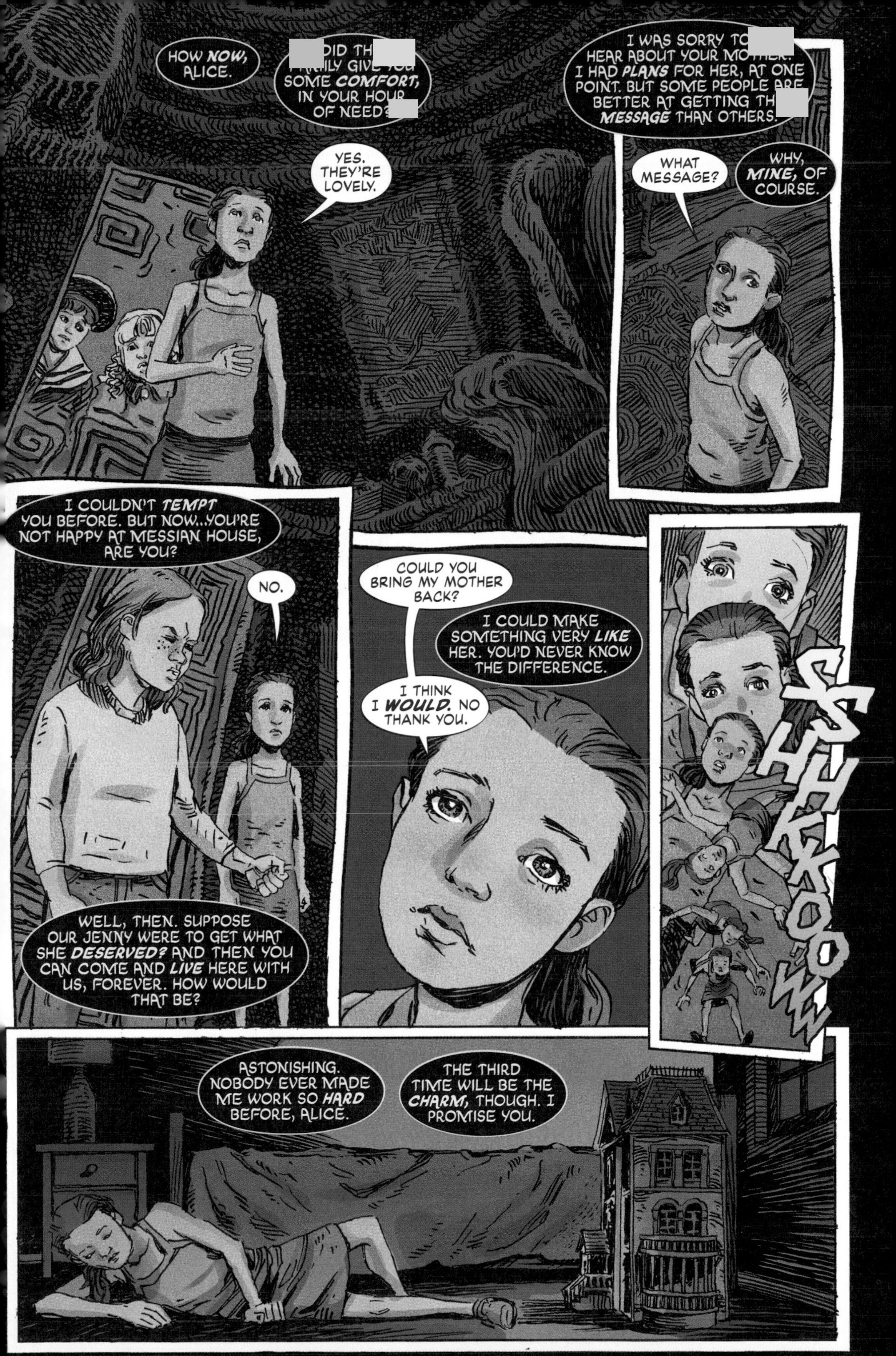
HOW NOW, ALICE.
DID TH FAMILY GIVE YOU SOME COMFORT, IN YOUR HOUR OF NEED?
YES. THEY'RE LOVELY.
I WAS SORRY TO HEAR ABOUT YOUR MOTHER. I HAD PLANS FOR HER, AT ONE POINT. BUT SOME PEOPLE ARE BETTER AT GETTING TH MESSAGE THAN OTHERS.
WHAT MESSAGE?
WHY, MINE, OF COURSE.
I COULDN'T TEMPT YOU BEFORE. BUT NOW...YOU'RE NOT HAPPY AT MESSIAN HOUSE, ARE YOU?
NO.
WELL, THEN. SUPPOSE OUR JENNY WERE TO GET WHAT SHE DESERVED? AND THEN YOU CAN COME AND LIVE HERE WITH US, FOREVER. HOW WOULD THAT BE?
COULD YOU BRING MY MOTHER BACK?
I COULD MAKE SOMETHING VERY LIKE HER. YOU'D NEVER KNOW THE DIFFERENCE.
I THINK I WOULD. NO THANK YOU.
SSHHKKOOOWW
ASTONISHING. NOBODY EVER MADE ME WORK SO HARD BEFORE, ALICE.
THE THIRD TIME WILL BE THE CHARM, THOUGH. I PROMISE YOU.

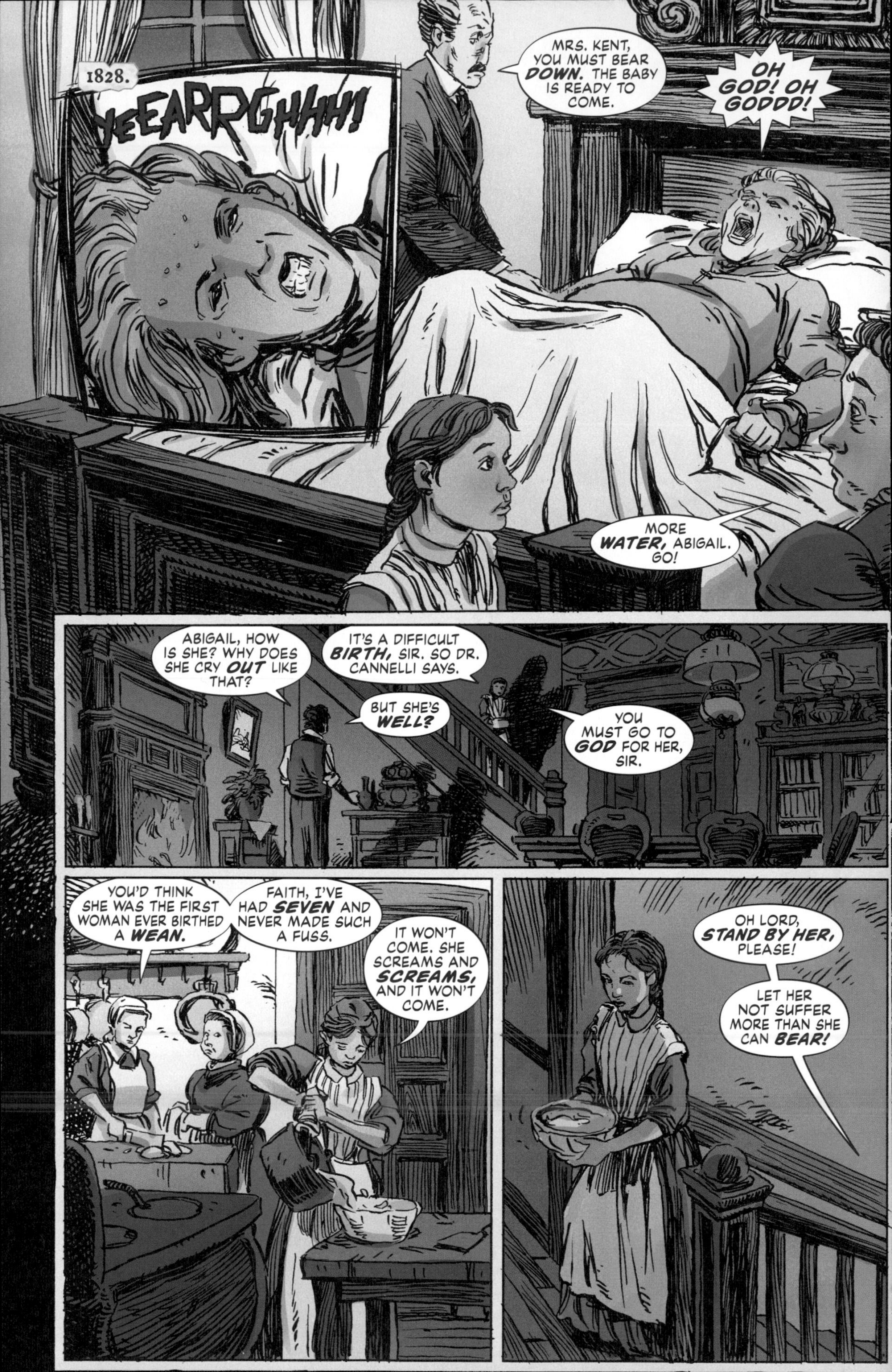
1828.
YEEARRGHHH!
MRS. KENT, YOU MUST BEAR DOWN. THE BABY IS READY TO COME.
OH GOD! OH GODDD!
MORE WATER, ABIGAIL. GO!
ABIGAIL, HOW IS SHE? WHY DOES SHE CRY OUT LIKE THAT?
IT'S A DIFFICULT BIRTH, SIR. SO DR. CANNELLI SAYS.
BUT SHE'S WELL?
YOU MUST GO TO GOD FOR HER, SIR.
YOU'D THINK SHE WAS THE FIRST WOMAN EVER BIRTHED A WEAN.
FAITH, I'VE HAD SEVEN AND NEVER MADE SUCH A FUSS.
IT WON'T COME. SHE SCREAMS AND SCREAMS, AND IT WON'T COME.
OH LORD, STAND BY HER, PLEASE!
LET HER NOT SUFFER MORE THAN SHE CAN BEAR!

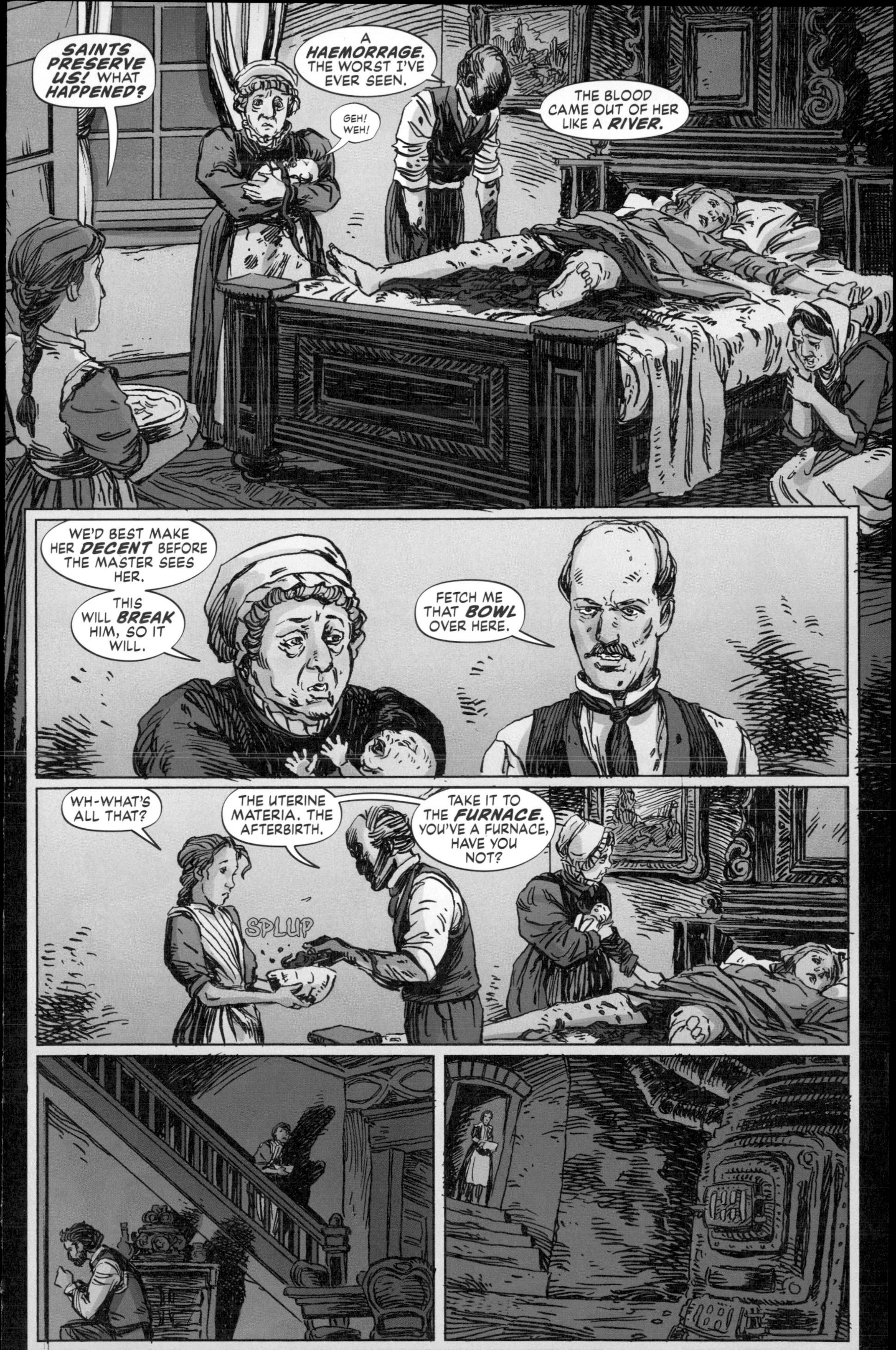
SAINTS PRESERVE US! WHAT HAPPENED?
A HAEMORRAGE. THE WORST I'VE EVER SEEN.
GEH! WEH!
THE BLOOD CAME OUT OF HER LIKE A RIVER.
WE'D BEST MAKE HER DECENT BEFORE THE MASTER SEES HER.
THIS WILL BREAK HIM, SO IT WILL.
FETCH ME THAT BOWL OVER HERE.
WH-WHAT'S ALL THAT?
THE UTERINE MATERIA. THE AFTERBIRTH.
TAKE IT TO THE FURNACE. YOU'VE A FURNACE, HAVE YOU NOT?
SPLUP

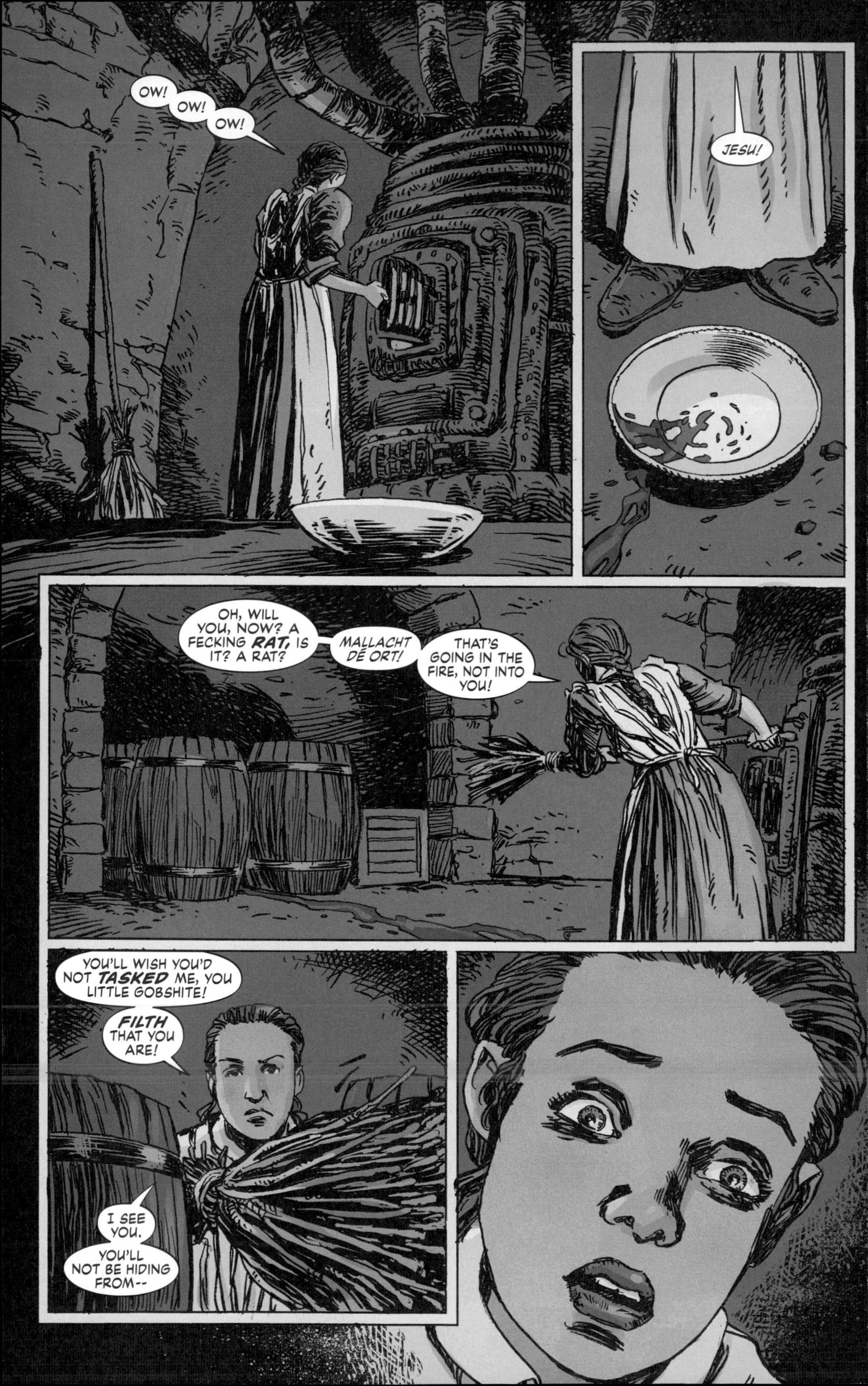
OW! OW! OW!
JESU!
OH, WILL YOU, NOW? A FECKING RAT, IS IT? A RAT?
MALLACHT DÉ ORT!
THAT'S GOING IN THE FIRE, NOT INTO YOU!
YOU'LL WISH YOU'D NOT TASKED ME, YOU LITTLE GOBSHITE!
FILTH THAT YOU ARE!
I SEE YOU.
YOU'LL NOT BE HIDING FROM--

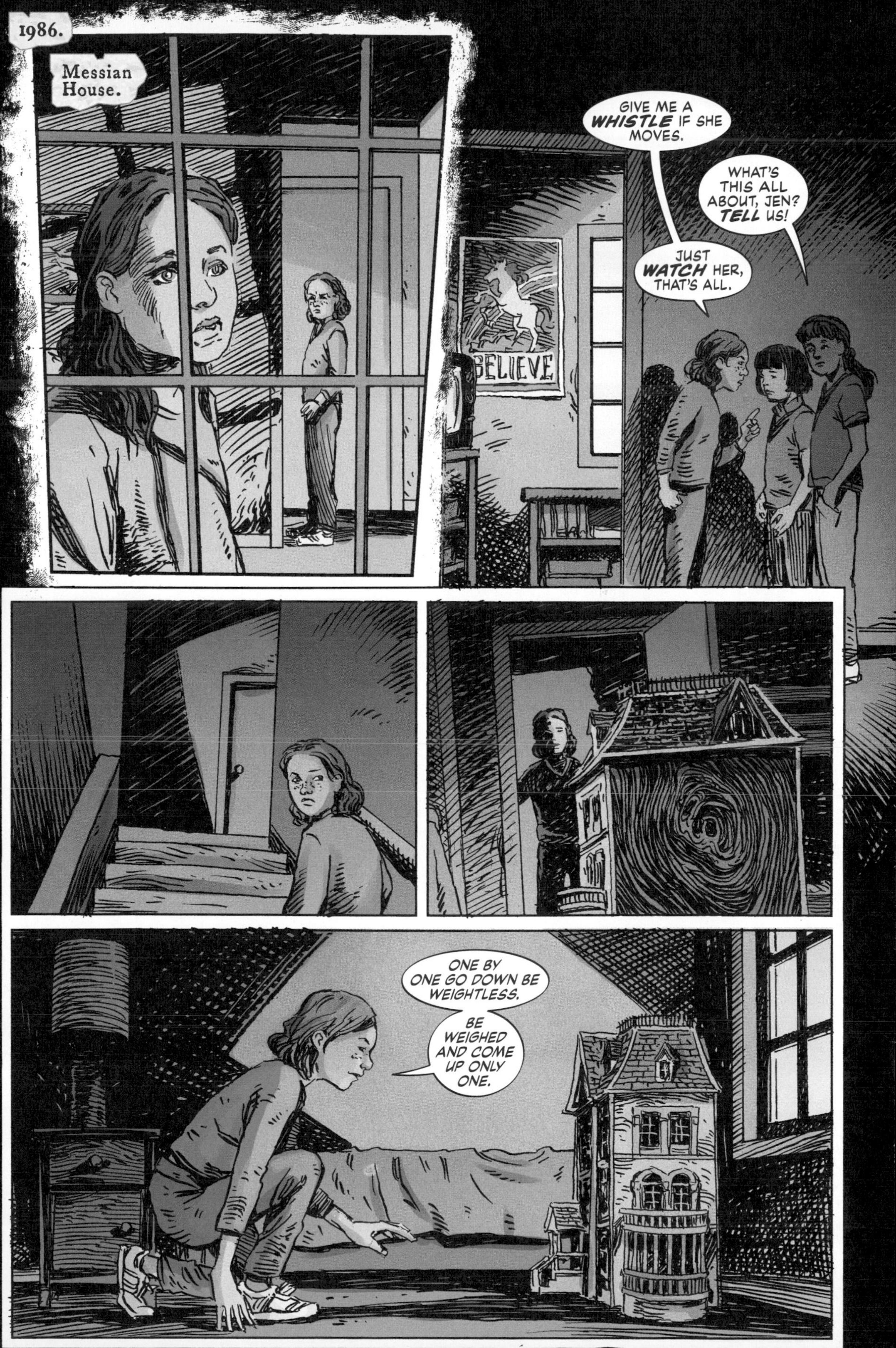
1986.
Messian House.
GIVE ME A WHISTLE IF SHE MOVES.
WHAT'S THIS ALL ABOUT, JEN? TELL US!
JUST WATCH HER, THAT'S ALL.
BELIEVE
ONE BY ONE GO DOWN BE WEIGHTLESS.
BE WEIGHED AND COME UP ONLY ONE.

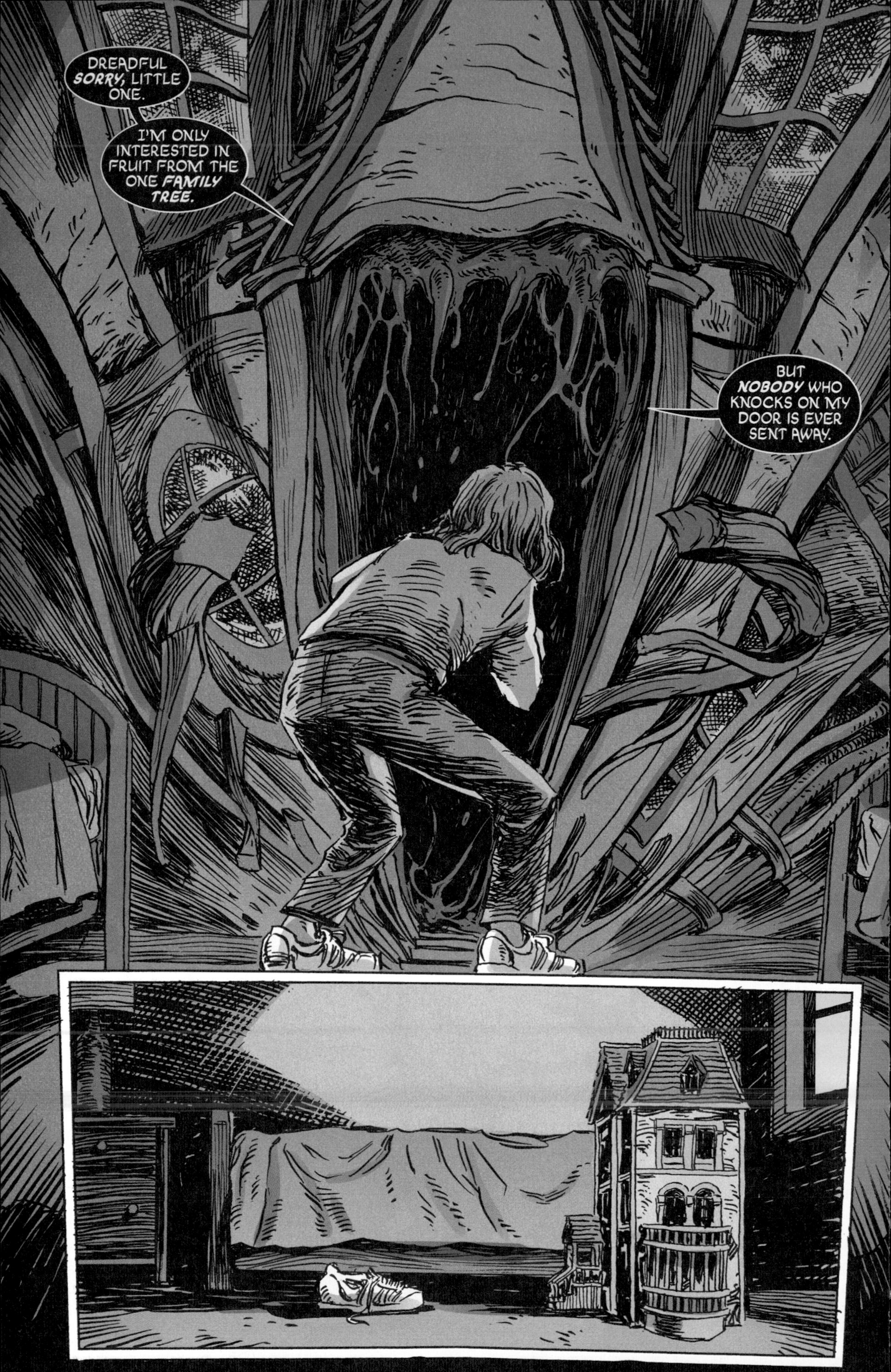
DREADFUL SORRY, LITTLE ONE.
I'M ONLY INTERESTED IN FRUIT FROM THE ONE FAMILY TREE.
BUT NOBODY WHO KNOCKS ON MY DOOR IS EVER SENT AWAY.

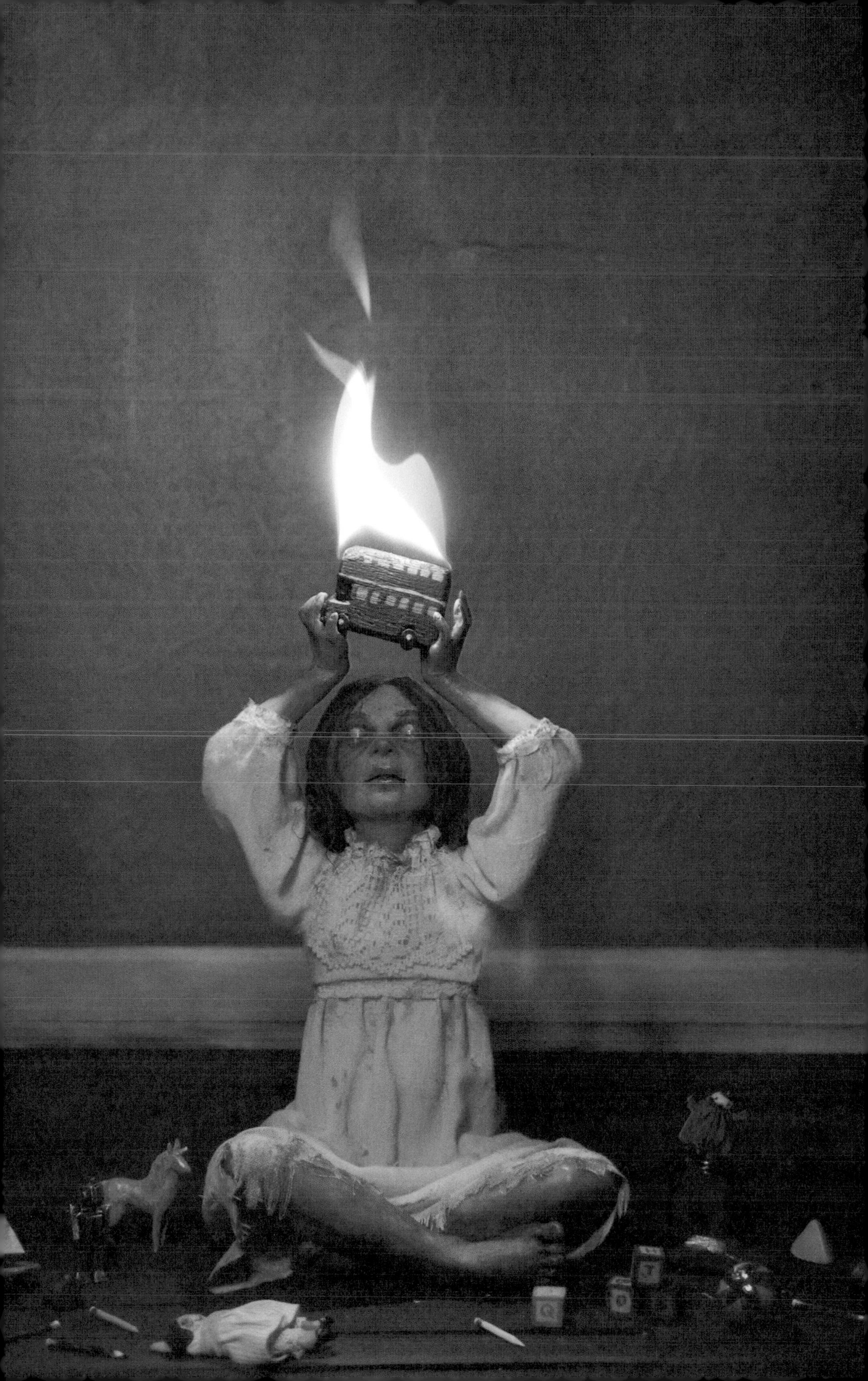

BE WEIGHTLESS

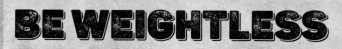

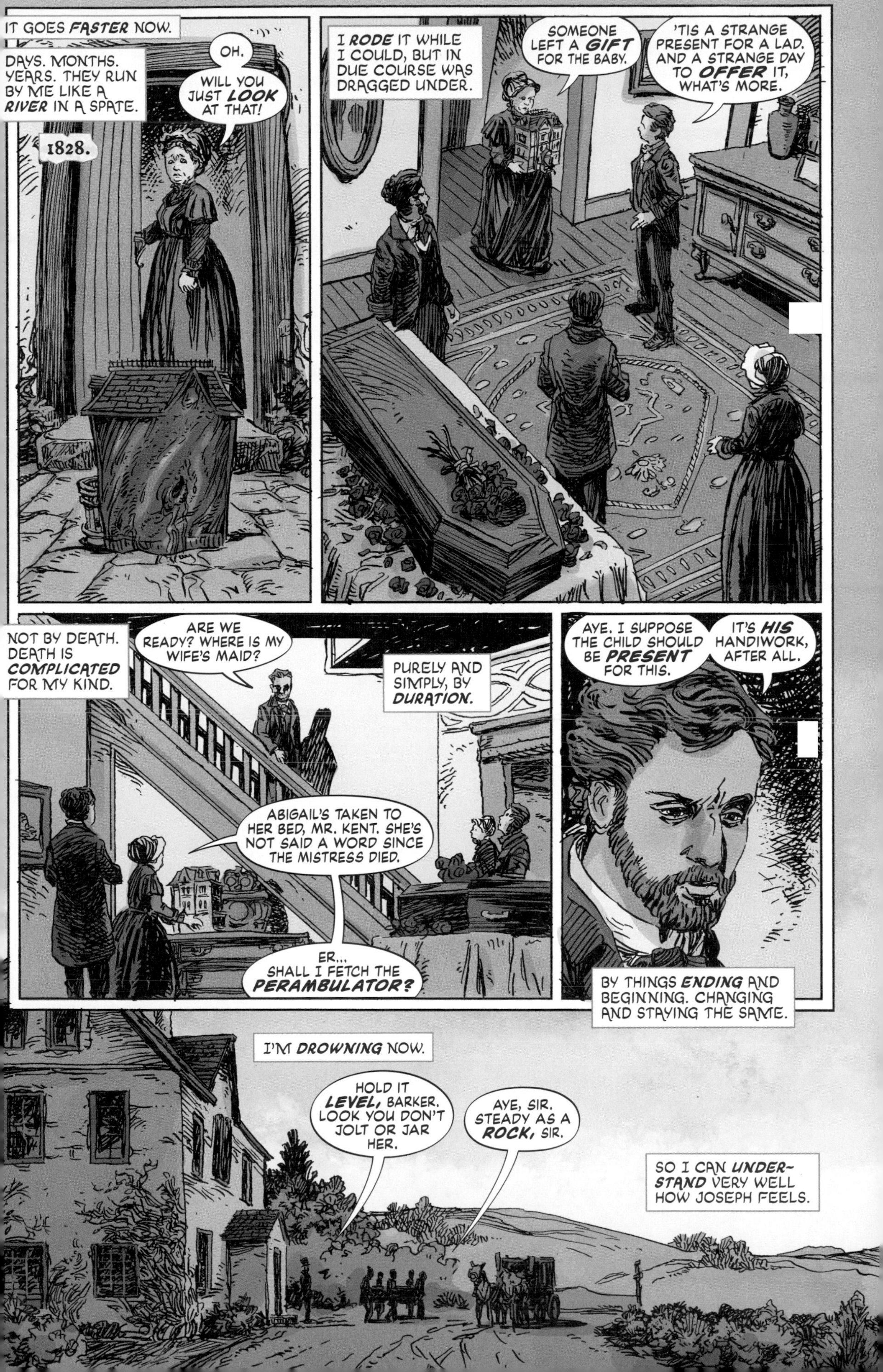
IT GOES FASTER NOW.
DAYS. MONTHS. YEARS. THEY RUN BY ME LIKE A RIVER IN A SPATE.
OH.
WILL YOU JUST LOOK AT THAT!
1828.
I RODE IT WHILE I COULD, BUT IN DUE COURSE WAS DRAGGED UNDER.
SOMEONE LEFT A GIFT FOR THE BABY.
'TIS A STRANGE PRESENT FOR A LAD. AND A STRANGE DAY TO OFFER IT, WHAT'S MORE.
NOT BY DEATH. DEATH IS COMPLICATED FOR MY KIND.
ARE WE READY? WHERE IS MY WIFE'S MAID?
PURELY AND SIMPLY, BY DURATION.
ABIGAIL'S TAKEN TO HER BED, MR. KENT. SHE'S NOT SAID A WORD SINCE THE MISTRESS DIED.
ER... SHALL I FETCH THE PERAMBULATOR?
AYE. I SUPPOSE THE CHILD SHOULD BE PRESENT FOR THIS.
IT'S HIS HANDIWORK, AFTER ALL.
BY THINGS ENDING AND BEGINNING. CHANGING AND STAYING THE SAME.
I'M DROWNING NOW.
HOLD IT LEVEL, BARKER. LOOK YOU DON'T JOLT OR JAR HER.
AYE, SIR. STEADY AS A ROCK, SIR.
SO I CAN UNDERSTAND VERY WELL HOW JOSEPH FEELS.

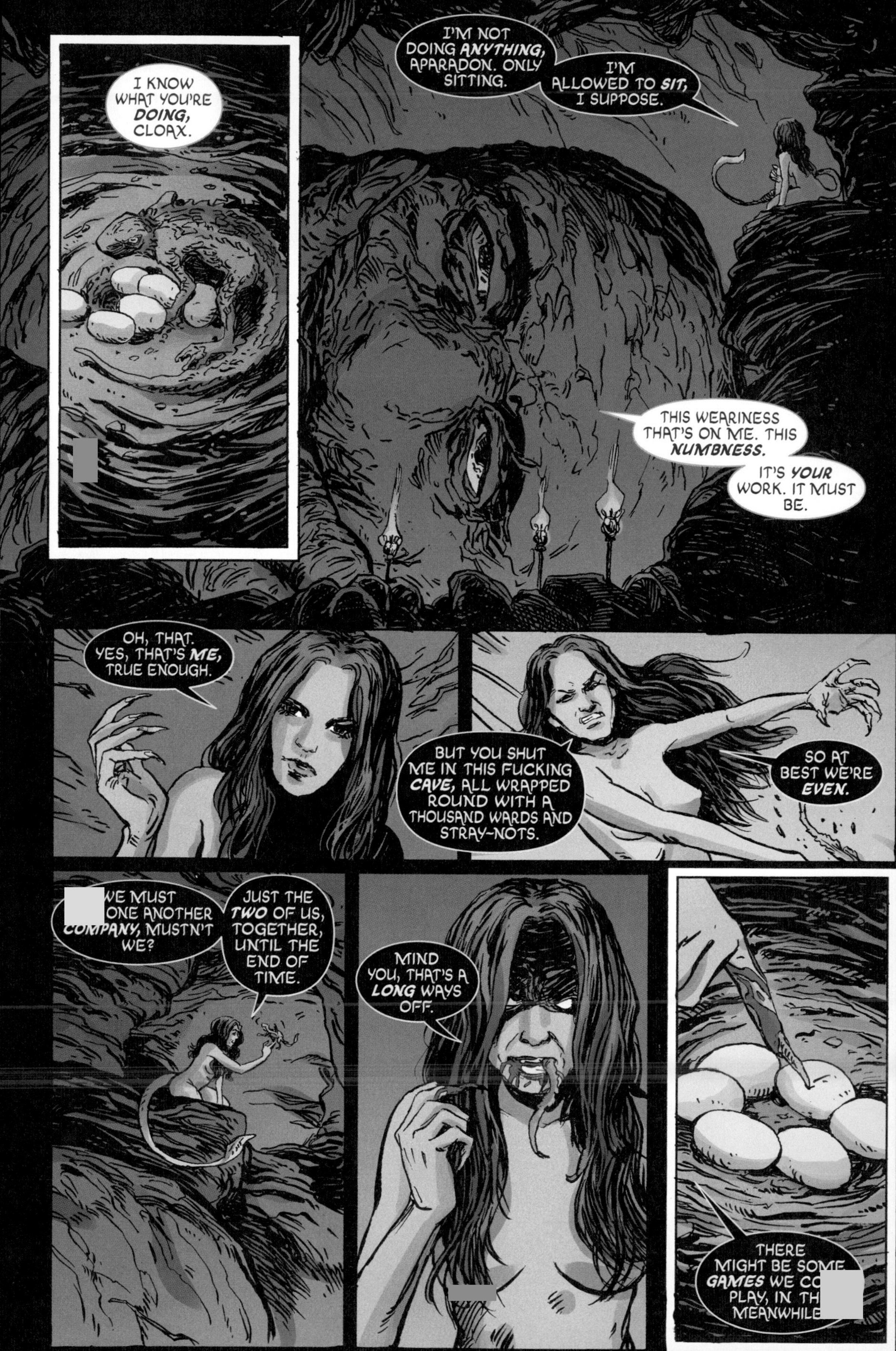

I KNOW WHAT YOU'RE DOING, CLOAX.
I'M NOT DOING ANYTHING, APARADON. ONLY SITTING.
I'M ALLOWED TO SIT, I SUPPOSE.
THIS WEARINESS THAT'S ON ME. THIS NUMBNESS.
IT'S YOUR WORK. IT MUST BE.
OH, THAT. YES, THAT'S ME, TRUE ENOUGH.
BUT YOU SHUT ME IN THIS FUCKING CAVE, ALL WRAPPED ROUND WITH A THOUSAND WARDS AND STRAY-NOTS.
SO AT BEST WE'RE EVEN.
WE MUST ONE ANOTHER COMPANY, MUSTN'T WE?
JUST THE TWO OF US, TOGETHER, UNTIL THE END OF TIME.
MIND YOU, THAT'S A LONG WAYS OFF.
THERE MIGHT BE SOME GAMES WE CO PLAY, IN TH MEANWHILE

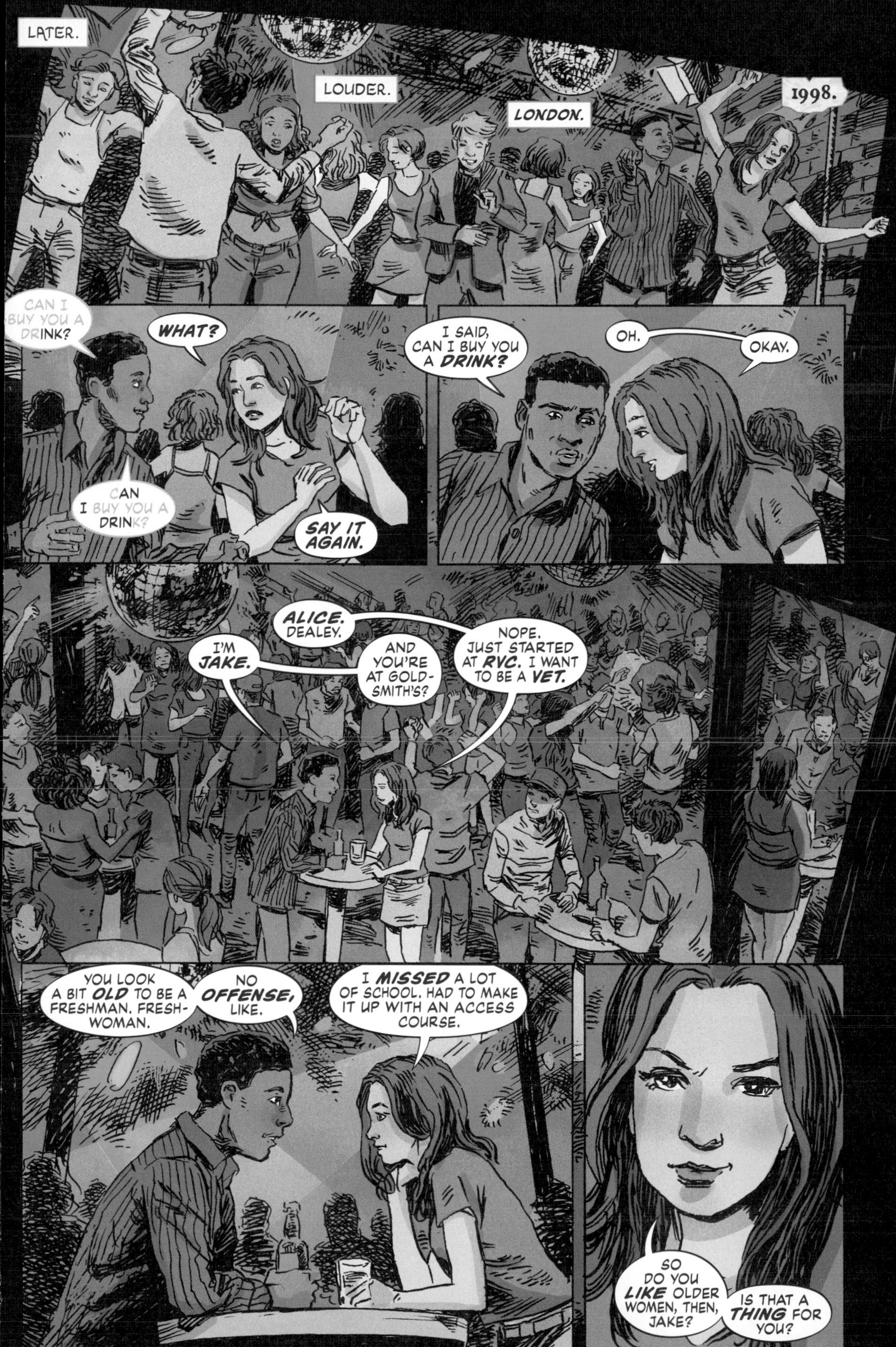
LATER.
LOUDER.
LONDON.
1998.
CAN I BUY YOU A DRINK?
WHAT?
CAN I BUY YOU A DRINK?
SAY IT AGAIN.
I SAID, CAN I BUY YOU A DRINK?
OH.
OKAY.
I'M JAKE.
ALICE. DEALEY.
AND YOU'RE AT GOLD-SMITH'S?
NOPE. JUST STARTED AT RVC. I WANT TO BE A VET.
YOU LOOK A BIT OLD TO BE A FRESHMAN. FRESH-WOMAN.
NO OFFENSE, LIKE.
I MISSED A LOT OF SCHOOL. HAD TO MAKE IT UP WITH AN ACCESS COURSE.
SO DO YOU LIKE OLDER WOMEN, THEN, JAKE?
IS THAT A THING FOR YOU?

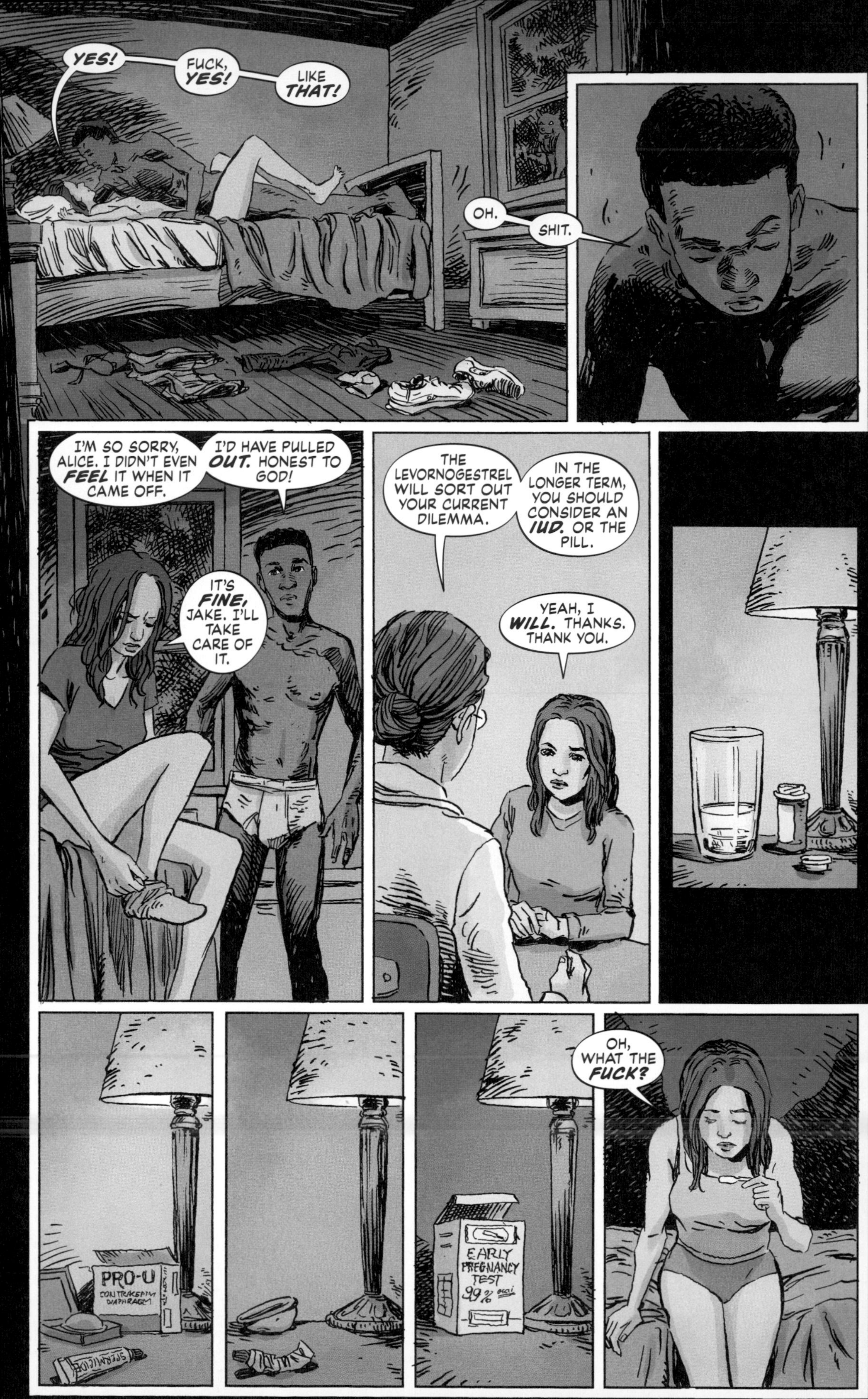
YES!
FUCK, YES!
LIKE THAT!
OH.
SHIT.
I'M SO SORRY, ALICE. I DIDN'T EVEN FEEL IT WHEN IT CAME OFF.
I'D HAVE PULLED OUT. HONEST TO GOD!
IT'S FINE, JAKE. I'LL TAKE CARE OF IT.
THE LEVORNOGESTREL WILL SORT OUT YOUR CURRENT DILEMMA.
IN THE LONGER TERM, YOU SHOULD CONSIDER AN IUD. OR THE PILL.
YEAH, I WILL. THANKS. THANK YOU.
PRO-U
CONTRACEPTIVE DIAPHRAGM
SPERMICIDE
EARLY PREGNANCY TEST
99%
OH, WHAT THE FUCK?

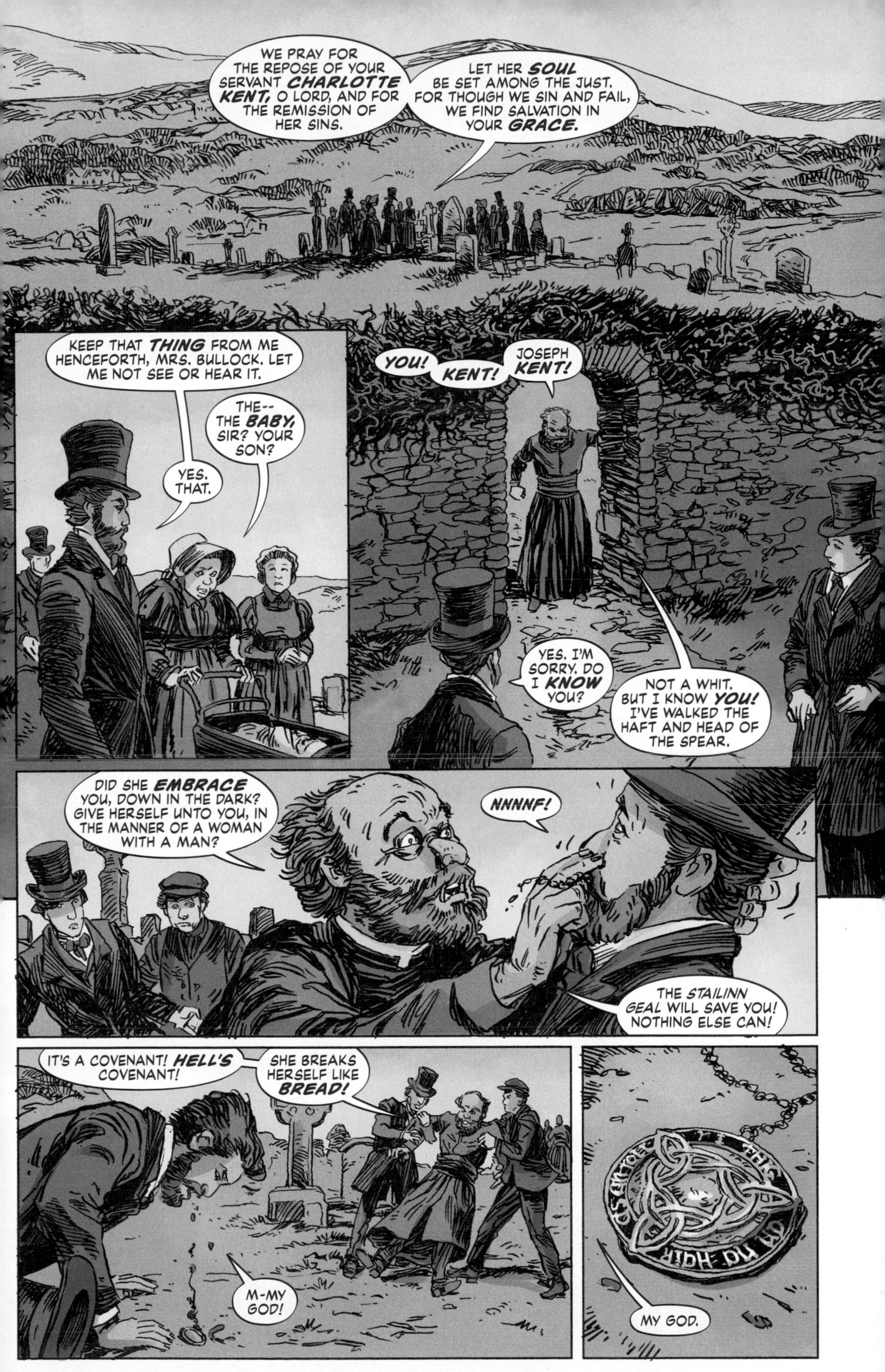
WE PRAY FOR THE REPOSE OF YOUR SERVANT CHARLOTTE KENT, O LORD, AND FOR THE REMISSION OF HER SINS.
LET HER SOUL BE SET AMONG THE JUST. FOR THOUGH WE SIN AND FAIL, WE FIND SALVATION IN YOUR GRACE.
KEEP THAT THING FROM ME HENCEFORTH, MRS. BULLOCK. LET ME NOT SEE OR HEAR IT.
THE-- THE BABY, SIR? YOUR SON?
YES. THAT.
YOU!
KENT!
JOSEPH KENT!
YES. I'M SORRY. DO I KNOW YOU?
NOT A WHIT. BUT I KNOW YOU! I'VE WALKED THE HAFT AND HEAD OF THE SPEAR.
DID SHE EMBRACE YOU, DOWN IN THE DARK? GIVE HERSELF UNTO YOU, IN THE MANNER OF A WOMAN WITH A MAN?
NNNNF!
THE STAILINN GEAL WILL SAVE YOU! NOTHING ELSE CAN!
IT'S A COVENANT! HELL'S COVENANT!
SHE BREAKS HERSELF LIKE BREAD!
M-MY GOD!
MY GOD.

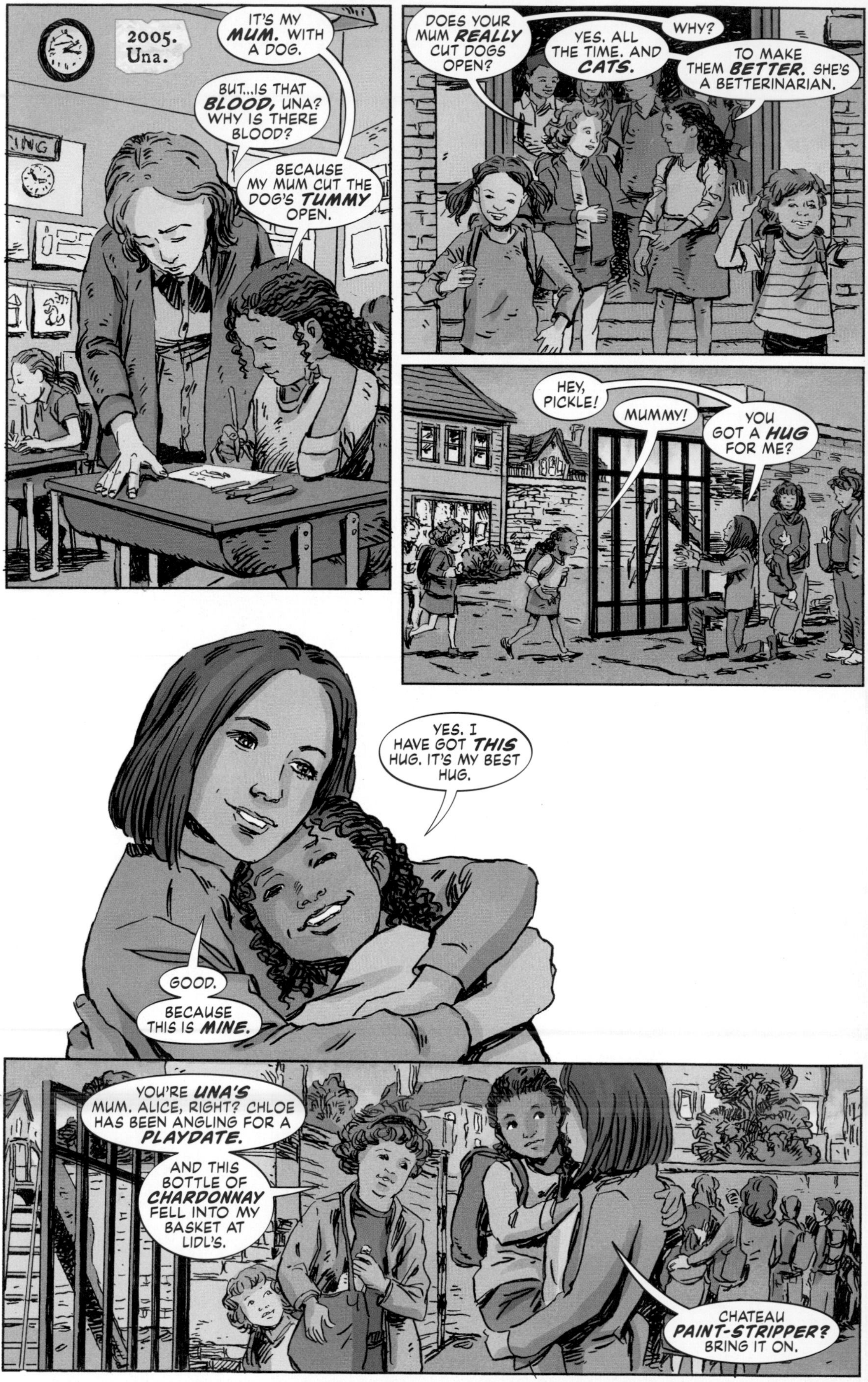
2005. Una.
IT'S MY MUM. WITH A DOG.
BUT...IS THAT BLOOD, UNA? WHY IS THERE BLOOD?
BECAUSE MY MUM CUT THE DOG'S TUMMY OPEN.
DOES YOUR MUM REALLY CUT DOGS OPEN?
WHY?
YES. ALL THE TIME. AND CATS.
TO MAKE THEM BETTER. SHE'S A BETTERINARIAN.
HEY, PICKLE!
MUMMY!
YOU GOT A HUG FOR ME?
YES. I HAVE GOT THIS HUG. IT'S MY BEST HUG.
GOOD.
BECAUSE THIS IS MINE.
YOU'RE UNA'S MUM. ALICE, RIGHT? CHLOE HAS BEEN ANGLING FOR A PLAYDATE.
AND THIS BOTTLE OF CHARDONNAY FELL INTO MY BASKET AT LIDL'S.
CHATEAU PAINT-STRIPPER? BRING IT ON.

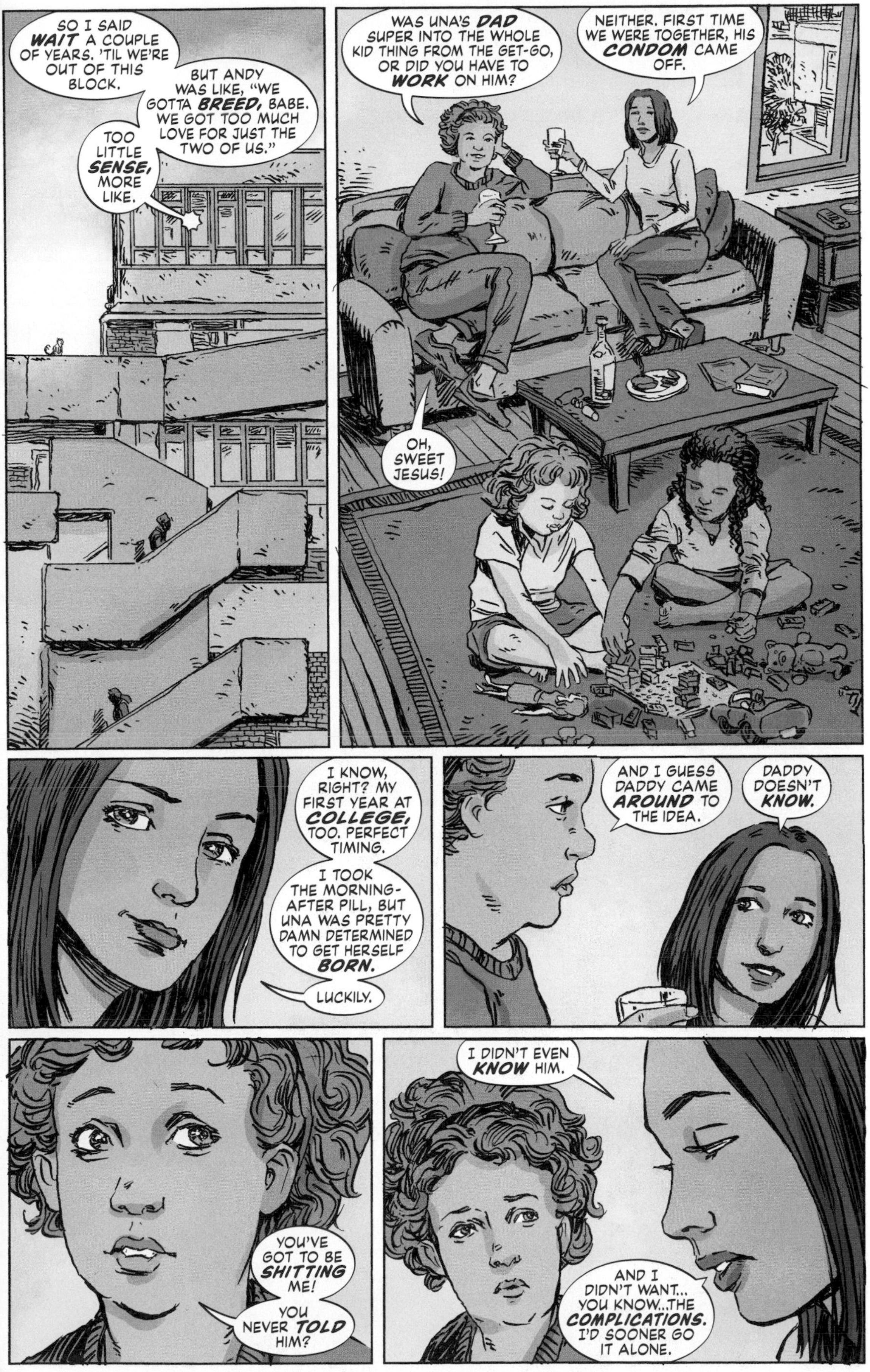
SO I SAID WAIT A COUPLE OF YEARS. 'TIL WE'RE OUT OF THIS BLOCK.
BUT ANDY WAS LIKE, "WE GOTTA BREED, BABE. WE GOT TOO MUCH LOVE FOR JUST THE TWO OF US."
TOO LITTLE SENSE, MORE LIKE.
WAS UNA'S DAD SUPER INTO THE WHOLE KID THING FROM THE GET-GO, OR DID YOU HAVE TO WORK ON HIM?
NEITHER. FIRST TIME WE WERE TOGETHER, HIS CONDOM CAME OFF.
OH, SWEET JESUS!
I KNOW, RIGHT? MY FIRST YEAR AT COLLEGE, TOO. PERFECT TIMING.
I TOOK THE MORNING-AFTER PILL, BUT UNA WAS PRETTY DAMN DETERMINED TO GET HERSELF BORN.
LUCKILY.
AND I GUESS DADDY CAME AROUND TO THE IDEA.
DADDY DOESN'T KNOW.
YOU'VE GOT TO BE SHITTING ME!
YOU NEVER TOLD HIM?
I DIDN'T EVEN KNOW HIM.
AND I DIDN'T WANT... YOU KNOW...THE COMPLICATIONS. I'D SOONER GO IT ALONE.

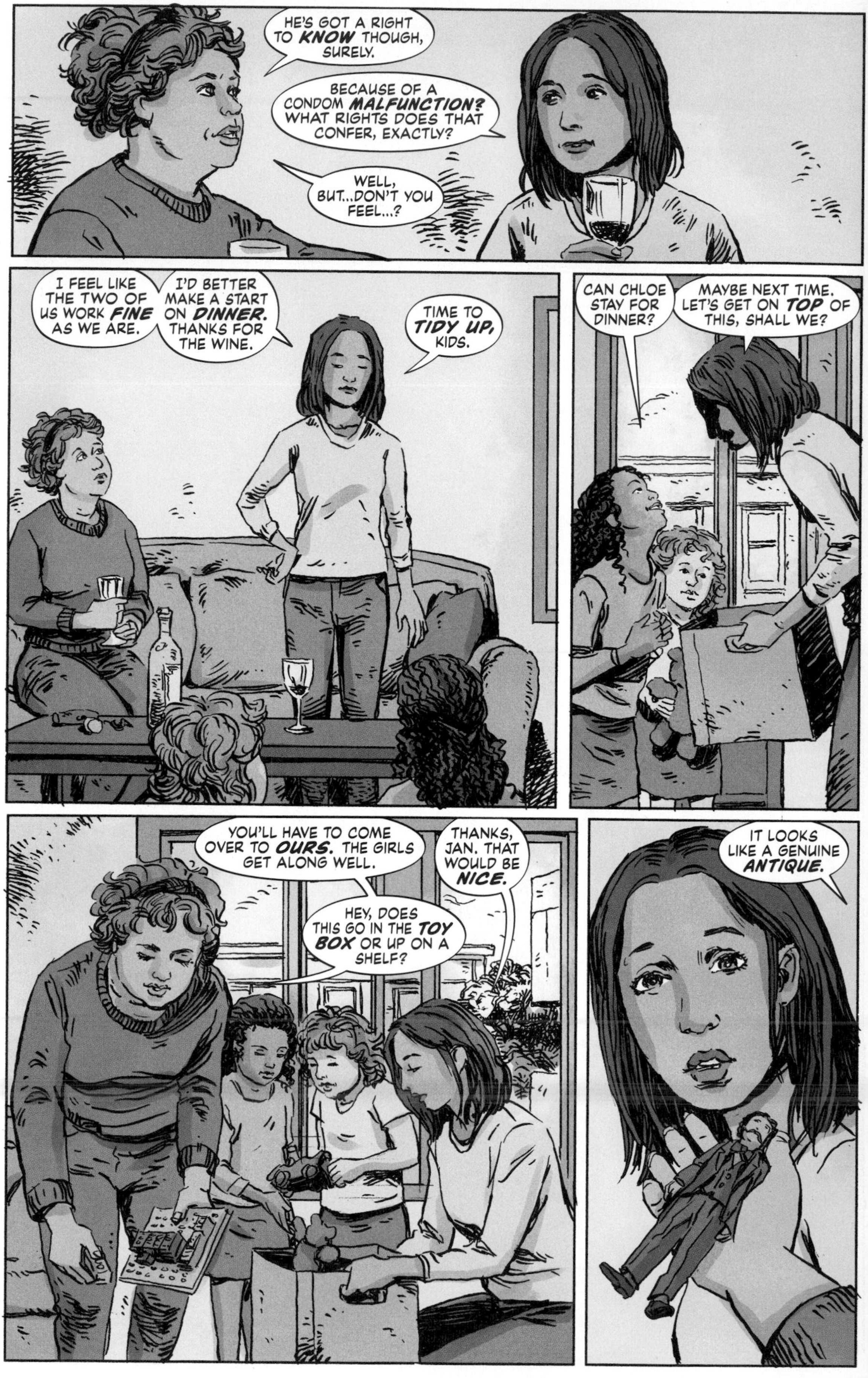
HE'S GOT A RIGHT TO KNOW THOUGH, SURELY.
BECAUSE OF A CONDOM MALFUNCTION? WHAT RIGHTS DOES THAT CONFER, EXACTLY?
WELL, BUT...DON'T YOU FEEL...?
I FEEL LIKE THE TWO OF US WORK FINE AS WE ARE.
I'D BETTER MAKE A START ON DINNER. THANKS FOR THE WINE.
TIME TO TIDY UP, KIDS.
CAN CHLOE STAY FOR DINNER?
MAYBE NEXT TIME. LET'S GET ON TOP OF THIS, SHALL WE?
YOU'LL HAVE TO COME OVER TO OURS. THE GIRLS GET ALONG WELL.
THANKS, JAN. THAT WOULD BE NICE.
HEY, DOES THIS GO IN THE TOY BOX OR UP ON A SHELF?
IT LOOKS LIKE A GENUINE ANTIQUE.

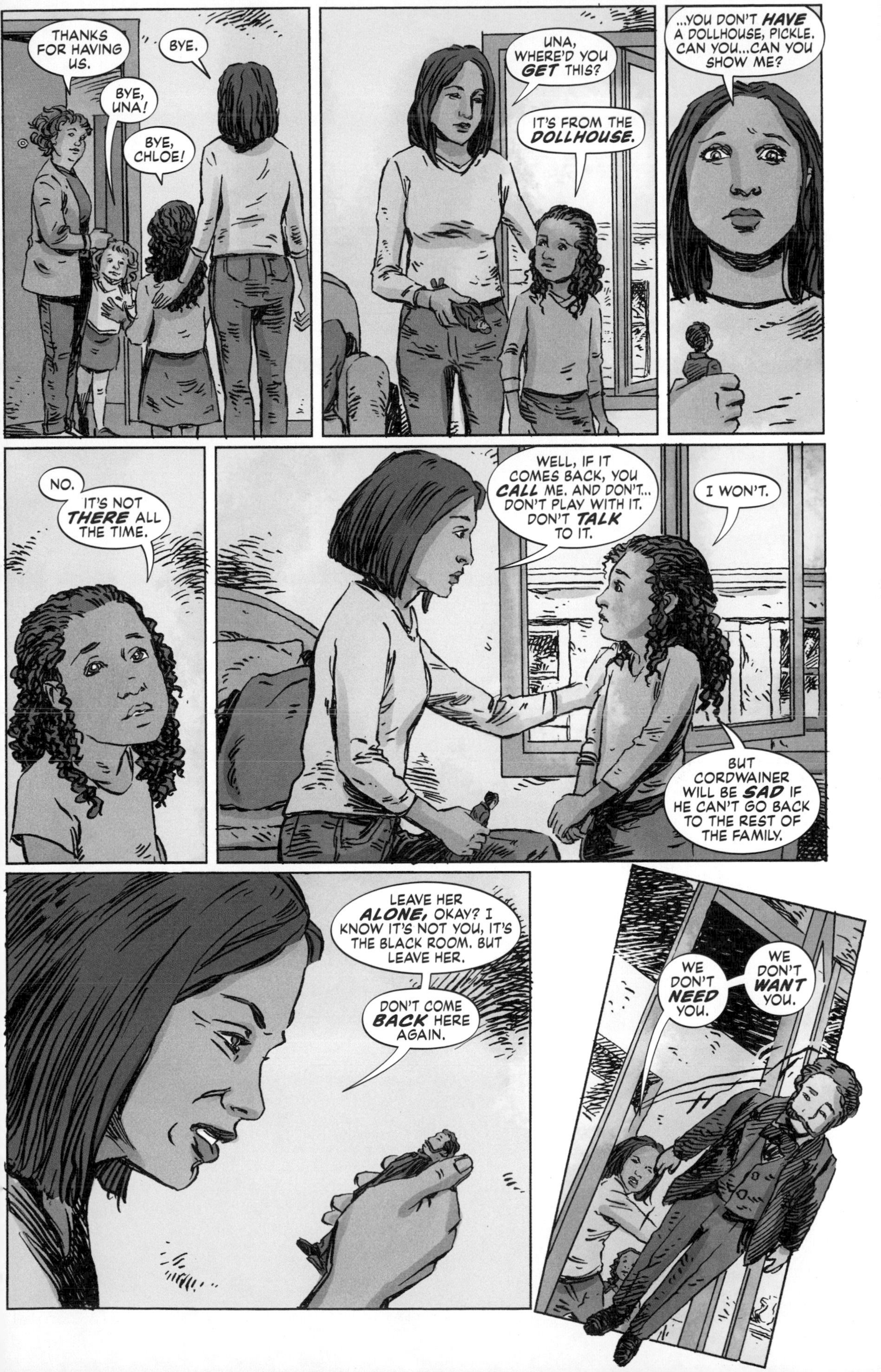
THANKS FOR HAVING US.
BYE.
BYE, UNA!
BYE, CHLOE!
UNA, WHERE'D YOU GET THIS?
IT'S FROM THE DOLLHOUSE.
...YOU DON'T HAVE A DOLLHOUSE, PICKLE. CAN YOU...CAN YOU SHOW ME?
NO.
IT'S NOT THERE ALL THE TIME.
WELL, IF IT COMES BACK, YOU CALL ME. AND DON'T... DON'T PLAY WITH IT. DON'T TALK TO IT.
I WON'T.
BUT CORDWAINER WILL BE SAD IF HE CAN'T GO BACK TO THE REST OF THE FAMILY.
LEAVE HER ALONE, OKAY? I KNOW IT'S NOT YOU, IT'S THE BLACK ROOM. BUT LEAVE HER.
DON'T COME BACK HERE AGAIN.
WE DON'T NEED YOU.
WE DON'T WANT YOU.

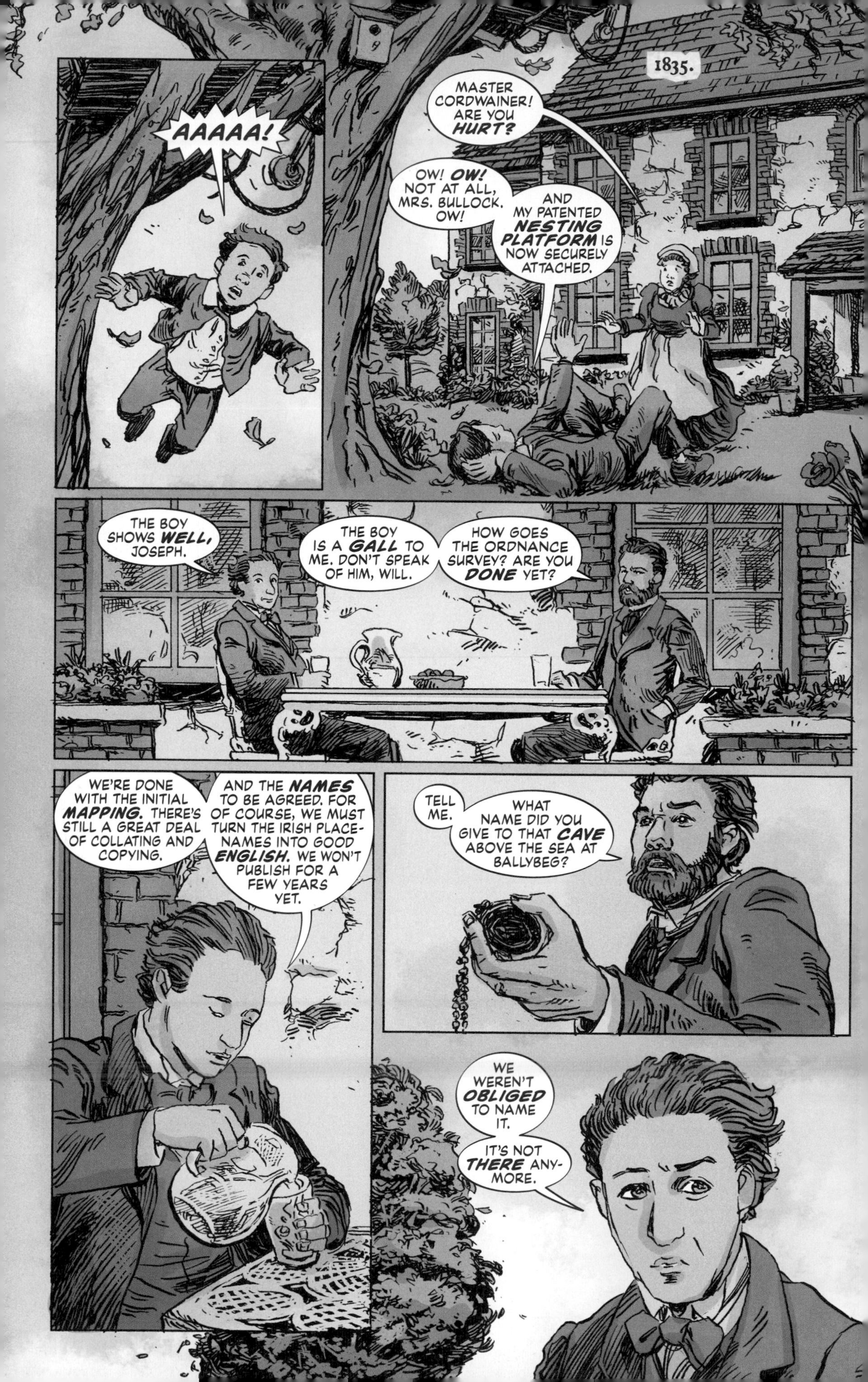
1835.
AAAAA!
MASTER CORDWAINER! ARE YOU HURT?
OW! OW! NOT AT ALL, MRS. BULLOCK. OW!
AND MY PATENTED NESTING PLATFORM IS NOW SECURELY ATTACHED.
THE BOY SHOWS WELL, JOSEPH.
THE BOY IS A GALL TO ME. DON'T SPEAK OF HIM, WILL.
HOW GOES THE ORDNANCE SURVEY? ARE YOU DONE YET?
WE'RE DONE WITH THE INITIAL MAPPING. THERE'S STILL A GREAT DEAL OF COLLATING AND COPYING.
AND THE NAMES TO BE AGREED. FOR OF COURSE, WE MUST TURN THE IRISH PLACE-NAMES INTO GOOD ENGLISH. WE WON'T PUBLISH FOR A FEW YEARS YET.
TELL ME.
WHAT NAME DID YOU GIVE TO THAT CAVE ABOVE THE SEA AT BALLYBEG?
WE WEREN'T OBLIGED TO NAME IT.
IT'S NOT THERE ANYMORE.

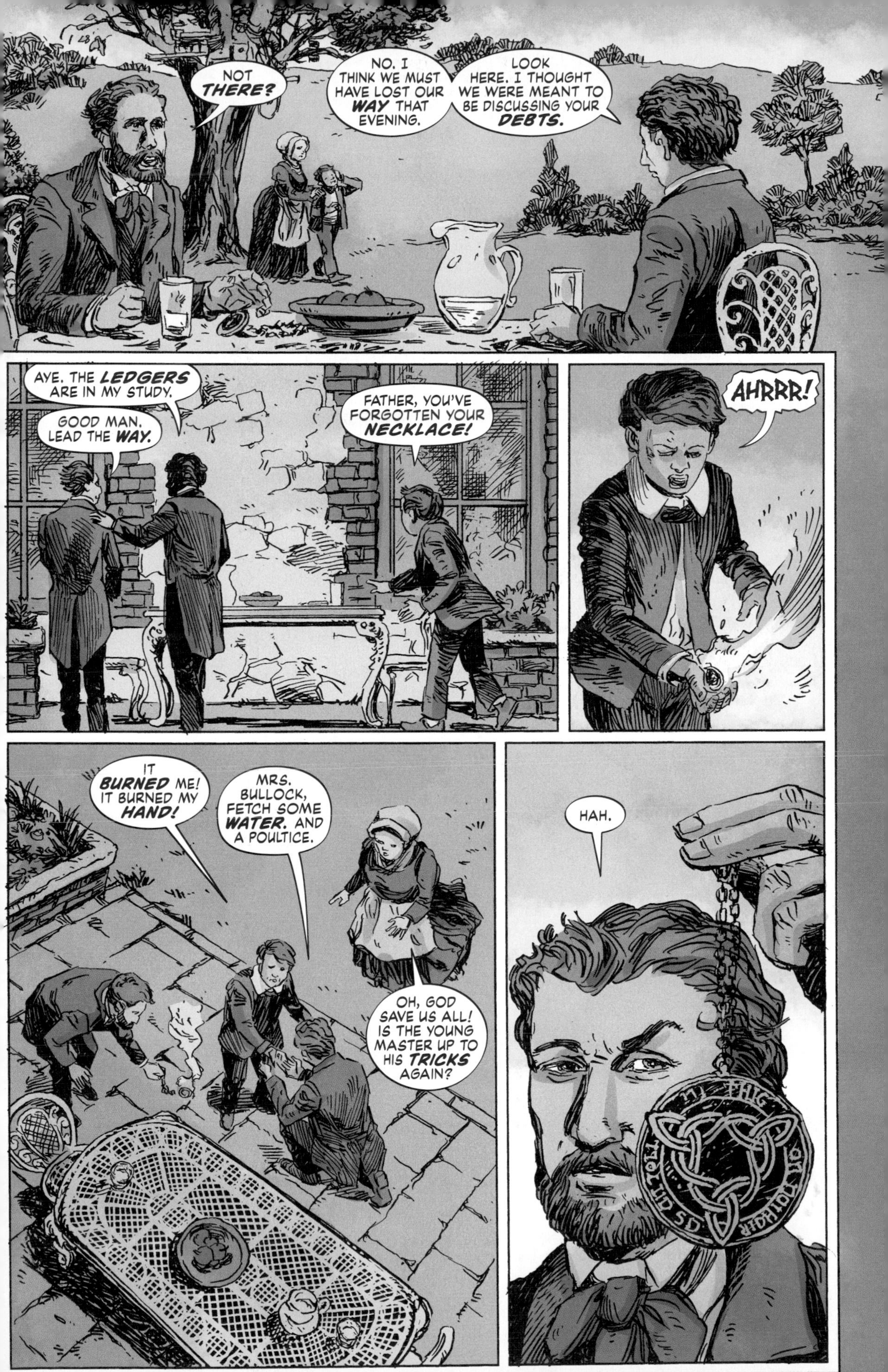
NOT THERE?
NO. I THINK WE MUST HAVE LOST OUR WAY THAT EVENING.
LOOK HERE. I THOUGHT WE WERE MEANT TO BE DISCUSSING YOUR DEBTS.
AYE. THE LEDGERS ARE IN MY STUDY.
GOOD MAN. LEAD THE WAY.
FATHER, YOU'VE FORGOTTEN YOUR NECKLACE!
AHRRR!
IT BURNED ME! IT BURNED MY HAND!
MRS. BULLOCK, FETCH SOME WATER. AND A POULTICE.
OH, GOD SAVE US ALL! IS THE YOUNG MASTER UP TO HIS TRICKS AGAIN?
HAH.

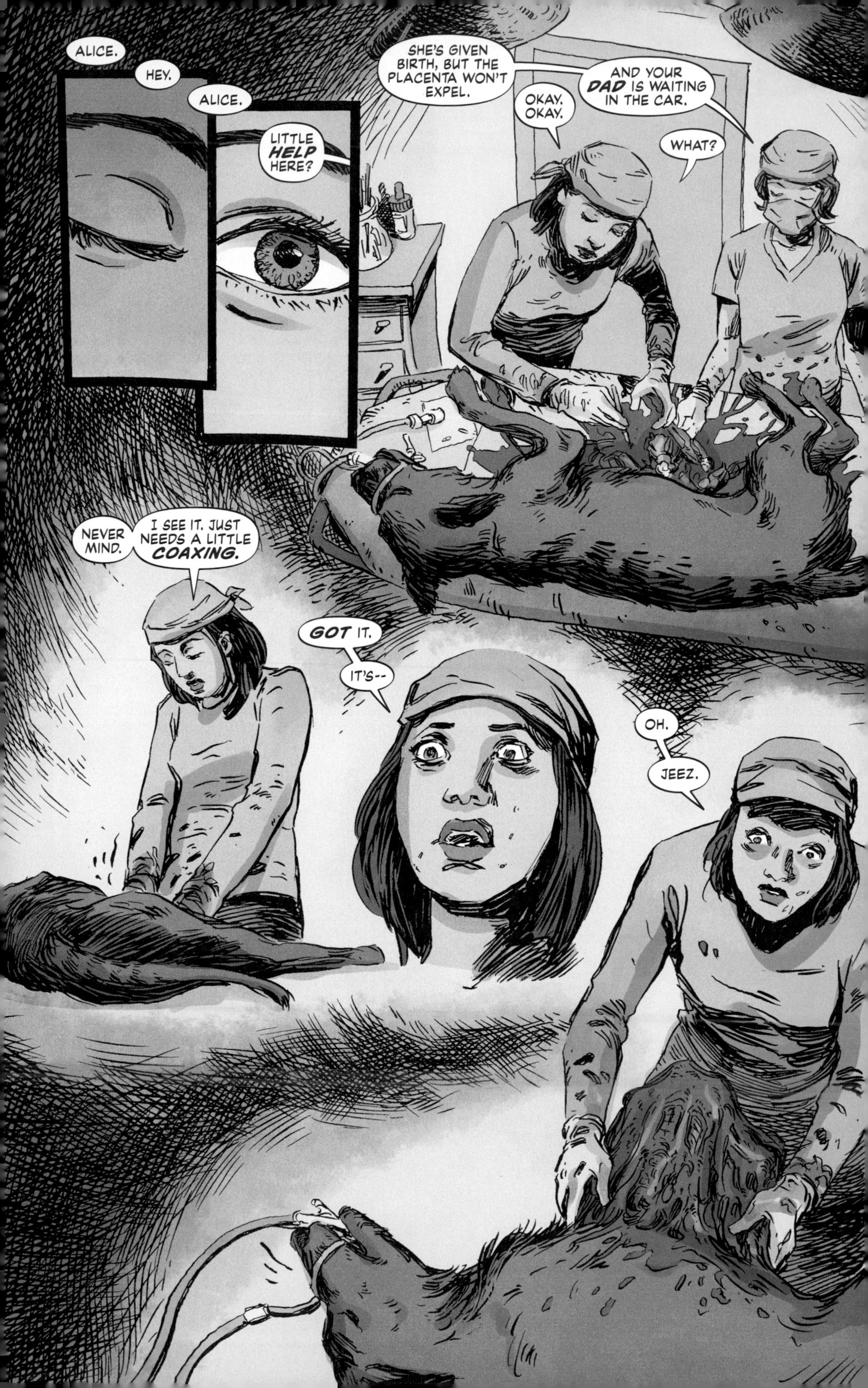
ALICE.
HEY.
ALICE.
LITTLE HELP HERE?
SHE'S GIVEN BIRTH, BUT THE PLACENTA WON'T EXPEL.
AND YOUR DAD IS WAITING IN THE CAR.
OKAY. OKAY.
WHAT?
NEVER MIND.
I SEE IT. JUST NEEDS A LITTLE COAXING.
GOT IT.
IT'S--
OH.
JEEZ.

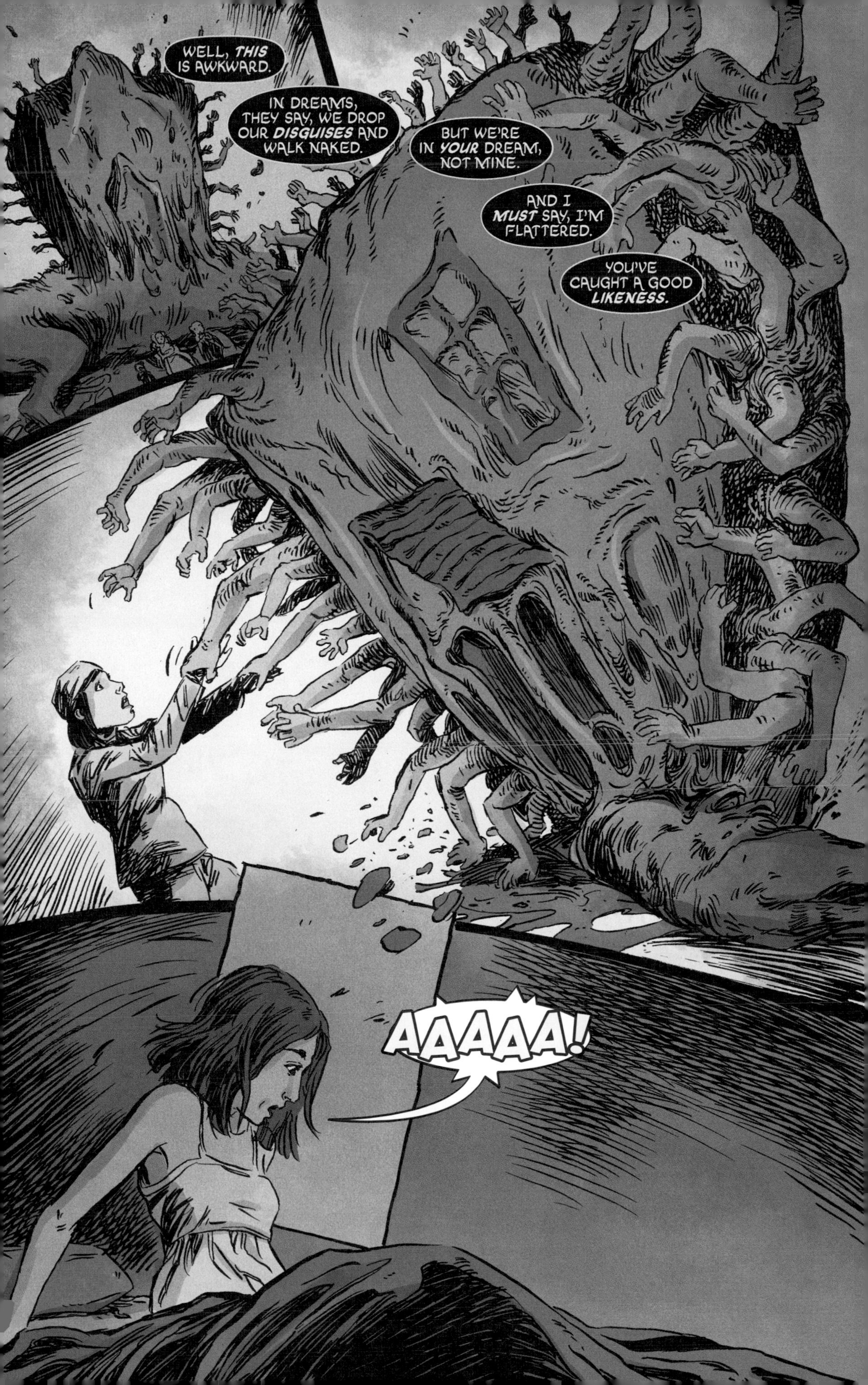
WELL, THIS IS AWKWARD.
IN DREAMS, THEY SAY, WE DROP OUR DISGUISES AND WALK NAKED.
BUT WE'RE IN YOUR DREAM, NOT MINE.
AND I MUST SAY, I'M FLATTERED.
YOU'VE CAUGHT A GOOD LIKENESS.
AAAAA!

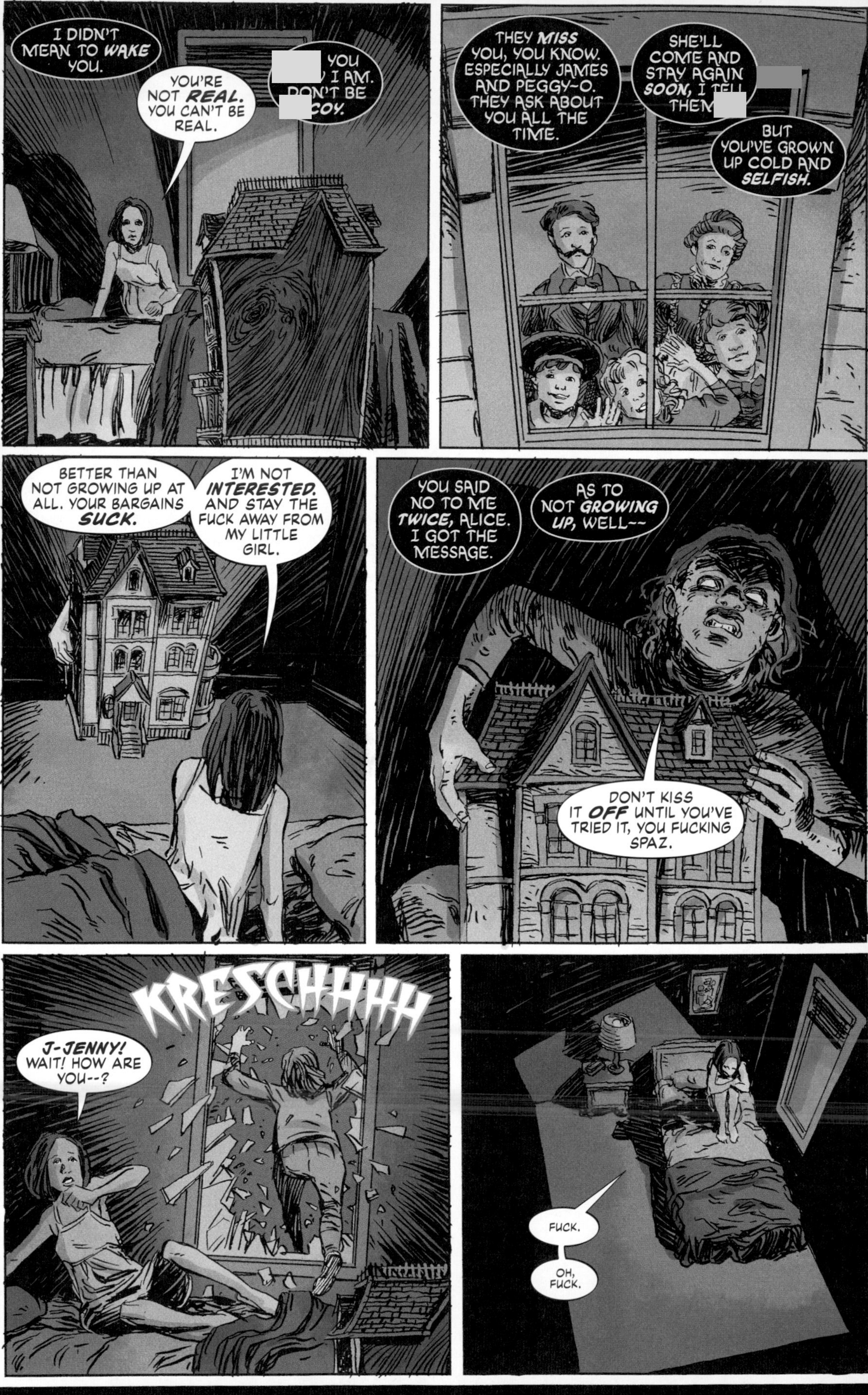
I DIDN'T MEAN TO WAKE YOU.
YOU'RE NOT REAL. YOU CAN'T BE REAL.
[redacted] YOU [redacted] I AM. DON'T BE [redacted]COY.
THEY MISS YOU, YOU KNOW. ESPECIALLY JAMES AND PEGGY-O. THEY ASK ABOUT YOU ALL THE TIME.
SHE'LL COME AND STAY AGAIN [redacted] SOON, I TELL THEM[redacted]
BUT YOU'VE GROWN UP COLD AND SELFISH.
BETTER THAN NOT GROWING UP AT ALL. YOUR BARGAINS SUCK.
I'M NOT INTERESTED. AND STAY THE FUCK AWAY FROM MY LITTLE GIRL.
YOU SAID NO TO ME TWICE, ALICE. I GOT THE MESSAGE.
AS TO NOT GROWING UP, WELL--
DON'T KISS IT OFF UNTIL YOU'VE TRIED IT, YOU FUCKING SPAZ.
KRESCHHHH
J-JENNY! WAIT! HOW ARE YOU--?
FUCK.
OH, FUCK.

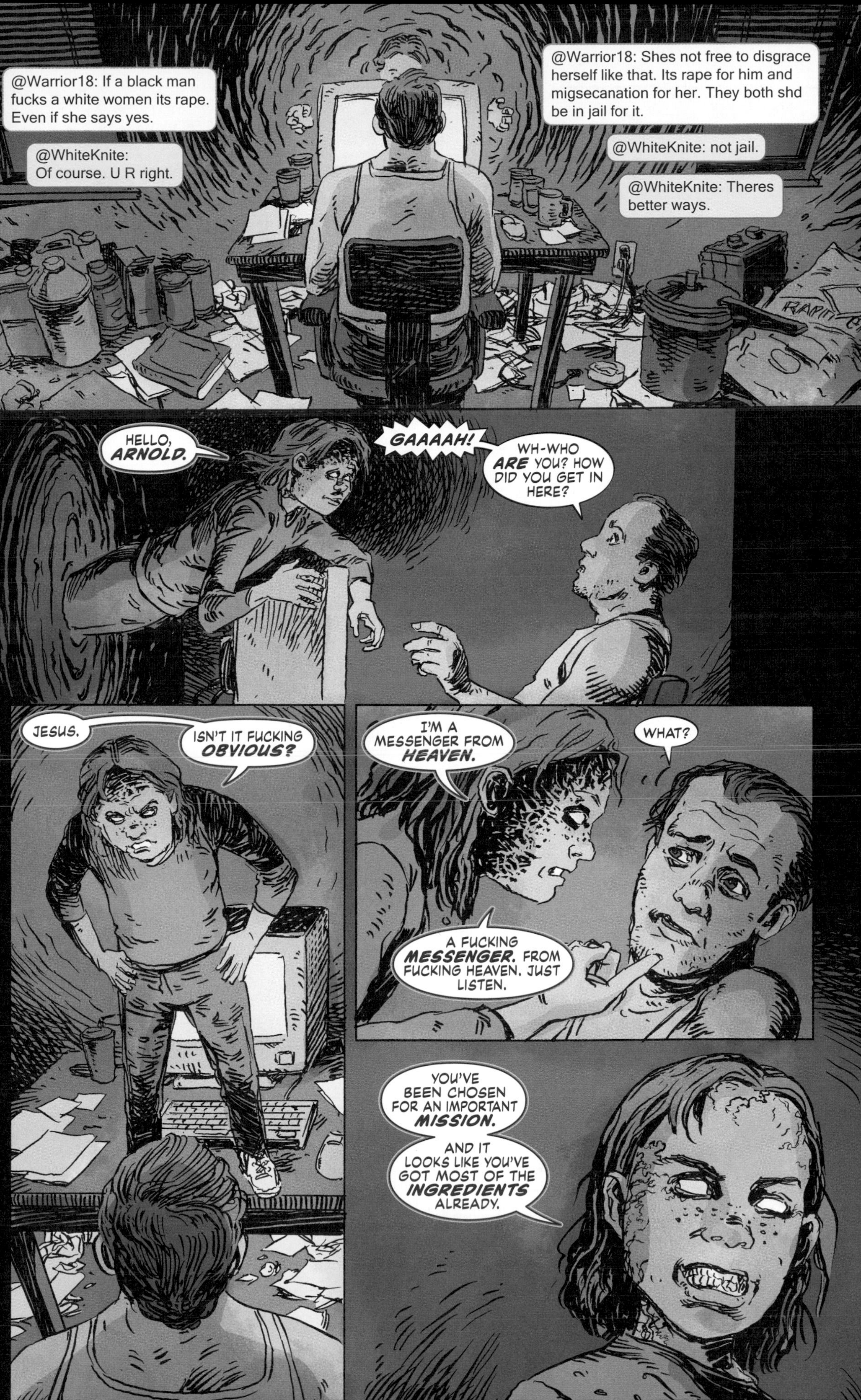
@Warrior18: If a black man fucks a white women its rape. Even if she says yes.
@WhiteKnite: Of course. U R right.
@Warrior18: Shes not free to disgrace herself like that. Its rape for him and migsecanation for her. They both shd be in jail for it.
@WhiteKnite: not jail.
@WhiteKnite: Theres better ways.
HELLO, ARNOLD.
GAAAAH!
WH-WHO ARE YOU? HOW DID YOU GET IN HERE?
JESUS.
ISN'T IT FUCKING OBVIOUS?
I'M A MESSENGER FROM HEAVEN.
WHAT?
A FUCKING MESSENGER. FROM FUCKING HEAVEN. JUST LISTEN.
YOU'VE BEEN CHOSEN FOR AN IMPORTANT MISSION.
AND IT LOOKS LIKE YOU'VE GOT MOST OF THE INGREDIENTS ALREADY.

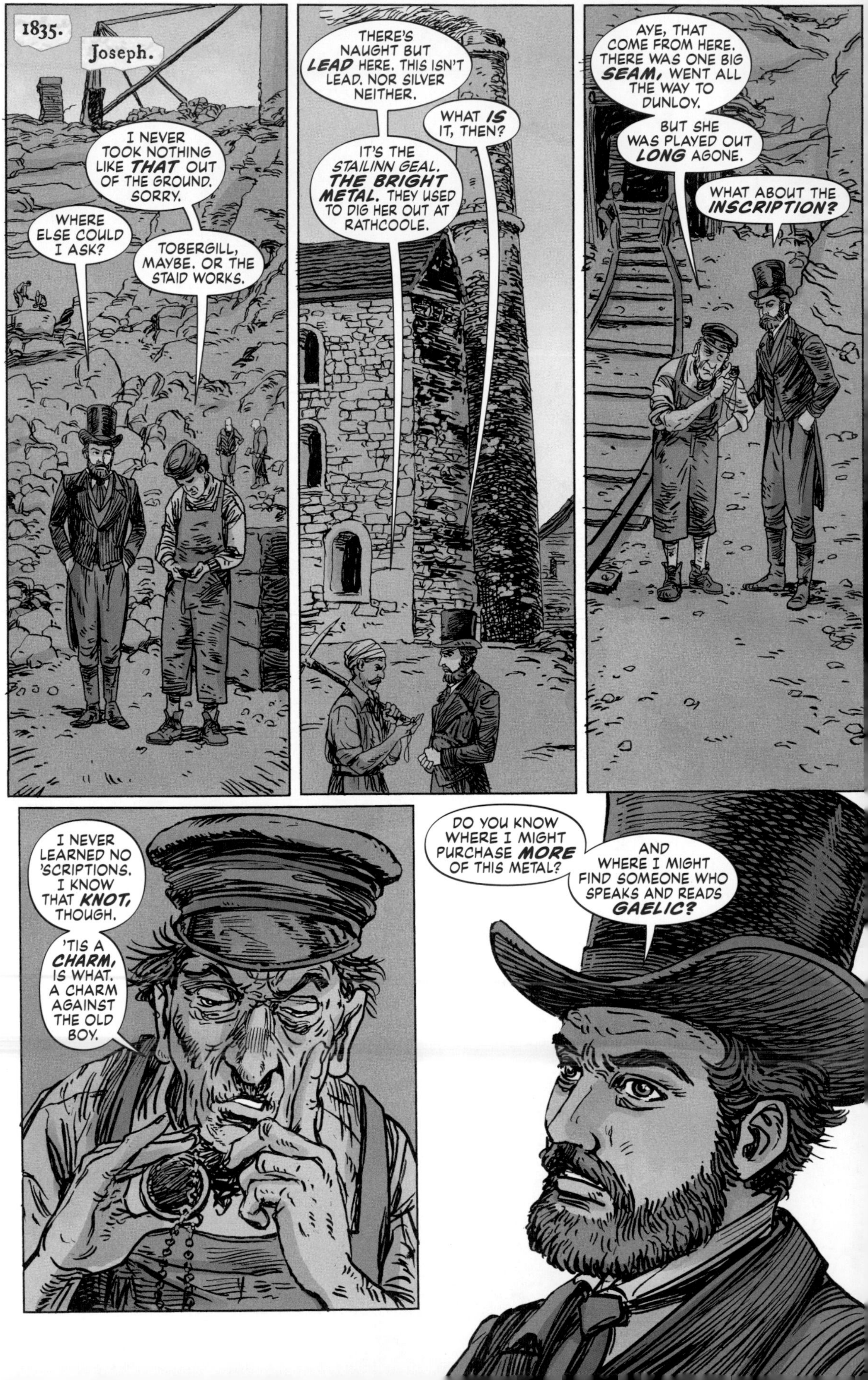
1835.
Joseph.
I NEVER TOOK NOTHING LIKE THAT OUT OF THE GROUND. SORRY.
WHERE ELSE COULD I ASK?
TOBERGILL, MAYBE. OR THE STAID WORKS.
THERE'S NAUGHT BUT LEAD HERE. THIS ISN'T LEAD. NOR SILVER NEITHER.
WHAT IS IT, THEN?
IT'S THE STAILINN GEAL. THE BRIGHT METAL. THEY USED TO DIG HER OUT AT RATHCOOLE.
AYE, THAT COME FROM HERE. THERE WAS ONE BIG SEAM, WENT ALL THE WAY TO DUNLOY.
BUT SHE WAS PLAYED OUT LONG AGONE.
WHAT ABOUT THE INSCRIPTION?
I NEVER LEARNED NO 'SCRIPTIONS. I KNOW THAT KNOT, THOUGH.
'TIS A CHARM, IS WHAT. A CHARM AGAINST THE OLD BOY.
DO YOU KNOW WHERE I MIGHT PURCHASE MORE OF THIS METAL?
AND WHERE I MIGHT FIND SOMEONE WHO SPEAKS AND READS GAELIC?

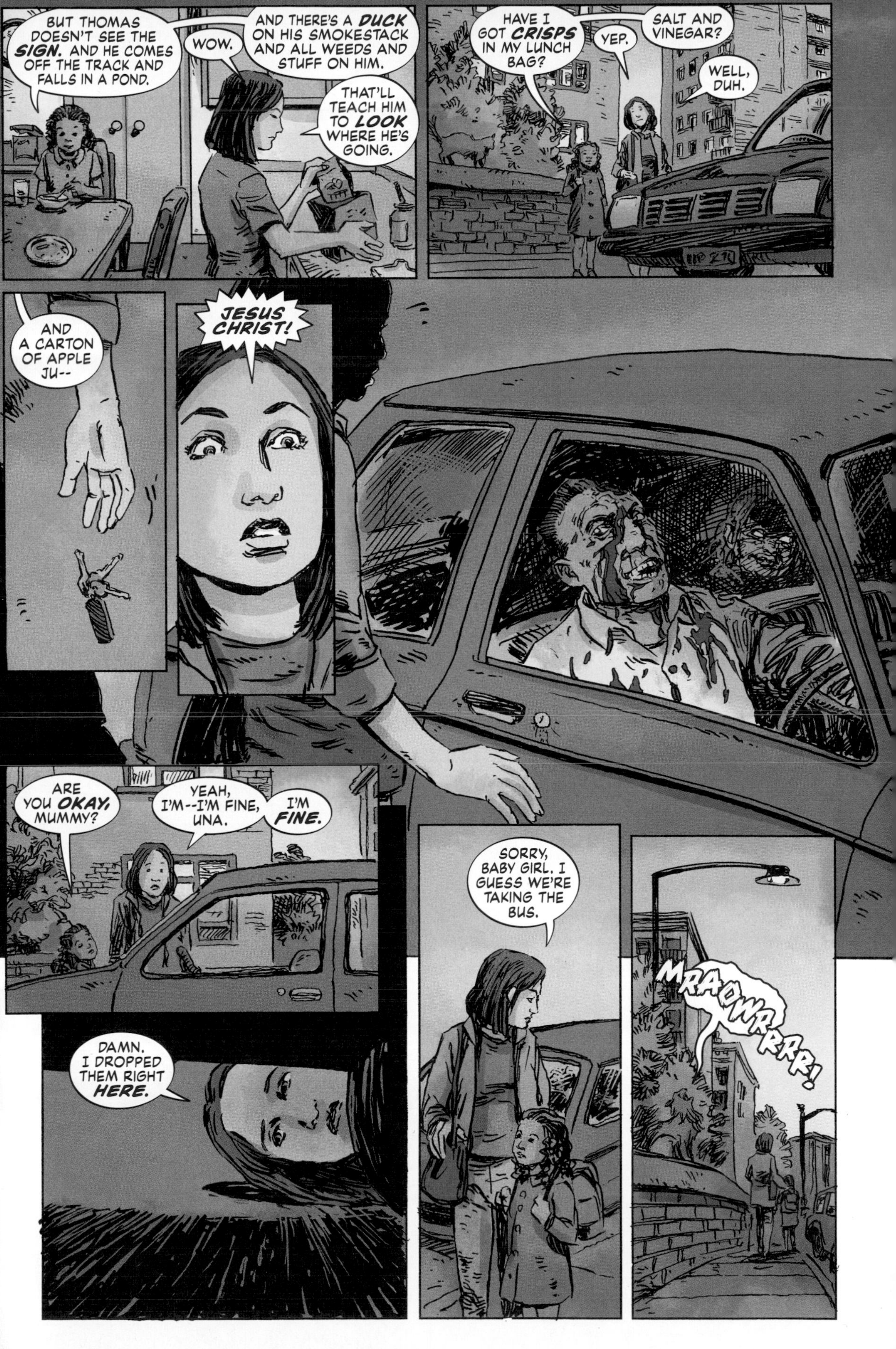
BUT THOMAS DOESN'T SEE THE SIGN. AND HE COMES OFF THE TRACK AND FALLS IN A POND.
WOW.
AND THERE'S A DUCK ON HIS SMOKESTACK AND ALL WEEDS AND STUFF ON HIM.
THAT'LL TEACH HIM TO LOOK WHERE HE'S GOING.
HAVE I GOT CRISPS IN MY LUNCH BAG?
YEP.
SALT AND VINEGAR?
WELL, DUH.
AND A CARTON OF APPLE JU--
JESUS CHRIST!
ARE YOU OKAY, MUMMY?
YEAH, I'M--I'M FINE, UNA.
I'M FINE.
DAMN. I DROPPED THEM RIGHT HERE.
SORRY, BABY GIRL. I GUESS WE'RE TAKING THE BUS.
MRAOWRRRR!

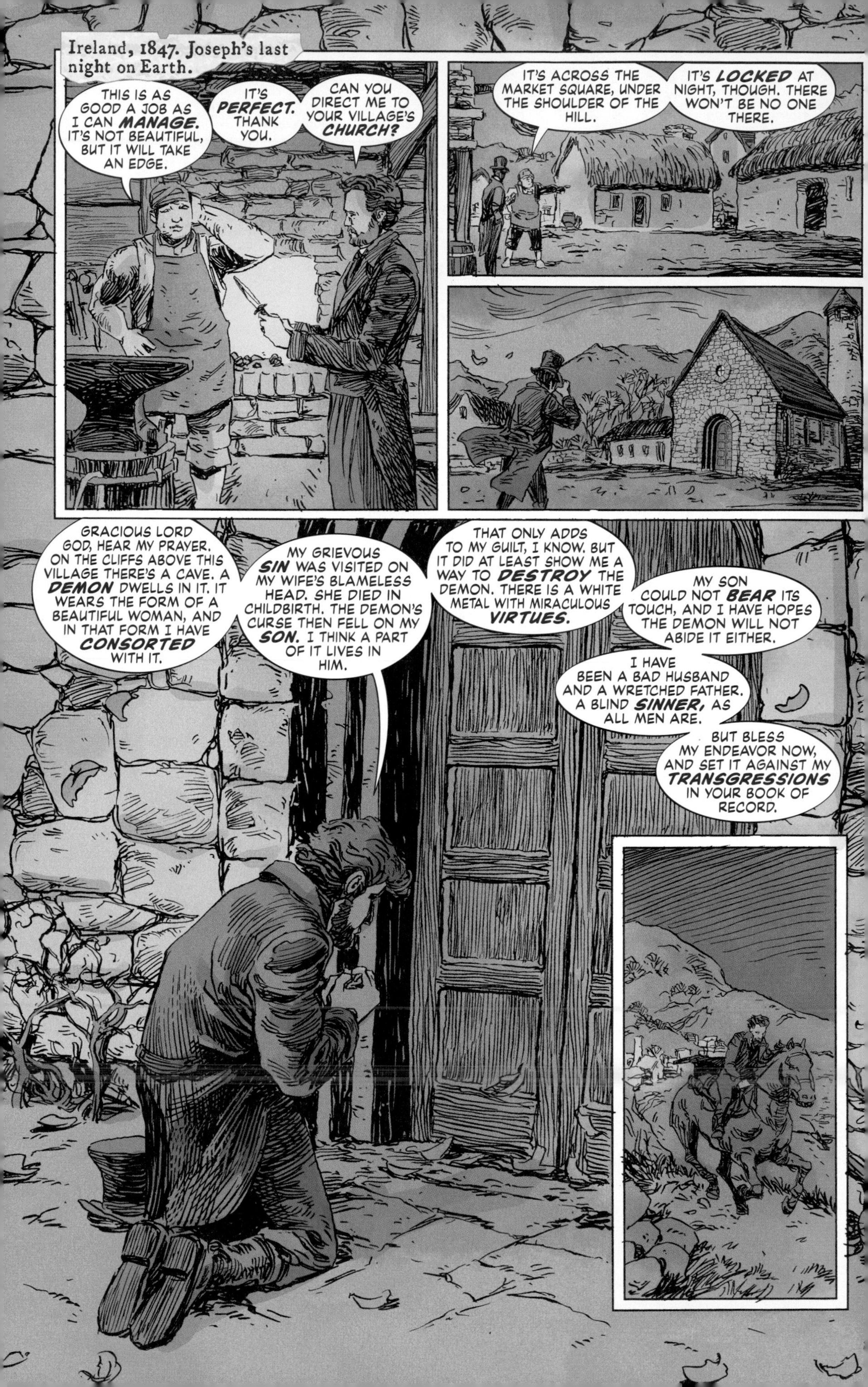
Ireland, 1847. Joseph's last night on Earth.
THIS IS AS GOOD A JOB AS I CAN MANAGE. IT'S NOT BEAUTIFUL, BUT IT WILL TAKE AN EDGE.
IT'S PERFECT. THANK YOU.
CAN YOU DIRECT ME TO YOUR VILLAGE'S CHURCH?
IT'S ACROSS THE MARKET SQUARE, UNDER THE SHOULDER OF THE HILL.
IT'S LOCKED AT NIGHT, THOUGH. THERE WON'T BE NO ONE THERE.
GRACIOUS LORD GOD, HEAR MY PRAYER. ON THE CLIFFS ABOVE THIS VILLAGE THERE'S A CAVE. A DEMON DWELLS IN IT. IT WEARS THE FORM OF A BEAUTIFUL WOMAN, AND IN THAT FORM I HAVE CONSORTED WITH IT.
MY GRIEVOUS SIN WAS VISITED ON MY WIFE'S BLAMELESS HEAD. SHE DIED IN CHILDBIRTH. THE DEMON'S CURSE THEN FELL ON MY SON. I THINK A PART OF IT LIVES IN HIM.
THAT ONLY ADDS TO MY GUILT, I KNOW. BUT IT DID AT LEAST SHOW ME A WAY TO DESTROY THE DEMON. THERE IS A WHITE METAL WITH MIRACULOUS VIRTUES.
MY SON COULD NOT BEAR ITS TOUCH, AND I HAVE HOPES THE DEMON WILL NOT ABIDE IT EITHER.
I HAVE BEEN A BAD HUSBAND AND A WRETCHED FATHER. A BLIND SINNER, AS ALL MEN ARE.
BUT BLESS MY ENDEAVOR NOW, AND SET IT AGAINST MY TRANSGRESSIONS IN YOUR BOOK OF RECORD.

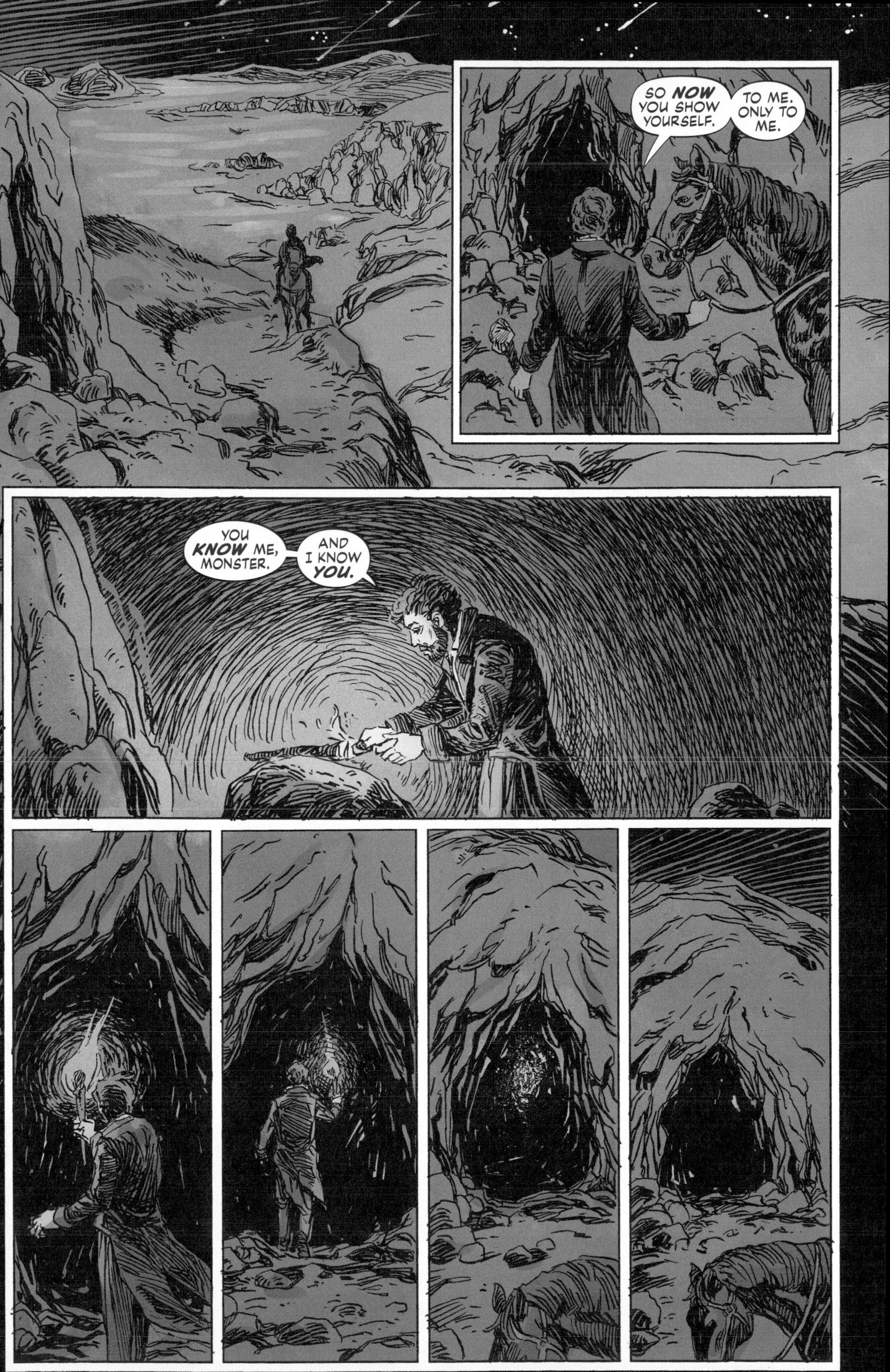
SO NOW YOU SHOW YOURSELF.
TO ME. ONLY TO ME.
YOU KNOW ME, MONSTER.
AND I KNOW YOU.

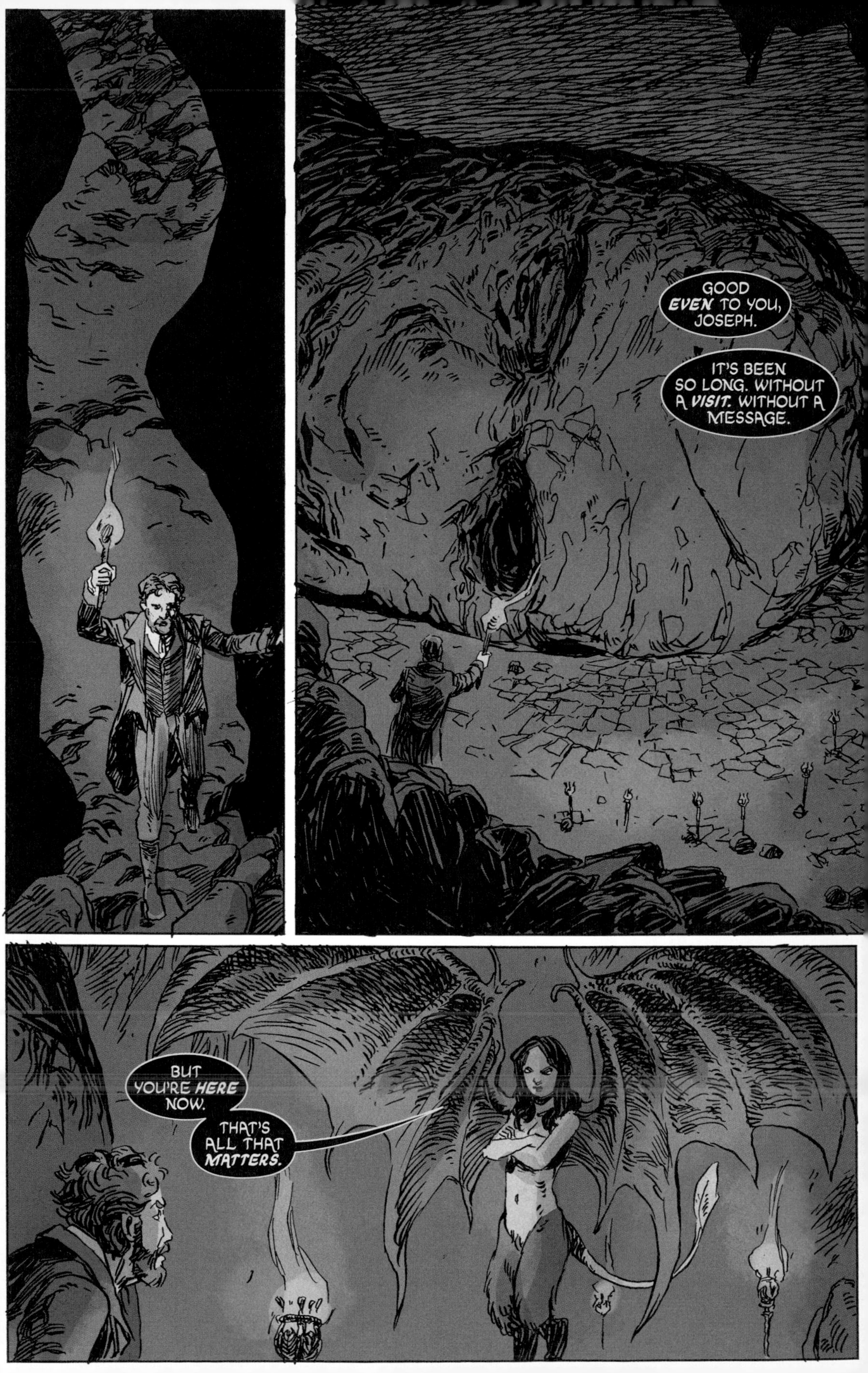
GOOD *EVEN* TO YOU, JOSEPH.
IT'S BEEN SO LONG. WITHOUT A *VISIT.* WITHOUT A MESSAGE.
BUT YOU'RE *HERE* NOW.
THAT'S ALL THAT *MATTERS.*

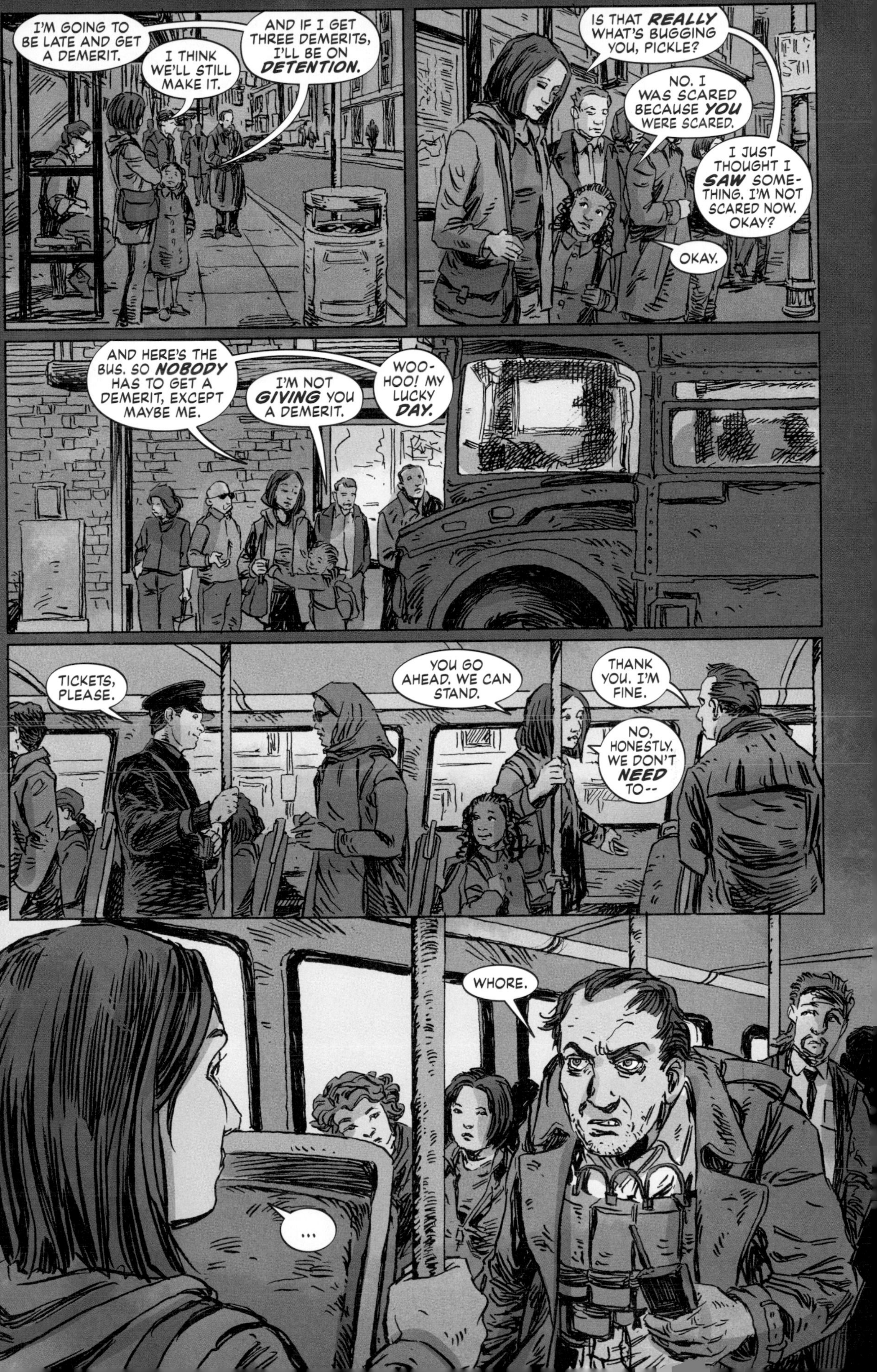
I'M GOING TO BE LATE AND GET A DEMERIT.
I THINK WE'LL STILL MAKE IT.
AND IF I GET THREE DEMERITS, I'LL BE ON *DETENTION*.
IS THAT *REALLY* WHAT'S BUGGING YOU, PICKLE?
NO. I WAS SCARED BECAUSE *YOU* WERE SCARED.
I JUST THOUGHT I *SAW* SOMETHING. I'M NOT SCARED NOW. OKAY?
OKAY.
AND HERE'S THE BUS. SO *NOBODY* HAS TO GET A DEMERIT, EXCEPT MAYBE ME.
I'M NOT *GIVING* YOU A DEMERIT.
WOO-HOO! MY LUCKY *DAY*.
TICKETS, PLEASE.
YOU GO AHEAD. WE CAN STAND.
THANK YOU. I'M FINE.
NO, HONESTLY, WE DON'T *NEED* TO--
WHORE.
...

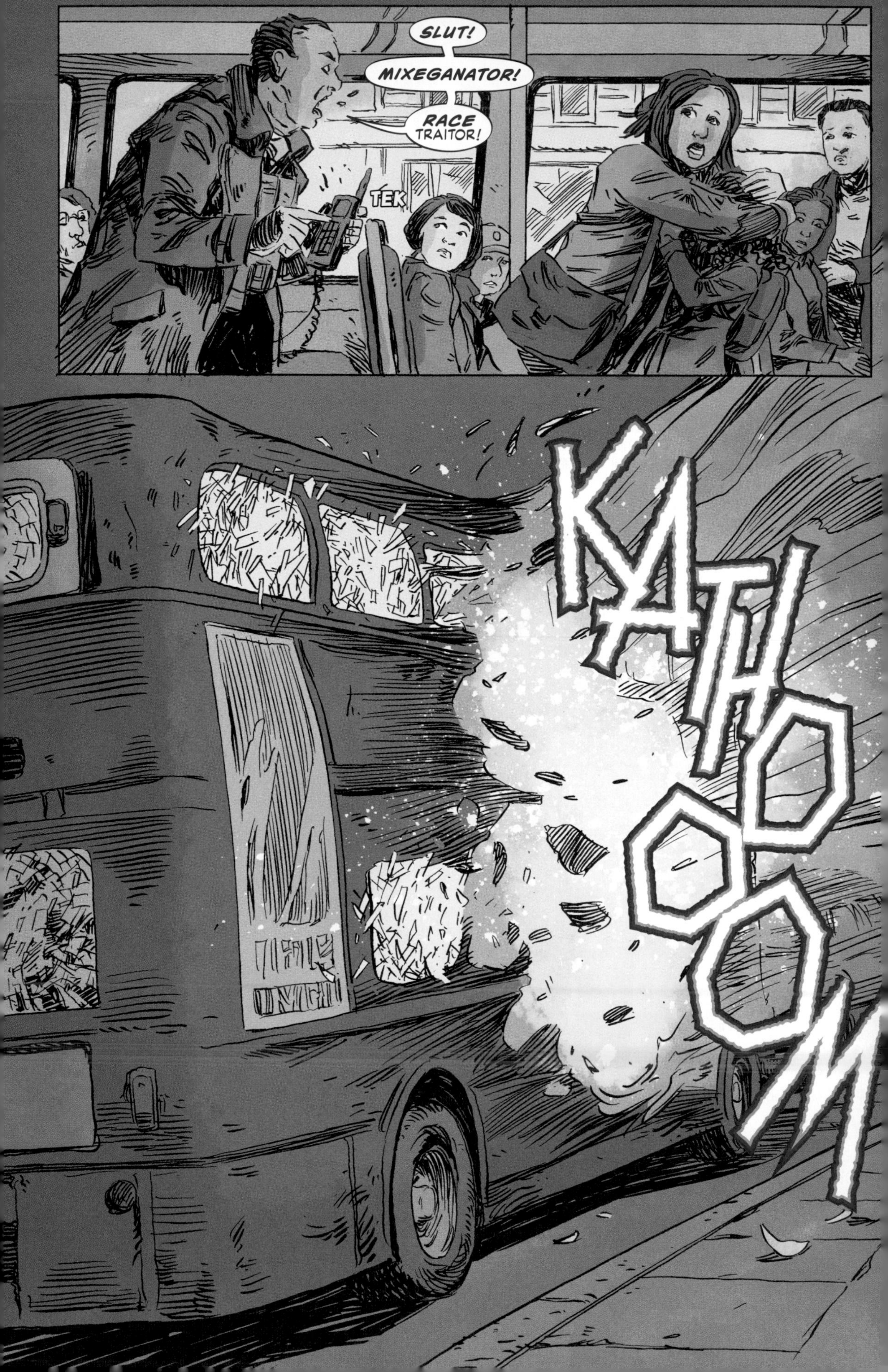
SLUT!
MIXEGANATOR!
RACE TRAITOR!
TEK
KATHOOOOM

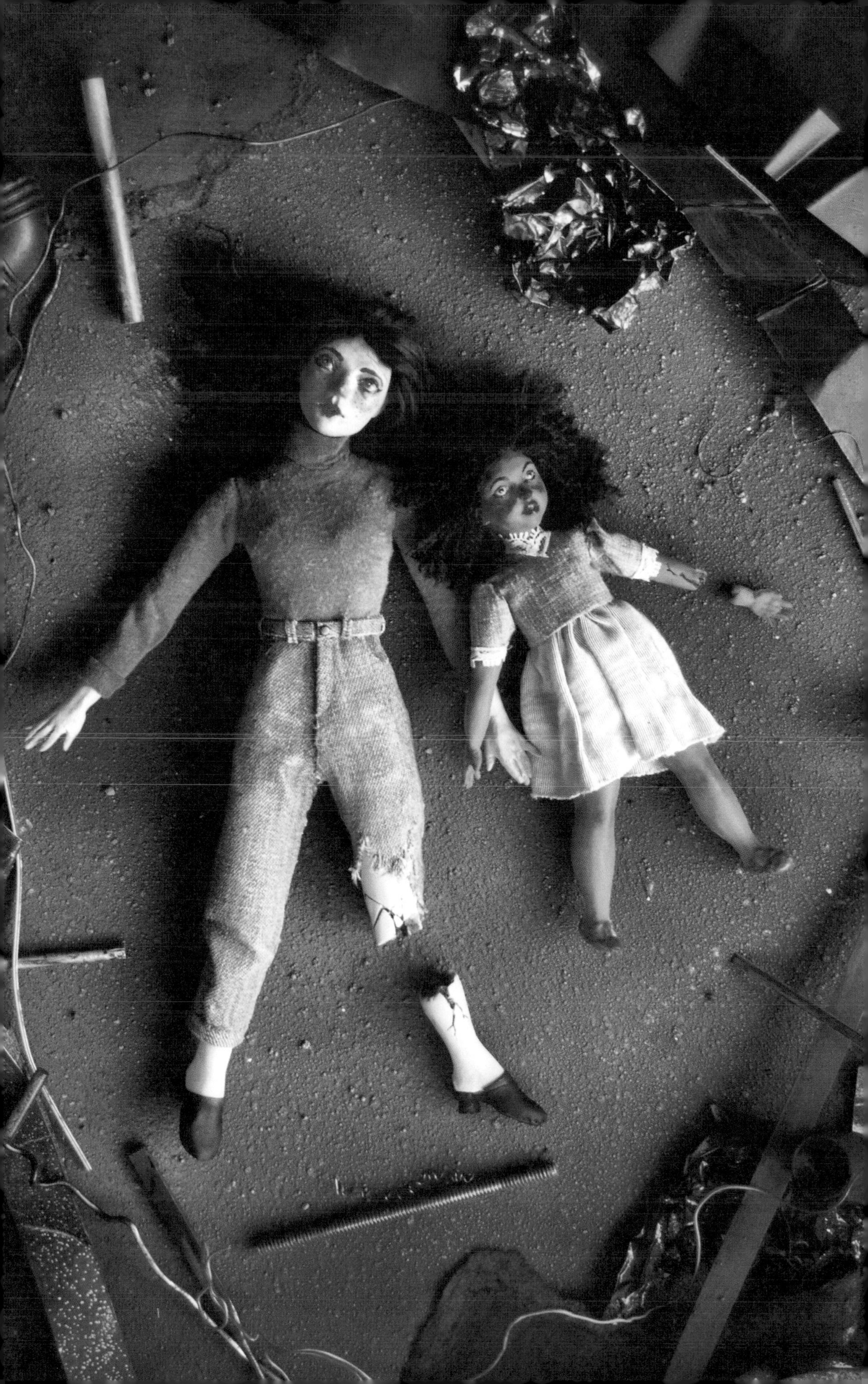

COME UP

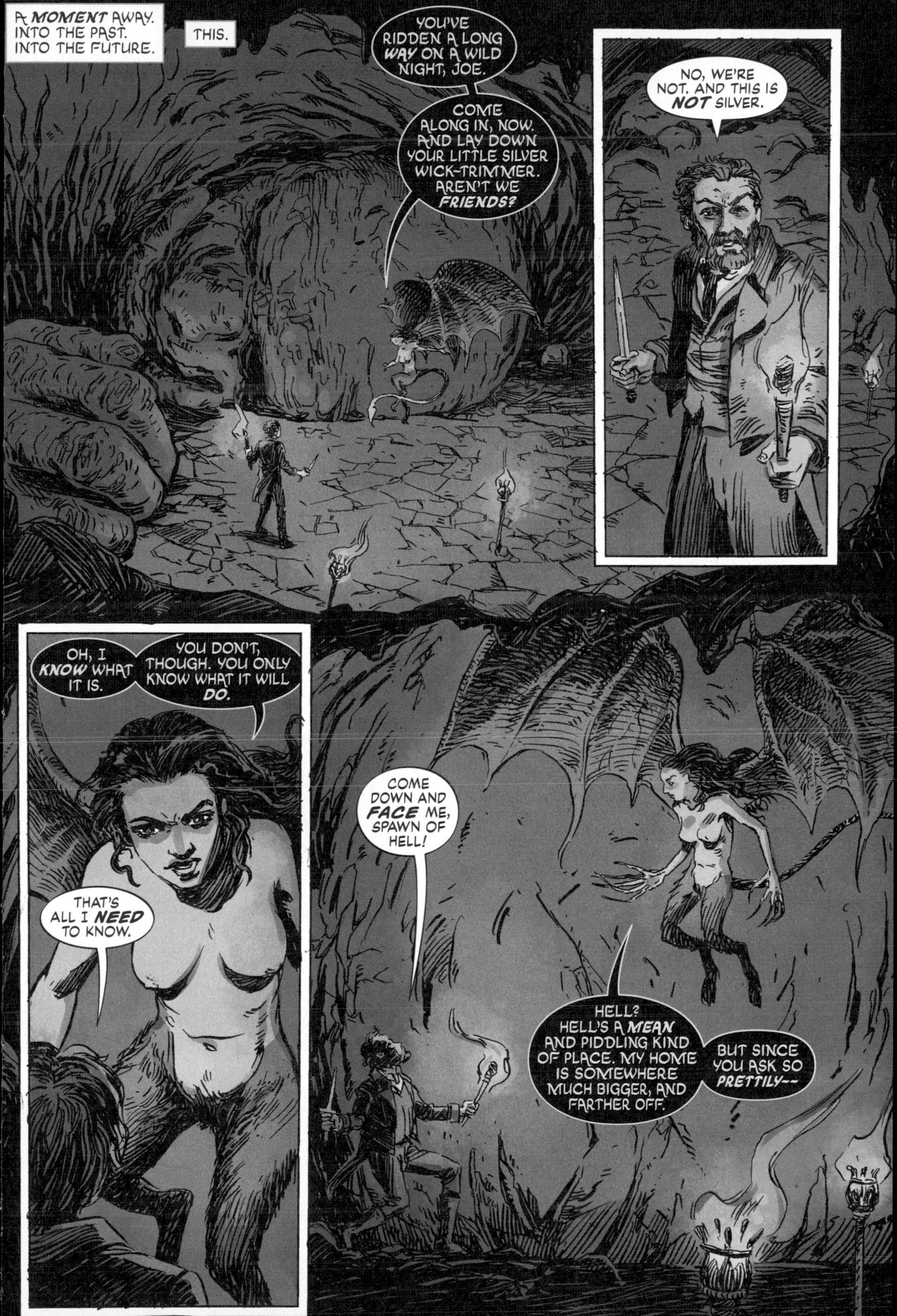
A *MOMENT* AWAY. INTO THE PAST. INTO THE FUTURE.
THIS.
YOU'VE RIDDEN A LONG *WAY* ON A WILD NIGHT, JOE.
COME ALONG IN, NOW. AND LAY DOWN YOUR LITTLE SILVER WICK-TRIMMER. AREN'T WE *FRIENDS?*
NO, WE'RE NOT. AND THIS IS *NOT* SILVER.
OH, I *KNOW* WHAT IT IS.
YOU DON'T, THOUGH. YOU ONLY KNOW WHAT IT WILL *DO.*
THAT'S ALL I *NEED* TO KNOW.
COME DOWN AND *FACE* ME, SPAWN OF HELL!
HELL? HELL'S A *MEAN* AND PIDDLING KIND OF PLACE. MY HOME IS SOMEWHERE MUCH BIGGER, AND FARTHER OFF.
BUT SINCE YOU ASK SO *PRETTILY--*

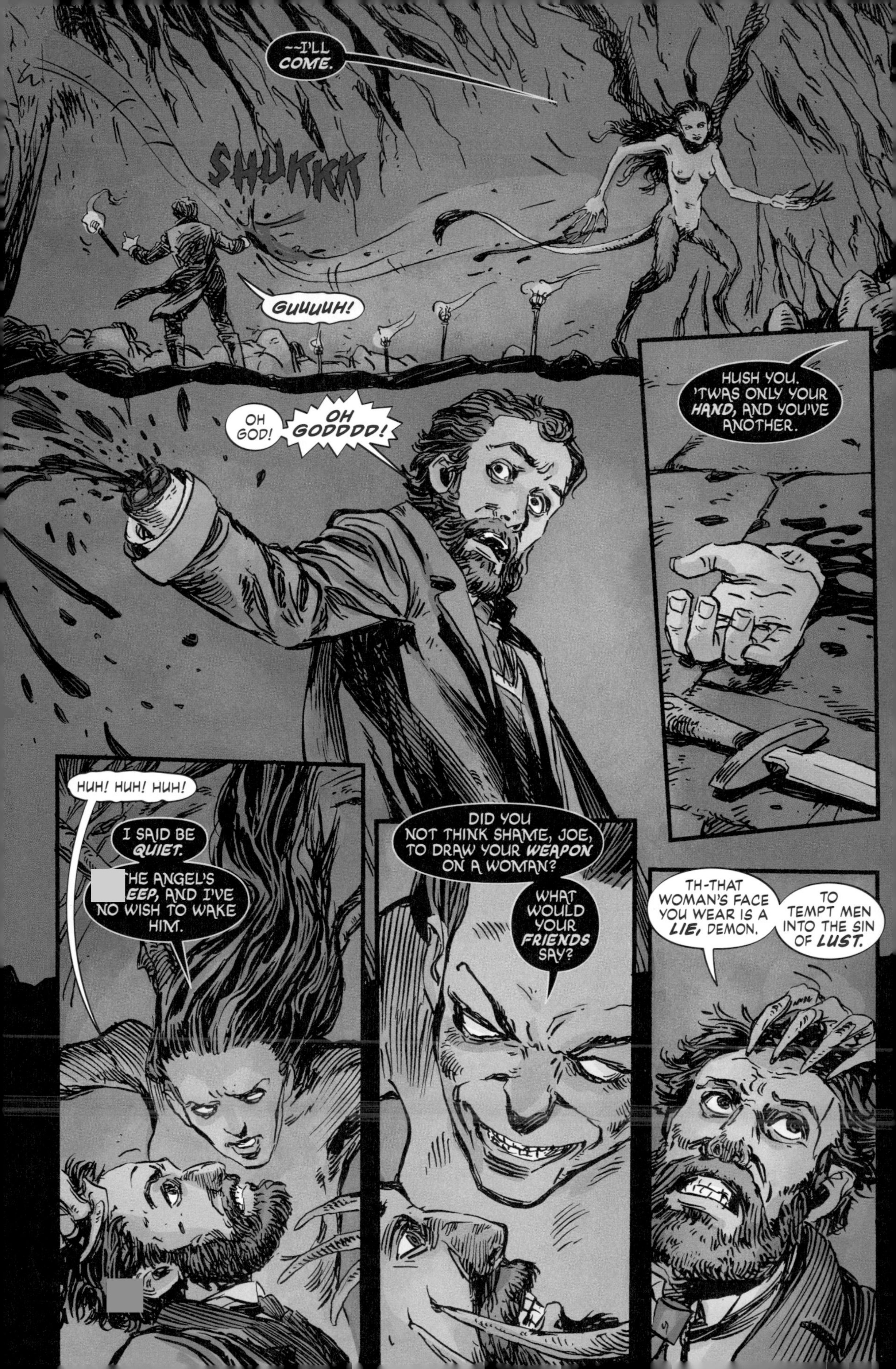
--I'LL COME.
SHUKKK
GUUUUH!
OH GOD!
OH GODDDD!
HUSH YOU. 'TWAS ONLY YOUR HAND, AND YOU'VE ANOTHER.
HUH! HUH! HUH!
I SAID BE QUIET.
THE ANGEL'S EEP, AND I'VE NO WISH TO WAKE HIM.
DID YOU NOT THINK SHAME, JOE, TO DRAW YOUR WEAPON ON A WOMAN?
WHAT WOULD YOUR FRIENDS SAY?
TH-THAT WOMAN'S FACE YOU WEAR IS A LIE, DEMON.
TO TEMPT MEN INTO THE SIN OF LUST.

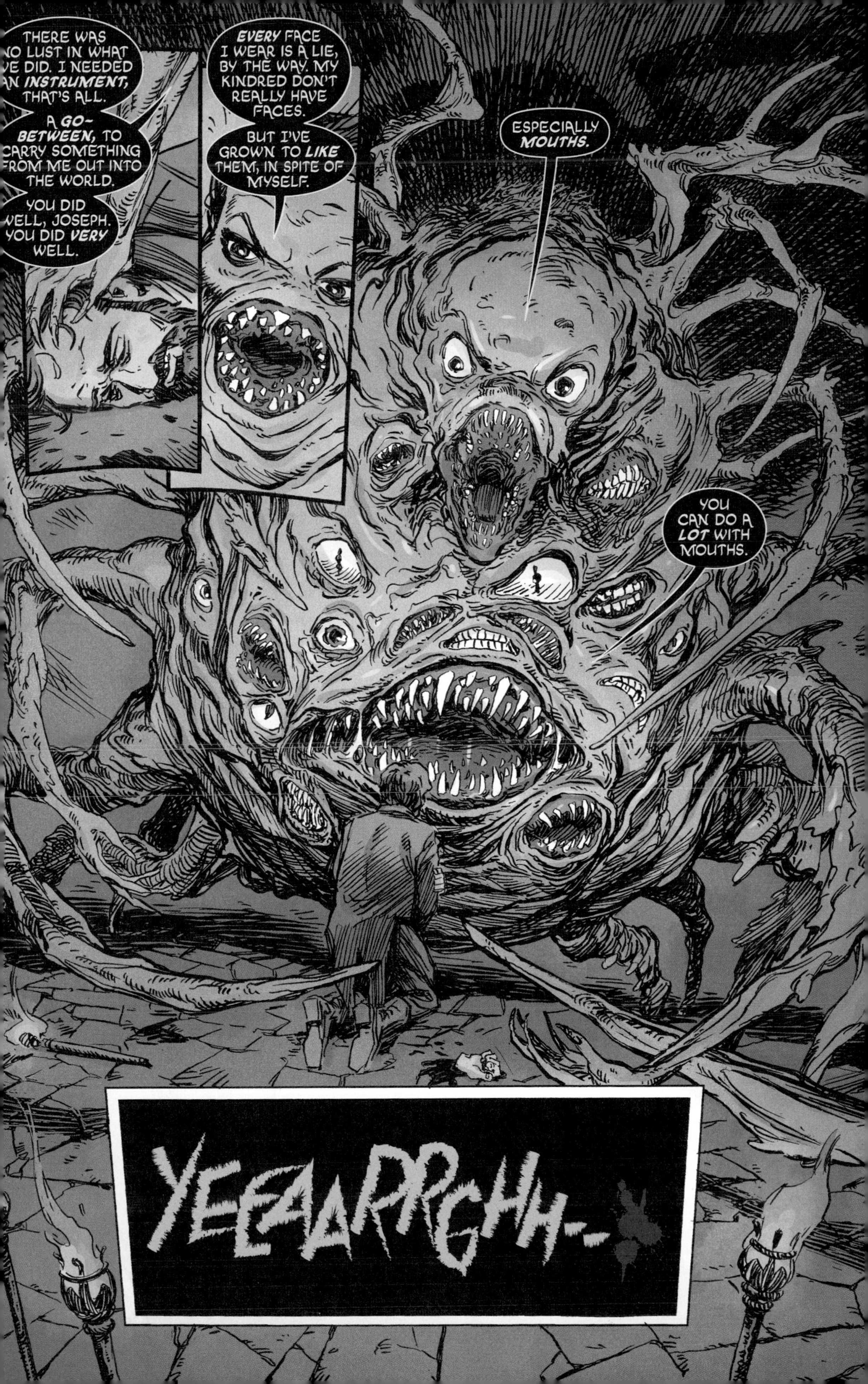
THERE WAS NO LUST IN WHAT WE DID. I NEEDED AN INSTRUMENT, THAT'S ALL.
A GO-BETWEEN, TO CARRY SOMETHING FROM ME OUT INTO THE WORLD.
YOU DID WELL, JOSEPH. YOU DID VERY WELL.
EVERY FACE I WEAR IS A LIE, BY THE WAY. MY KINDRED DON'T REALLY HAVE FACES.
BUT I'VE GROWN TO LIKE THEM, IN SPITE OF MYSELF.
ESPECIALLY MOUTHS.
YOU CAN DO A LOT WITH MOUTHS.
YEEAARRGHH--

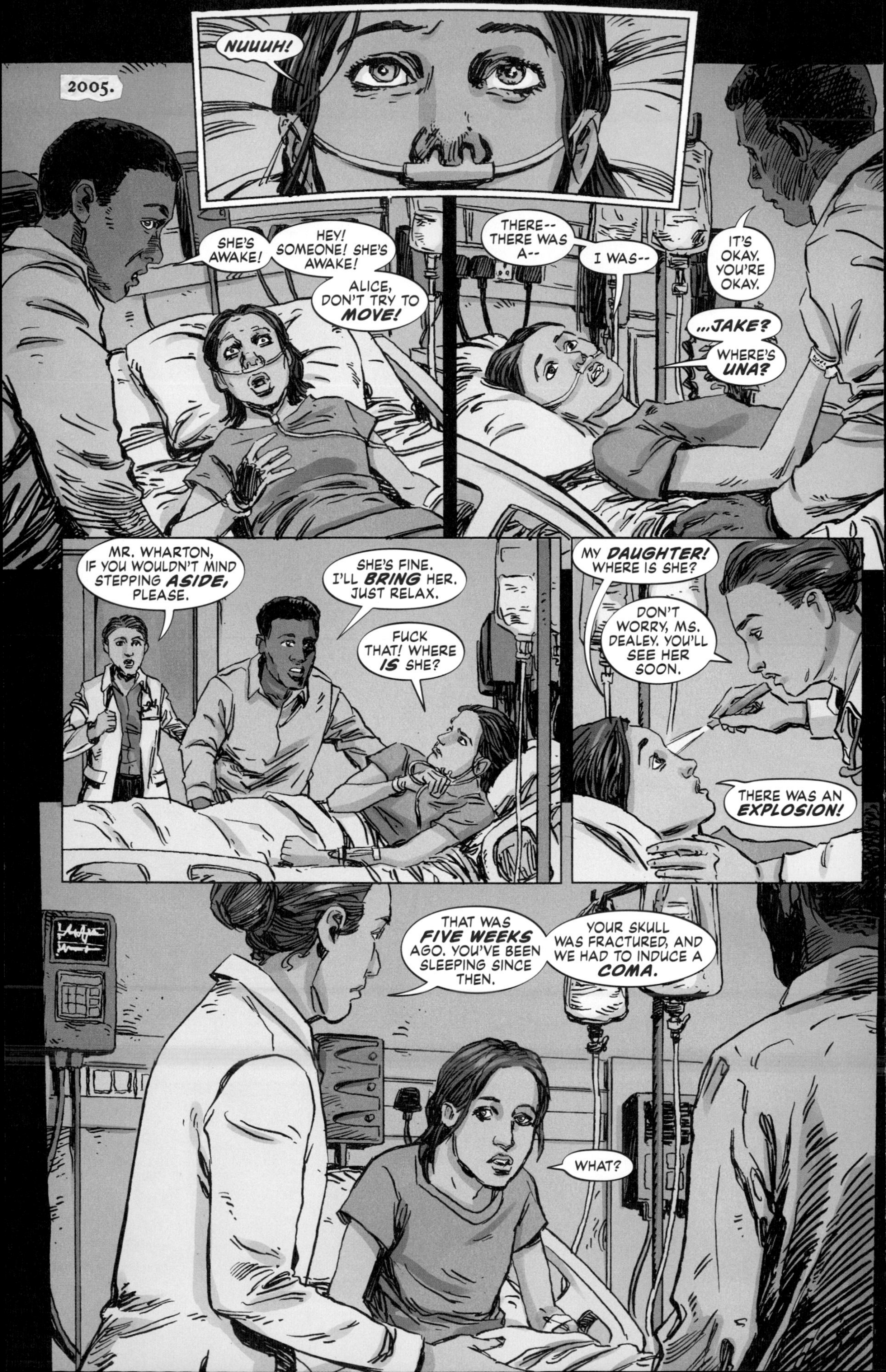
NUUUH!
2005.
SHE'S AWAKE!
HEY! SOMEONE! SHE'S AWAKE!
ALICE, DON'T TRY TO MOVE!
THERE-- THERE WAS A--
I WAS--
IT'S OKAY. YOU'RE OKAY.
...JAKE?
WHERE'S UNA?
MR. WHARTON, IF YOU WOULDN'T MIND STEPPING ASIDE, PLEASE.
SHE'S FINE. I'LL BRING HER. JUST RELAX.
FUCK THAT! WHERE IS SHE?
MY DAUGHTER! WHERE IS SHE?
DON'T WORRY, MS. DEALEY. YOU'LL SEE HER SOON.
THERE WAS AN EXPLOSION!
THAT WAS FIVE WEEKS AGO. YOU'VE BEEN SLEEPING SINCE THEN.
YOUR SKULL WAS FRACTURED, AND WE HAD TO INDUCE A COMA.
WHAT?

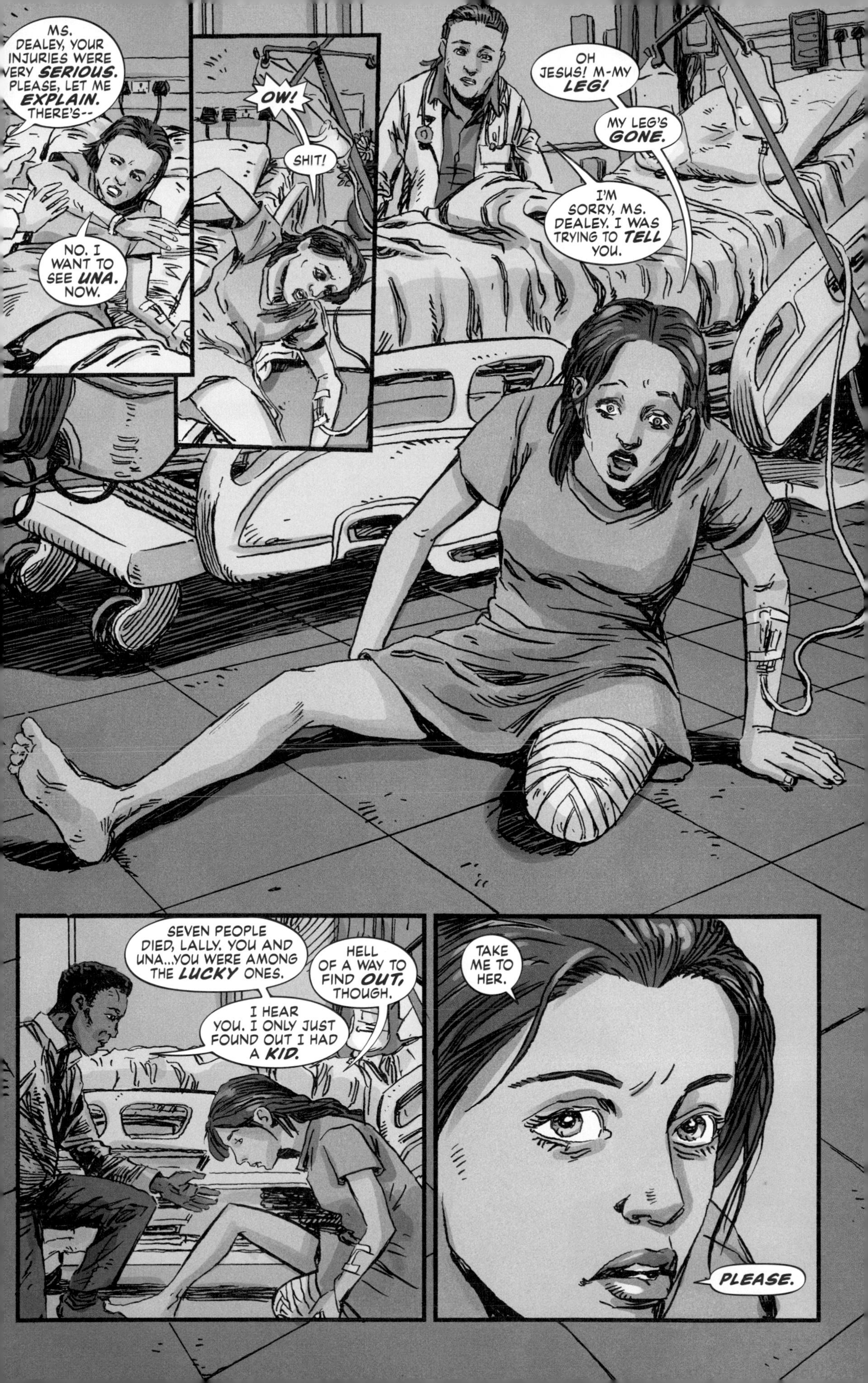
MS. DEALEY, YOUR INJURIES WERE VERY SERIOUS. PLEASE, LET ME EXPLAIN. THERE'S--
NO. I WANT TO SEE UNA. NOW.
OW!
SHIT!
OH JESUS! M-MY LEG!
MY LEG'S GONE.
I'M SORRY, MS. DEALEY. I WAS TRYING TO TELL YOU.
SEVEN PEOPLE DIED, LALLY. YOU AND UNA...YOU WERE AMONG THE LUCKY ONES.
I HEAR YOU. I ONLY JUST FOUND OUT I HAD A KID.
HELL OF A WAY TO FIND OUT, THOUGH.
TAKE ME TO HER.
PLEASE.

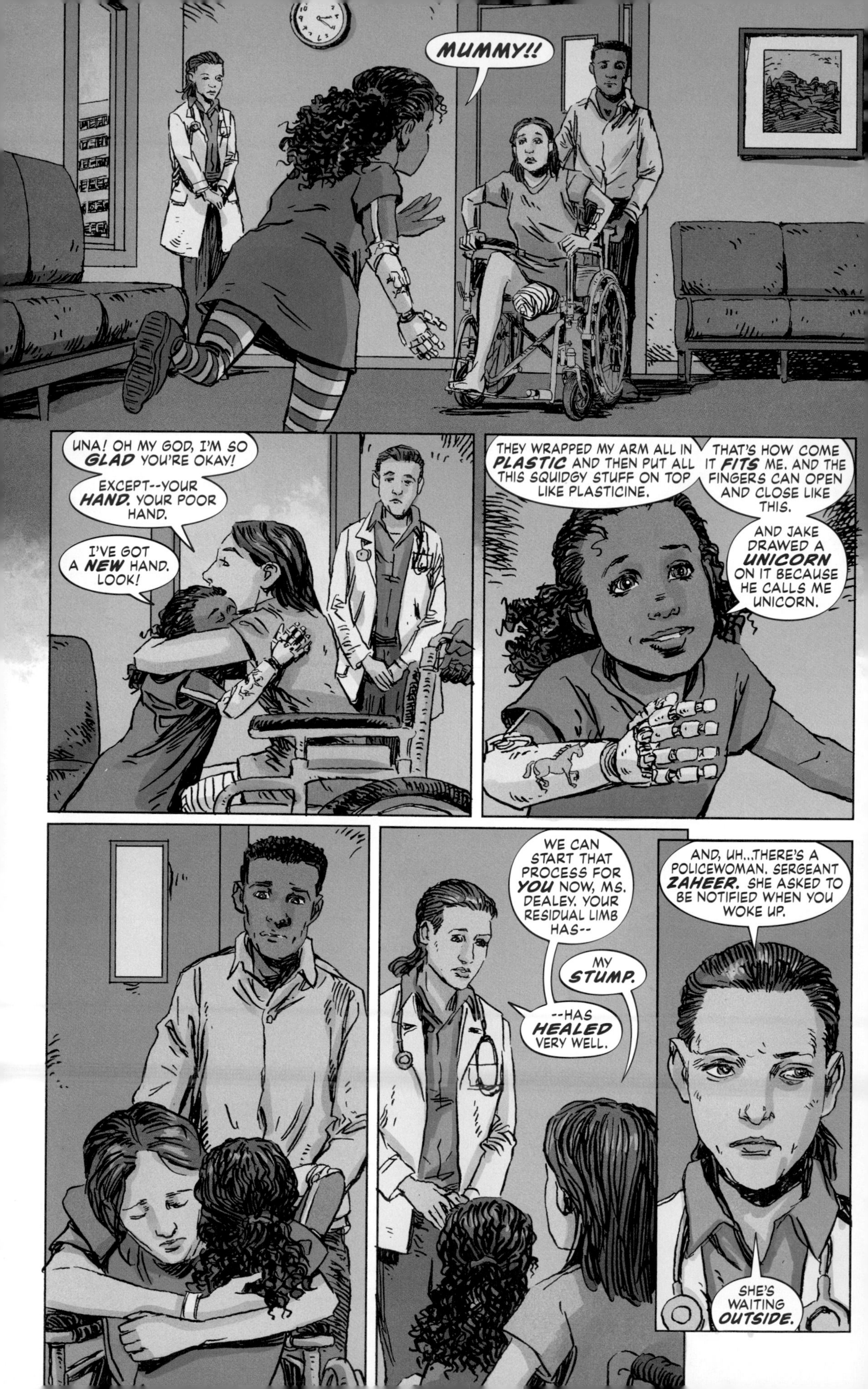

MUMMY!!
UNA! OH MY GOD, I'M SO GLAD YOU'RE OKAY!
EXCEPT--YOUR HAND. YOUR POOR HAND.
I'VE GOT A NEW HAND. LOOK!
THEY WRAPPED MY ARM ALL IN PLASTIC AND THEN PUT ALL THIS SQUIDGY STUFF ON TOP LIKE PLASTICINE.
THAT'S HOW COME IT FITS ME. AND THE FINGERS CAN OPEN AND CLOSE LIKE THIS.
AND JAKE DRAWED A UNICORN ON IT BECAUSE HE CALLS ME UNICORN.
WE CAN START THAT PROCESS FOR YOU NOW, MS. DEALEY. YOUR RESIDUAL LIMB HAS--
MY STUMP.
--HAS HEALED VERY WELL.
AND, UH...THERE'S A POLICEWOMAN. SERGEANT ZAHEER. SHE ASKED TO BE NOTIFIED WHEN YOU WOKE UP.
SHE'S WAITING OUTSIDE.

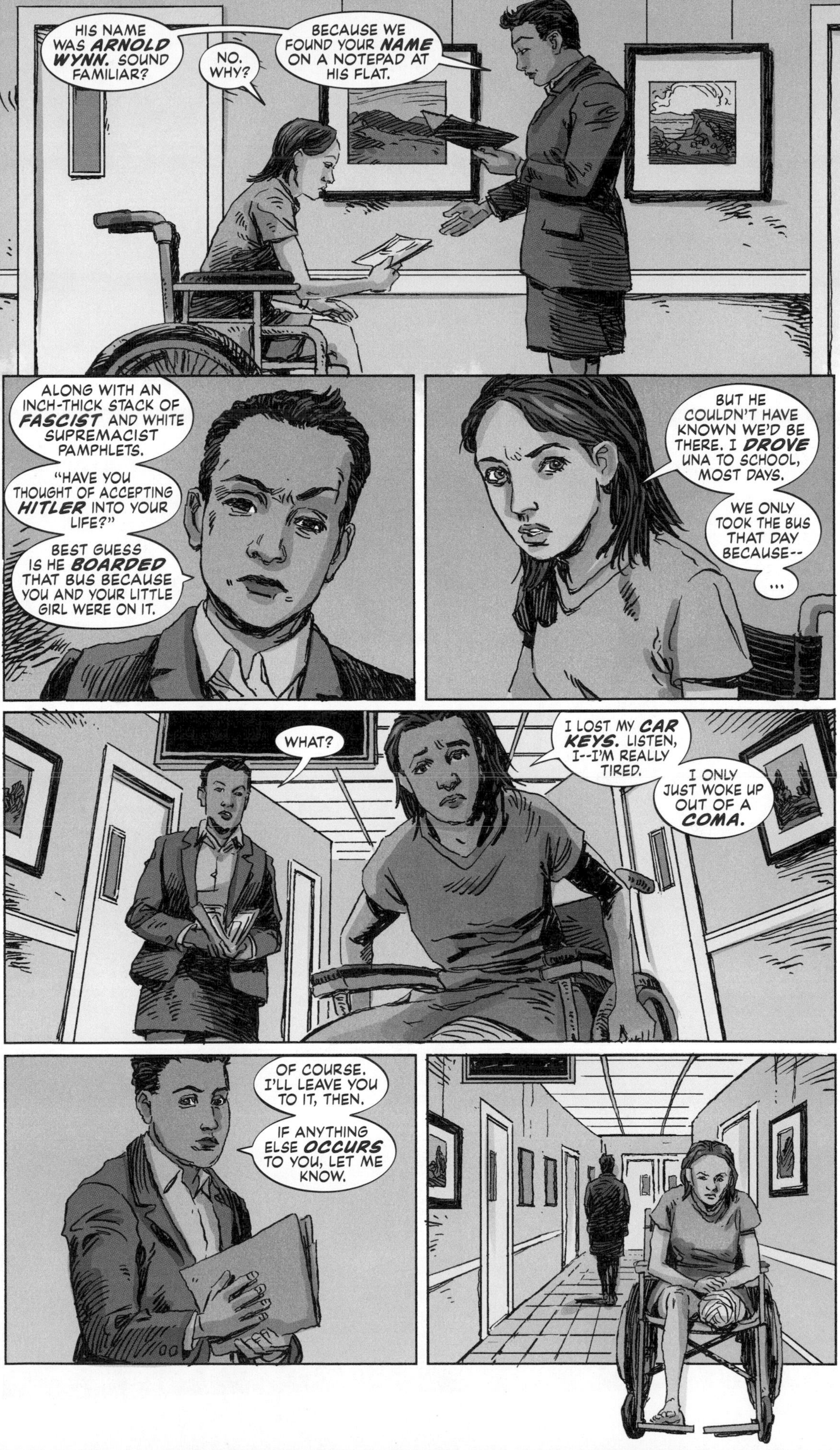
HIS NAME WAS ARNOLD WYNN. SOUND FAMILIAR?
NO. WHY?
BECAUSE WE FOUND YOUR NAME ON A NOTEPAD AT HIS FLAT.
ALONG WITH AN INCH-THICK STACK OF FASCIST AND WHITE SUPREMACIST PAMPHLETS.
"HAVE YOU THOUGHT OF ACCEPTING HITLER INTO YOUR LIFE?"
BEST GUESS IS HE BOARDED THAT BUS BECAUSE YOU AND YOUR LITTLE GIRL WERE ON IT.
BUT HE COULDN'T HAVE KNOWN WE'D BE THERE. I DROVE UNA TO SCHOOL, MOST DAYS.
WE ONLY TOOK THE BUS THAT DAY BECAUSE--
...
WHAT?
I LOST MY CAR KEYS. LISTEN, I--I'M REALLY TIRED.
I ONLY JUST WOKE UP OUT OF A COMA.
OF COURSE. I'LL LEAVE YOU TO IT, THEN.
IF ANYTHING ELSE OCCURS TO YOU, LET ME KNOW.

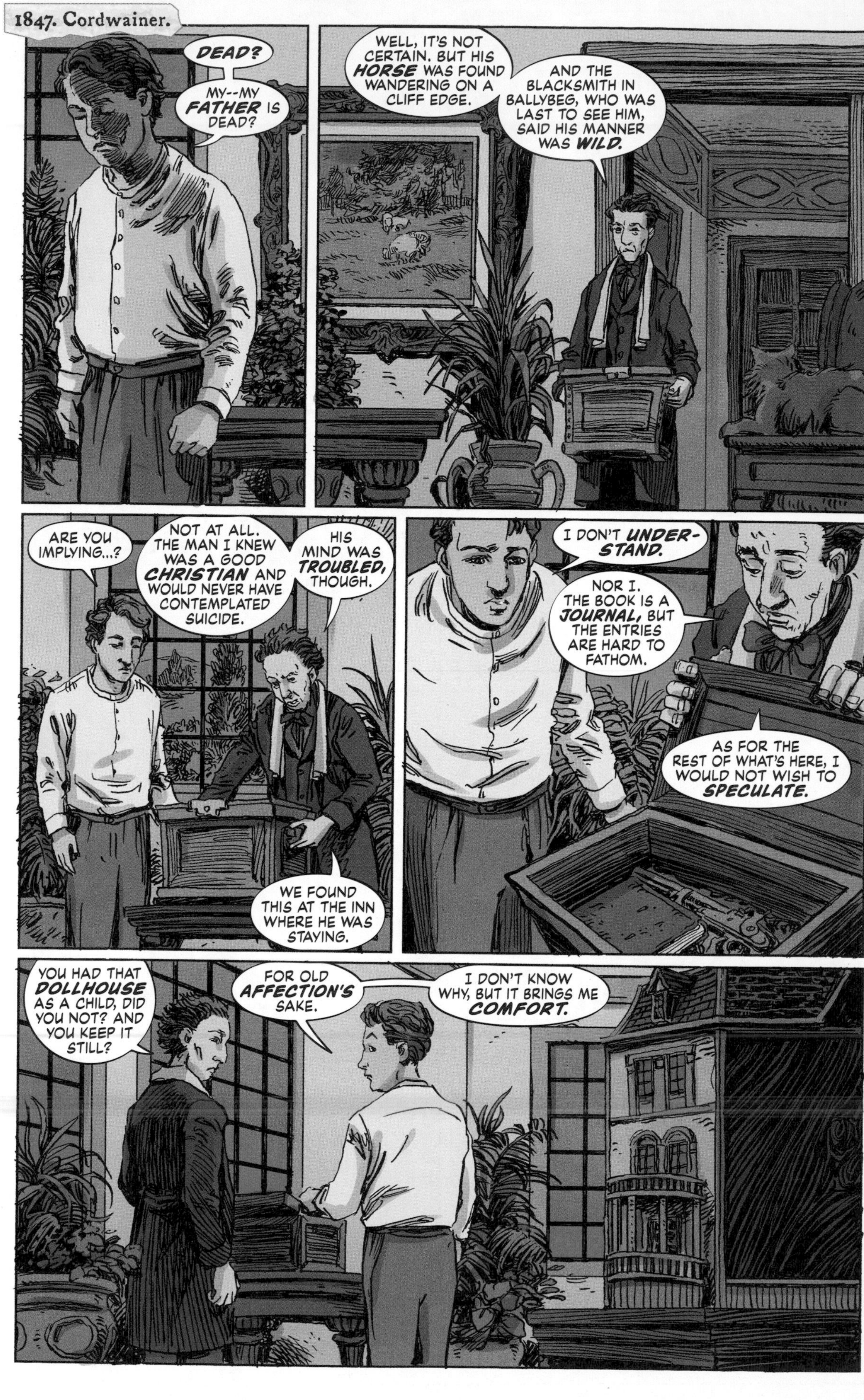
1847. Cordwainer.
DEAD?
MY--MY FATHER IS DEAD?
WELL, IT'S NOT CERTAIN. BUT HIS HORSE WAS FOUND WANDERING ON A CLIFF EDGE.
AND THE BLACKSMITH IN BALLYBEG, WHO WAS LAST TO SEE HIM, SAID HIS MANNER WAS WILD.
ARE YOU IMPLYING...?
NOT AT ALL. THE MAN I KNEW WAS A GOOD CHRISTIAN AND WOULD NEVER HAVE CONTEMPLATED SUICIDE.
HIS MIND WAS TROUBLED, THOUGH.
WE FOUND THIS AT THE INN WHERE HE WAS STAYING.
I DON'T UNDER-STAND.
NOR I. THE BOOK IS A JOURNAL, BUT THE ENTRIES ARE HARD TO FATHOM.
AS FOR THE REST OF WHAT'S HERE, I WOULD NOT WISH TO SPECULATE.
YOU HAD THAT DOLLHOUSE AS A CHILD, DID YOU NOT? AND YOU KEEP IT STILL?
FOR OLD AFFECTION'S SAKE.
I DON'T KNOW WHY, BUT IT BRINGS ME COMFORT.

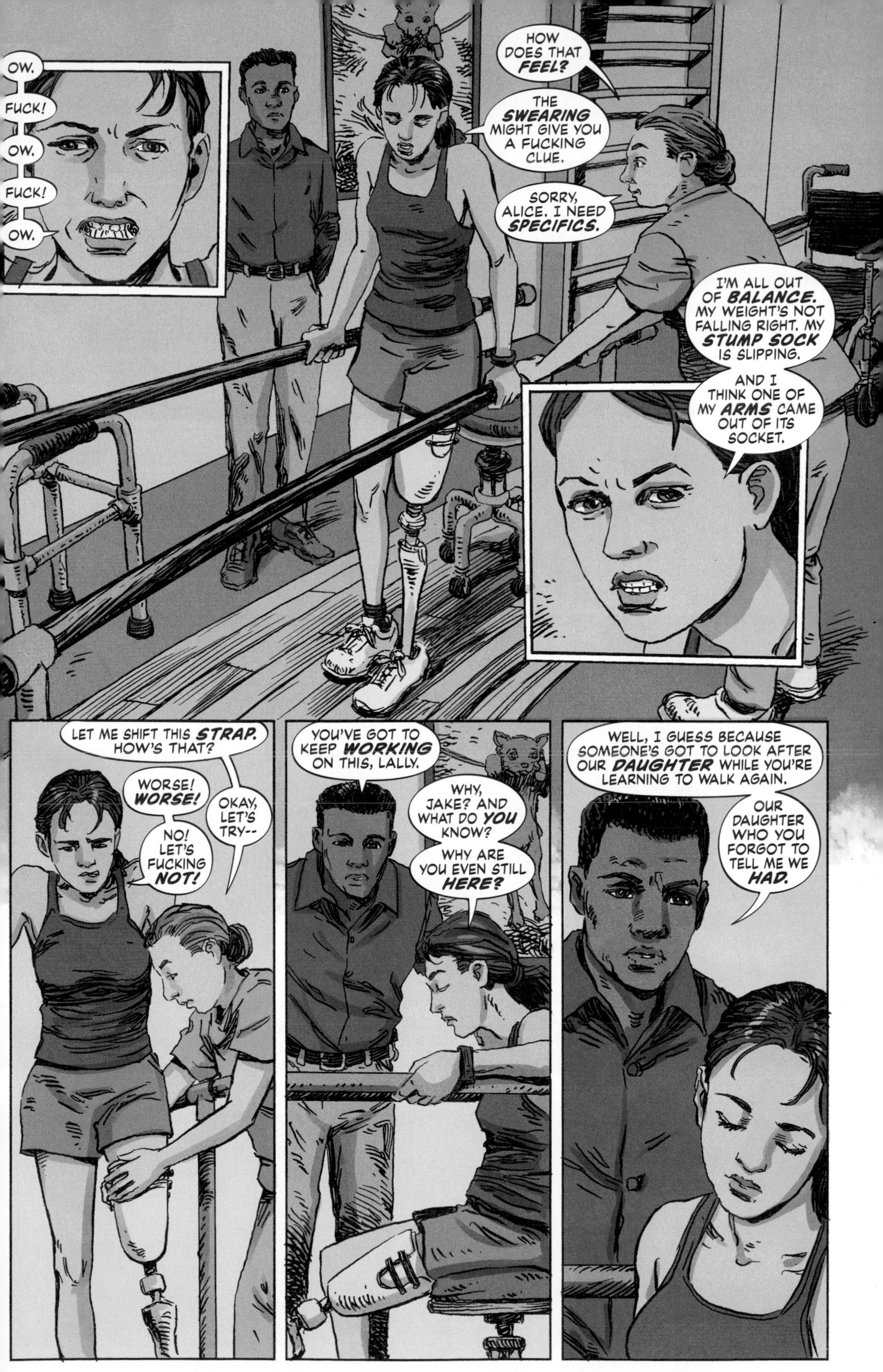
OW.
FUCK!
OW.
FUCK!
OW.
HOW DOES THAT FEEL?
THE SWEARING MIGHT GIVE YOU A FUCKING CLUE.
SORRY, ALICE. I NEED SPECIFICS.
I'M ALL OUT OF BALANCE. MY WEIGHT'S NOT FALLING RIGHT. MY STUMP SOCK IS SLIPPING.
AND I THINK ONE OF MY ARMS CAME OUT OF ITS SOCKET.
LET ME SHIFT THIS STRAP. HOW'S THAT?
WORSE! WORSE!
OKAY, LET'S TRY--
NO! LET'S FUCKING NOT!
YOU'VE GOT TO KEEP WORKING ON THIS, LALLY.
WHY, JAKE? AND WHAT DO YOU KNOW?
WHY ARE YOU EVEN STILL HERE?
WELL, I GUESS BECAUSE SOMEONE'S GOT TO LOOK AFTER OUR DAUGHTER WHILE YOU'RE LEARNING TO WALK AGAIN.
OUR DAUGHTER WHO YOU FORGOT TO TELL ME WE HAD.

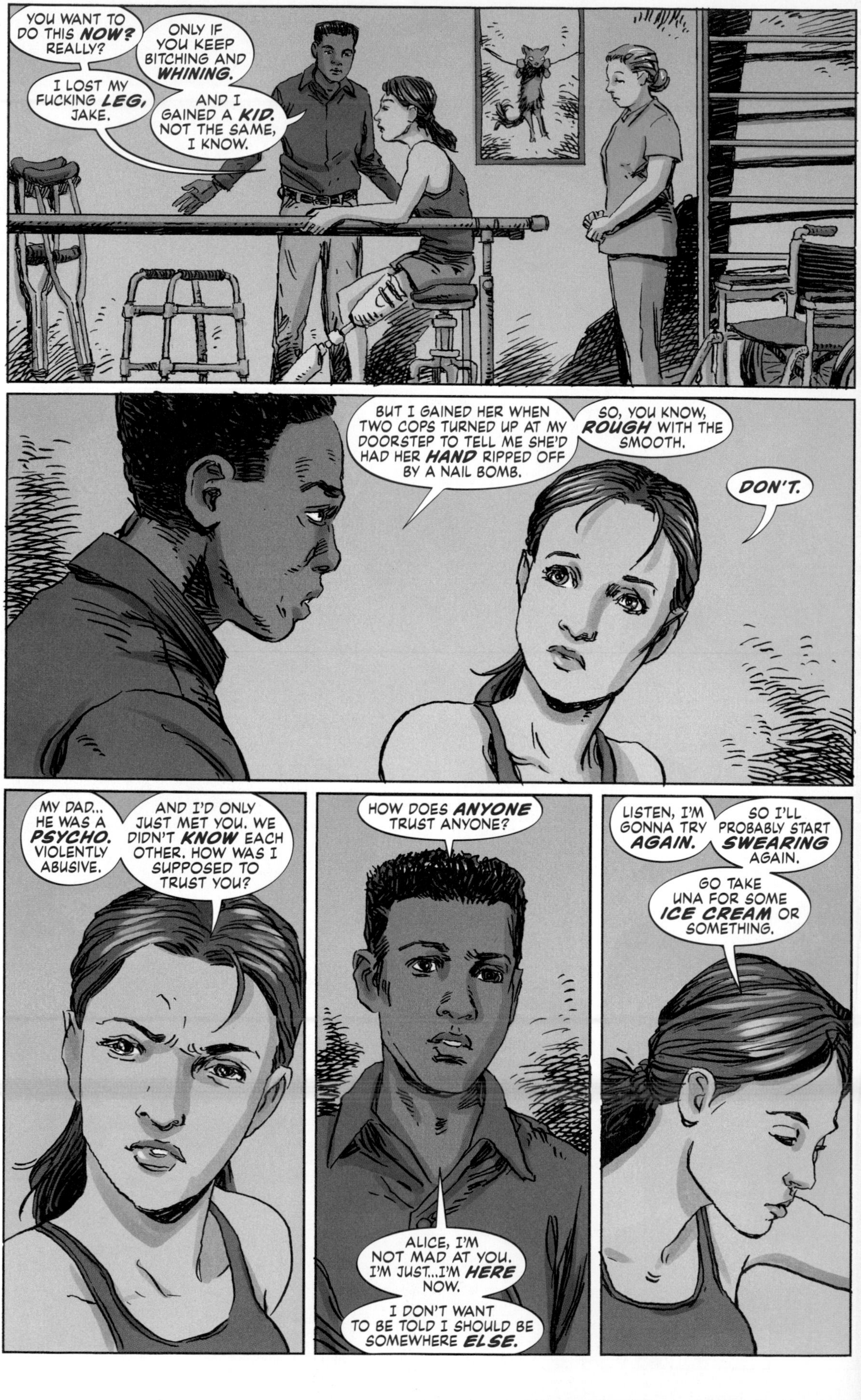
YOU WANT TO DO THIS NOW? REALLY?
ONLY IF YOU KEEP BITCHING AND WHINING.
I LOST MY FUCKING LEG, JAKE.
AND I GAINED A KID. NOT THE SAME, I KNOW.
BUT I GAINED HER WHEN TWO COPS TURNED UP AT MY DOORSTEP TO TELL ME SHE'D HAD HER HAND RIPPED OFF BY A NAIL BOMB.
SO, YOU KNOW, ROUGH WITH THE SMOOTH.
DON'T.
MY DAD... HE WAS A PSYCHO. VIOLENTLY ABUSIVE.
AND I'D ONLY JUST MET YOU. WE DIDN'T KNOW EACH OTHER. HOW WAS I SUPPOSED TO TRUST YOU?
HOW DOES ANYONE TRUST ANYONE?
ALICE, I'M NOT MAD AT YOU. I'M JUST...I'M HERE NOW.
I DON'T WANT TO BE TOLD I SHOULD BE SOMEWHERE ELSE.
LISTEN, I'M GONNA TRY AGAIN.
SO I'LL PROBABLY START SWEARING AGAIN.
GO TAKE UNA FOR SOME ICE CREAM OR SOMETHING.

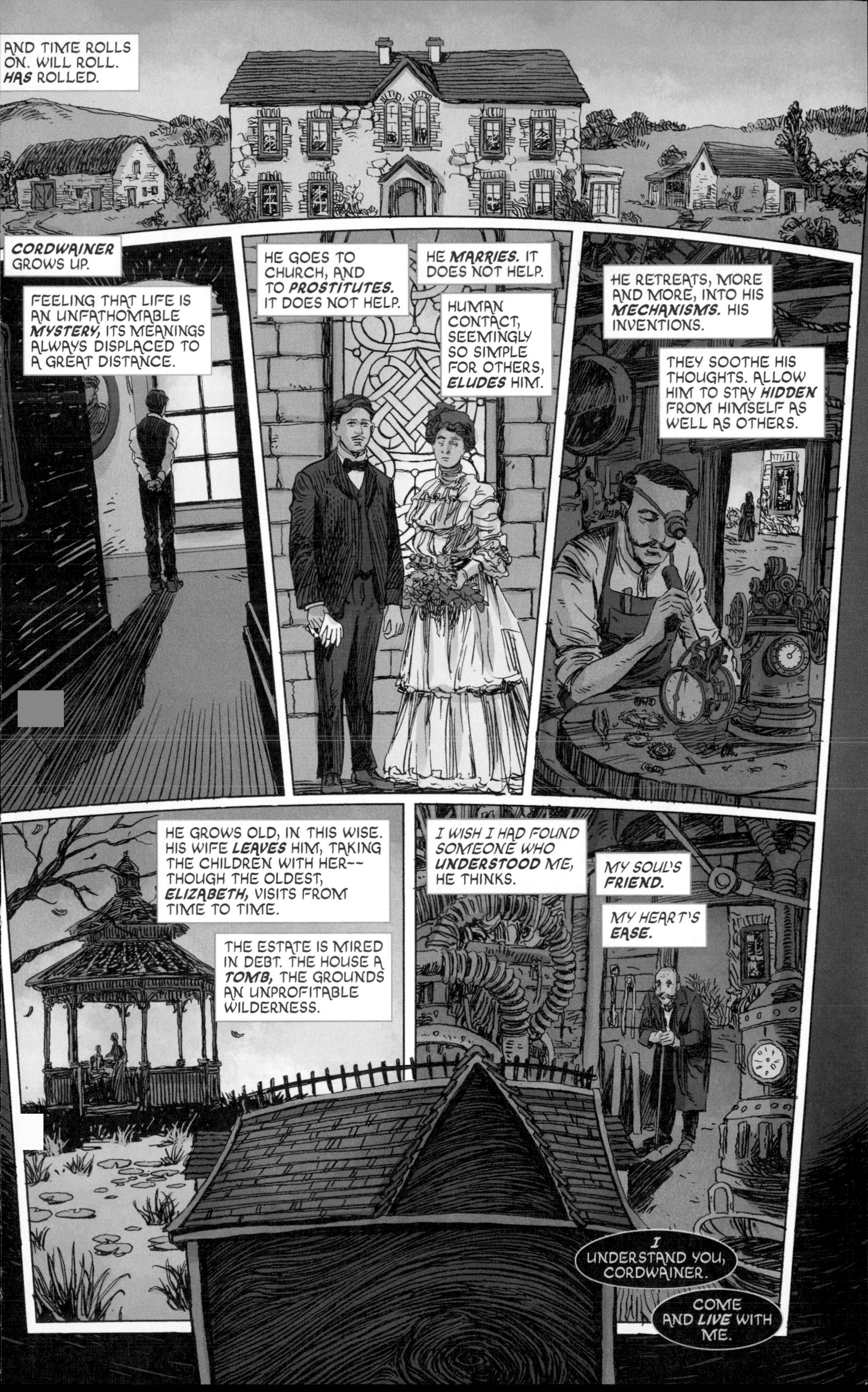
AND TIME ROLLS ON. WILL ROLL. HAS ROLLED.
CORDWAINER GROWS UP.
FEELING THAT LIFE IS AN UNFATHOMABLE MYSTERY, ITS MEANINGS ALWAYS DISPLACED TO A GREAT DISTANCE.
HE GOES TO CHURCH, AND TO PROSTITUTES. IT DOES NOT HELP.
HE MARRIES. IT DOES NOT HELP.
HUMAN CONTACT, SEEMINGLY SO SIMPLE FOR OTHERS, ELUDES HIM.
HE RETREATS, MORE AND MORE, INTO HIS MECHANISMS. HIS INVENTIONS.
THEY SOOTHE HIS THOUGHTS. ALLOW HIM TO STAY HIDDEN FROM HIMSELF AS WELL AS OTHERS.
HE GROWS OLD, IN THIS WISE. HIS WIFE LEAVES HIM, TAKING THE CHILDREN WITH HER-- THOUGH THE OLDEST, ELIZABETH, VISITS FROM TIME TO TIME.
THE ESTATE IS MIRED IN DEBT. THE HOUSE A TOMB, THE GROUNDS AN UNPROFITABLE WILDERNESS.
I WISH I HAD FOUND SOMEONE WHO UNDERSTOOD ME, HE THINKS.
MY SOUL'S FRIEND.
MY HEART'S EASE.
I UNDERSTAND YOU, CORDWAINER.
COME AND LIVE WITH ME.

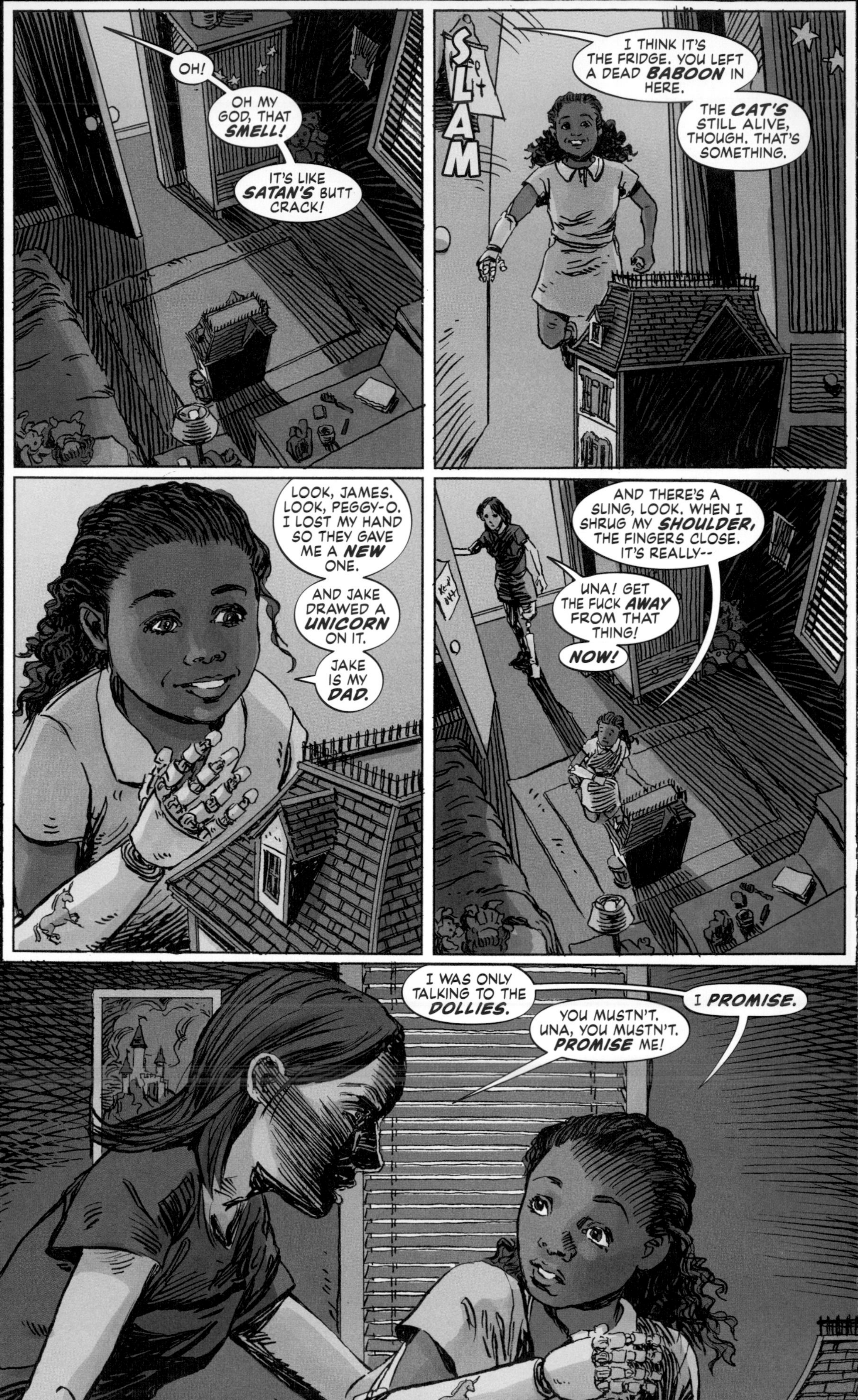

OH!
OH MY GOD, THAT **SMELL!**
IT'S LIKE **SATAN'S** BUTT CRACK!
SLAM
I THINK IT'S THE FRIDGE. YOU LEFT A DEAD **BABOON** IN HERE.
THE **CAT'S** STILL ALIVE, THOUGH. THAT'S SOMETHING.
LOOK, JAMES. LOOK, PEGGY-O. I LOST MY HAND SO THEY GAVE ME A **NEW** ONE.
AND JAKE DRAWED A **UNICORN** ON IT.
JAKE IS MY **DAD.**
AND THERE'S A SLING, LOOK. WHEN I SHRUG MY **SHOULDER,** THE FINGERS CLOSE. IT'S REALLY--
UNA! GET THE FUCK **AWAY** FROM THAT THING!
NOW!
I WAS ONLY TALKING TO THE **DOLLIES.**
YOU MUSTN'T. UNA, YOU MUSTN'T. **PROMISE** ME!
I **PROMISE.**

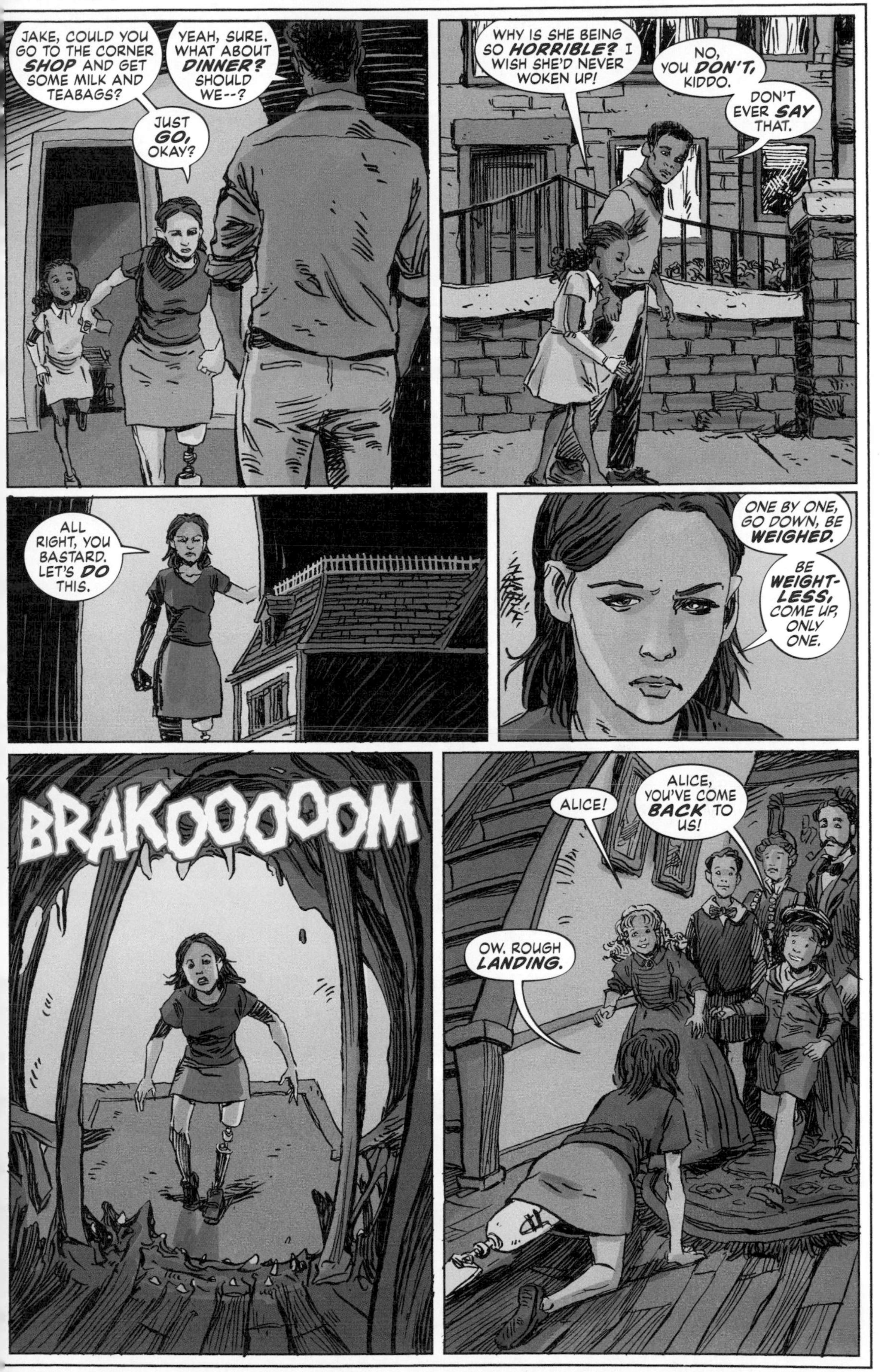
JAKE, COULD YOU GO TO THE CORNER SHOP AND GET SOME MILK AND TEABAGS?
YEAH, SURE. WHAT ABOUT DINNER? SHOULD WE--?
JUST GO, OKAY?
WHY IS SHE BEING SO HORRIBLE? I WISH SHE'D NEVER WOKEN UP!
NO, YOU DON'T, KIDDO.
DON'T EVER SAY THAT.
ALL RIGHT, YOU BASTARD. LET'S DO THIS.
ONE BY ONE, GO DOWN, BE WEIGHED.
BE WEIGHTLESS, COME UP, ONLY ONE.
BRAKOOOOOM
ALICE!
ALICE, YOU'VE COME BACK TO US!
OW. ROUGH LANDING.

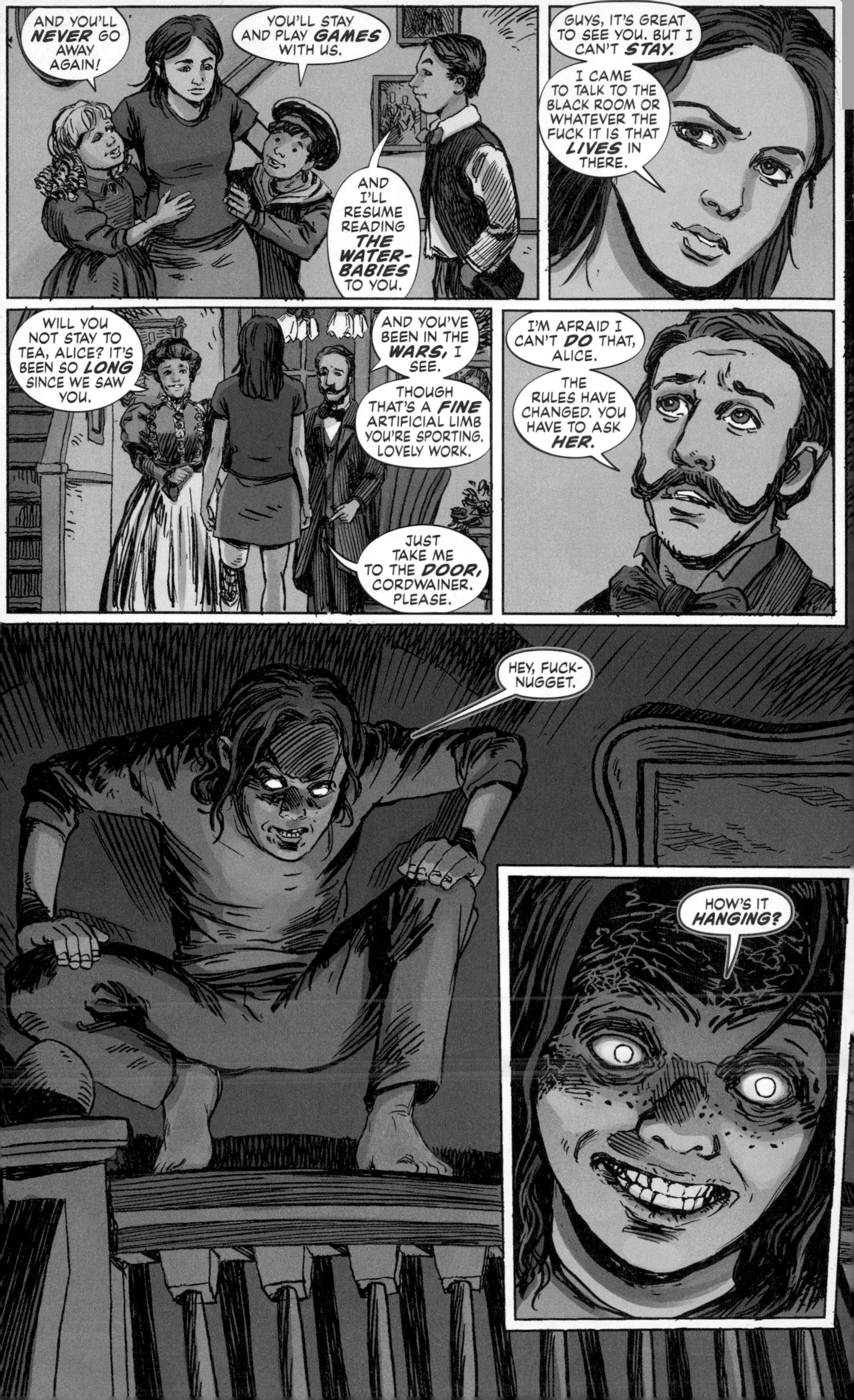
AND YOU'LL NEVER GO AWAY AGAIN!
YOU'LL STAY AND PLAY GAMES WITH US.
AND I'LL RESUME READING THE WATER-BABIES TO YOU.
GUYS, IT'S GREAT TO SEE YOU. BUT I CAN'T STAY.
I CAME TO TALK TO THE BLACK ROOM OR WHATEVER THE FUCK IT IS THAT LIVES IN THERE.
WILL YOU NOT STAY TO TEA, ALICE? IT'S BEEN SO LONG SINCE WE SAW YOU.
AND YOU'VE BEEN IN THE WARS, I SEE.
THOUGH THAT'S A FINE ARTIFICIAL LIMB YOU'RE SPORTING. LOVELY WORK.
JUST TAKE ME TO THE DOOR, CORDWAINER. PLEASE.
I'M AFRAID I CAN'T DO THAT, ALICE.
THE RULES HAVE CHANGED. YOU HAVE TO ASK HER.
HEY, FUCK-NUGGET.
HOW'S IT HANGING?

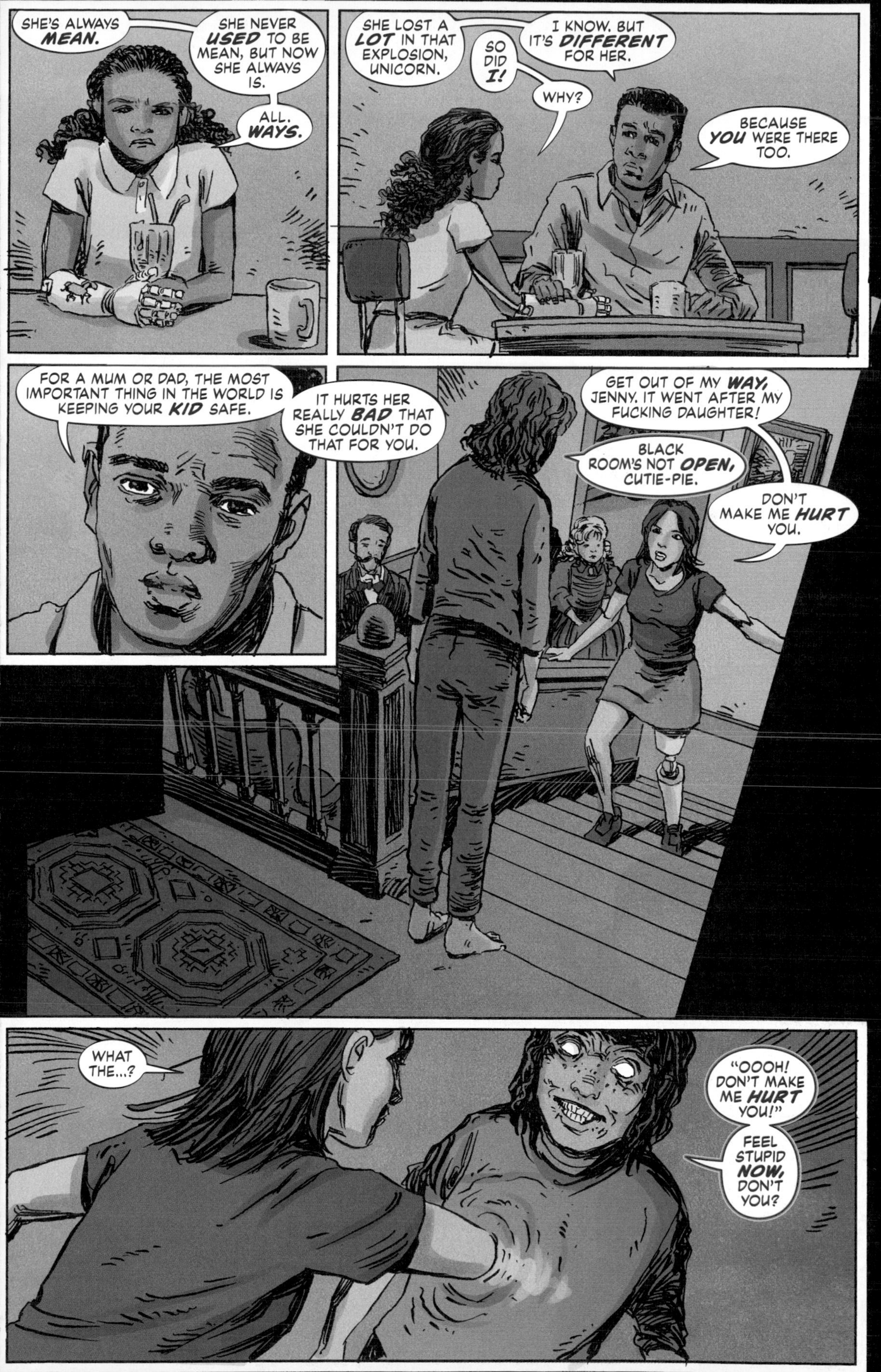

SHE'S ALWAYS MEAN.
SHE NEVER USED TO BE MEAN, BUT NOW SHE ALWAYS IS.
ALL. WAYS.
SHE LOST A LOT IN THAT EXPLOSION, UNICORN.
SO DID I!
I KNOW. BUT IT'S DIFFERENT FOR HER.
WHY?
BECAUSE YOU WERE THERE TOO.
FOR A MUM OR DAD, THE MOST IMPORTANT THING IN THE WORLD IS KEEPING YOUR KID SAFE.
IT HURTS HER REALLY BAD THAT SHE COULDN'T DO THAT FOR YOU.
GET OUT OF MY WAY, JENNY. IT WENT AFTER MY FUCKING DAUGHTER!
BLACK ROOM'S NOT OPEN, CUTIE-PIE.
DON'T MAKE ME HURT YOU.
WHAT THE...?
"OOOH! DON'T MAKE ME HURT YOU!"
FEEL STUPID NOW, DON'T YOU?

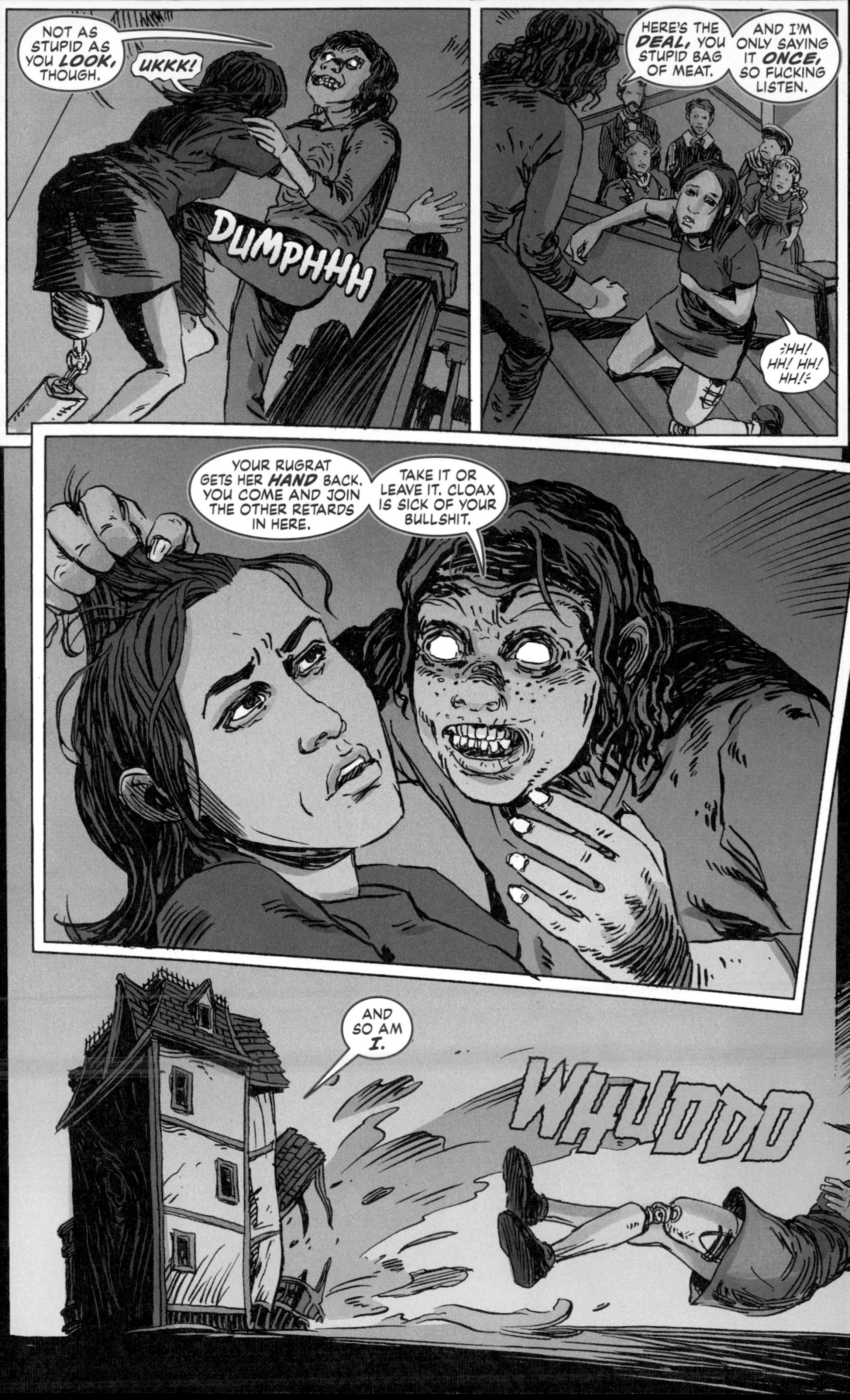
NOT AS STUPID AS YOU *LOOK,* THOUGH.
UKKK!
DUMPHHH
HERE'S THE *DEAL,* YOU STUPID BAG OF MEAT.
AND I'M ONLY SAYING IT *ONCE,* SO FUCKING LISTEN.
HH! HH! HH! HH!
YOUR RUGRAT GETS HER *HAND* BACK. YOU COME AND JOIN THE OTHER RETARDS IN HERE.
TAKE IT OR LEAVE IT. CLOAX IS SICK OF YOUR BULLSHIT.
AND SO AM *I.*
WHUDDD

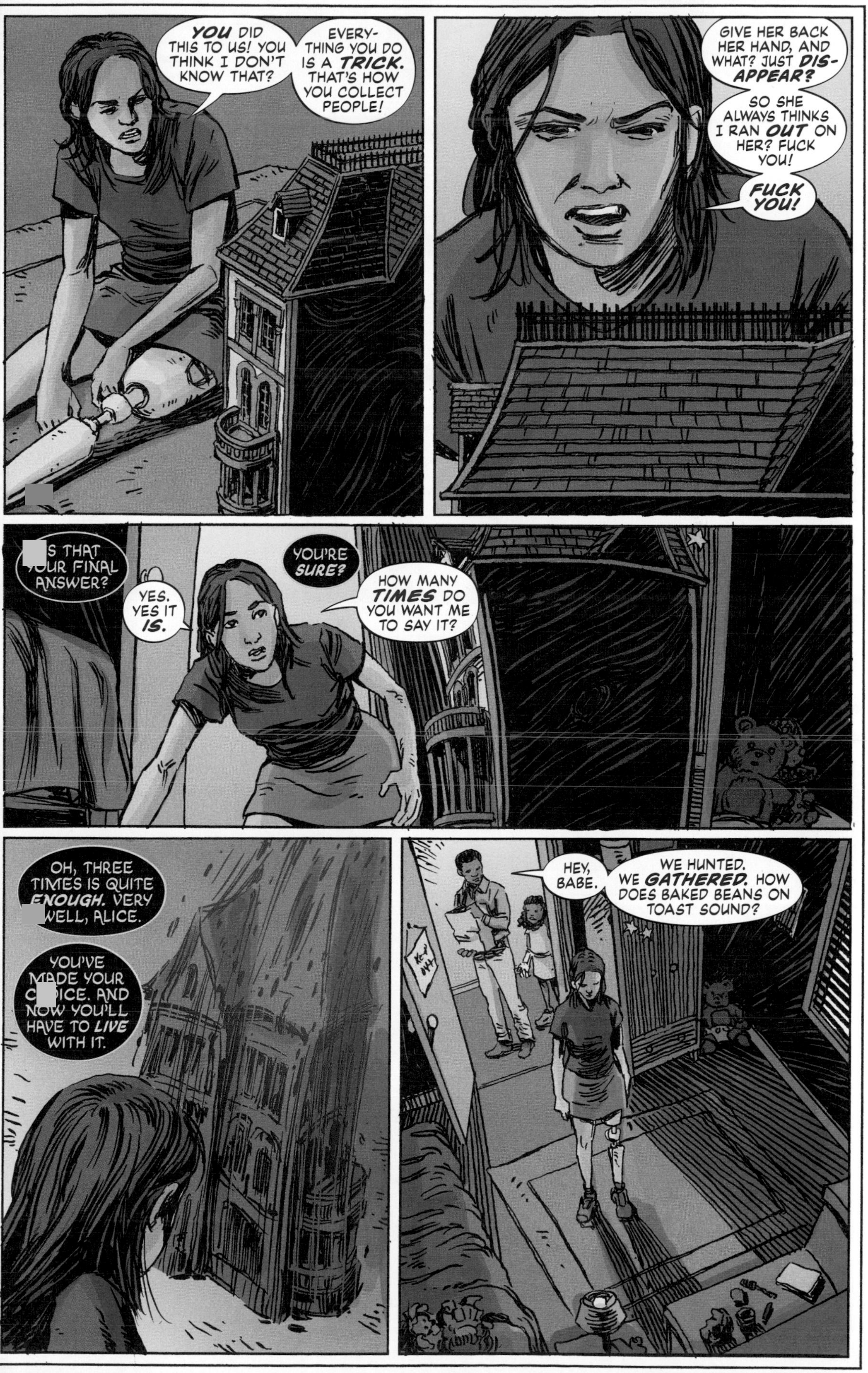
YOU DID THIS TO US! YOU THINK I DON'T KNOW THAT?
EVERY-THING YOU DO IS A TRICK. THAT'S HOW YOU COLLECT PEOPLE!
GIVE HER BACK HER HAND, AND WHAT? JUST DIS-APPEAR?
SO SHE ALWAYS THINKS I RAN OUT ON HER? FUCK YOU!
FUCK YOU!
IS THAT YOUR FINAL ANSWER?
YES. YES IT IS.
YOU'RE SURE?
HOW MANY TIMES DO YOU WANT ME TO SAY IT?
OH, THREE TIMES IS QUITE ENOUGH. VERY WELL, ALICE.
YOU'VE MADE YOUR CHOICE. AND NOW YOU'LL HAVE TO LIVE WITH IT.
HEY, BABE.
WE HUNTED. WE GATHERED. HOW DOES BAKED BEANS ON TOAST SOUND?

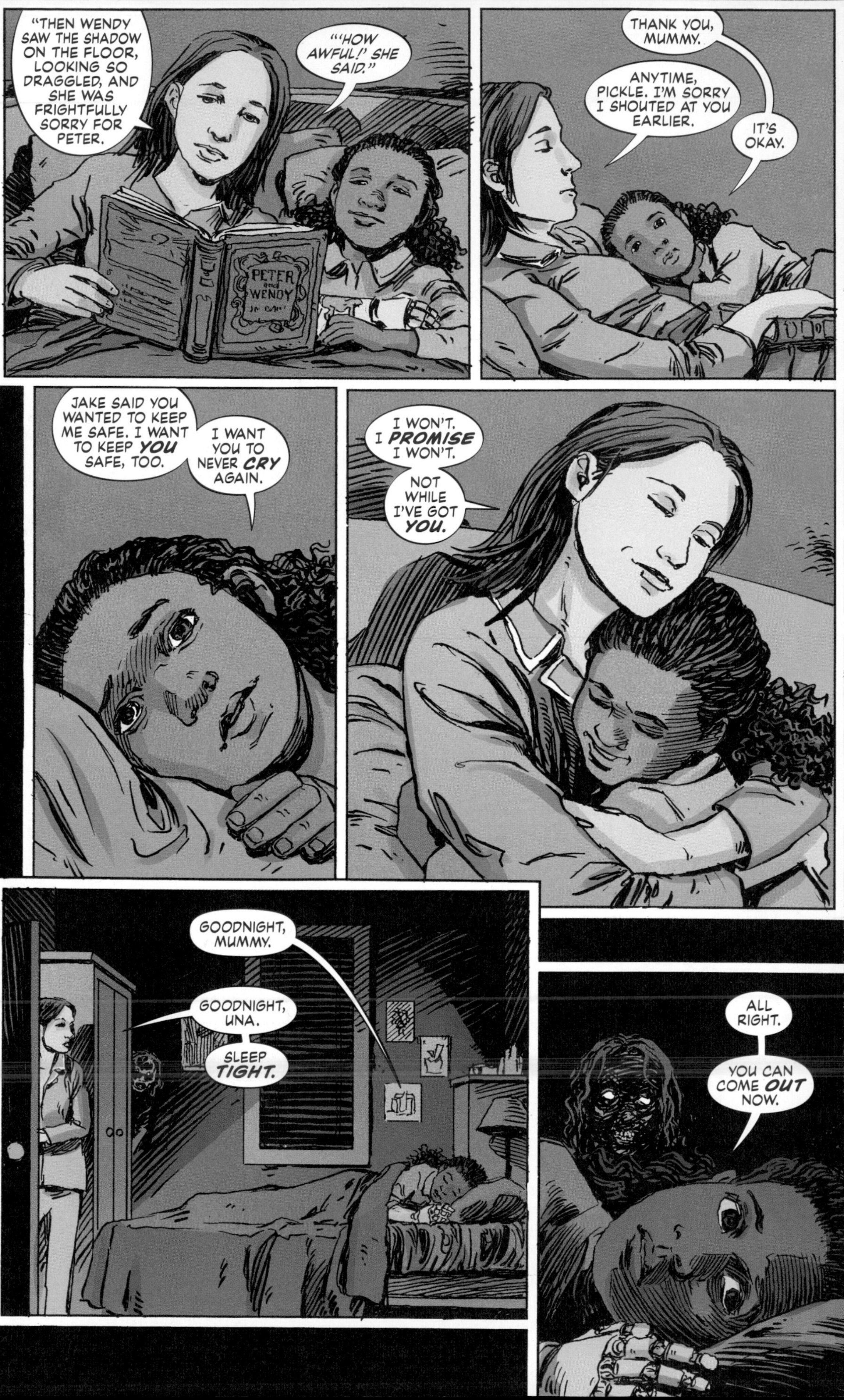
"THEN WENDY SAW THE SHADOW ON THE FLOOR, LOOKING SO DRAGGLED, AND SHE WAS FRIGHTFULLY SORRY FOR PETER.
"'HOW AWFUL!' SHE SAID."
PETER and WENDY
THANK YOU, MUMMY.
ANYTIME, PICKLE. I'M SORRY I SHOUTED AT YOU EARLIER.
IT'S OKAY.
JAKE SAID YOU WANTED TO KEEP ME SAFE. I WANT TO KEEP *YOU* SAFE, TOO.
I WANT YOU TO NEVER *CRY* AGAIN.
I WON'T. I *PROMISE* I WON'T.
NOT WHILE I'VE GOT *YOU.*
GOODNIGHT, MUMMY.
GOODNIGHT, UNA.
SLEEP *TIGHT.*
ALL RIGHT.
YOU CAN COME *OUT* NOW.

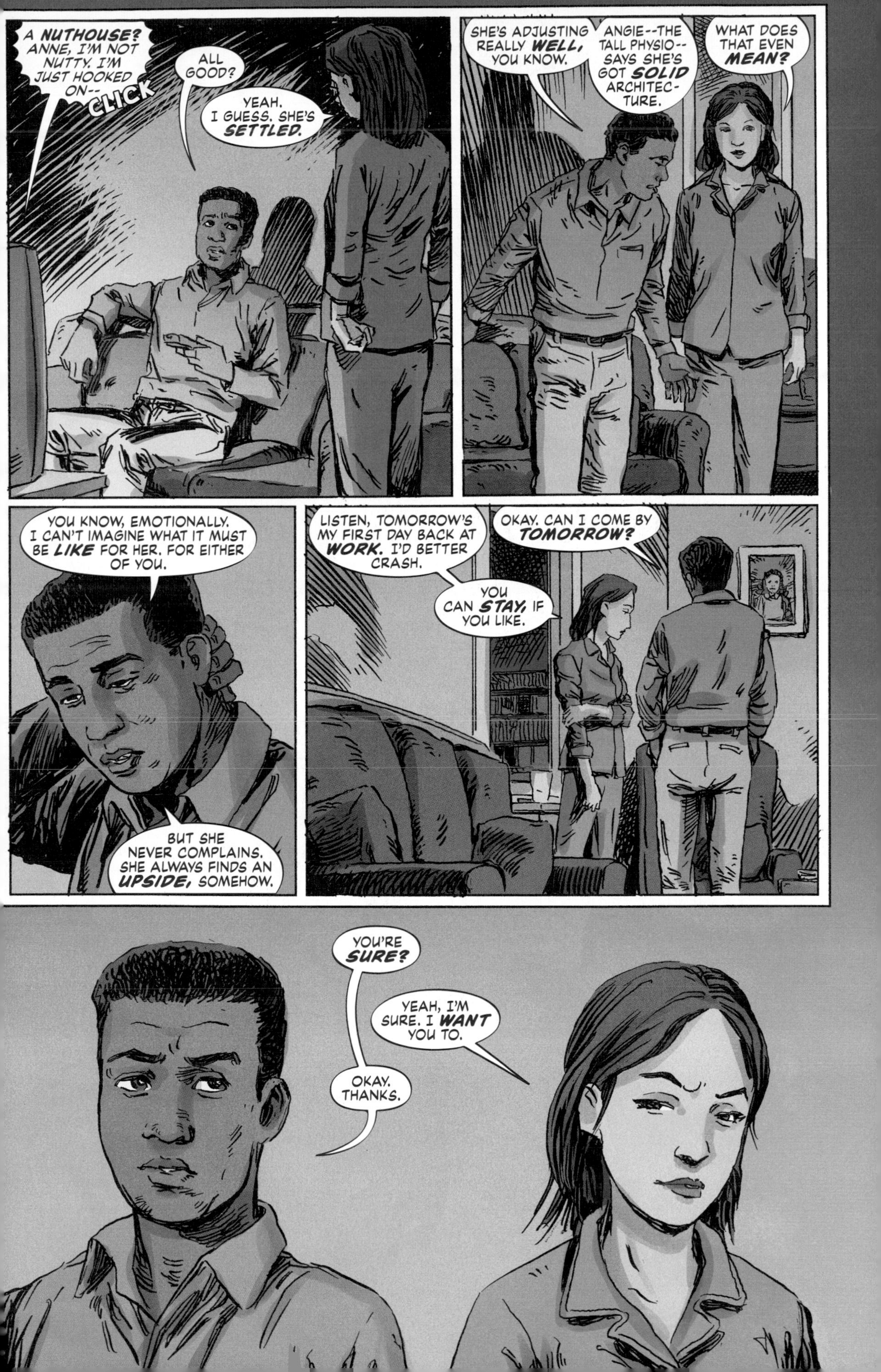
A NUTHOUSE? ANNE, I'M NOT NUTTY. I'M JUST HOOKED ON--
CLICK
ALL GOOD?
YEAH. I GUESS. SHE'S SETTLED.
SHE'S ADJUSTING REALLY WELL, YOU KNOW.
ANGIE--THE TALL PHYSIO--SAYS SHE'S GOT SOLID ARCHITEC-TURE.
WHAT DOES THAT EVEN MEAN?
YOU KNOW, EMOTIONALLY. I CAN'T IMAGINE WHAT IT MUST BE LIKE FOR HER. FOR EITHER OF YOU.
BUT SHE NEVER COMPLAINS. SHE ALWAYS FINDS AN UPSIDE, SOMEHOW.
LISTEN, TOMORROW'S MY FIRST DAY BACK AT WORK. I'D BETTER CRASH.
OKAY. CAN I COME BY TOMORROW?
YOU CAN STAY, IF YOU LIKE.
YOU'RE SURE?
YEAH, I'M SURE. I WANT YOU TO.
OKAY. THANKS.

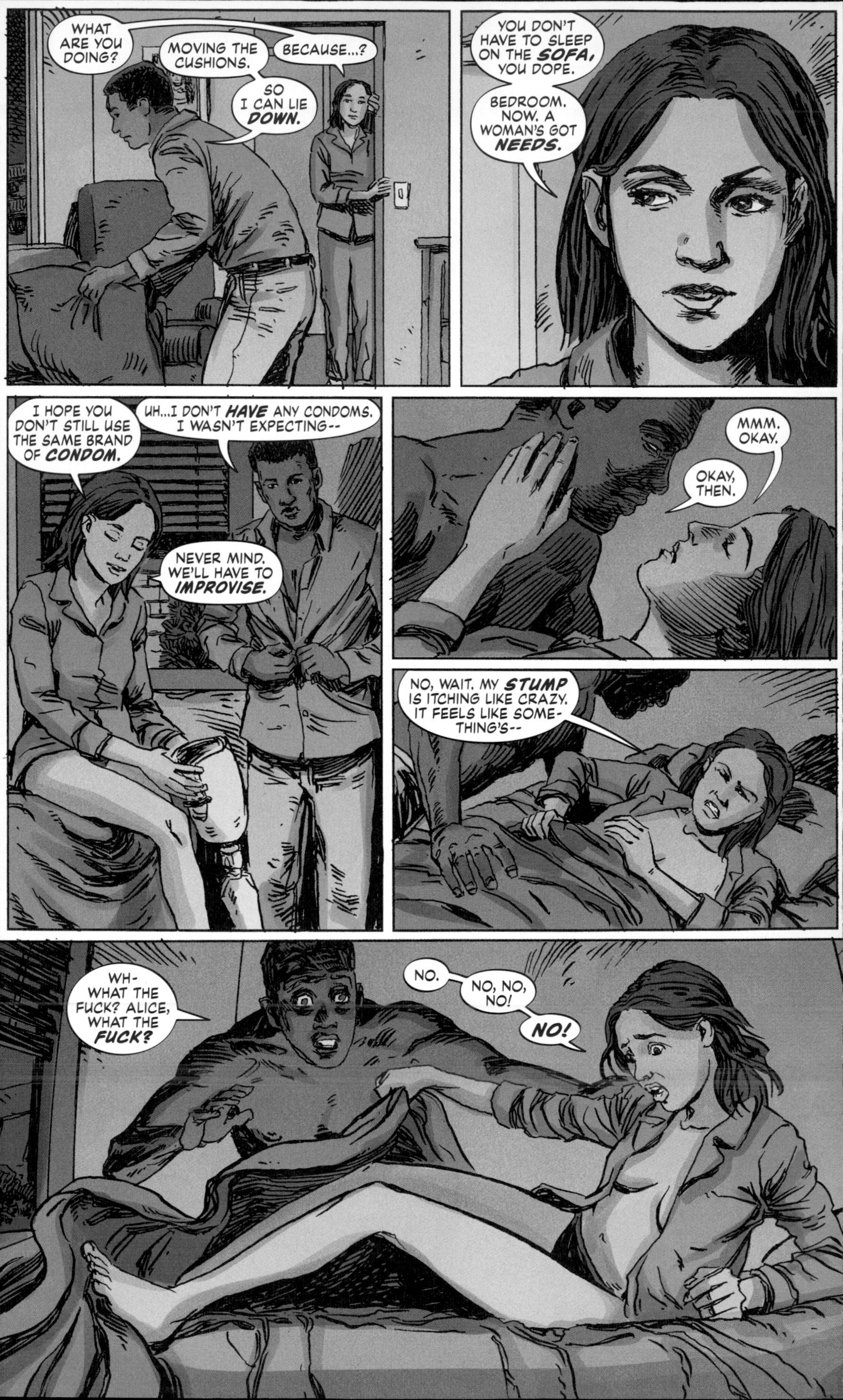
WHAT ARE YOU DOING?
MOVING THE CUSHIONS.
BECAUSE...?
SO I CAN LIE **DOWN.**
YOU DON'T HAVE TO SLEEP ON THE **SOFA,** YOU DOPE.
BEDROOM. NOW. A WOMAN'S GOT **NEEDS.**
I HOPE YOU DON'T STILL USE THE SAME BRAND OF **CONDOM.**
UH...I DON'T **HAVE** ANY CONDOMS. I WASN'T EXPECTING--
NEVER MIND. WE'LL HAVE TO **IMPROVISE.**
MMM. OKAY.
OKAY, THEN.
NO, WAIT. MY **STUMP** IS ITCHING LIKE CRAZY. IT FEELS LIKE SOME-THING'S--
WH- WHAT THE FUCK? ALICE, WHAT THE **FUCK?**
NO.
NO, NO, NO!
NO!

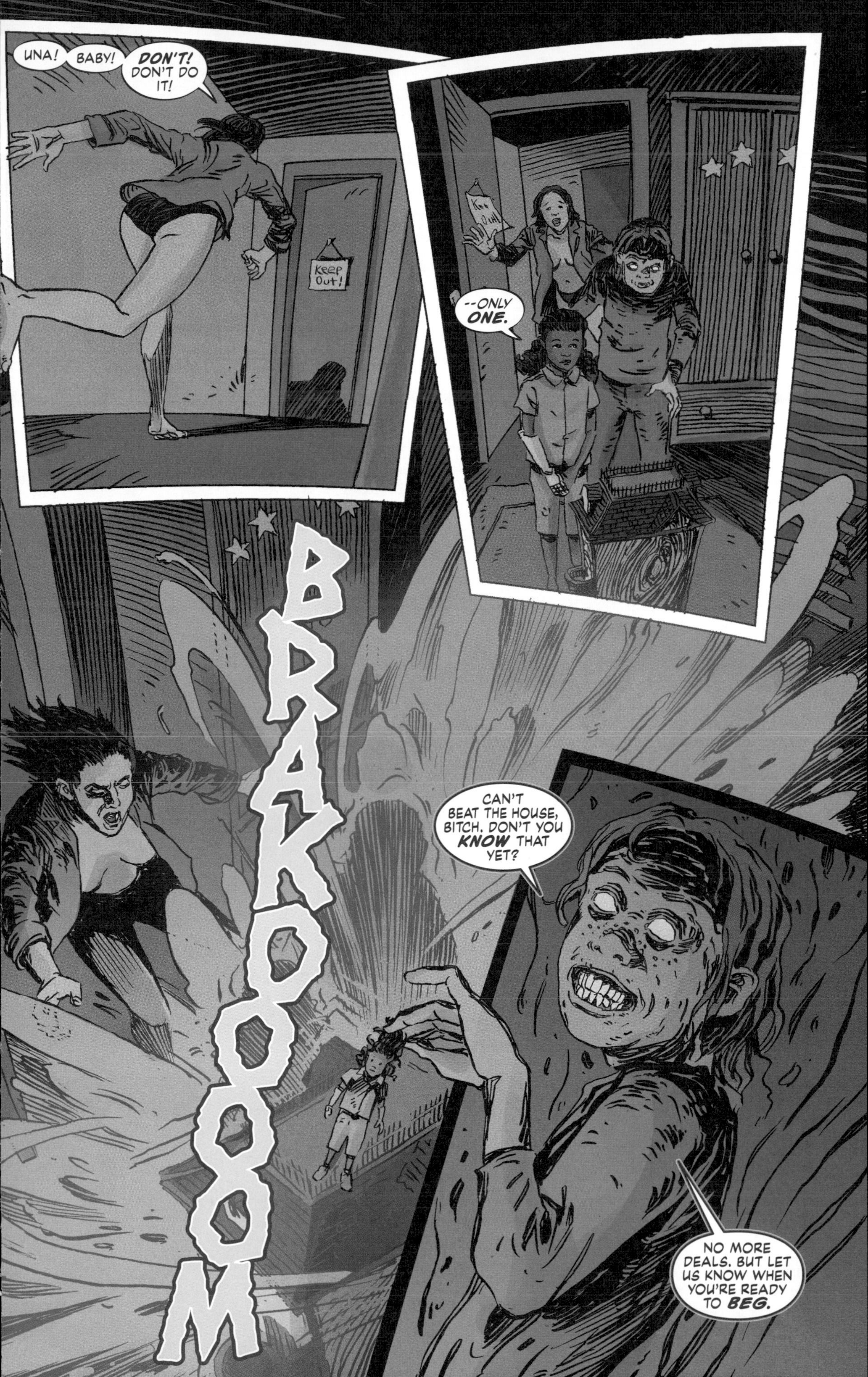
UNA!
BABY!
DON'T! DON'T DO IT!
Keep Out!
--ONLY ONE.
BRAKOOOOOM
CAN'T BEAT THE HOUSE, BITCH. DON'T YOU KNOW THAT YET?
NO MORE DEALS. BUT LET US KNOW WHEN YOU'RE READY TO BEG.

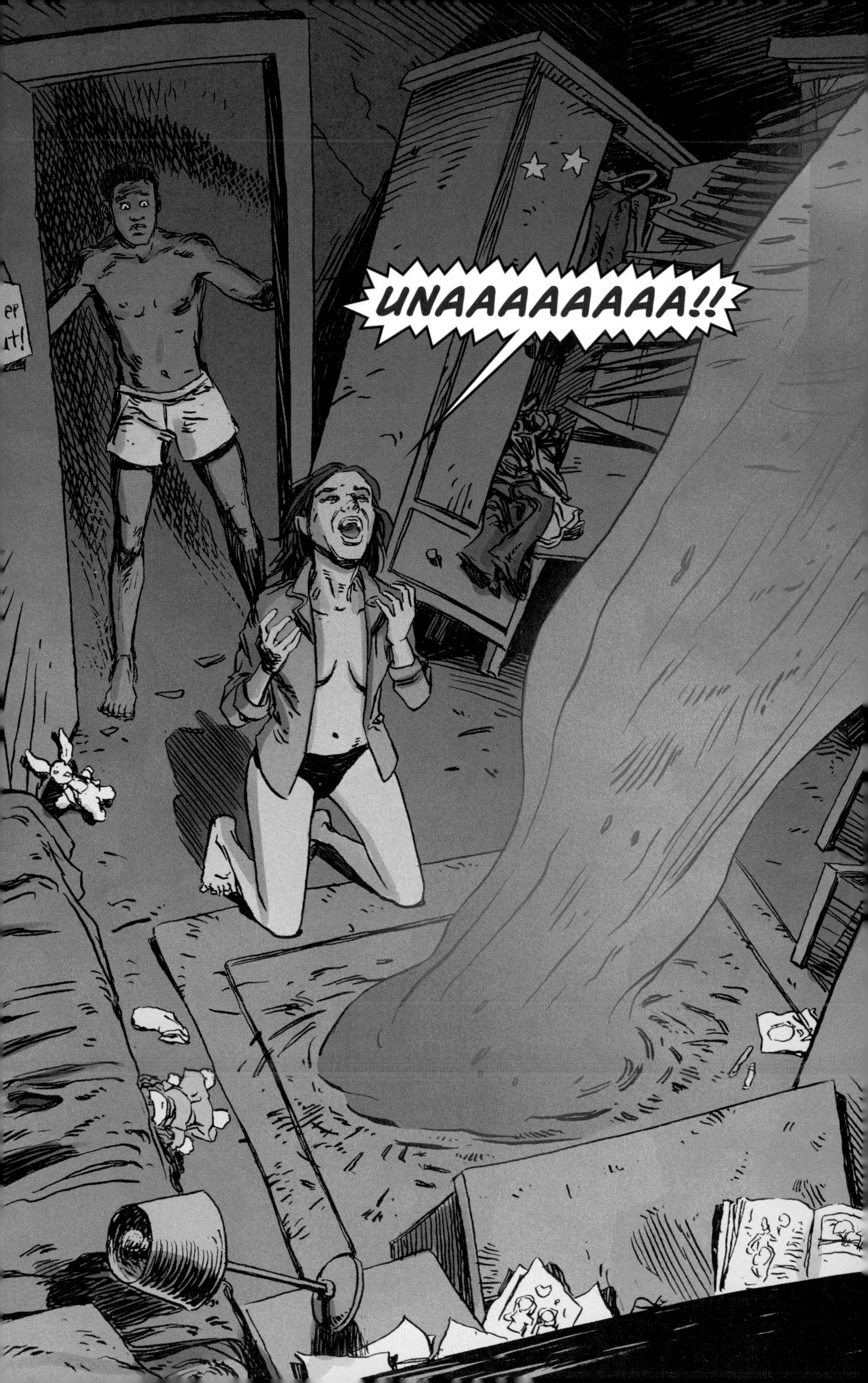
UNAAAAAAA!!

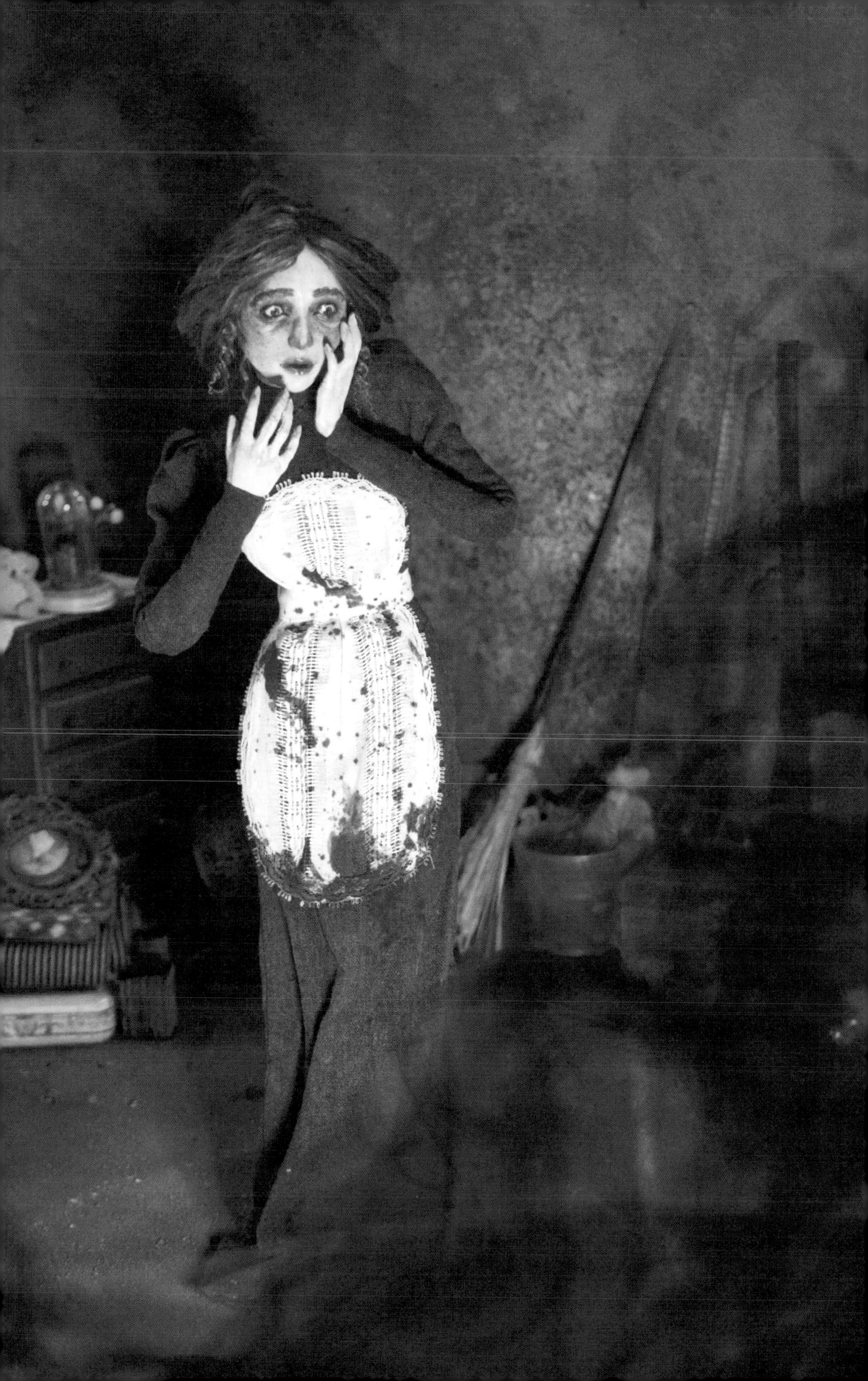

ONLY ONE

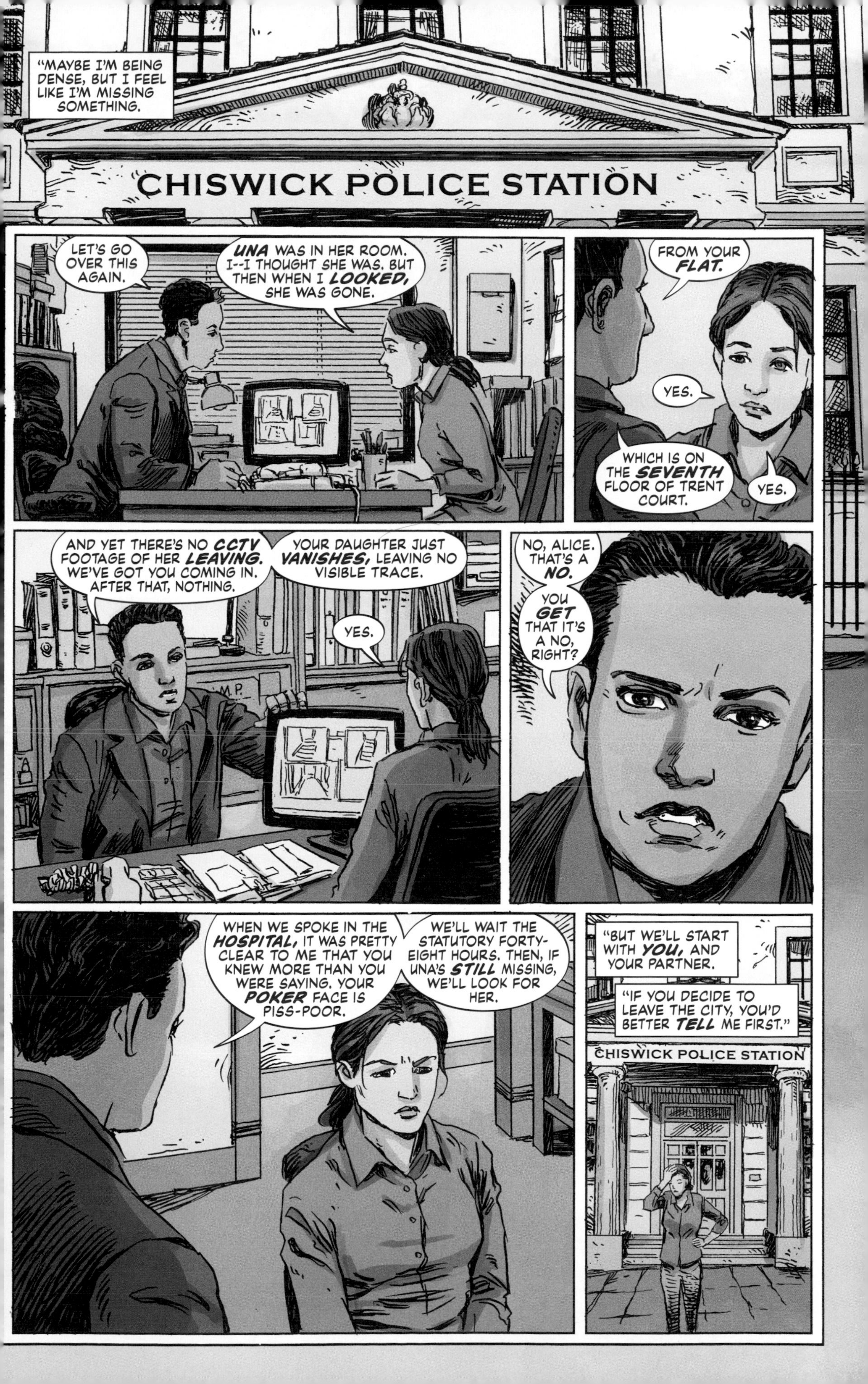
"MAYBE I'M BEING DENSE, BUT I FEEL LIKE I'M MISSING SOMETHING.
CHISWICK POLICE STATION
LET'S GO OVER THIS AGAIN.
UNA WAS IN HER ROOM. I--I THOUGHT SHE WAS. BUT THEN WHEN I LOOKED, SHE WAS GONE.
FROM YOUR FLAT.
YES.
WHICH IS ON THE SEVENTH FLOOR OF TRENT COURT.
YES.
AND YET THERE'S NO CCTV FOOTAGE OF HER LEAVING. WE'VE GOT YOU COMING IN. AFTER THAT, NOTHING.
YOUR DAUGHTER JUST VANISHES, LEAVING NO VISIBLE TRACE.
YES.
NO, ALICE. THAT'S A NO.
YOU GET THAT IT'S A NO, RIGHT?
WHEN WE SPOKE IN THE HOSPITAL, IT WAS PRETTY CLEAR TO ME THAT YOU KNEW MORE THAN YOU WERE SAYING. YOUR POKER FACE IS PISS-POOR.
WE'LL WAIT THE STATUTORY FORTY-EIGHT HOURS. THEN, IF UNA'S STILL MISSING, WE'LL LOOK FOR HER.
"BUT WE'LL START WITH YOU, AND YOUR PARTNER.
"IF YOU DECIDE TO LEAVE THE CITY, YOU'D BETTER TELL ME FIRST."
CHISWICK POLICE STATION

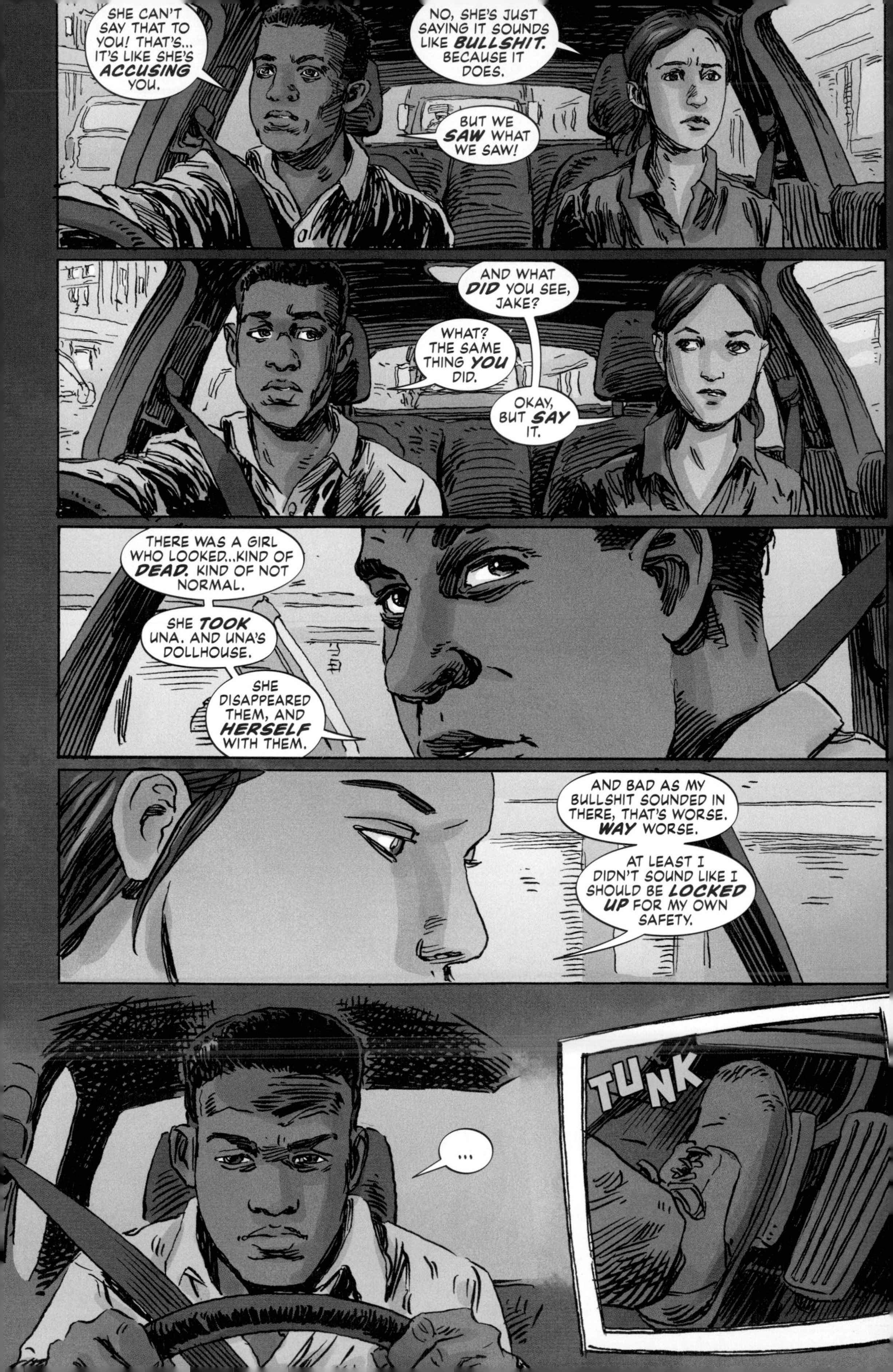
SHE CAN'T SAY THAT TO YOU! THAT'S... IT'S LIKE SHE'S ACCUSING YOU.
NO, SHE'S JUST SAYING IT SOUNDS LIKE BULLSHIT. BECAUSE IT DOES.
BUT WE SAW WHAT WE SAW!
AND WHAT DID YOU SEE, JAKE?
WHAT? THE SAME THING YOU DID.
OKAY, BUT SAY IT.
THERE WAS A GIRL WHO LOOKED...KIND OF DEAD. KIND OF NOT NORMAL.
SHE TOOK UNA. AND UNA'S DOLLHOUSE.
SHE DISAPPEARED THEM, AND HERSELF WITH THEM.
AND BAD AS MY BULLSHIT SOUNDED IN THERE, THAT'S WORSE. WAY WORSE.
AT LEAST I DIDN'T SOUND LIKE I SHOULD BE LOCKED UP FOR MY OWN SAFETY.
...
TUNK

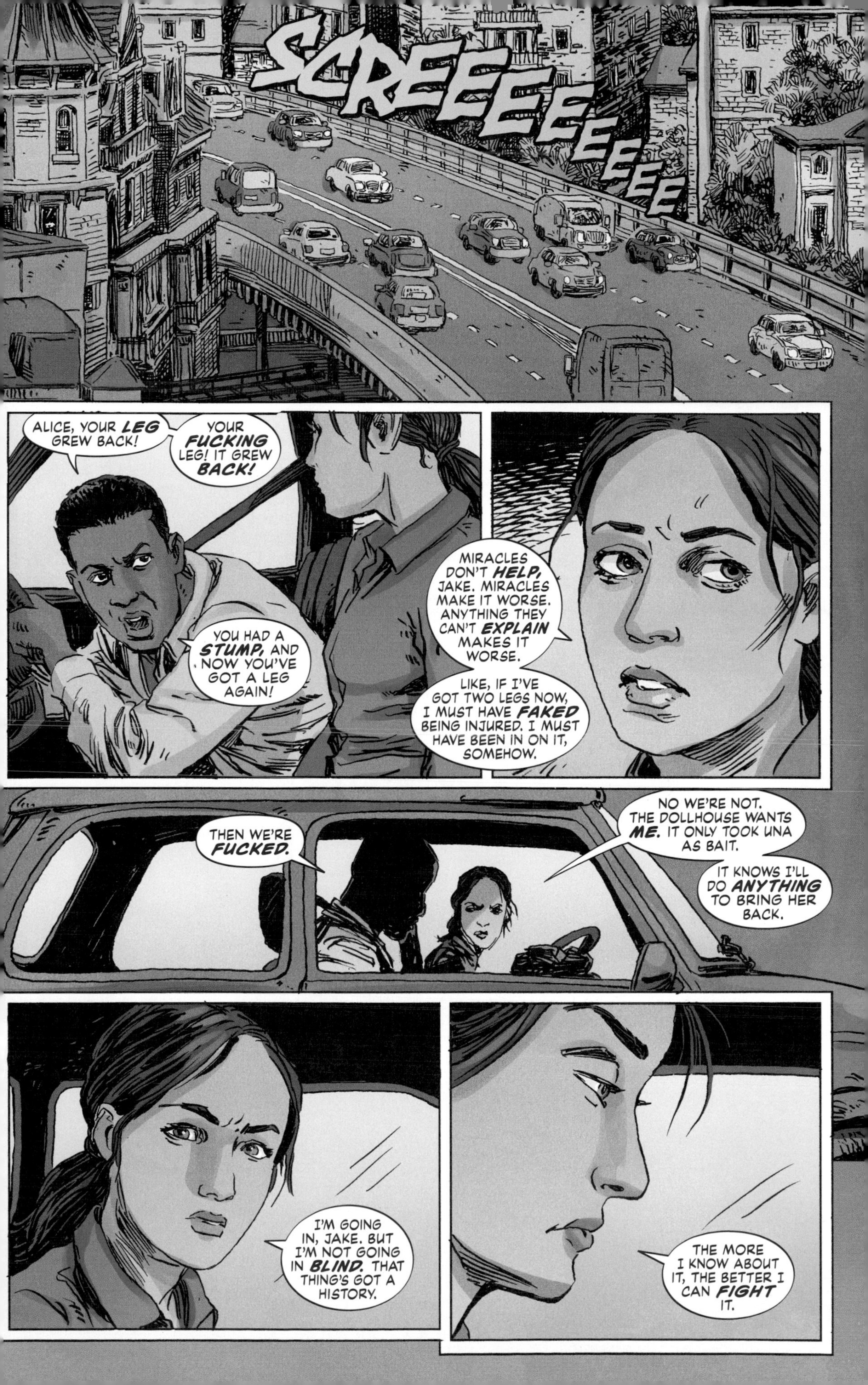
SCREEEEEEEEE
ALICE, YOUR LEG GREW BACK!
YOUR FUCKING LEG! IT GREW BACK!
YOU HAD A STUMP, AND NOW YOU'VE GOT A LEG AGAIN!
MIRACLES DON'T HELP, JAKE. MIRACLES MAKE IT WORSE. ANYTHING THEY CAN'T EXPLAIN MAKES IT WORSE.
LIKE, IF I'VE GOT TWO LEGS NOW, I MUST HAVE FAKED BEING INJURED. I MUST HAVE BEEN IN ON IT, SOMEHOW.
THEN WE'RE FUCKED.
NO WE'RE NOT. THE DOLLHOUSE WANTS ME. IT ONLY TOOK UNA AS BAIT.
IT KNOWS I'LL DO ANYTHING TO BRING HER BACK.
I'M GOING IN, JAKE. BUT I'M NOT GOING IN BLIND. THAT THING'S GOT A HISTORY.
THE MORE I KNOW ABOUT IT, THE BETTER I CAN FIGHT IT.

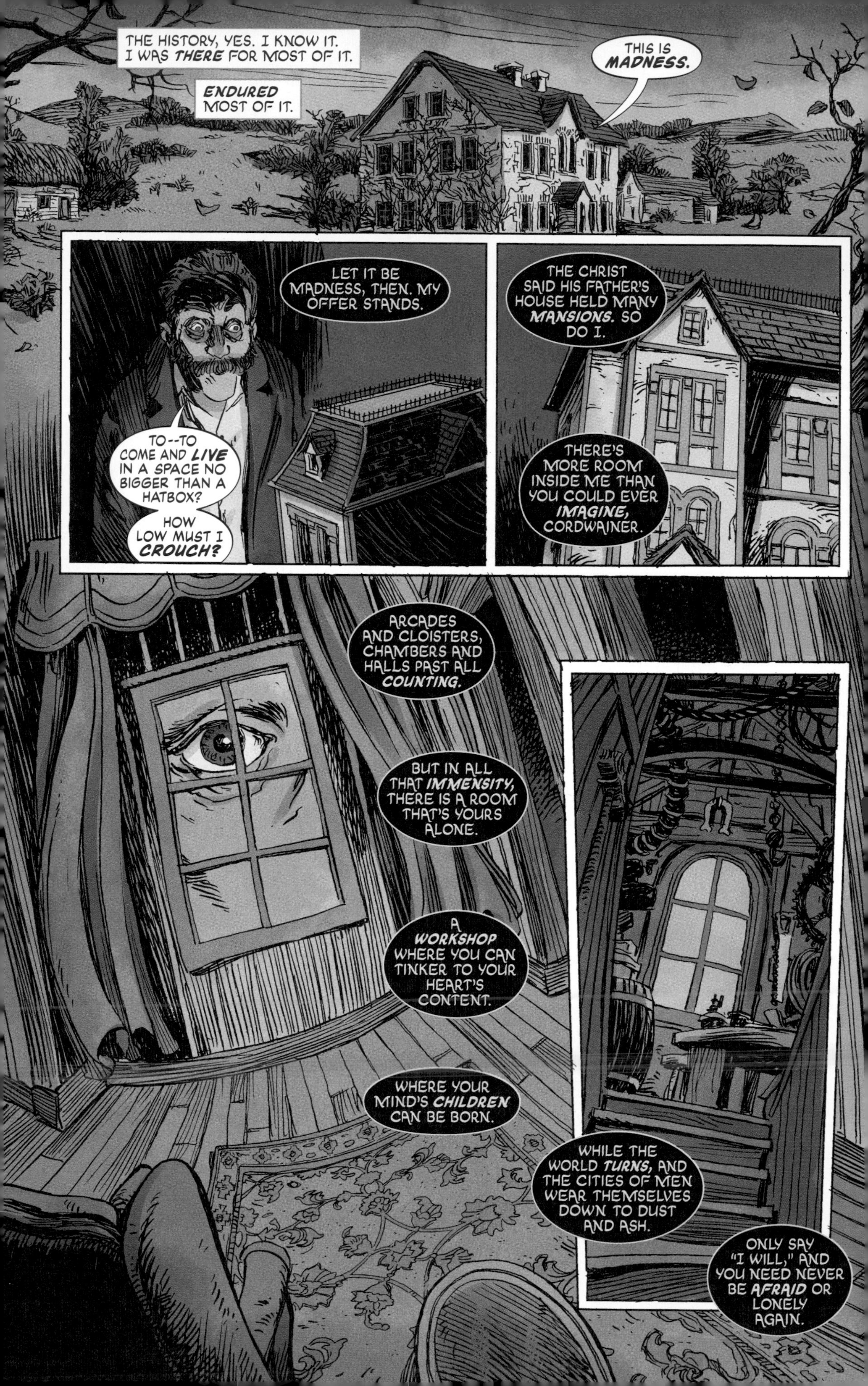
THE HISTORY, YES. I KNOW IT. I WAS *THERE* FOR MOST OF IT.
ENDURED MOST OF IT.
THIS IS *MADNESS.*
LET IT BE MADNESS, THEN. MY OFFER STANDS.
TO--TO COME AND *LIVE* IN A SPACE NO BIGGER THAN A HATBOX?
HOW LOW MUST I *CROUCH?*
THE CHRIST SAID HIS FATHER'S HOUSE HELD MANY *MANSIONS.* SO DO I.
THERE'S MORE ROOM INSIDE ME THAN YOU COULD EVER *IMAGINE,* CORDWAINER.
ARCADES AND CLOISTERS, CHAMBERS AND HALLS PAST ALL *COUNTING.*
BUT IN ALL THAT *IMMENSITY,* THERE IS A ROOM THAT'S YOURS ALONE.
A *WORKSHOP* WHERE YOU CAN TINKER TO YOUR HEART'S CONTENT.
WHERE YOUR MIND'S *CHILDREN* CAN BE BORN.
WHILE THE WORLD *TURNS,* AND THE CITIES OF MEN WEAR THEMSELVES DOWN TO DUST AND ASH.
ONLY SAY "I WILL," AND YOU NEED NEVER BE *AFRAID* OR LONELY AGAIN.

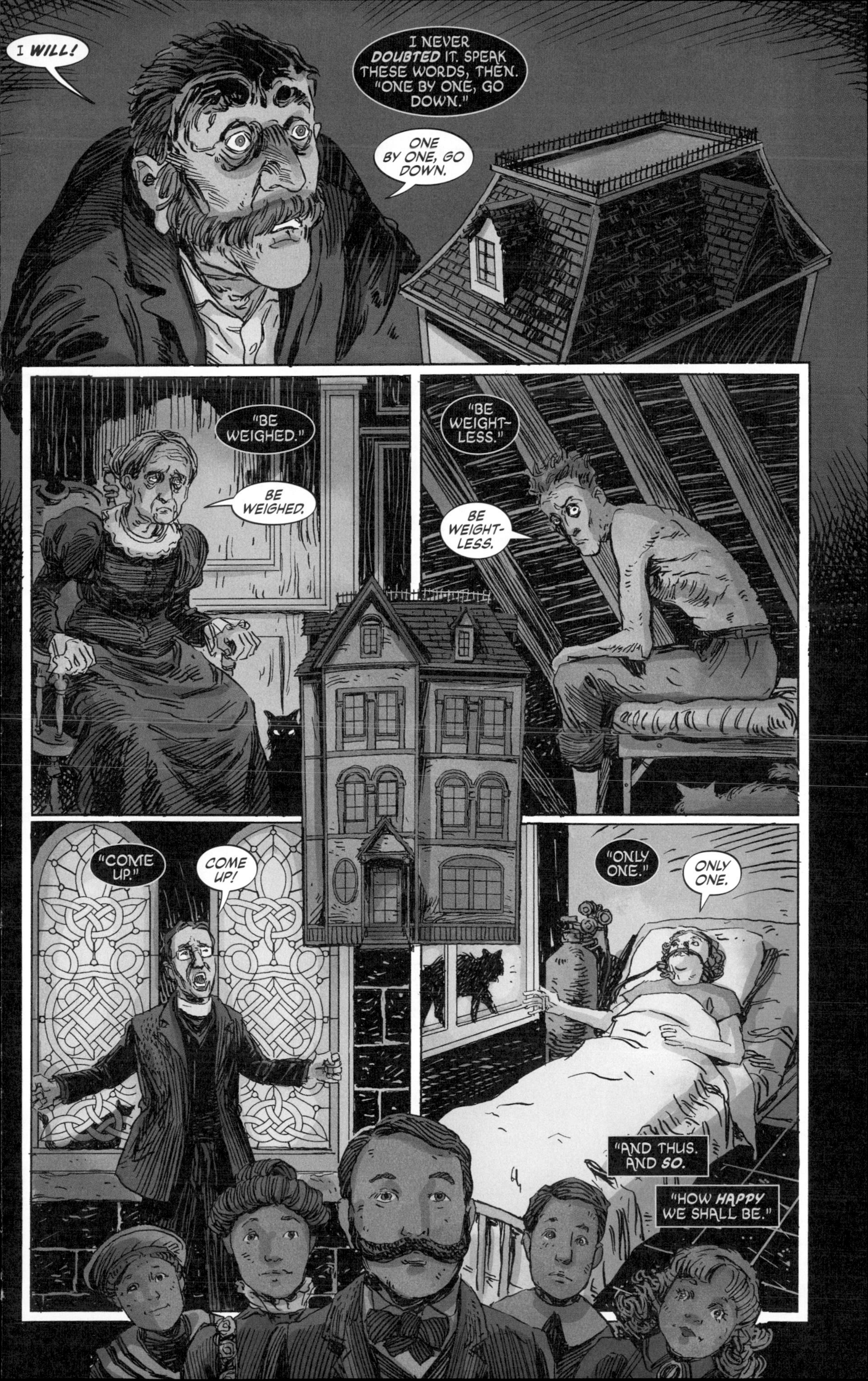
I WILL!
I NEVER DOUBTED IT. SPEAK THESE WORDS, THEN. "ONE BY ONE, GO DOWN."
ONE BY ONE, GO DOWN.
"BE WEIGHED."
BE WEIGHED.
"BE WEIGHT-LESS."
BE WEIGHT-LESS.
"COME UP."
COME UP!
"ONLY ONE."
ONLY ONE.
"AND THUS. AND SO.
"HOW HAPPY WE SHALL BE."

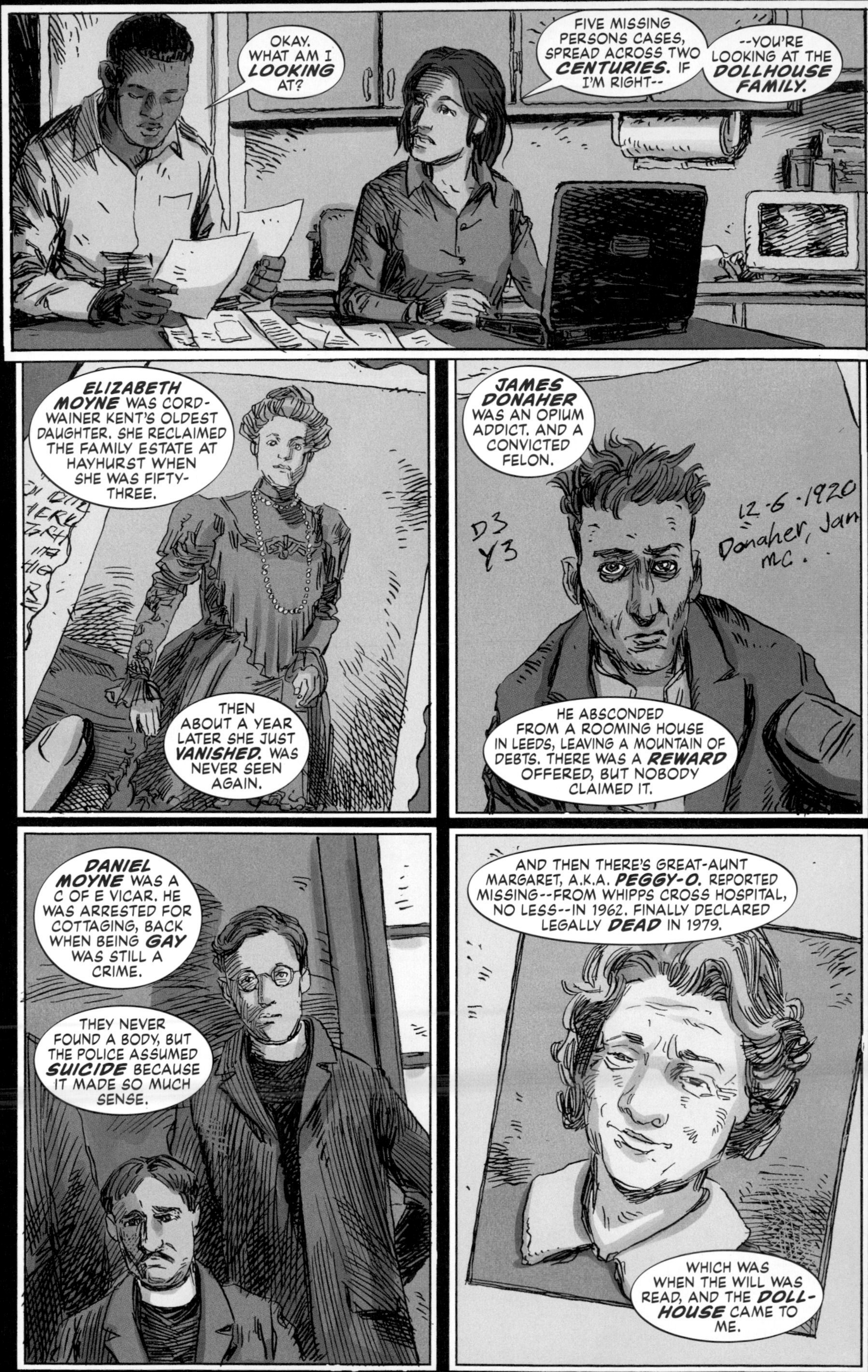
OKAY. WHAT AM I LOOKING AT?
FIVE MISSING PERSONS CASES, SPREAD ACROSS TWO CENTURIES. IF I'M RIGHT--
--YOU'RE LOOKING AT THE DOLLHOUSE FAMILY.
ELIZABETH MOYNE WAS CORD-WAINER KENT'S OLDEST DAUGHTER. SHE RECLAIMED THE FAMILY ESTATE AT HAYHURST WHEN SHE WAS FIFTY-THREE.
THEN ABOUT A YEAR LATER SHE JUST VANISHED. WAS NEVER SEEN AGAIN.
JAMES DONAHER WAS AN OPIUM ADDICT. AND A CONVICTED FELON.
D3 Y3
12-6-1920 Donaher, Jam MC.
HE ABSCONDED FROM A ROOMING HOUSE IN LEEDS, LEAVING A MOUNTAIN OF DEBTS. THERE WAS A REWARD OFFERED, BUT NOBODY CLAIMED IT.
DANIEL MOYNE WAS A C OF E VICAR. HE WAS ARRESTED FOR COTTAGING, BACK WHEN BEING GAY WAS STILL A CRIME.
THEY NEVER FOUND A BODY, BUT THE POLICE ASSUMED SUICIDE BECAUSE IT MADE SO MUCH SENSE.
AND THEN THERE'S GREAT-AUNT MARGARET, A.K.A. PEGGY-O. REPORTED MISSING--FROM WHIPPS CROSS HOSPITAL, NO LESS--IN 1962. FINALLY DECLARED LEGALLY DEAD IN 1979.
WHICH WAS WHEN THE WILL WAS READ, AND THE DOLL-HOUSE CAME TO ME.

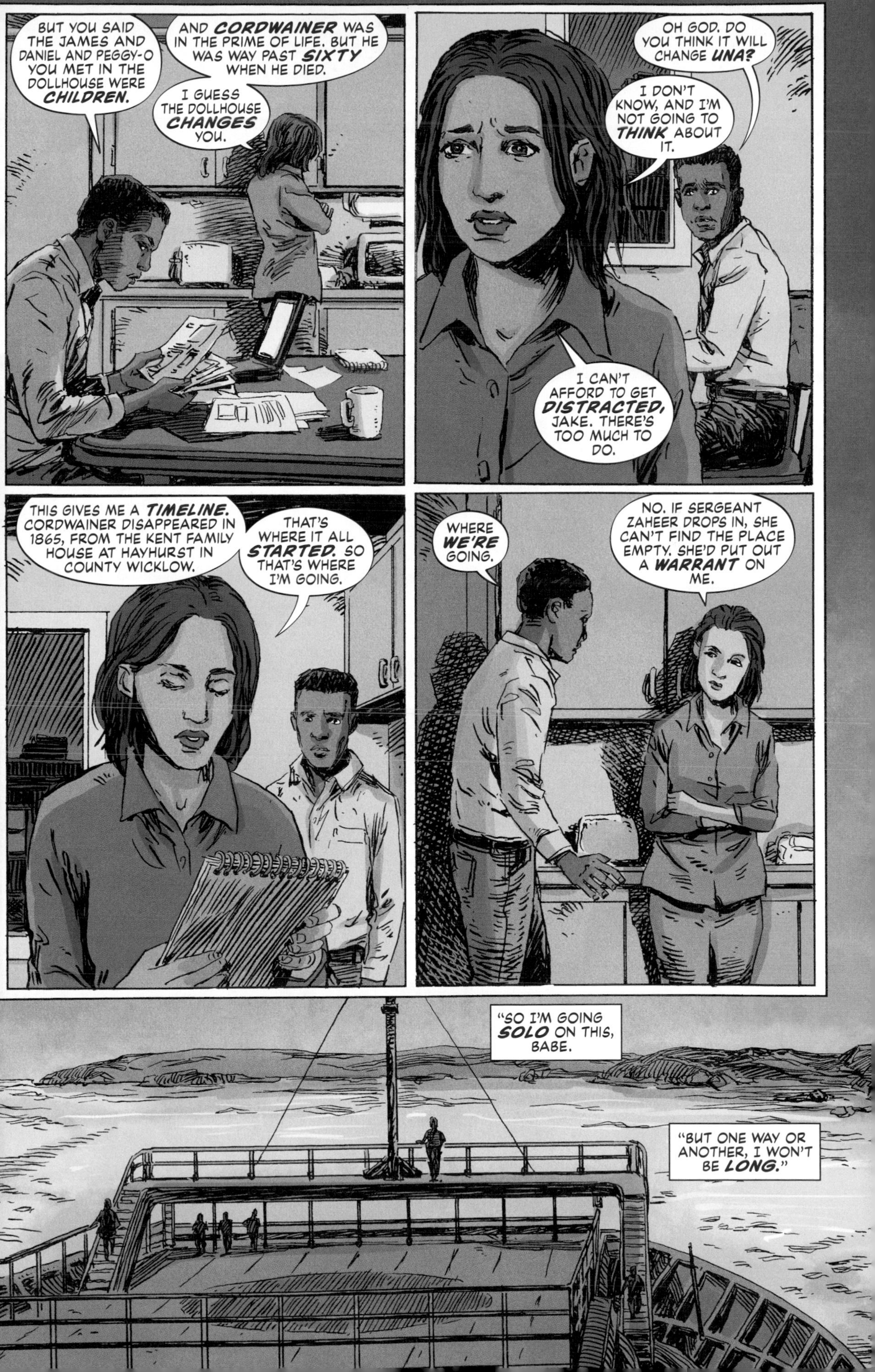
BUT YOU SAID THE JAMES AND DANIEL AND PEGGY-O YOU MET IN THE DOLLHOUSE WERE CHILDREN.
AND CORDWAINER WAS IN THE PRIME OF LIFE. BUT HE WAS WAY PAST SIXTY WHEN HE DIED.
I GUESS THE DOLLHOUSE CHANGES YOU.
OH GOD. DO YOU THINK IT WILL CHANGE UNA?
I DON'T KNOW, AND I'M NOT GOING TO THINK ABOUT IT.
I CAN'T AFFORD TO GET DISTRACTED, JAKE. THERE'S TOO MUCH TO DO.
THIS GIVES ME A TIMELINE. CORDWAINER DISAPPEARED IN 1865, FROM THE KENT FAMILY HOUSE AT HAYHURST IN COUNTY WICKLOW.
THAT'S WHERE IT ALL STARTED. SO THAT'S WHERE I'M GOING.
WHERE WE'RE GOING.
NO. IF SERGEANT ZAHEER DROPS IN, SHE CAN'T FIND THE PLACE EMPTY. SHE'D PUT OUT A WARRANT ON ME.
"SO I'M GOING SOLO ON THIS, BABE.
"BUT ONE WAY OR ANOTHER, I WON'T BE LONG."

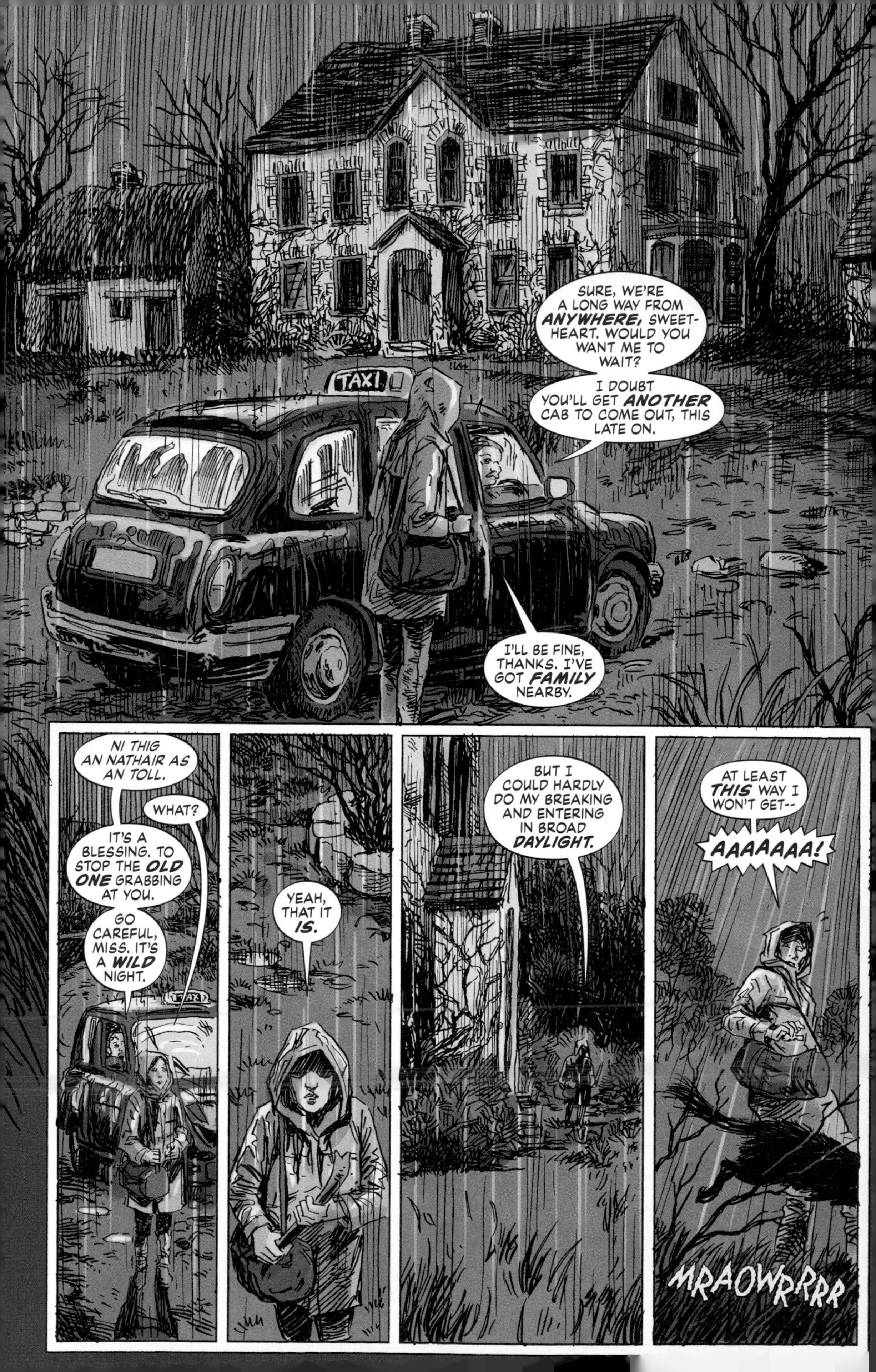
SURE, WE'RE A LONG WAY FROM ANYWHERE, SWEET-HEART. WOULD YOU WANT ME TO WAIT?
I DOUBT YOU'LL GET ANOTHER CAB TO COME OUT, THIS LATE ON.
TAXI
I'LL BE FINE, THANKS. I'VE GOT FAMILY NEARBY.
NI THIG AN NATHAIR AS AN TOLL.
WHAT?
IT'S A BLESSING. TO STOP THE OLD ONE GRABBING AT YOU.
GO CAREFUL, MISS. IT'S A WILD NIGHT.
YEAH, THAT IT IS.
BUT I COULD HARDLY DO MY BREAKING AND ENTERING IN BROAD DAYLIGHT.
AT LEAST THIS WAY I WON'T GET--
AAAAAAA!
MRAOWRRRR

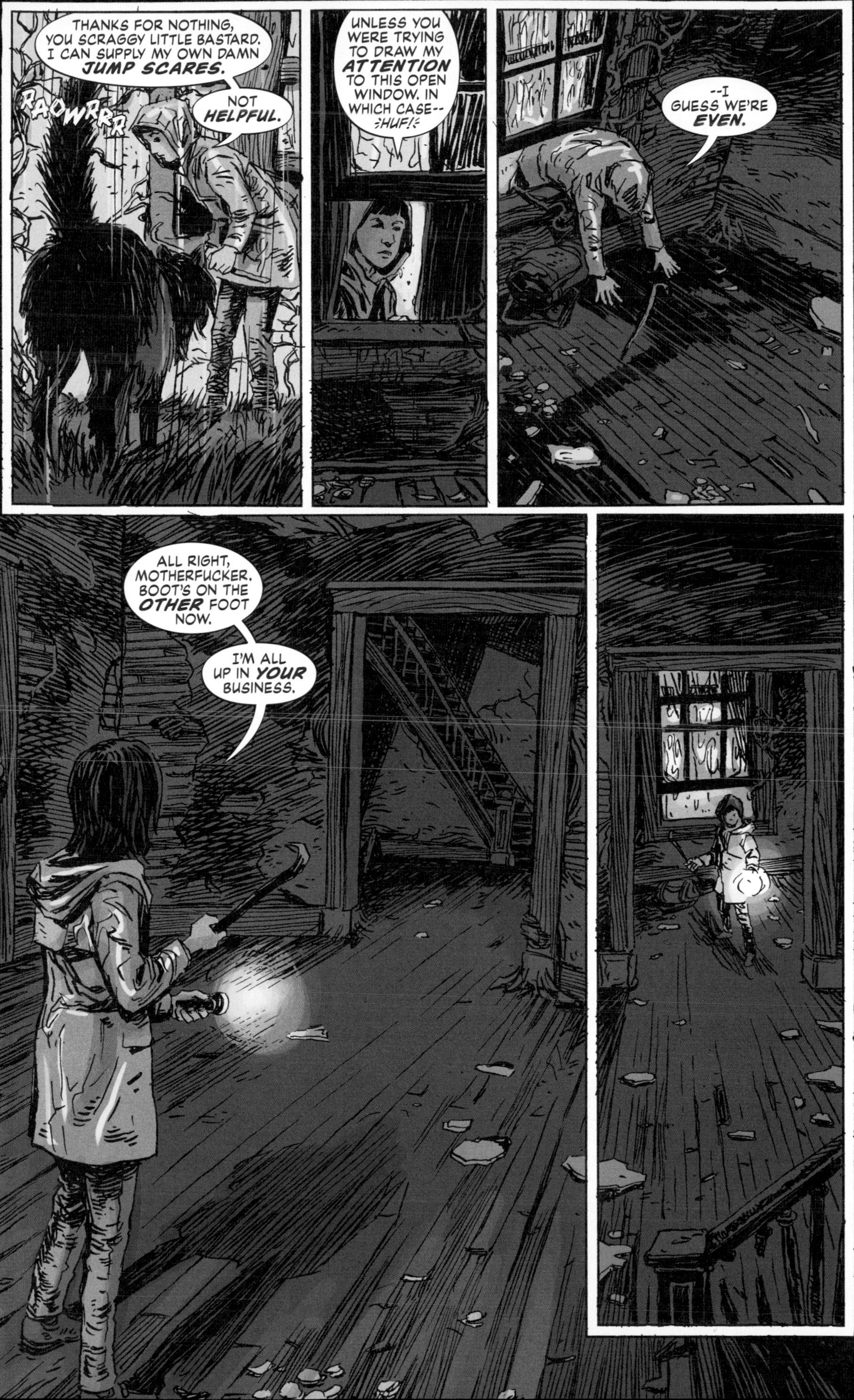
THANKS FOR NOTHING, YOU SCRAGGY LITTLE BASTARD. I CAN SUPPLY MY OWN DAMN JUMP SCARES.
RAOWRRR
NOT HELPFUL.
UNLESS YOU WERE TRYING TO DRAW MY ATTENTION TO THIS OPEN WINDOW. IN WHICH CASE--
HUF!
--I GUESS WE'RE EVEN.
ALL RIGHT, MOTHERFUCKER. BOOT'S ON THE OTHER FOOT NOW.
I'M ALL UP IN YOUR BUSINESS.

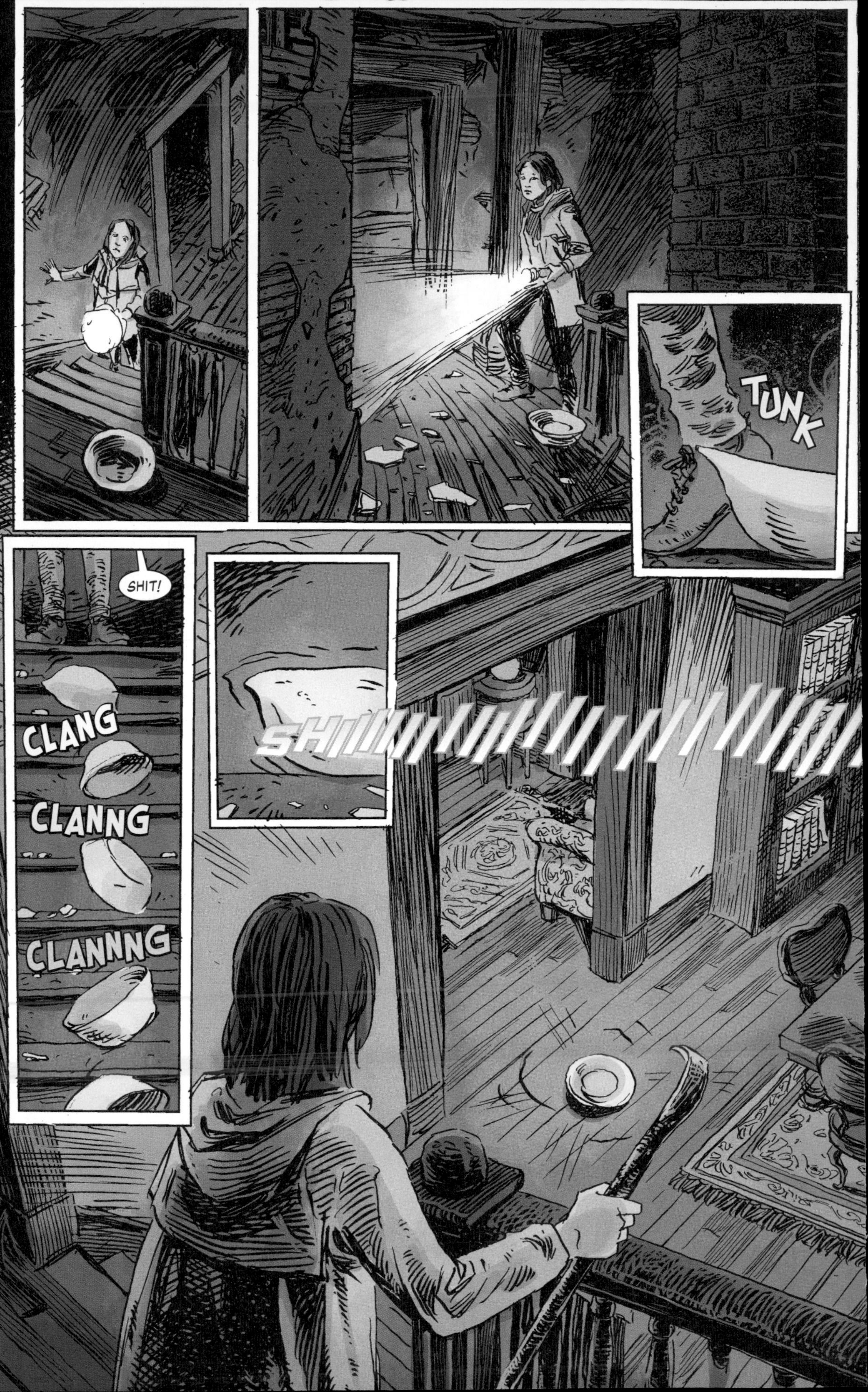
TUNK
SHIT!
CLANG
CLANNG
CLANNNG
SHI

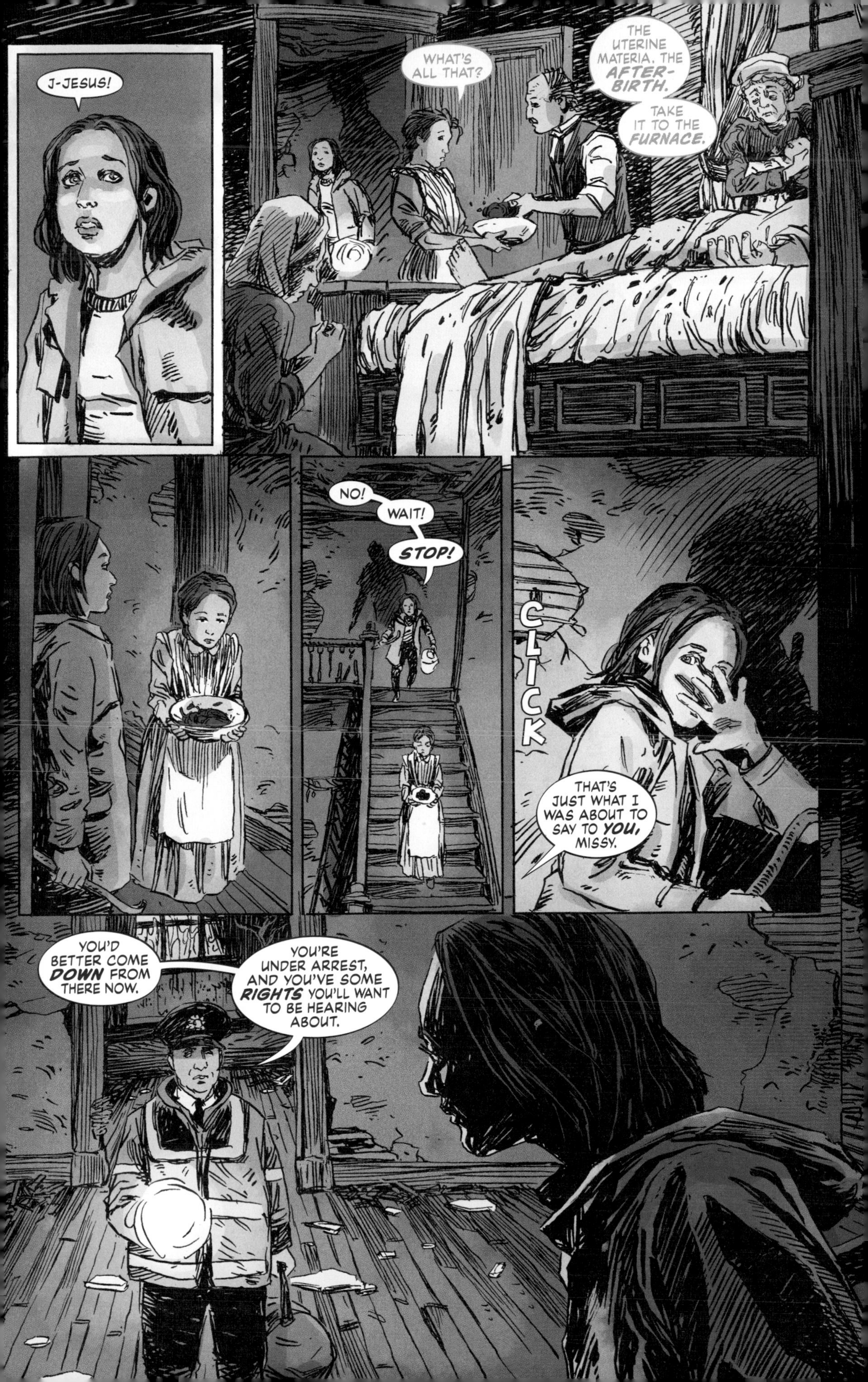
J-JESUS!
WHAT'S ALL THAT?
THE UTERINE MATERIA. THE AFTER-BIRTH.
TAKE IT TO THE FURNACE.
NO!
WAIT!
STOP!
CLICK
THAT'S JUST WHAT I WAS ABOUT TO SAY TO YOU, MISSY.
YOU'D BETTER COME DOWN FROM THERE NOW.
YOU'RE UNDER ARREST, AND YOU'VE SOME RIGHTS YOU'LL WANT TO BE HEARING ABOUT.

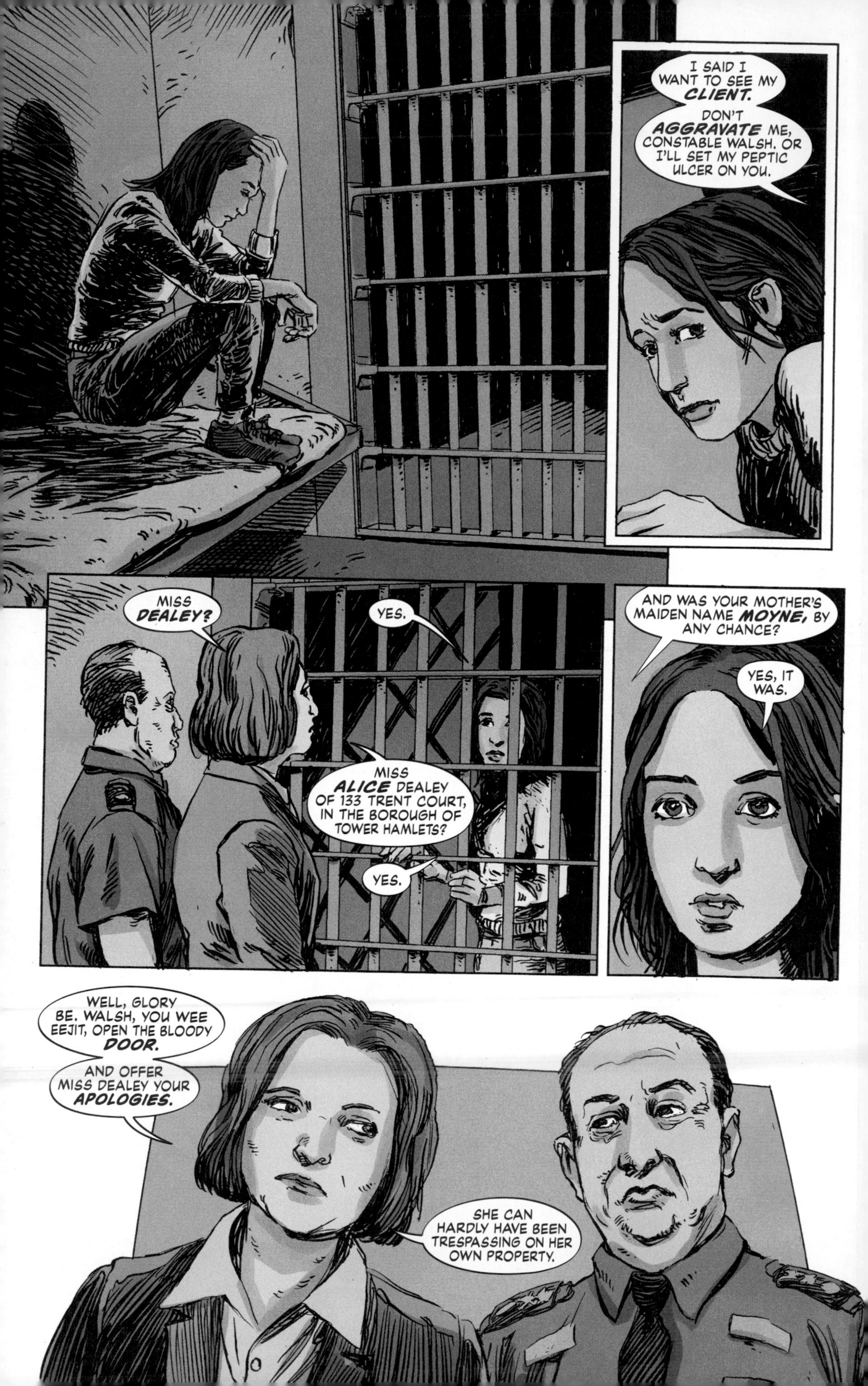
I SAID I WANT TO SEE MY CLIENT.
DON'T AGGRAVATE ME, CONSTABLE WALSH. OR I'LL SET MY PEPTIC ULCER ON YOU.
MISS DEALEY?
YES.
MISS ALICE DEALEY OF 133 TRENT COURT, IN THE BOROUGH OF TOWER HAMLETS?
YES.
AND WAS YOUR MOTHER'S MAIDEN NAME MOYNE, BY ANY CHANCE?
YES, IT WAS.
WELL, GLORY BE. WALSH, YOU WEE EEJIT, OPEN THE BLOODY DOOR.
AND OFFER MISS DEALEY YOUR APOLOGIES.
SHE CAN HARDLY HAVE BEEN TRESPASSING ON HER OWN PROPERTY.

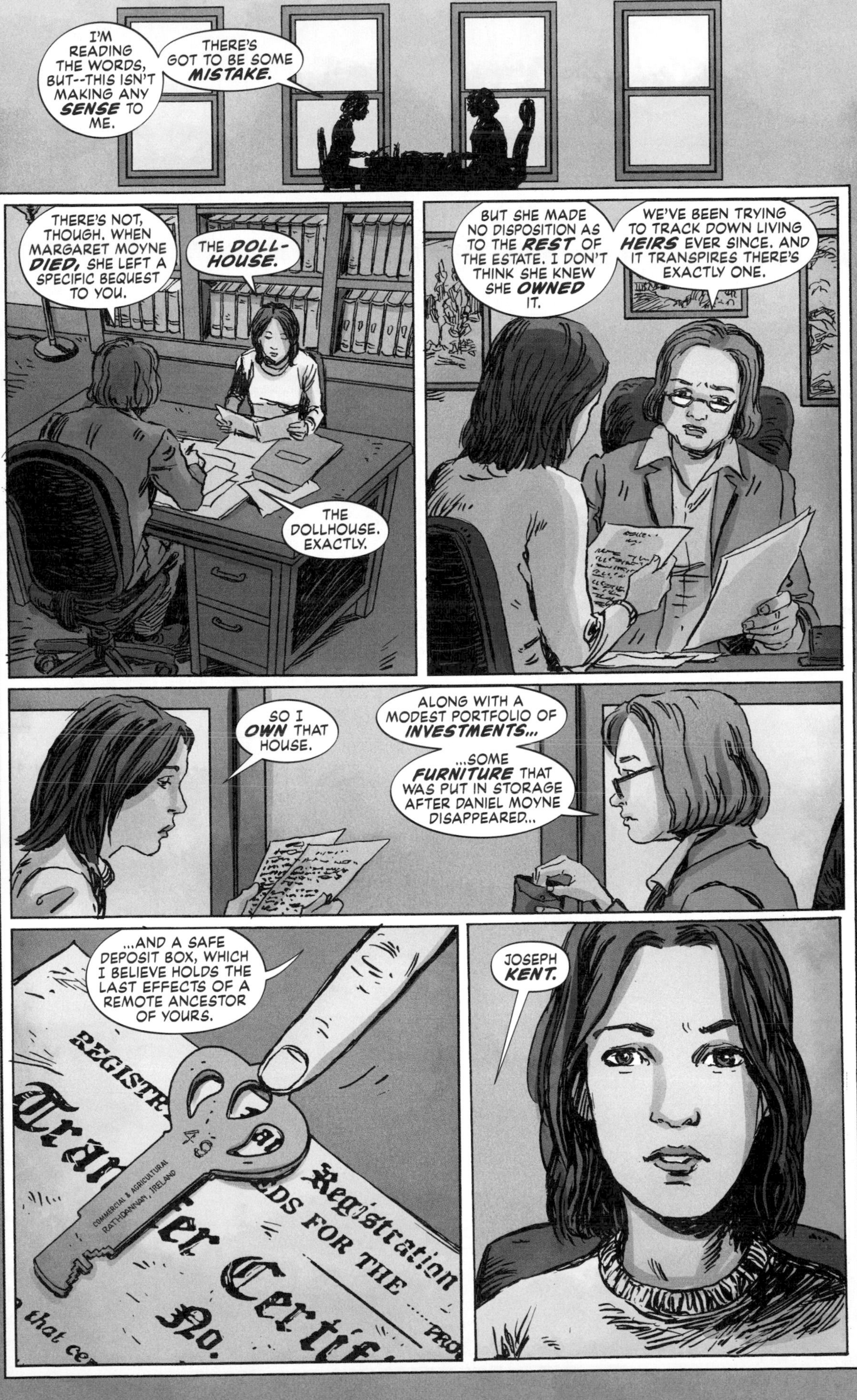
I'M READING THE WORDS, BUT--THIS ISN'T MAKING ANY SENSE TO ME.
THERE'S GOT TO BE SOME MISTAKE.
THERE'S NOT, THOUGH. WHEN MARGARET MOYNE DIED, SHE LEFT A SPECIFIC BEQUEST TO YOU.
THE DOLL-HOUSE.
THE DOLLHOUSE. EXACTLY.
BUT SHE MADE NO DISPOSITION AS TO THE REST OF THE ESTATE. I DON'T THINK SHE KNEW SHE OWNED IT.
WE'VE BEEN TRYING TO TRACK DOWN LIVING HEIRS EVER SINCE. AND IT TRANSPIRES THERE'S EXACTLY ONE.
SO I OWN THAT HOUSE.
ALONG WITH A MODEST PORTFOLIO OF INVESTMENTS...
...SOME FURNITURE THAT WAS PUT IN STORAGE AFTER DANIEL MOYNE DISAPPEARED...
...AND A SAFE DEPOSIT BOX, WHICH I BELIEVE HOLDS THE LAST EFFECTS OF A REMOTE ANCESTOR OF YOURS.
COMMERCIAL & AGRICULTURAL
RATHDANNAN, IRELAND
Registration
DS FOR THE
No.
JOSEPH KENT.

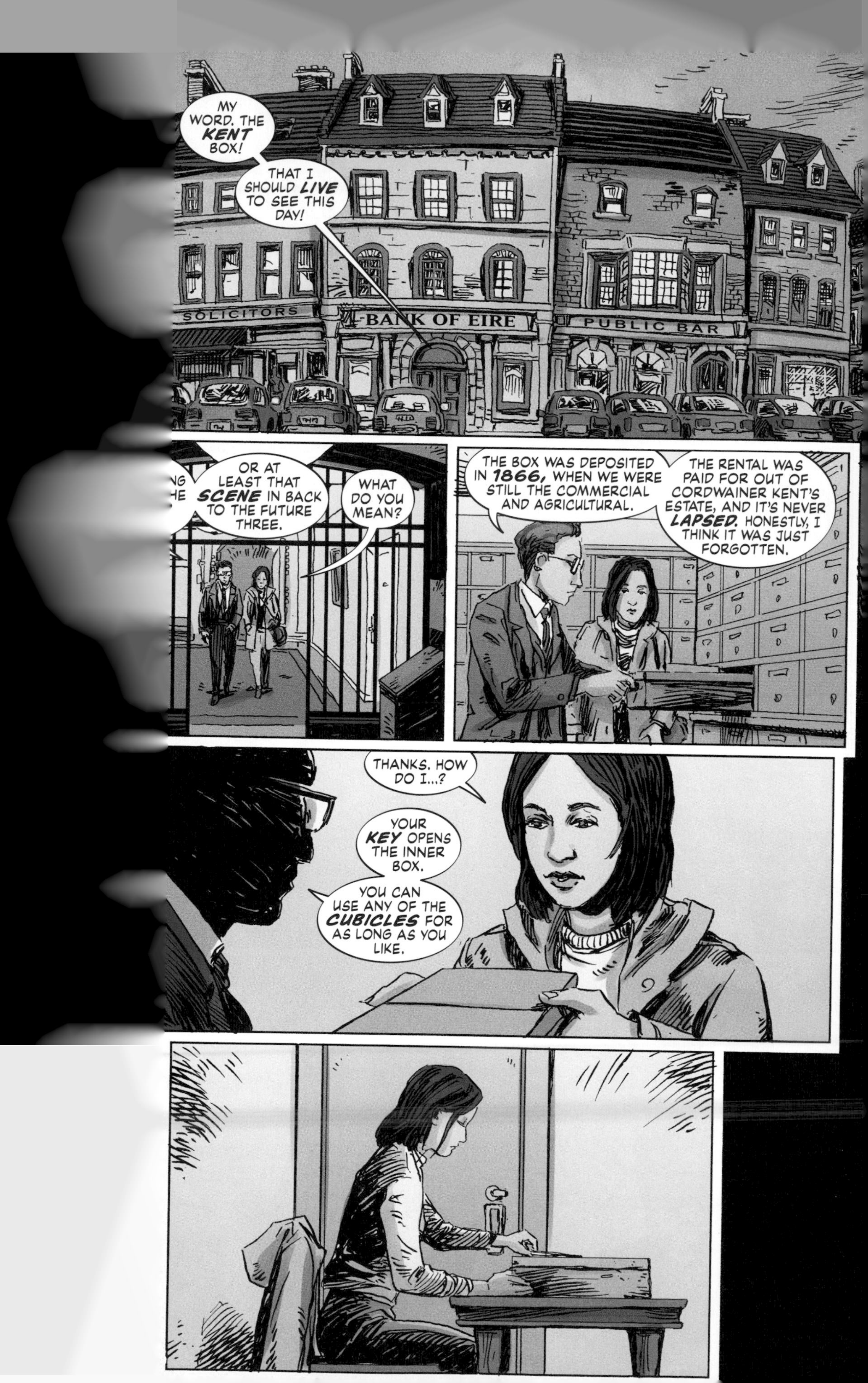
MY WORD. THE KENT BOX!
THAT I SHOULD LIVE TO SEE THIS DAY!
SOLICITORS
BANK OF EIRE
PUBLIC BAR
OR AT LEAST THAT SCENE IN BACK TO THE FUTURE THREE.
WHAT DO YOU MEAN?
THE BOX WAS DEPOSITED IN 1866, WHEN WE WERE STILL THE COMMERCIAL AND AGRICULTURAL.
THE RENTAL WAS PAID FOR OUT OF CORDWAINER KENT'S ESTATE, AND IT'S NEVER LAPSED. HONESTLY, I THINK IT WAS JUST FORGOTTEN.
THANKS. HOW DO I...?
YOUR KEY OPENS THE INNER BOX.
YOU CAN USE ANY OF THE CUBICLES FOR AS LONG AS YOU LIKE.

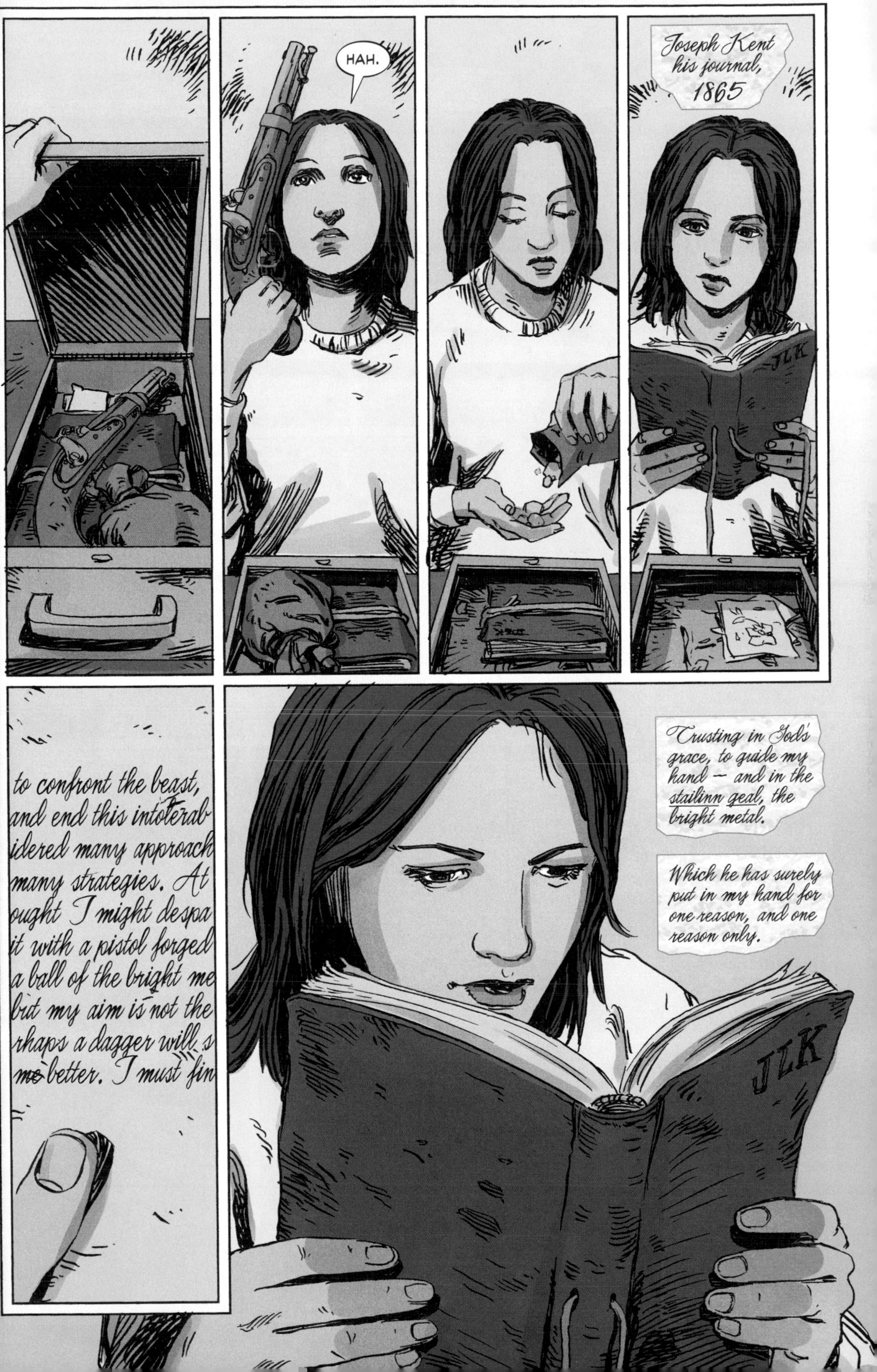
HAH.
Joseph Kent his journal, 1865
to confront the beast, and end this intoleral idered many approach many strategies. At ought I might despa it with a pistol forged a ball of the bright me but my aim is not the rhaps a dagger will s me better. I must fin
Trusting in God's grace, to guide my hand — and in the stailinn geal, the bright metal.
Which he has surely put in my hand for one reason, and one reason only.

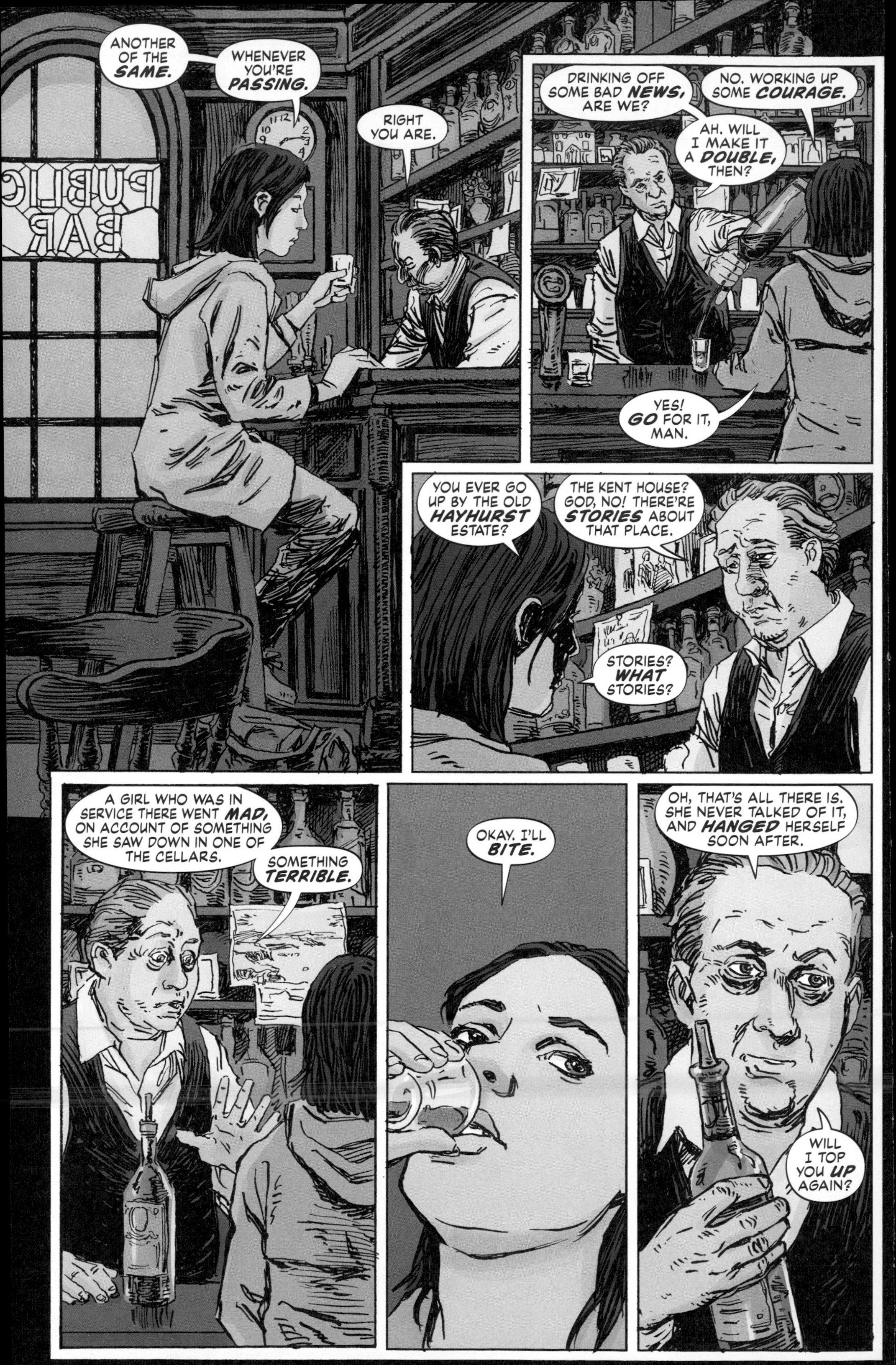
ANOTHER OF THE SAME.
WHENEVER YOU'RE PASSING.
RIGHT YOU ARE.
PUBLIC BAR
DRINKING OFF SOME BAD NEWS, ARE WE?
NO. WORKING UP SOME COURAGE.
AH. WILL I MAKE IT A DOUBLE, THEN?
YES! GO FOR IT, MAN.
YOU EVER GO UP BY THE OLD HAYHURST ESTATE?
THE KENT HOUSE? GOD, NO! THERE'RE STORIES ABOUT THAT PLACE.
STORIES? WHAT STORIES?
A GIRL WHO WAS IN SERVICE THERE WENT MAD, ON ACCOUNT OF SOMETHING SHE SAW DOWN IN ONE OF THE CELLARS.
SOMETHING TERRIBLE.
OKAY. I'LL BITE.
OH, THAT'S ALL THERE IS. SHE NEVER TALKED OF IT, AND HANGED HERSELF SOON AFTER.
WILL I TOP YOU UP AGAIN?

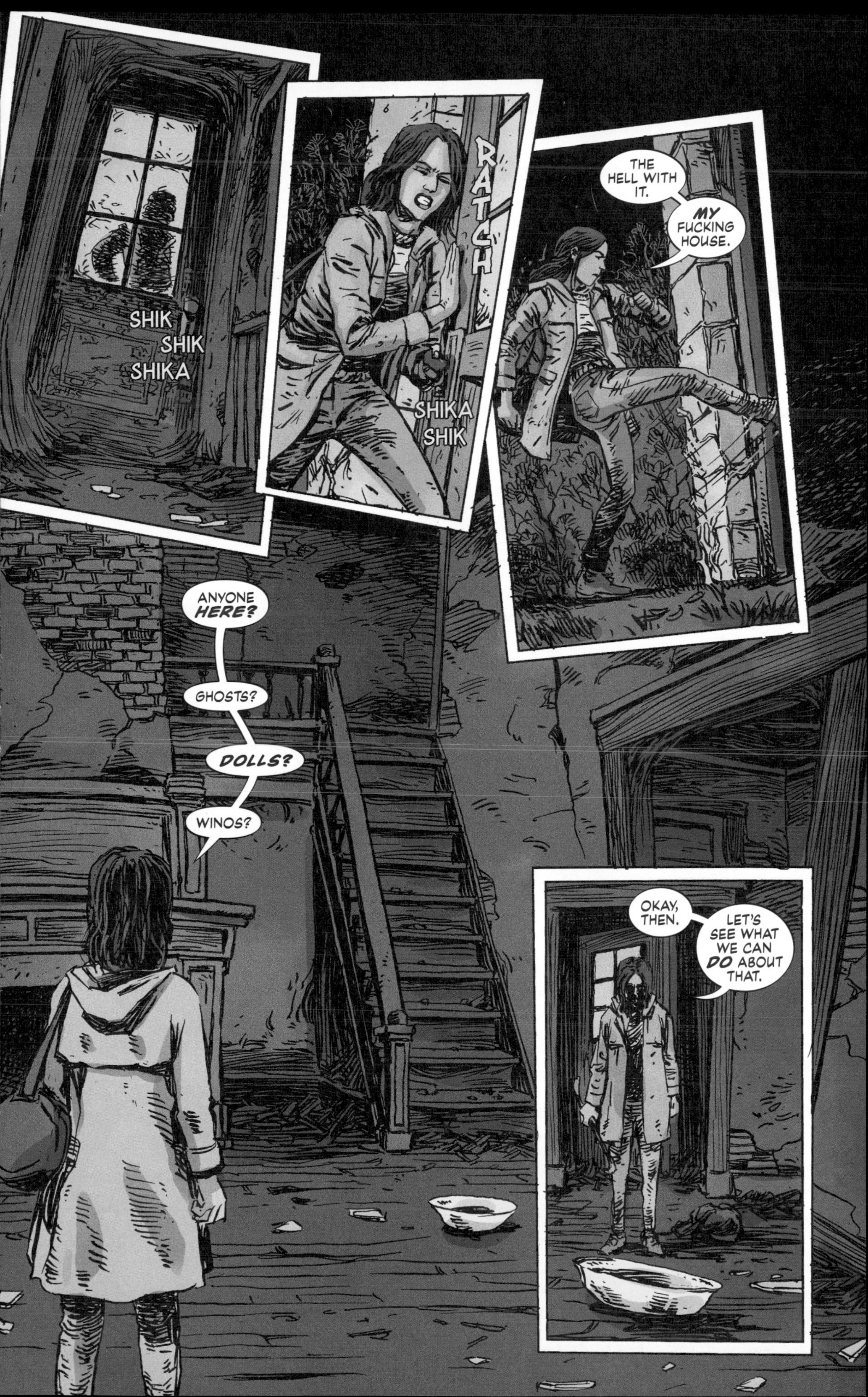
SHIK
SHIK
SHIKA
RATCH
SHIKA
SHIK
THE HELL WITH IT.
MY FUCKING HOUSE.
ANYONE HERE?
GHOSTS?
DOLLS?
WINOS?
OKAY, THEN.
LET'S SEE WHAT WE CAN DO ABOUT THAT.

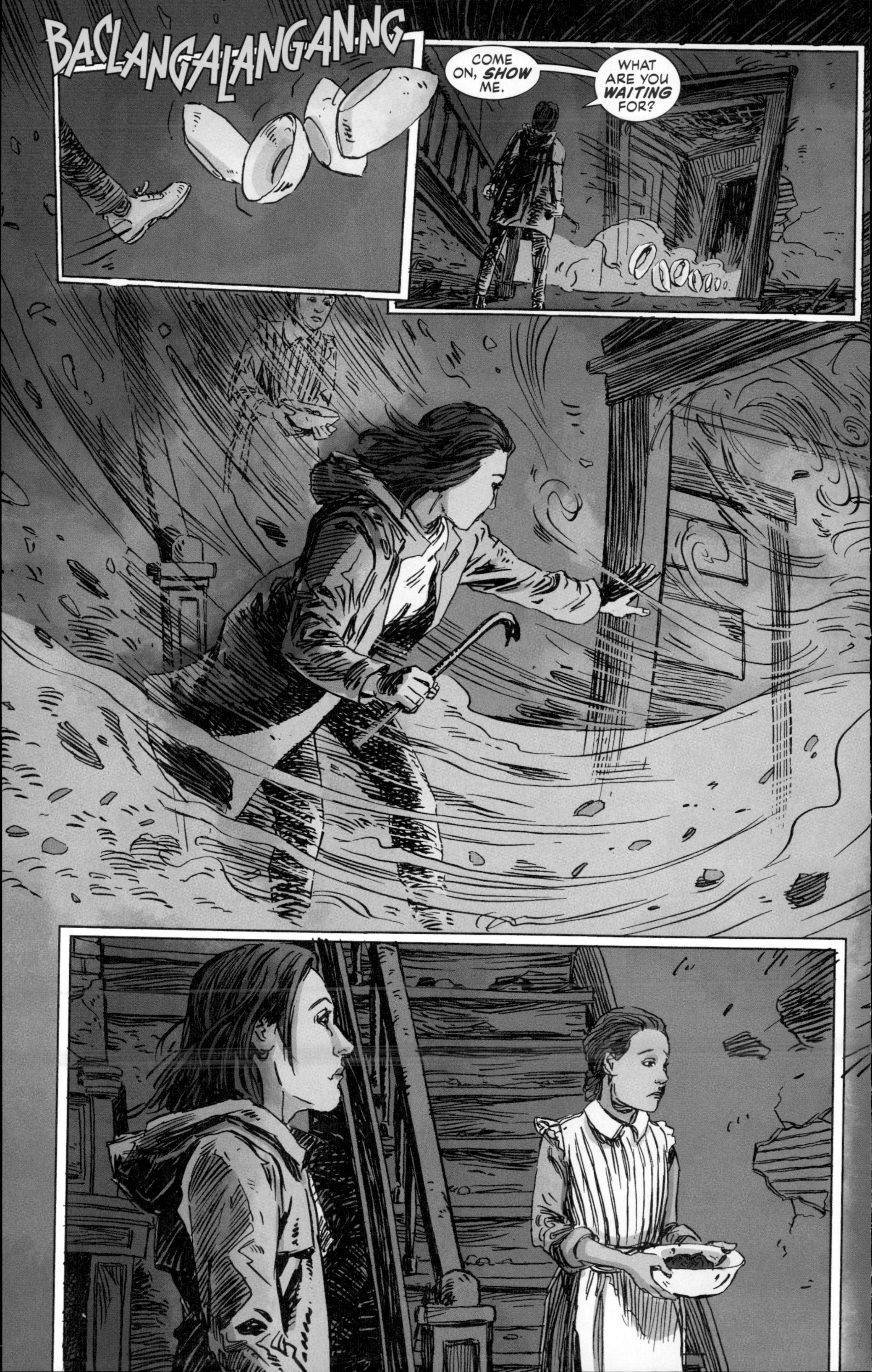
BASLANGALANGANNG
COME ON, SHOW ME.
WHAT ARE YOU WAITING FOR?

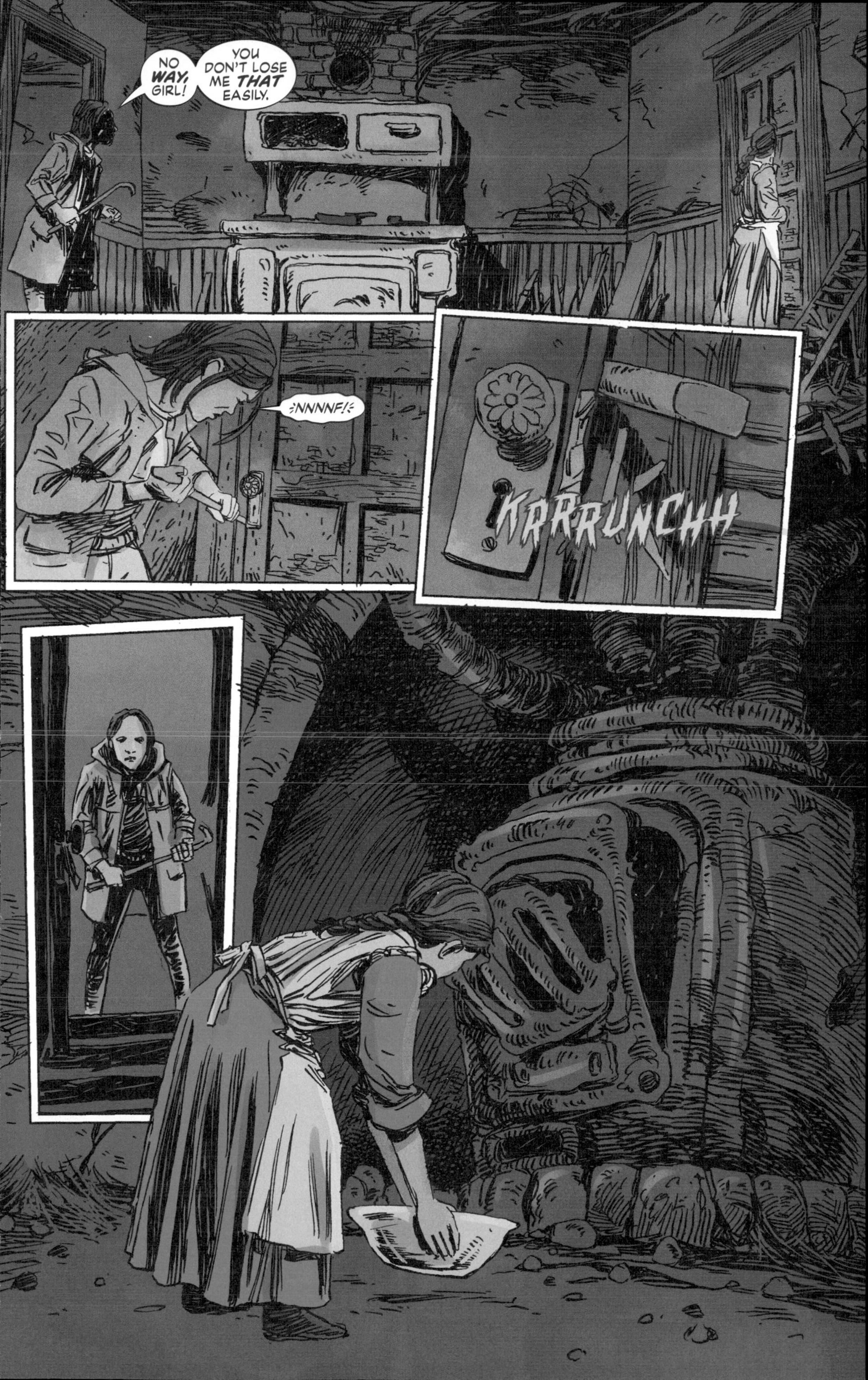
NO WAY, GIRL!
YOU DON'T LOSE ME THAT EASILY.
NNNNF!
KRRRUNCHH

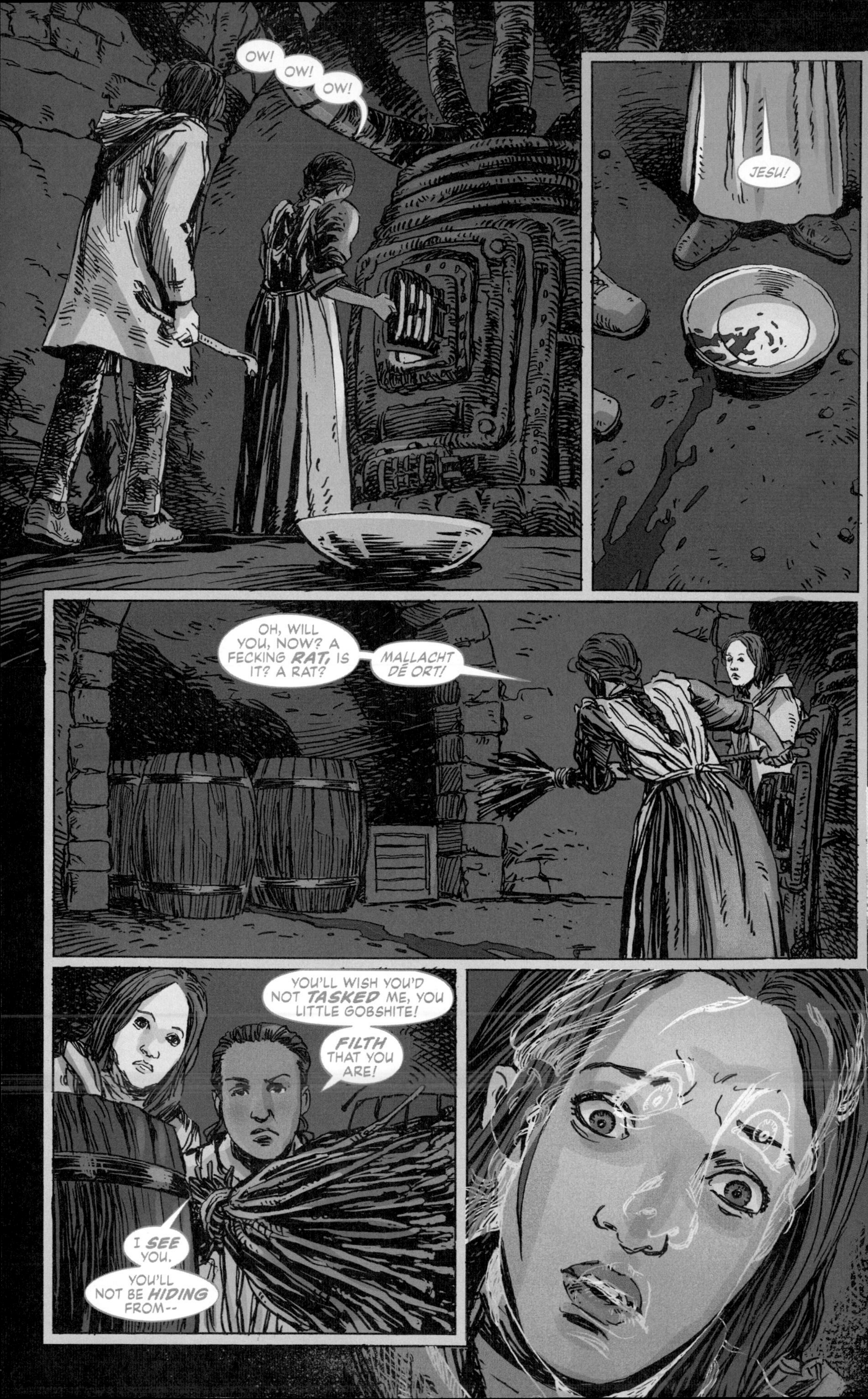
OW!
OW!
OW!
JESU!
OH, WILL YOU, NOW? A FECKING RAT, IS IT? A RAT?
MALLACHT DÉ ORT!
YOU'LL WISH YOU'D NOT TASKED ME, YOU LITTLE GOBSHITE!
FILTH THAT YOU ARE!
I SEE YOU.
YOU'LL NOT BE HIDING FROM--

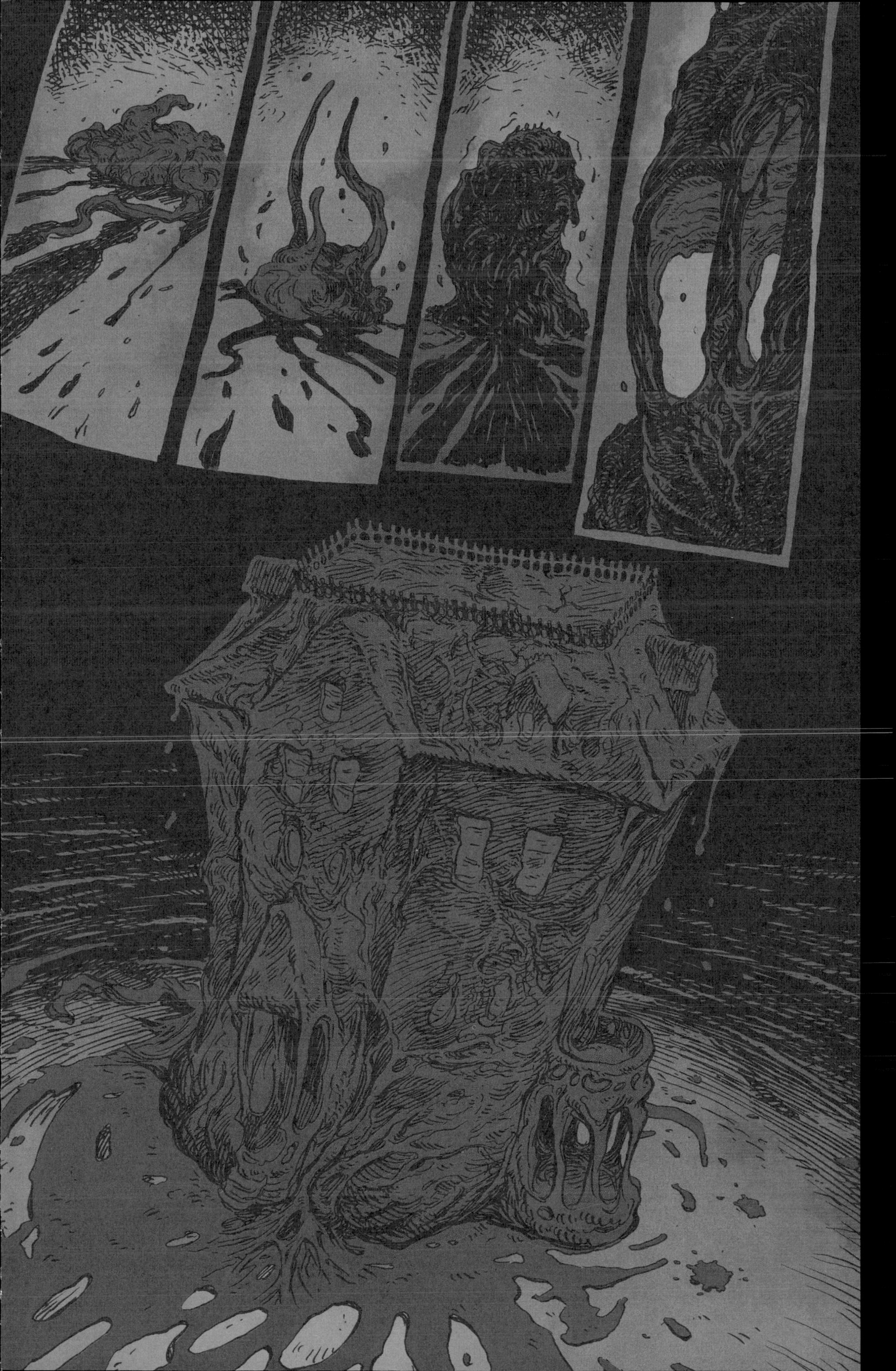

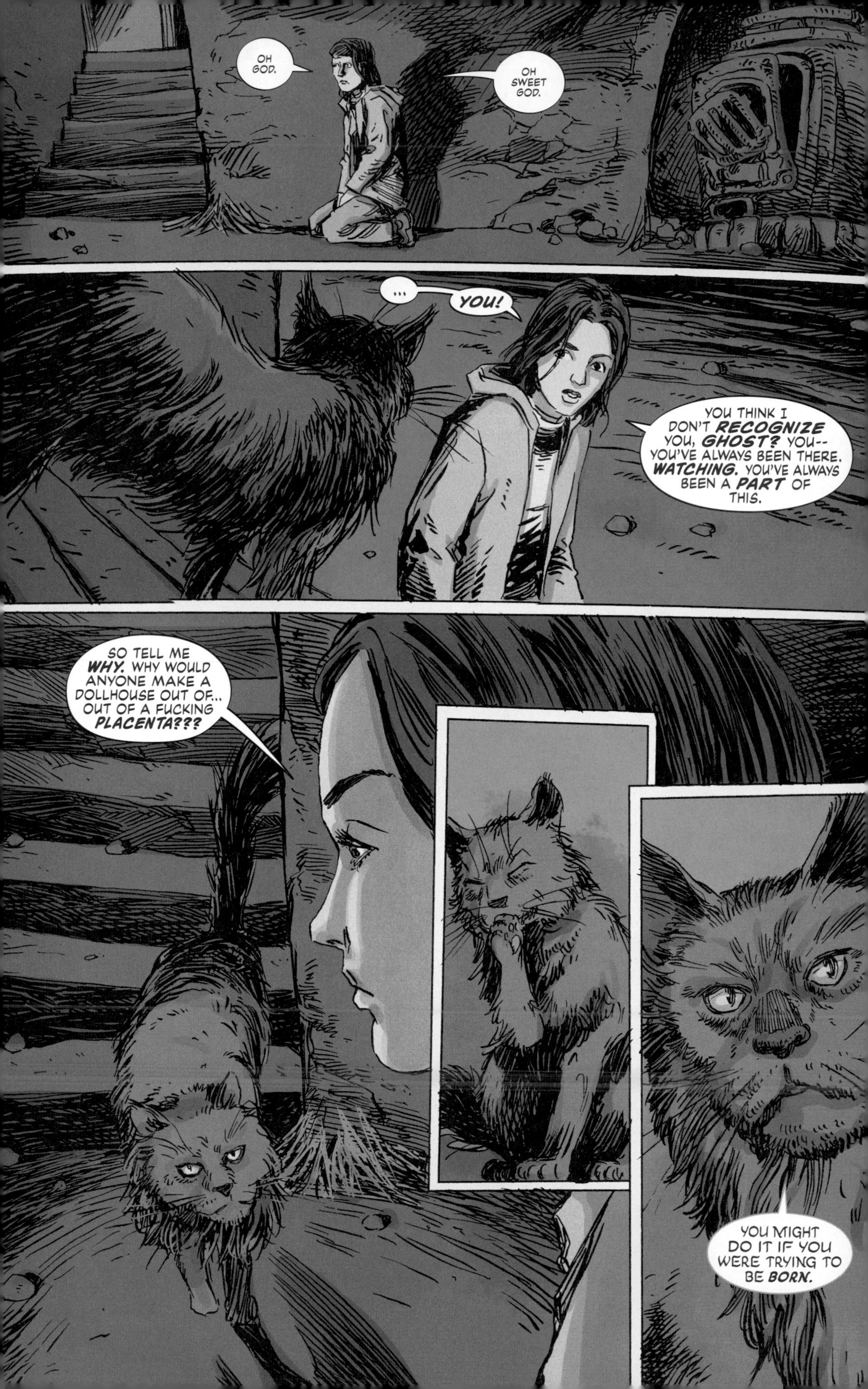
OH GOD.
OH SWEET GOD.
...
YOU!
YOU THINK I DON'T RECOGNIZE YOU, GHOST? YOU-- YOU'VE ALWAYS BEEN THERE. WATCHING. YOU'VE ALWAYS BEEN A PART OF THIS.
SO TELL ME WHY. WHY WOULD ANYONE MAKE A DOLLHOUSE OUT OF... OUT OF A FUCKING PLACENTA???
YOU MIGHT DO IT IF YOU WERE TRYING TO BE BORN.

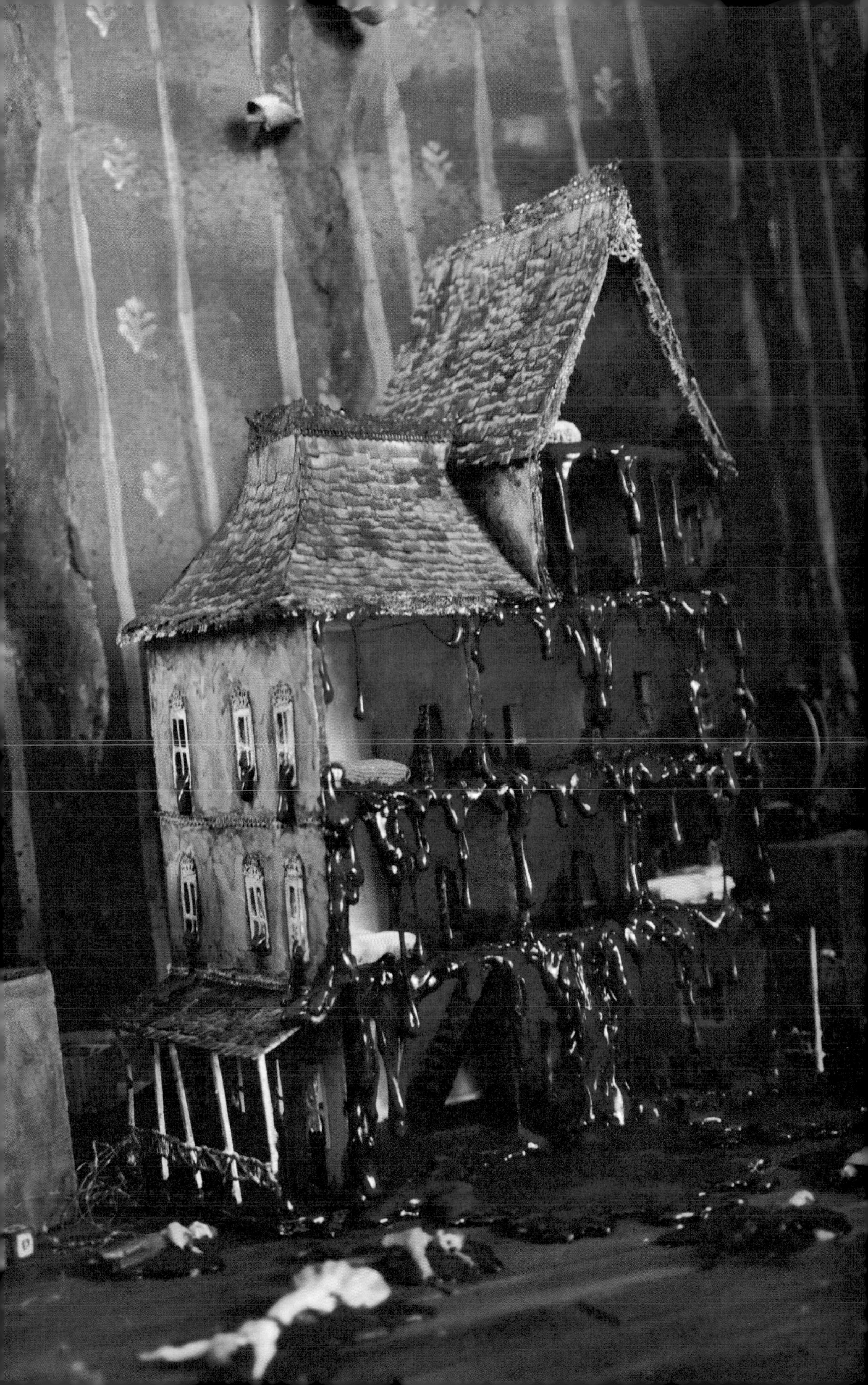

UNA

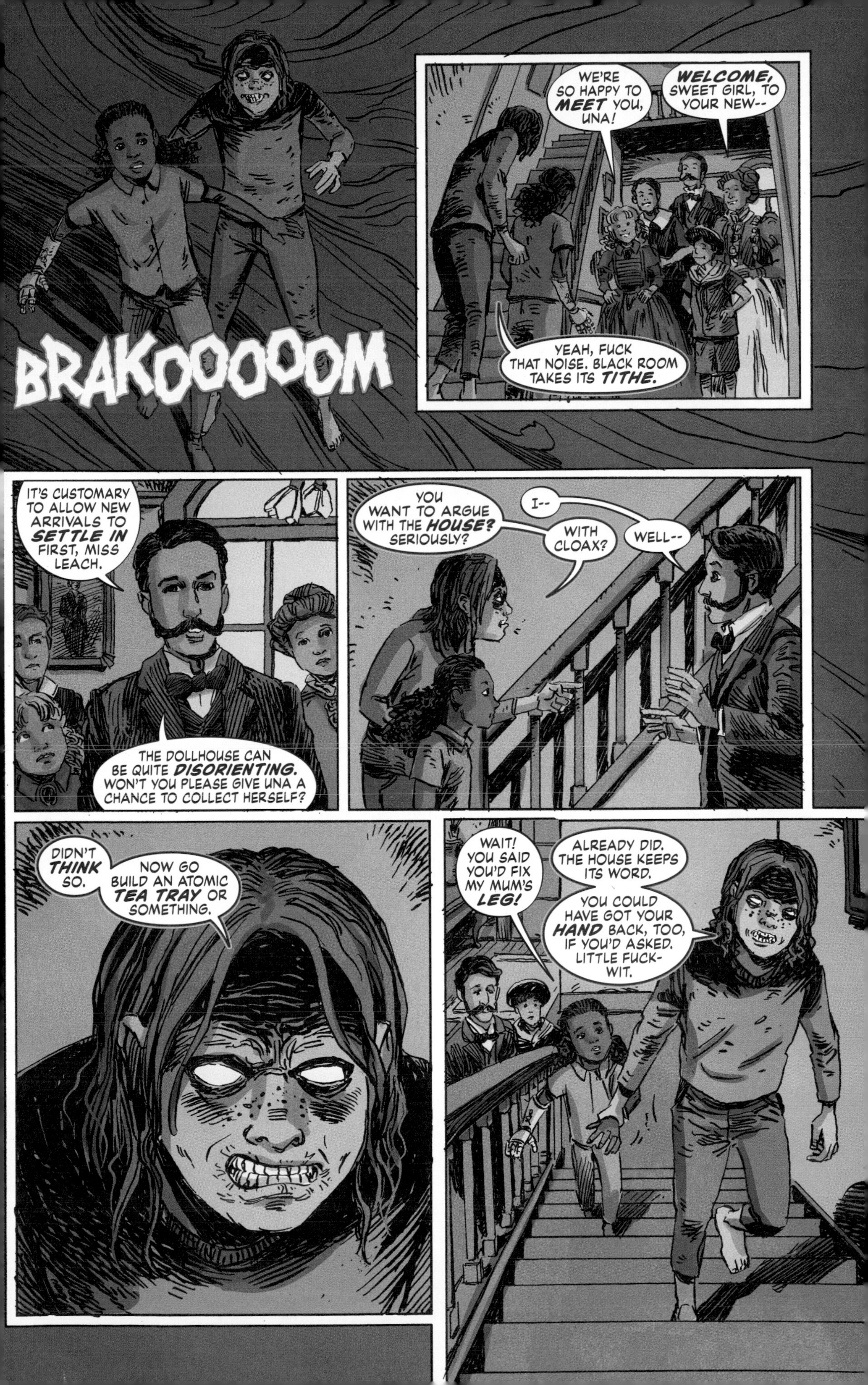
BRAKOOOOOM
WE'RE SO HAPPY TO MEET YOU, UNA!
WELCOME, SWEET GIRL, TO YOUR NEW--
YEAH, FUCK THAT NOISE. BLACK ROOM TAKES ITS TITHE.
IT'S CUSTOMARY TO ALLOW NEW ARRIVALS TO SETTLE IN FIRST, MISS LEACH.
THE DOLLHOUSE CAN BE QUITE DISORIENTING. WON'T YOU PLEASE GIVE UNA A CHANCE TO COLLECT HERSELF?
YOU WANT TO ARGUE WITH THE HOUSE? SERIOUSLY?
I--
WITH CLOAX?
WELL--
DIDN'T THINK SO.
NOW GO BUILD AN ATOMIC TEA TRAY OR SOMETHING.
WAIT! YOU SAID YOU'D FIX MY MUM'S LEG!
ALREADY DID. THE HOUSE KEEPS ITS WORD.
YOU COULD HAVE GOT YOUR HAND BACK, TOO, IF YOU'D ASKED. LITTLE FUCK-WIT.

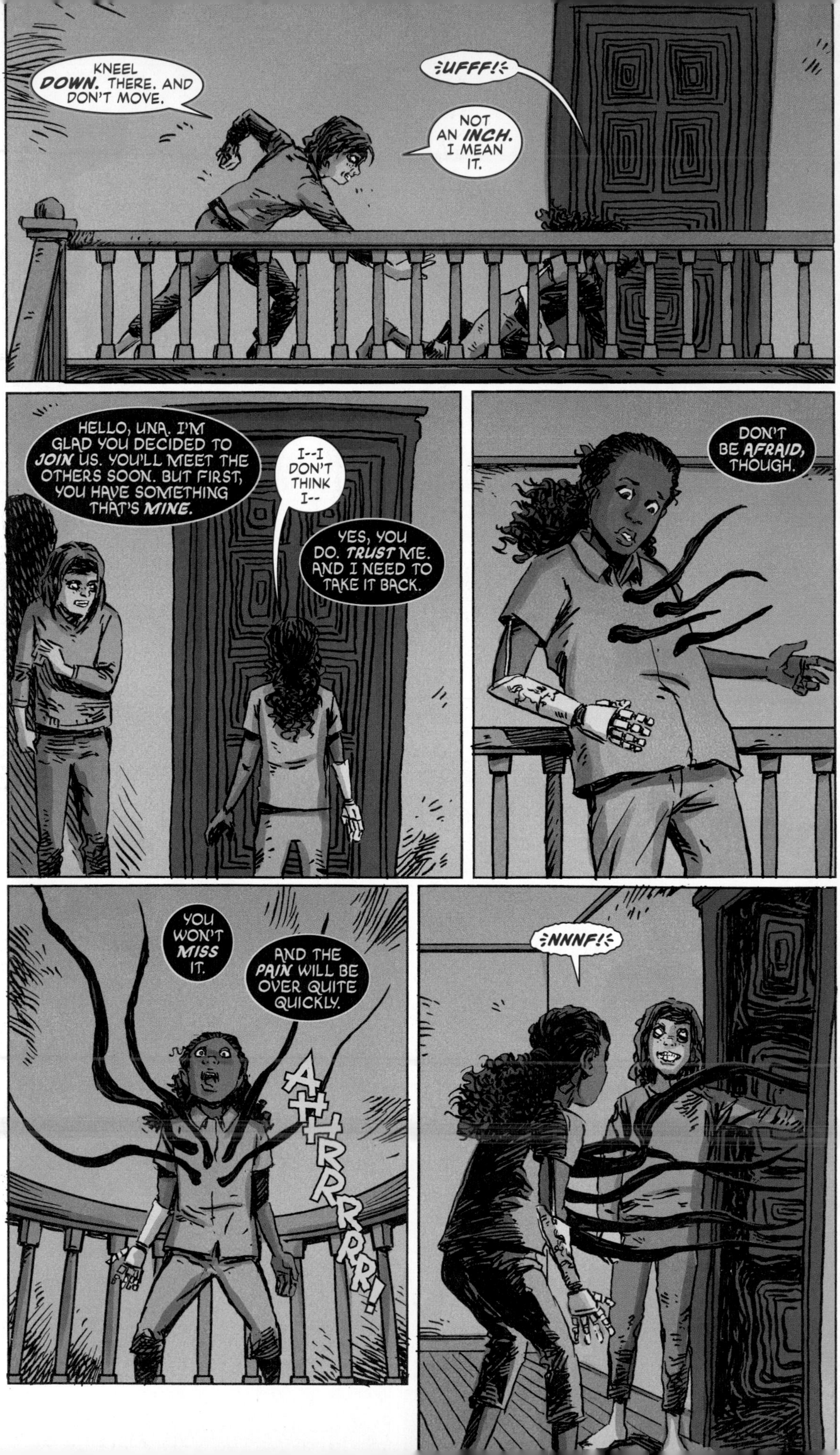
KNEEL DOWN. THERE. AND DON'T MOVE.
UFFF!
NOT AN INCH. I MEAN IT.
HELLO, UNA. I'M GLAD YOU DECIDED TO JOIN US. YOU'LL MEET THE OTHERS SOON. BUT FIRST, YOU HAVE SOMETHING THAT'S MINE.
I--I DON'T THINK I--
YES, YOU DO. TRUST ME. AND I NEED TO TAKE IT BACK.
DON'T BE AFRAID, THOUGH.
YOU WON'T MISS IT.
AND THE PAIN WILL BE OVER QUITE QUICKLY.
AHHRRRR!
NNNF!

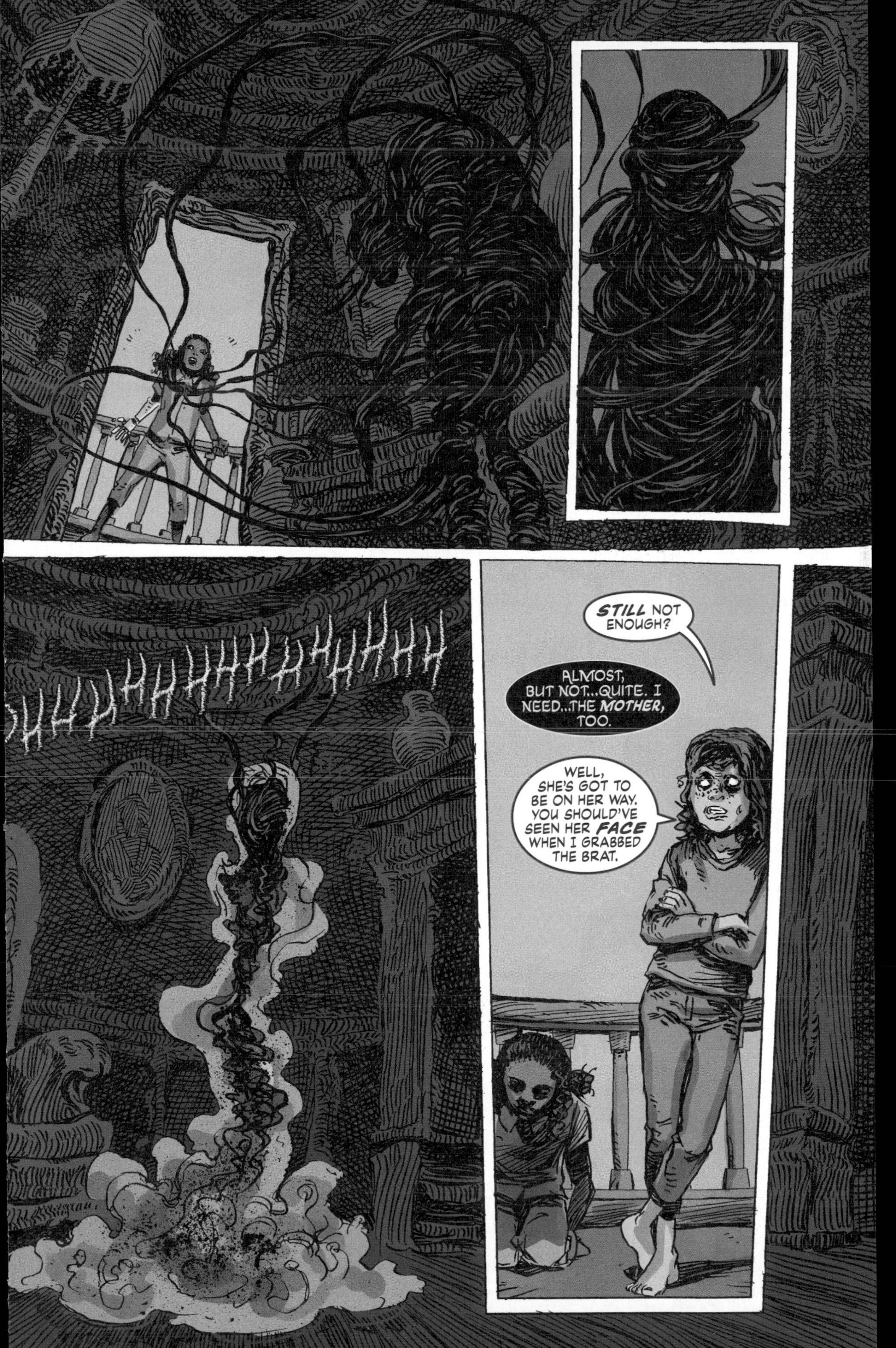
HHHHHHHHHHHHHHHHHHHHH
STILL NOT ENOUGH?
ALMOST, BUT NOT...QUITE. I NEED...THE MOTHER, TOO.
WELL, SHE'S GOT TO BE ON HER WAY. YOU SHOULD'VE SEEN HER FACE WHEN I GRABBED THE BRAT.

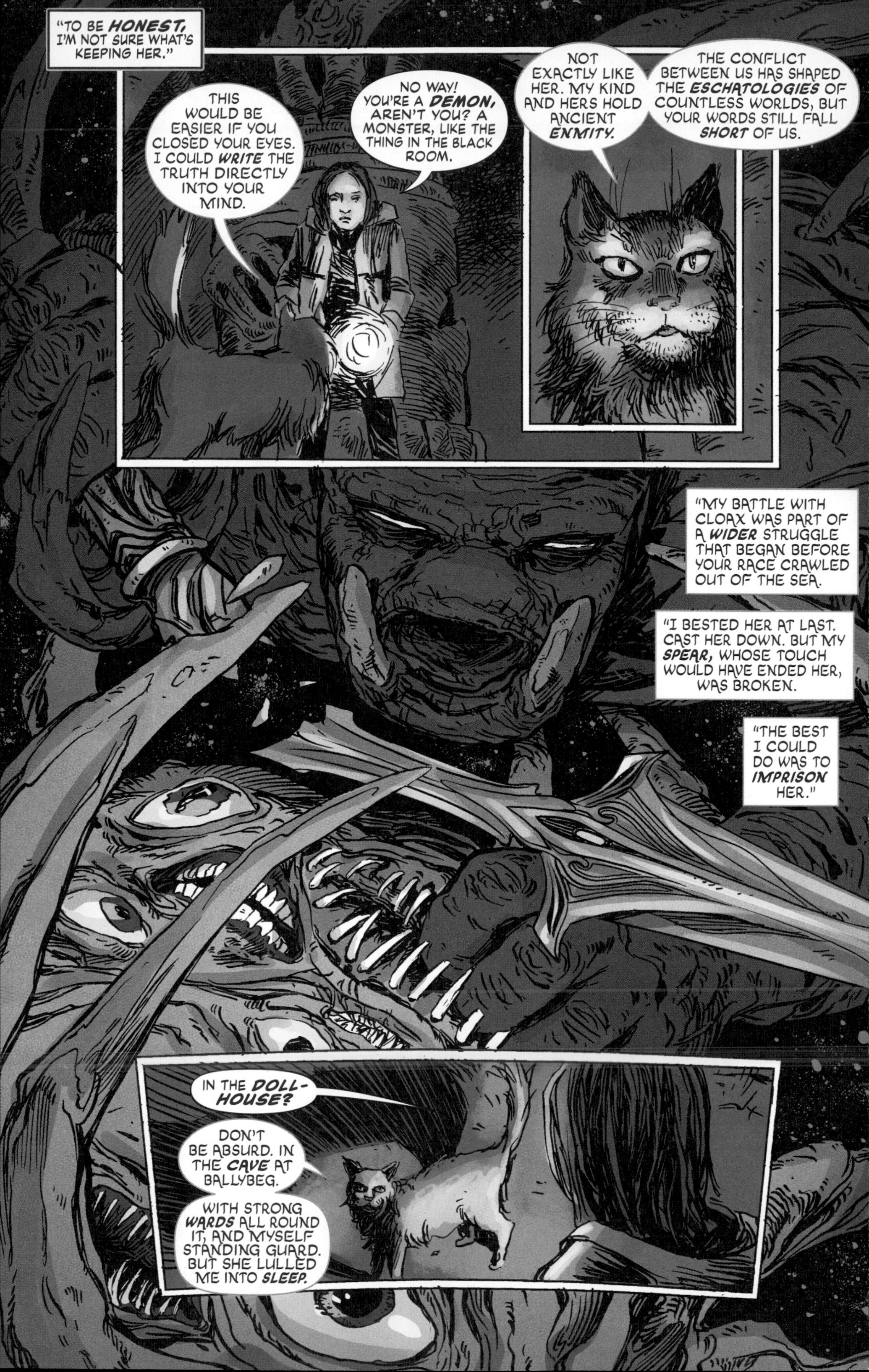
"TO BE HONEST, I'M NOT SURE WHAT'S KEEPING HER."
THIS WOULD BE EASIER IF YOU CLOSED YOUR EYES. I COULD WRITE THE TRUTH DIRECTLY INTO YOUR MIND.
NO WAY! YOU'RE A DEMON, AREN'T YOU? A MONSTER, LIKE THE THING IN THE BLACK ROOM.
NOT EXACTLY LIKE HER. MY KIND AND HERS HOLD ANCIENT ENMITY.
THE CONFLICT BETWEEN US HAS SHAPED THE ESCHATOLOGIES OF COUNTLESS WORLDS, BUT YOUR WORDS STILL FALL SHORT OF US.
"MY BATTLE WITH CLOAX WAS PART OF A WIDER STRUGGLE THAT BEGAN BEFORE YOUR RACE CRAWLED OUT OF THE SEA.
"I BESTED HER AT LAST. CAST HER DOWN. BUT MY SPEAR, WHOSE TOUCH WOULD HAVE ENDED HER, WAS BROKEN.
"THE BEST I COULD DO WAS TO IMPRISON HER."
IN THE DOLL-HOUSE?
DON'T BE ABSURD. IN THE CAVE AT BALLYBEG.
WITH STRONG WARDS ALL ROUND IT, AND MYSELF STANDING GUARD. BUT SHE LULLED ME INTO SLEEP.

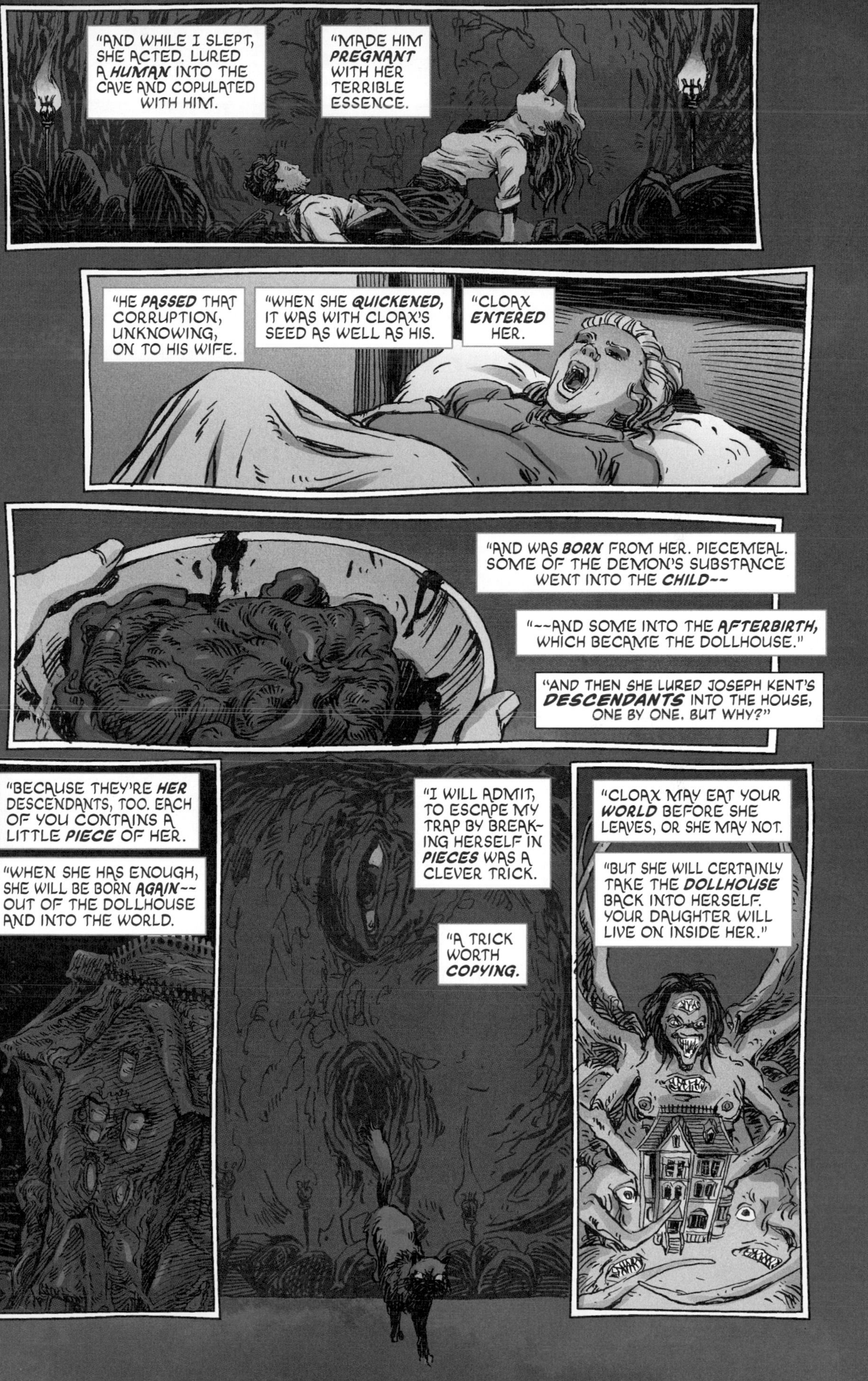
"AND WHILE I SLEPT, SHE ACTED. LURED A HUMAN INTO THE CAVE AND COPULATED WITH HIM.
"MADE HIM PREGNANT WITH HER TERRIBLE ESSENCE.
"HE PASSED THAT CORRUPTION, UNKNOWING, ON TO HIS WIFE.
"WHEN SHE QUICKENED, IT WAS WITH CLOAX'S SEED AS WELL AS HIS.
"CLOAX ENTERED HER.
"AND WAS BORN FROM HER. PIECEMEAL. SOME OF THE DEMON'S SUBSTANCE WENT INTO THE CHILD--
"--AND SOME INTO THE AFTERBIRTH, WHICH BECAME THE DOLLHOUSE."
"AND THEN SHE LURED JOSEPH KENT'S DESCENDANTS INTO THE HOUSE, ONE BY ONE. BUT WHY?"
"BECAUSE THEY'RE HER DESCENDANTS, TOO. EACH OF YOU CONTAINS A LITTLE PIECE OF HER.
"WHEN SHE HAS ENOUGH, SHE WILL BE BORN AGAIN-- OUT OF THE DOLLHOUSE AND INTO THE WORLD.
"I WILL ADMIT, TO ESCAPE MY TRAP BY BREAKING HERSELF IN PIECES WAS A CLEVER TRICK.
"A TRICK WORTH COPYING.
"CLOAX MAY EAT YOUR WORLD BEFORE SHE LEAVES, OR SHE MAY NOT.
"BUT SHE WILL CERTAINLY TAKE THE DOLLHOUSE BACK INTO HERSELF. YOUR DAUGHTER WILL LIVE ON INSIDE HER."

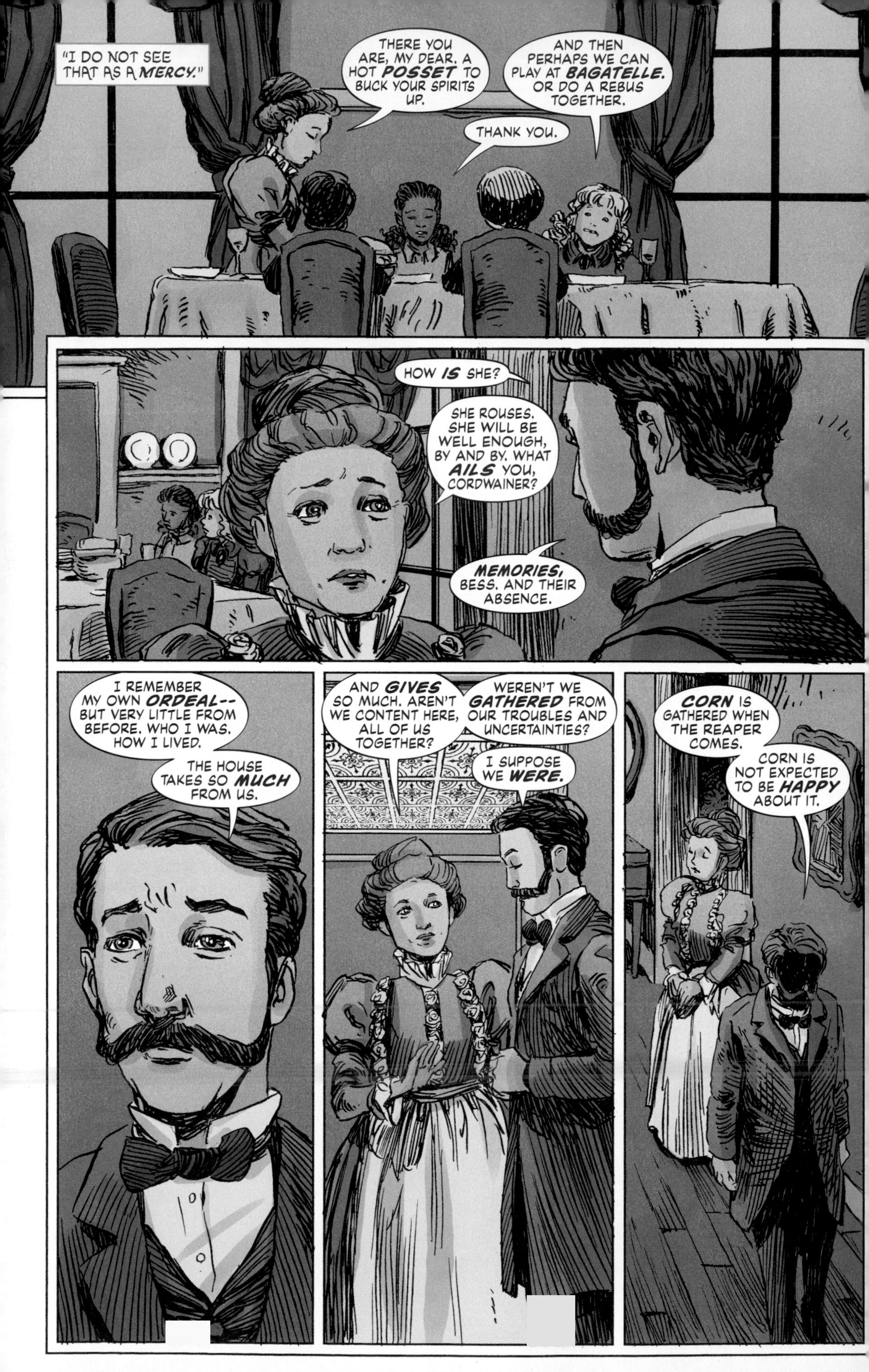
"I DO NOT SEE THAT AS A MERCY."
THERE YOU ARE, MY DEAR. A HOT POSSET TO BUCK YOUR SPIRITS UP.
AND THEN PERHAPS WE CAN PLAY AT BAGATELLE. OR DO A REBUS TOGETHER.
THANK YOU.
HOW IS SHE?
SHE ROUSES. SHE WILL BE WELL ENOUGH, BY AND BY. WHAT AILS YOU, CORDWAINER?
MEMORIES, BESS. AND THEIR ABSENCE.
I REMEMBER MY OWN ORDEAL-- BUT VERY LITTLE FROM BEFORE. WHO I WAS. HOW I LIVED.
THE HOUSE TAKES SO MUCH FROM US.
AND GIVES SO MUCH. AREN'T WE CONTENT HERE, ALL OF US TOGETHER?
WEREN'T WE GATHERED FROM OUR TROUBLES AND UNCERTAINTIES?
I SUPPOSE WE WERE.
CORN IS GATHERED WHEN THE REAPER COMES.
CORN IS NOT EXPECTED TO BE HAPPY ABOUT IT.

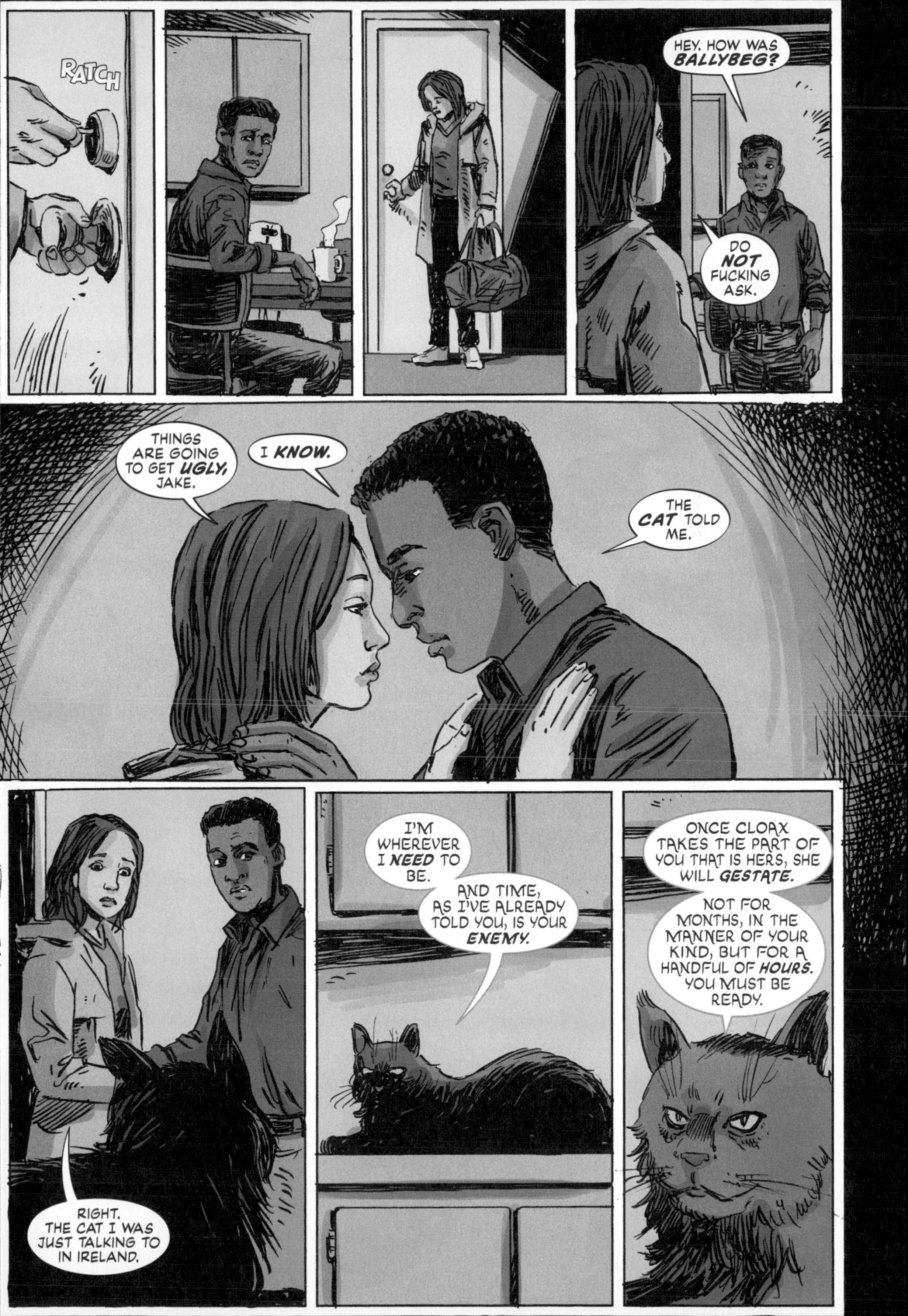

RATCH
HEY. HOW WAS BALLYBEG?
DO NOT FUCKING ASK.
THINGS ARE GOING TO GET UGLY, JAKE.
I KNOW.
THE CAT TOLD ME.
RIGHT. THE CAT I WAS JUST TALKING TO IN IRELAND.
I'M WHEREVER I NEED TO BE.
AND TIME, AS I'VE ALREADY TOLD YOU, IS YOUR ENEMY.
ONCE CLOAX TAKES THE PART OF YOU THAT IS HERS, SHE WILL GESTATE.
NOT FOR MONTHS, IN THE MANNER OF YOUR KIND, BUT FOR A HANDFUL OF HOURS. YOU MUST BE READY.

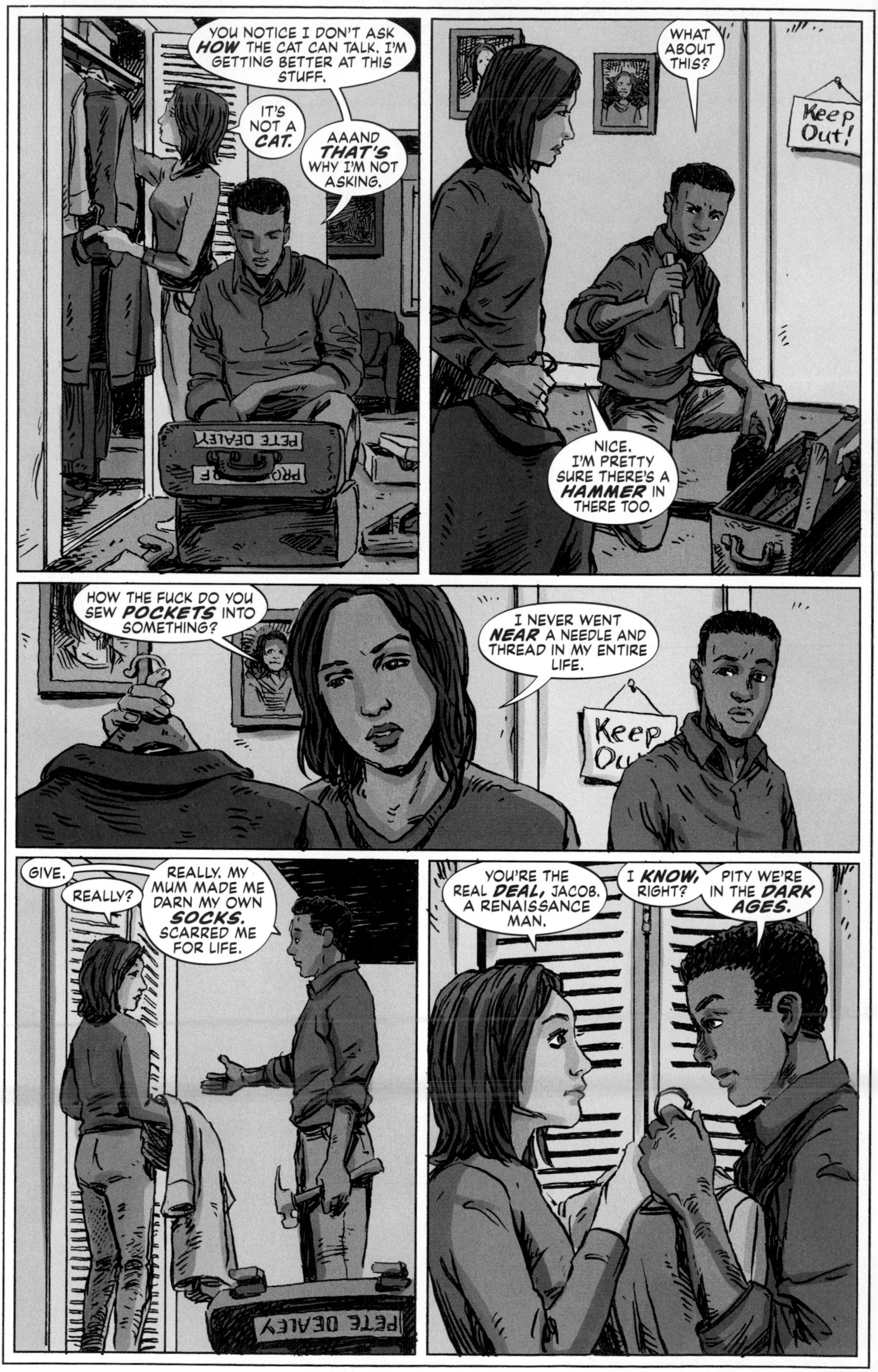
YOU NOTICE I DON'T ASK HOW THE CAT CAN TALK. I'M GETTING BETTER AT THIS STUFF.
IT'S NOT A CAT.
AAAND THAT'S WHY I'M NOT ASKING.
PETE DEALEY
WHAT ABOUT THIS?
Keep Out!
NICE. I'M PRETTY SURE THERE'S A HAMMER IN THERE TOO.
HOW THE FUCK DO YOU SEW POCKETS INTO SOMETHING?
I NEVER WENT NEAR A NEEDLE AND THREAD IN MY ENTIRE LIFE.
GIVE.
REALLY?
REALLY. MY MUM MADE ME DARN MY OWN SOCKS. SCARRED ME FOR LIFE.
PETE DEALEY
YOU'RE THE REAL DEAL, JACOB. A RENAISSANCE MAN.
I KNOW, RIGHT?
PITY WE'RE IN THE DARK AGES.

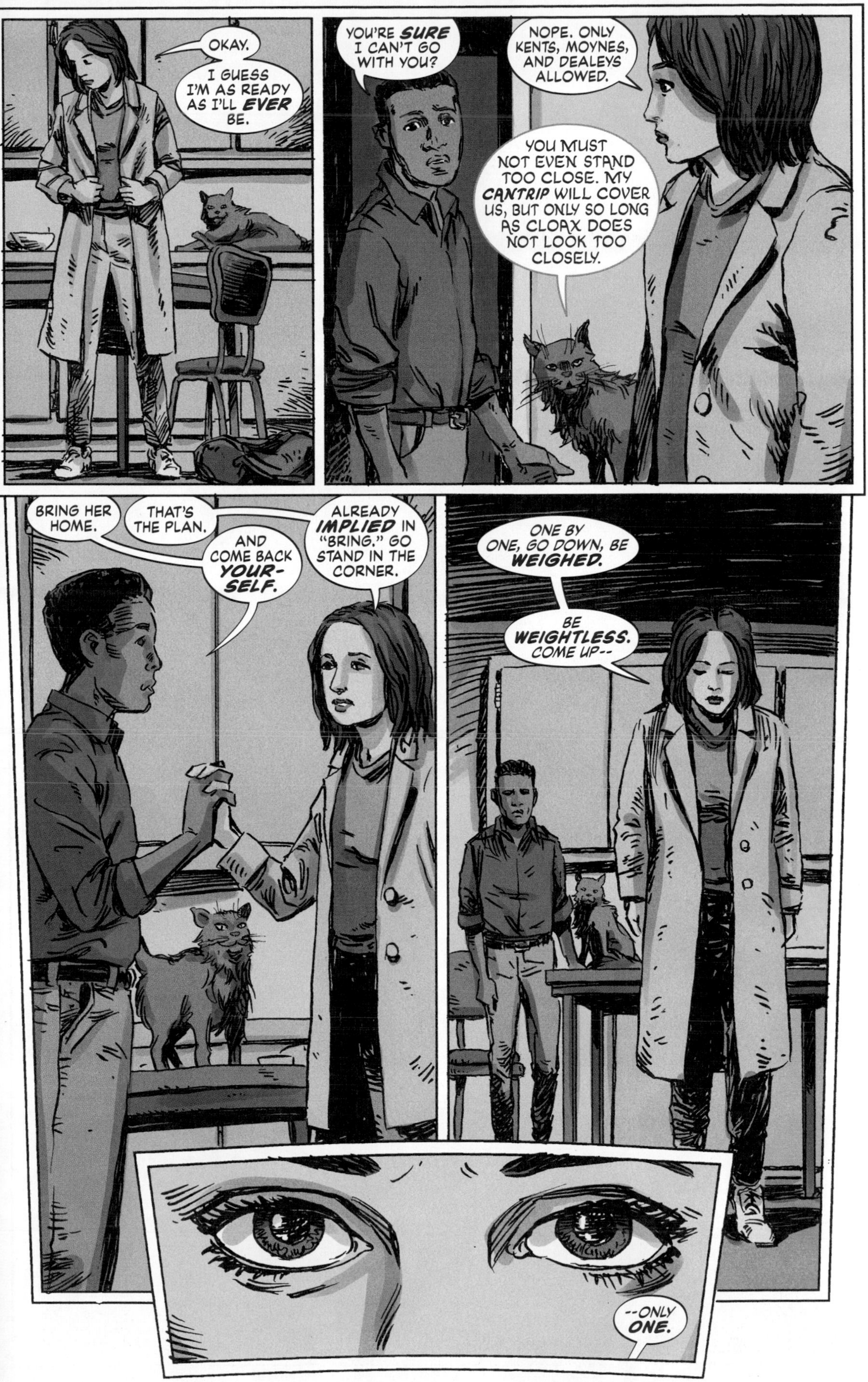
OKAY.
I GUESS I'M AS READY AS I'LL EVER BE.
YOU'RE SURE I CAN'T GO WITH YOU?
NOPE. ONLY KENTS, MOYNES, AND DEALEYS ALLOWED.
YOU MUST NOT EVEN STAND TOO CLOSE. MY CANTRIP WILL COVER US, BUT ONLY SO LONG AS CLOAX DOES NOT LOOK TOO CLOSELY.
BRING HER HOME.
THAT'S THE PLAN.
AND COME BACK YOURSELF.
ALREADY IMPLIED IN "BRING." GO STAND IN THE CORNER.
ONE BY ONE, GO DOWN, BE WEIGHED.
BE WEIGHTLESS. COME UP--
--ONLY ONE.

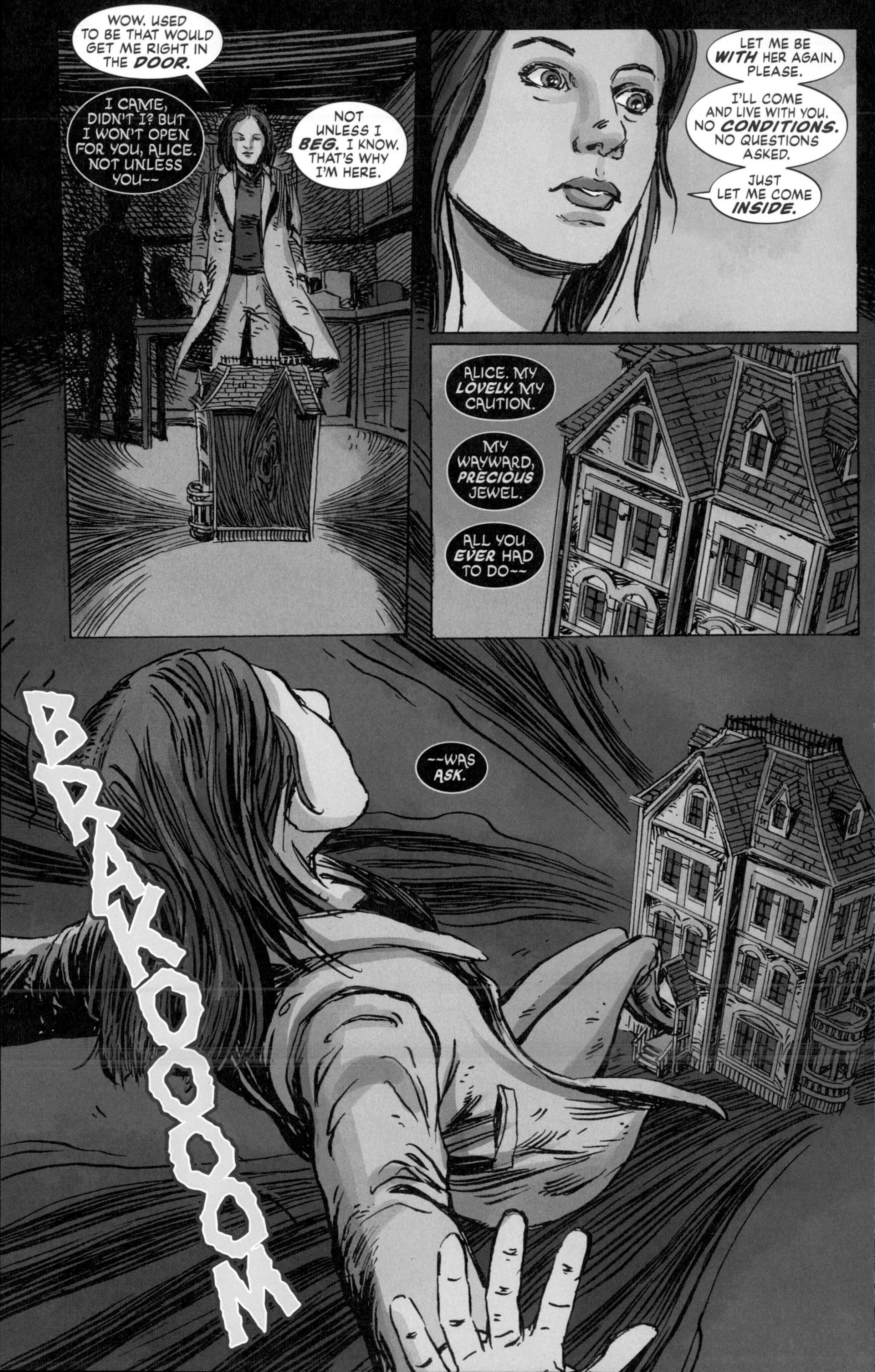
WOW. USED TO BE THAT WOULD GET ME RIGHT IN THE DOOR.
I CAME, DIDN'T I? BUT I WON'T OPEN FOR YOU, ALICE. NOT UNLESS YOU--
NOT UNLESS I BEG. I KNOW. THAT'S WHY I'M HERE.
LET ME BE WITH HER AGAIN. PLEASE.
I'LL COME AND LIVE WITH YOU. NO CONDITIONS. NO QUESTIONS ASKED.
JUST LET ME COME INSIDE.
ALICE. MY LOVELY. MY CAUTION.
MY WAYWARD, PRECIOUS JEWEL.
ALL YOU EVER HAD TO DO--
--WAS ASK.
BRAKOOOOM

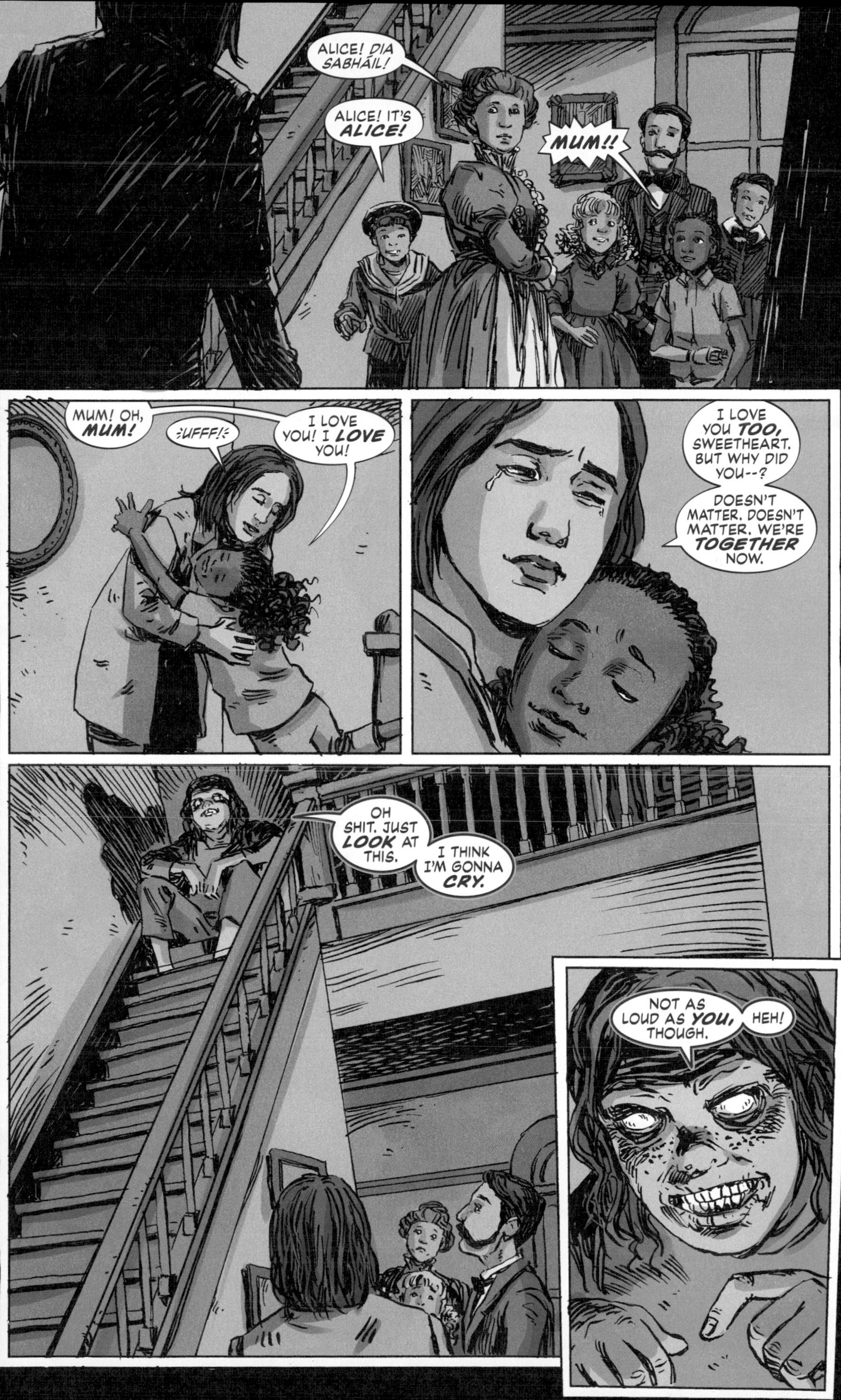
ALICE! DIA SABHÁIL!
ALICE! IT'S ALICE!
MUM!!
MUM! OH, MUM!
UFFF!
I LOVE YOU! I LOVE YOU!
I LOVE YOU TOO, SWEETHEART. BUT WHY DID YOU--?
DOESN'T MATTER. DOESN'T MATTER. WE'RE TOGETHER NOW.
OH SHIT. JUST LOOK AT THIS.
I THINK I'M GONNA CRY.
NOT AS LOUD AS YOU, THOUGH.
HEH!

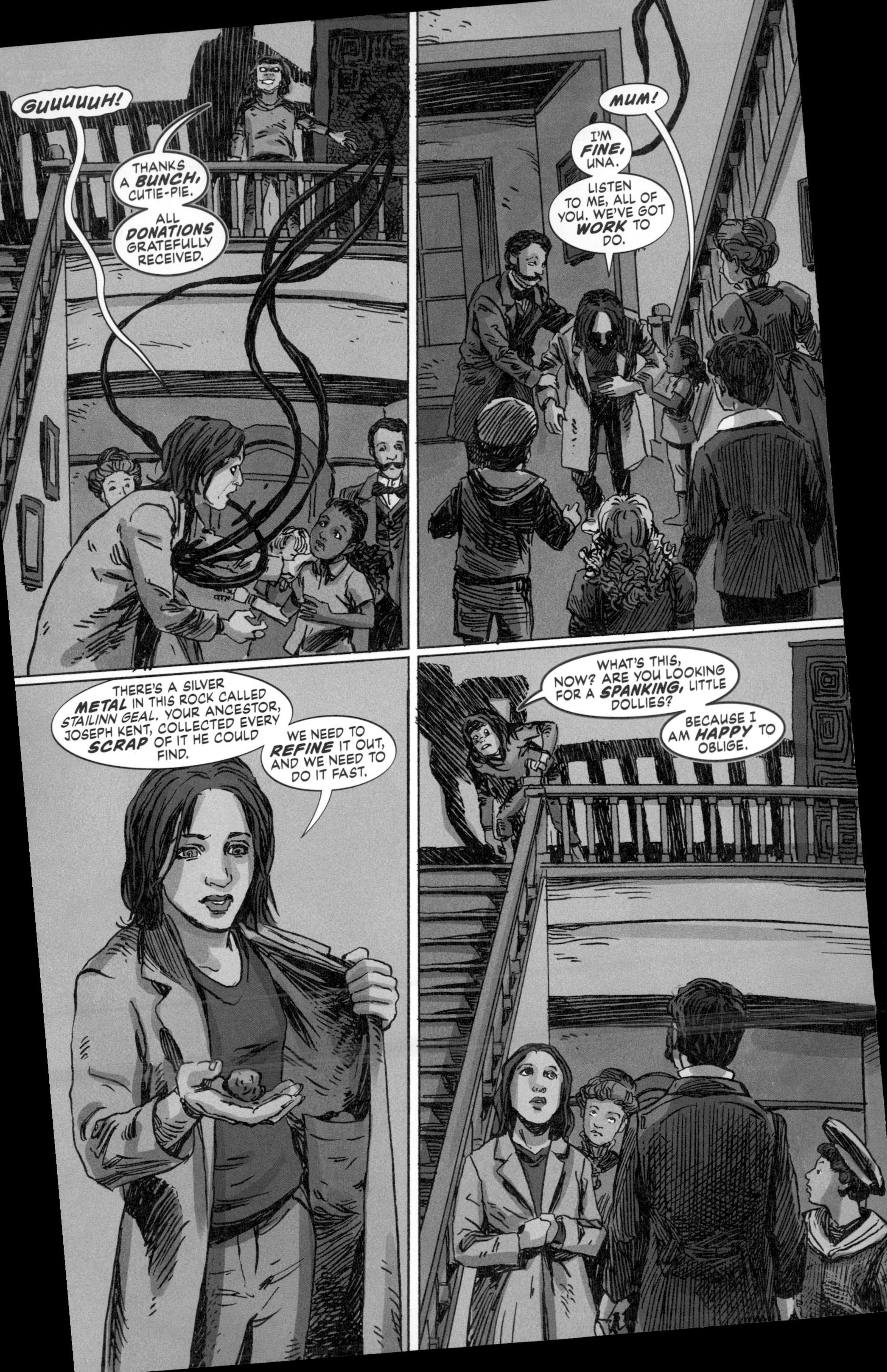
GUUUUUH!
THANKS A BUNCH, CUTIE-PIE.
ALL DONATIONS GRATEFULLY RECEIVED.
MUM!
I'M FINE, UNA.
LISTEN TO ME, ALL OF YOU. WE'VE GOT WORK TO DO.
THERE'S A SILVER METAL IN THIS ROCK CALLED STAILINN GEAL. YOUR ANCESTOR, JOSEPH KENT, COLLECTED EVERY SCRAP OF IT HE COULD FIND.
WE NEED TO REFINE IT OUT, AND WE NEED TO DO IT FAST.
WHAT'S THIS, NOW? ARE YOU LOOKING FOR A SPANKING, LITTLE DOLLIES?
BECAUSE I AM HAPPY TO OBLIGE.

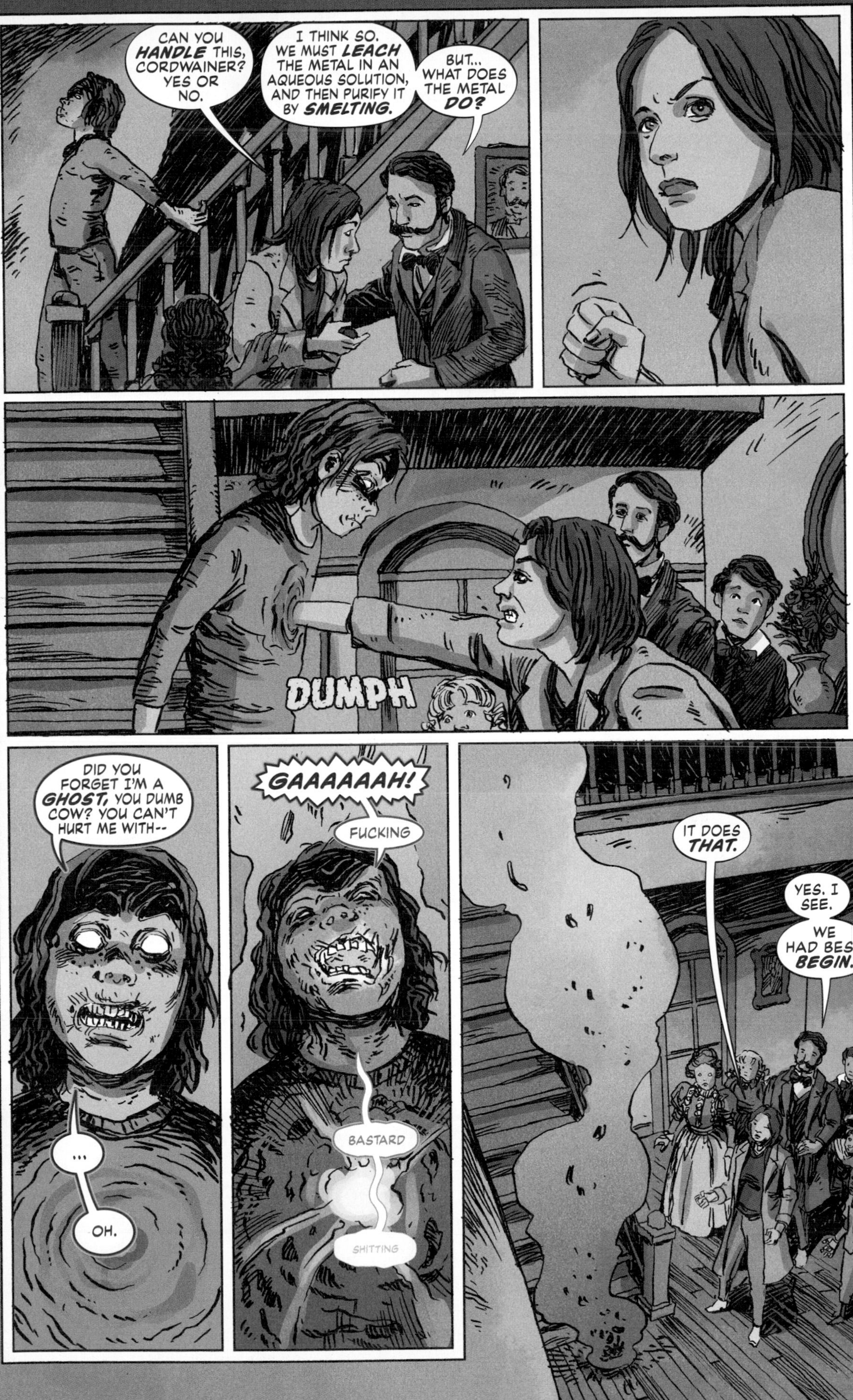

CAN YOU HANDLE THIS, CORDWAINER? YES OR NO.
I THINK SO. WE MUST LEACH THE METAL IN AN AQUEOUS SOLUTION, AND THEN PURIFY IT BY SMELTING.
BUT... WHAT DOES THE METAL DO?
DUMPH
DID YOU FORGET I'M A GHOST, YOU DUMB COW? YOU CAN'T HURT ME WITH--
...
OH.
GAAAAAAAH!
FUCKING
BASTARD
SHITTING
IT DOES THAT.
YES. I SEE.
WE HAD BEST BEGIN.

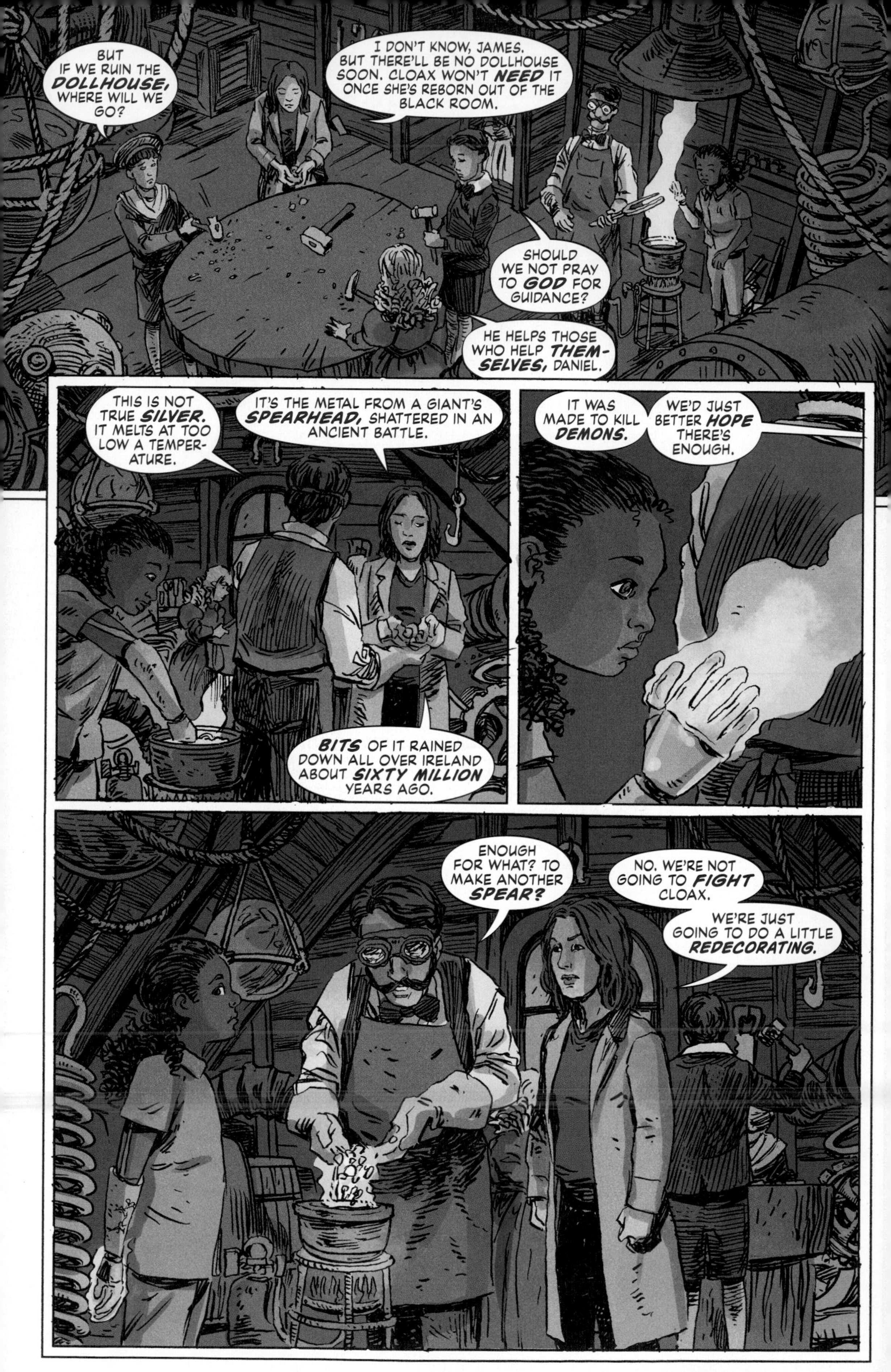

BUT IF WE RUIN THE DOLLHOUSE, WHERE WILL WE GO?
I DON'T KNOW, JAMES. BUT THERE'LL BE NO DOLLHOUSE SOON. CLOAX WON'T NEED IT ONCE SHE'S REBORN OUT OF THE BLACK ROOM.
SHOULD WE NOT PRAY TO GOD FOR GUIDANCE?
HE HELPS THOSE WHO HELP THEM-SELVES, DANIEL.
THIS IS NOT TRUE SILVER. IT MELTS AT TOO LOW A TEMPER-ATURE.
IT'S THE METAL FROM A GIANT'S SPEARHEAD, SHATTERED IN AN ANCIENT BATTLE.
BITS OF IT RAINED DOWN ALL OVER IRELAND ABOUT SIXTY MILLION YEARS AGO.
IT WAS MADE TO KILL DEMONS.
WE'D JUST BETTER HOPE THERE'S ENOUGH.
ENOUGH FOR WHAT? TO MAKE ANOTHER SPEAR?
NO. WE'RE NOT GOING TO FIGHT CLOAX.
WE'RE JUST GOING TO DO A LITTLE REDECORATING.

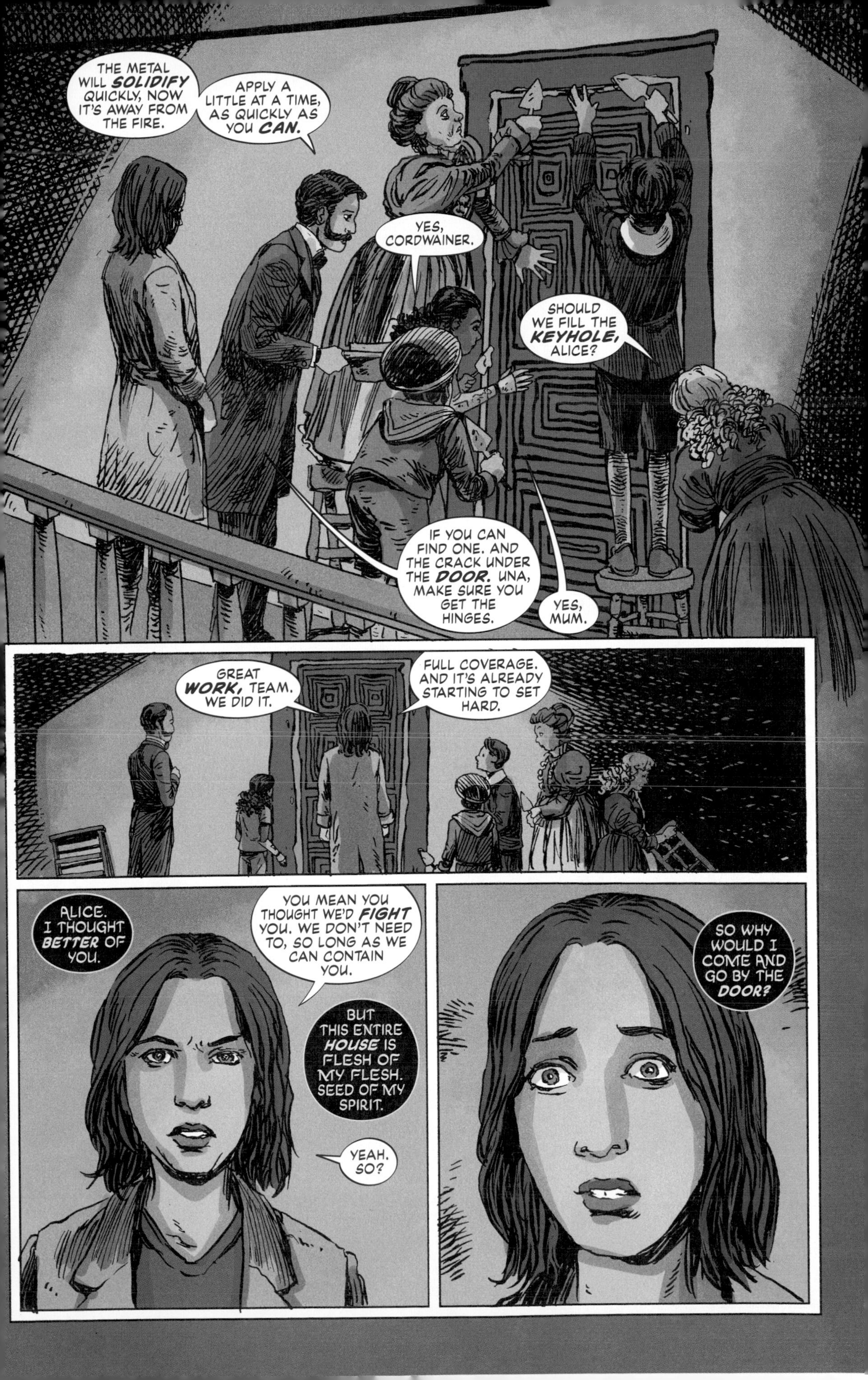
THE METAL WILL SOLIDIFY QUICKLY, NOW IT'S AWAY FROM THE FIRE.
APPLY A LITTLE AT A TIME, AS QUICKLY AS YOU CAN.
YES, CORDWAINER.
SHOULD WE FILL THE KEYHOLE, ALICE?
IF YOU CAN FIND ONE. AND THE CRACK UNDER THE DOOR. UNA, MAKE SURE YOU GET THE HINGES.
YES, MUM.
GREAT WORK, TEAM. WE DID IT.
FULL COVERAGE. AND IT'S ALREADY STARTING TO SET HARD.
ALICE. I THOUGHT BETTER OF YOU.
YOU MEAN YOU THOUGHT WE'D FIGHT YOU. WE DON'T NEED TO, SO LONG AS WE CAN CONTAIN YOU.
BUT THIS ENTIRE HOUSE IS FLESH OF MY FLESH. SEED OF MY SPIRIT.
YEAH. SO?
SO WHY WOULD I COME AND GO BY THE DOOR?

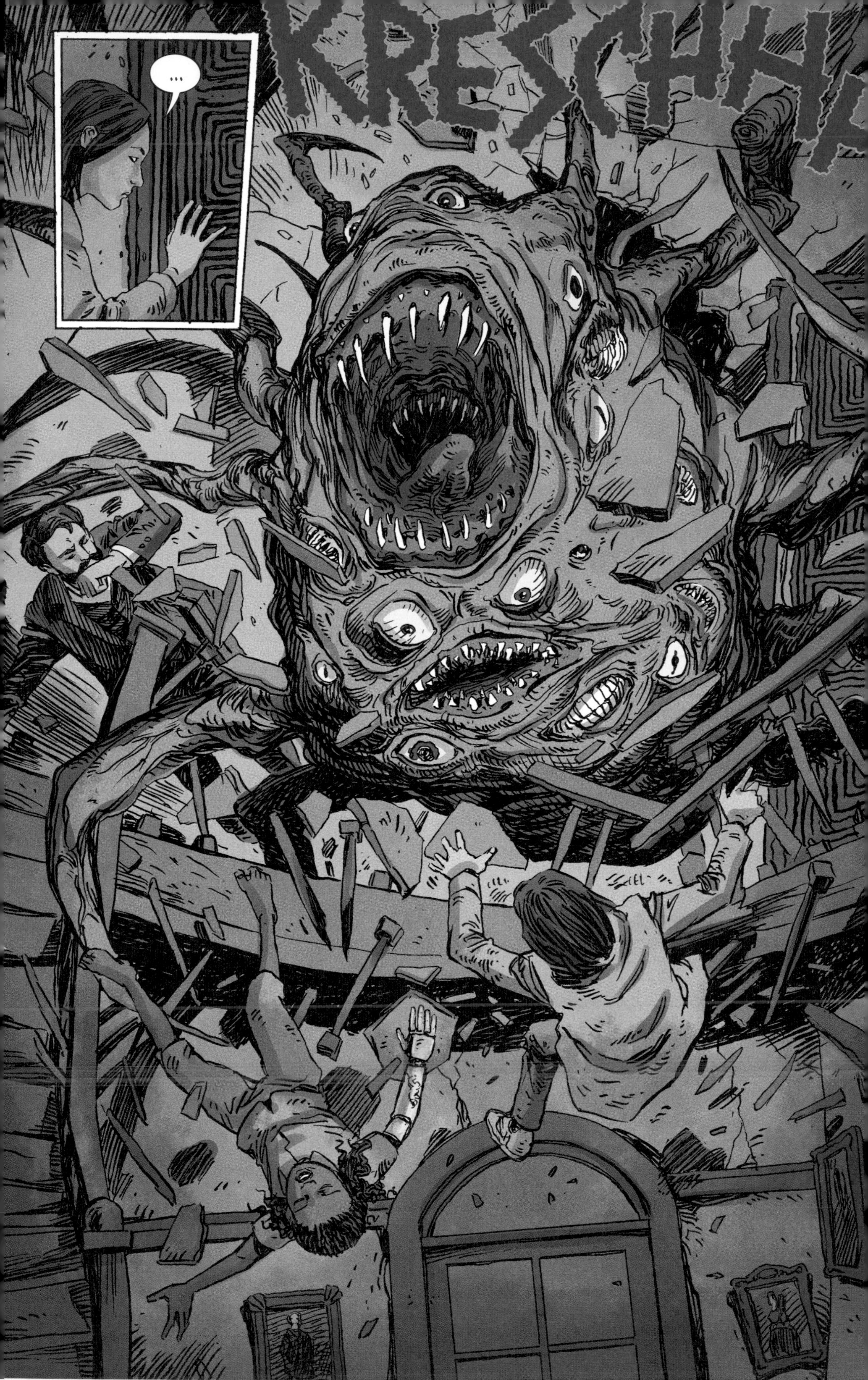
...
KRESCHH

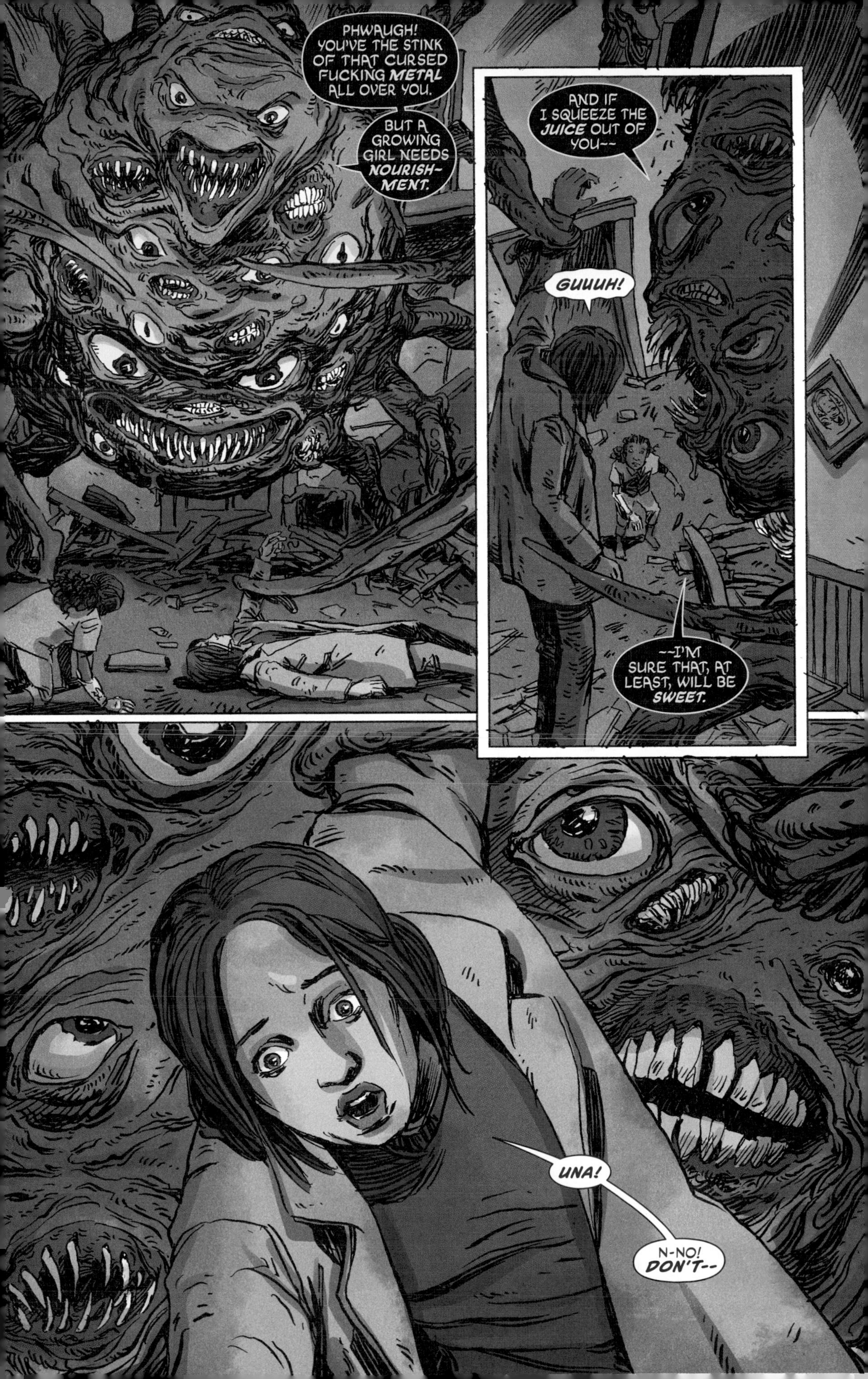
PHWAUGH! YOU'VE THE STINK OF THAT CURSED FUCKING METAL ALL OVER YOU.
BUT A GROWING GIRL NEEDS NOURISHMENT.
AND IF I SQUEEZE THE JUICE OUT OF YOU--
GUUUH!
--I'M SURE THAT, AT LEAST, WILL BE SWEET.
UNA!
N-NO! DON'T--

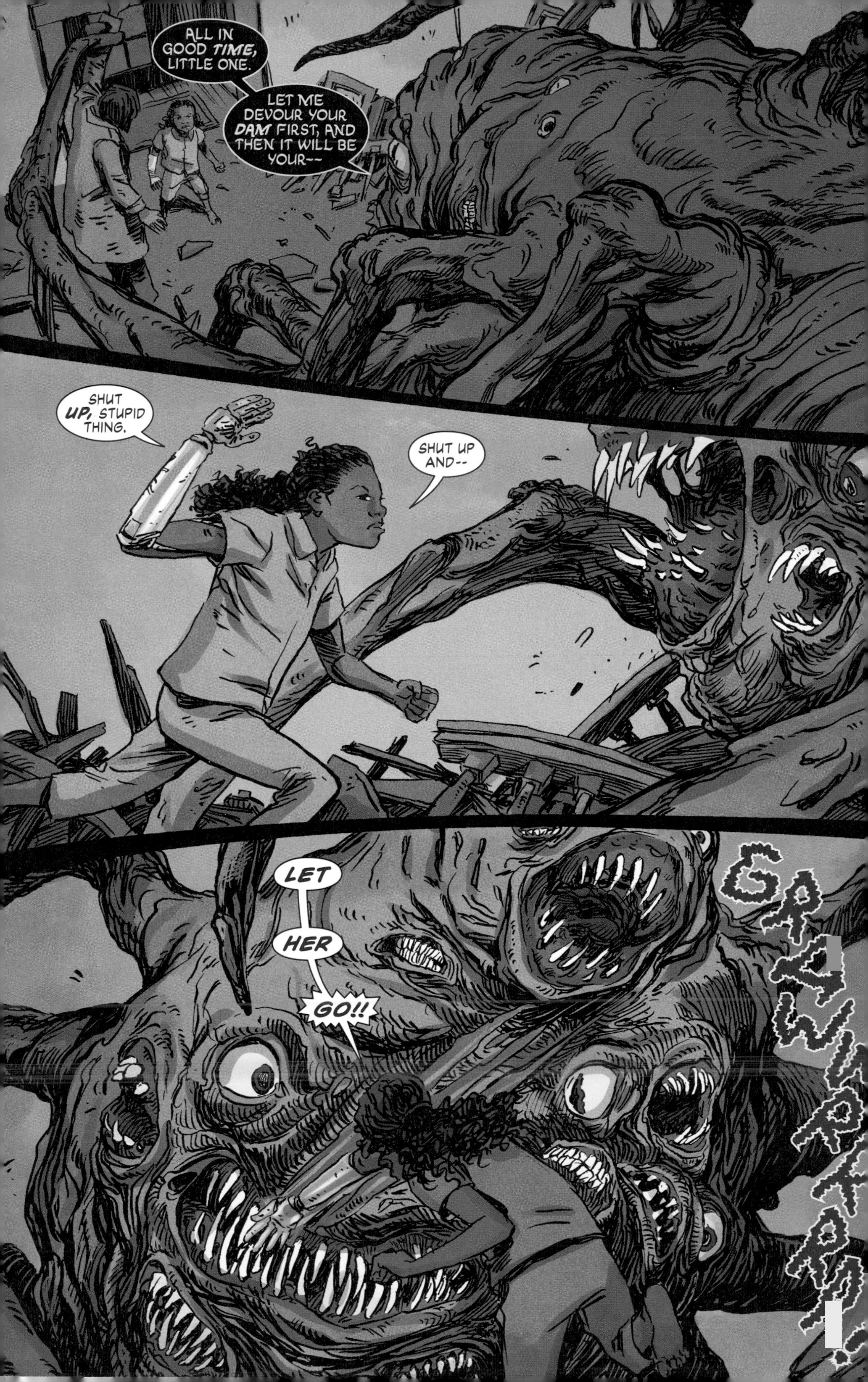
ALL IN GOOD *TIME,* LITTLE ONE.
LET ME DEVOUR YOUR *DAM* FIRST, AND THEN IT WILL BE YOUR--
SHUT *UP,* STUPID THING.
SHUT UP AND--
LET
HER
GO!!

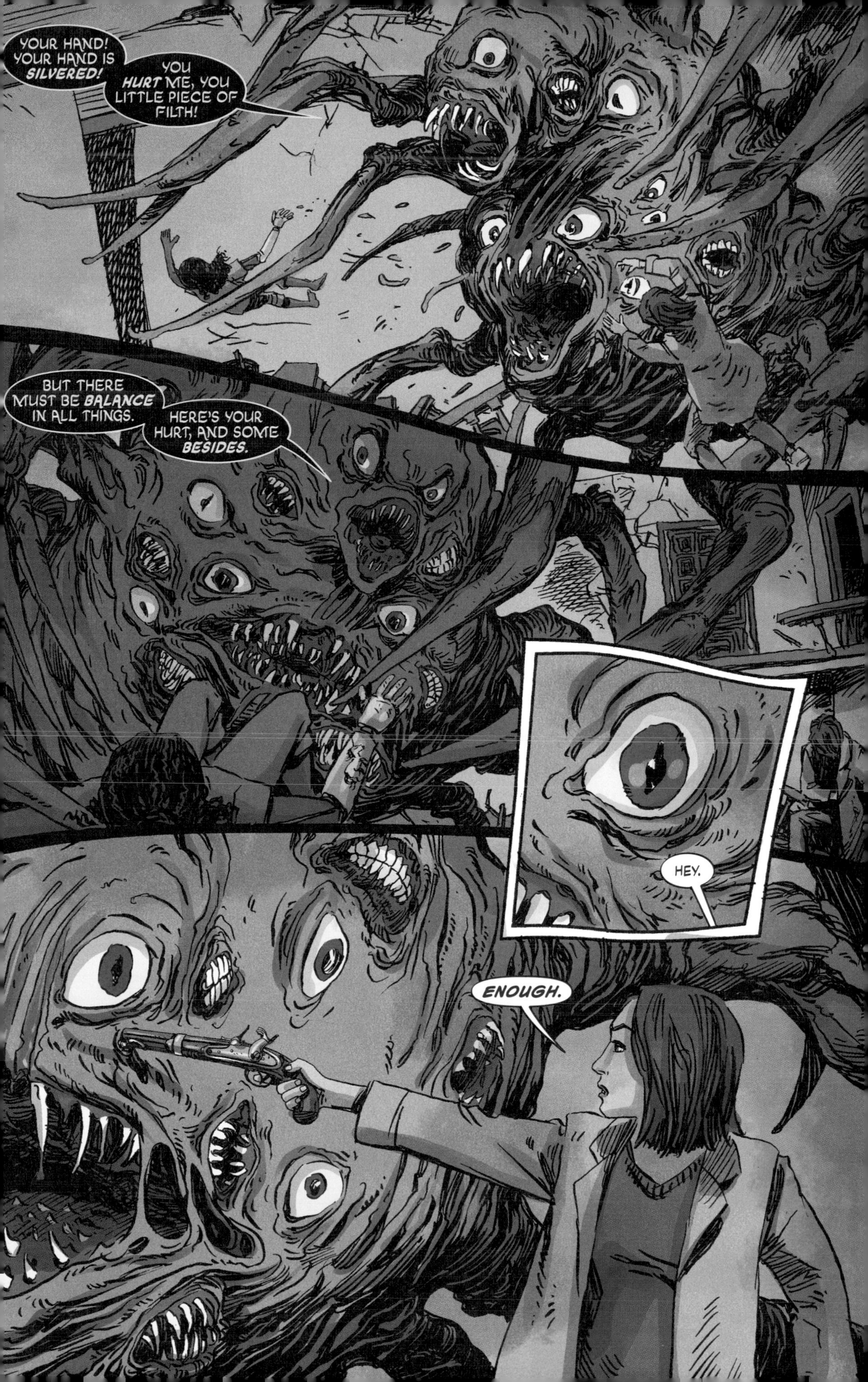
YOUR HAND! YOUR HAND IS SILVERED!
YOU HURT ME, YOU LITTLE PIECE OF FILTH!
BUT THERE MUST BE BALANCE IN ALL THINGS.
HERE'S YOUR HURT, AND SOME BESIDES.
HEY.
ENOUGH.

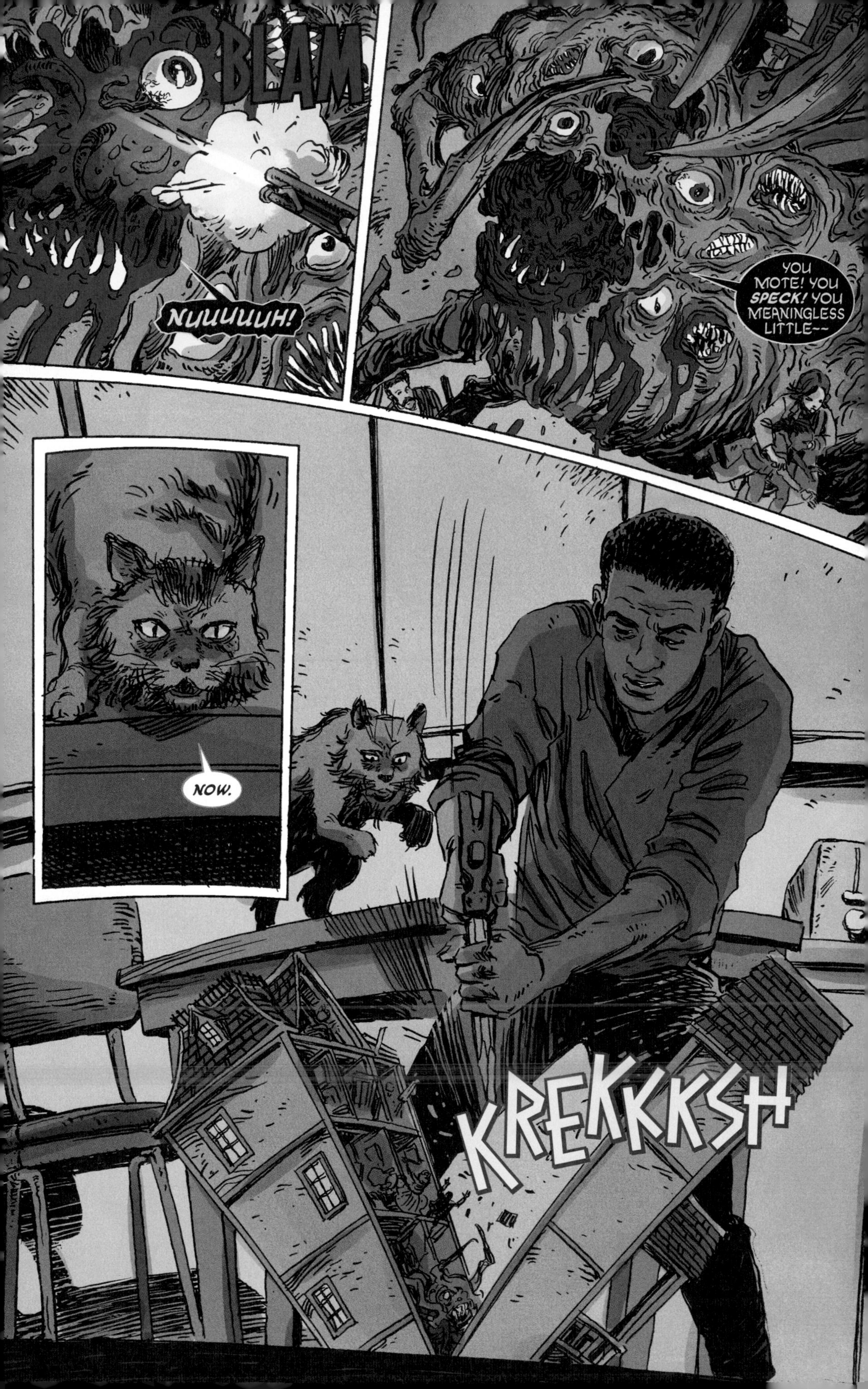
BLAM
NUUUUUH!
YOU MOTE! YOU SPECK! YOU MEANINGLESS LITTLE--
NOW.
KREKKKSH

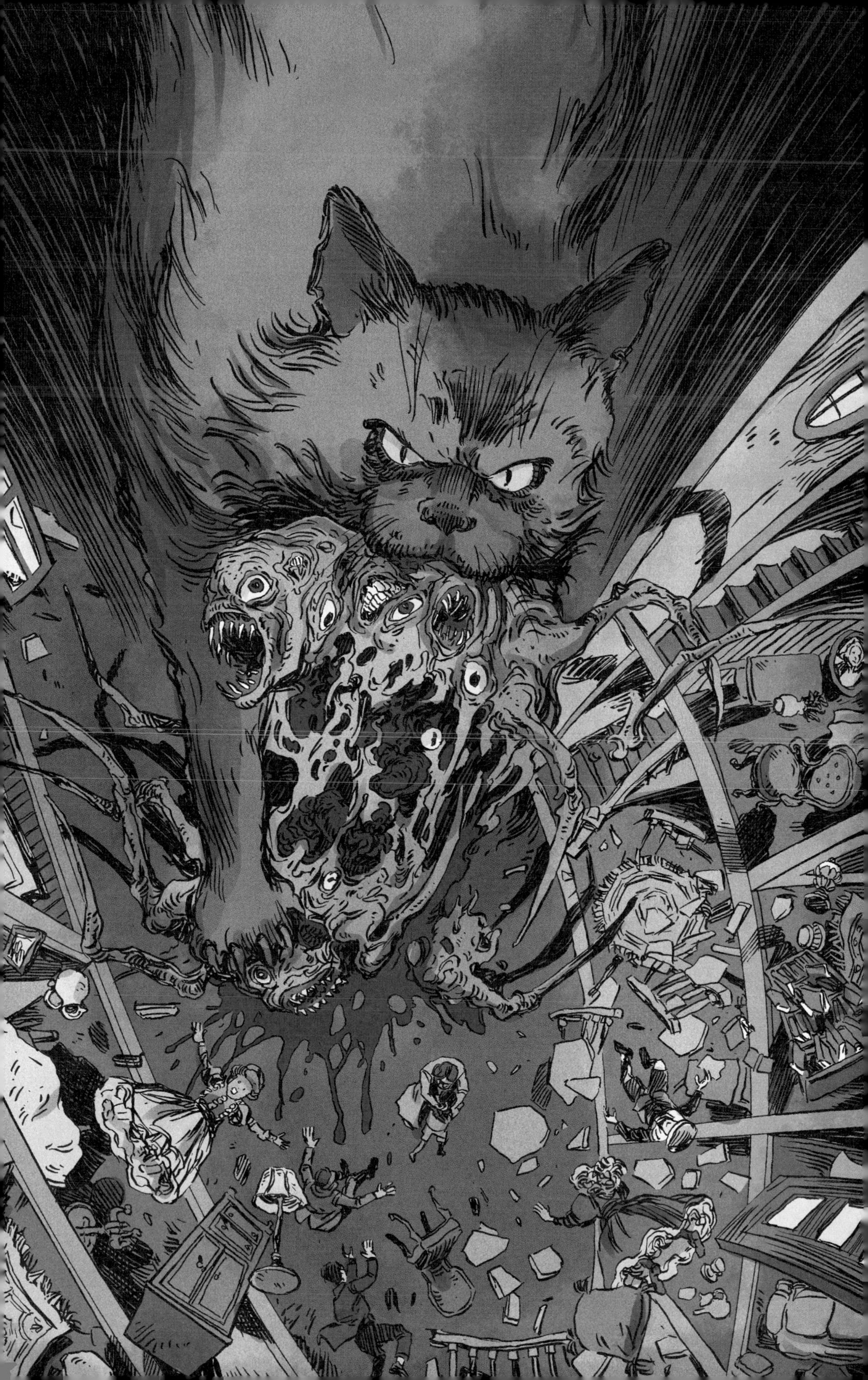

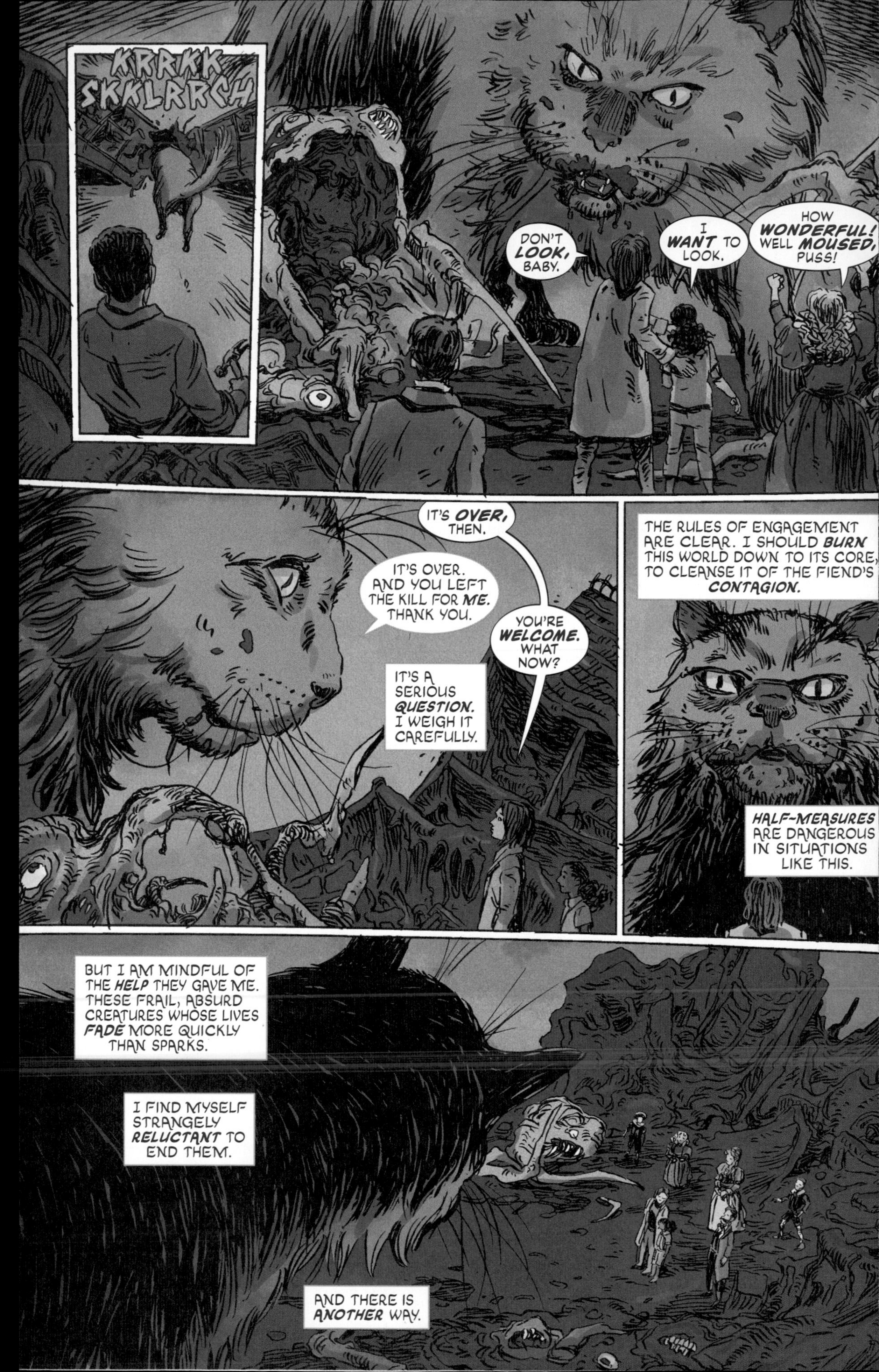

KRRKK SKKLRRCH
DON'T **LOOK,** BABY.
I **WANT** TO LOOK.
HOW **WONDERFUL!** WELL **MOUSED,** PUSS!
IT'S **OVER,** THEN.
IT'S OVER. AND YOU LEFT THE KILL FOR **ME.** THANK YOU.
YOU'RE **WELCOME.** WHAT NOW?
IT'S A SERIOUS **QUESTION.** I WEIGH IT CAREFULLY.
THE RULES OF ENGAGEMENT ARE CLEAR. I SHOULD **BURN** THIS WORLD DOWN TO ITS CORE, TO CLEANSE IT OF THE FIEND'S **CONTAGION.**
HALF-MEASURES ARE DANGEROUS IN SITUATIONS LIKE THIS.
BUT I AM MINDFUL OF THE **HELP** THEY GAVE ME. THESE FRAIL, ABSURD CREATURES WHOSE LIVES **FADE** MORE QUICKLY THAN SPARKS.
I FIND MYSELF STRANGELY **RELUCTANT** TO END THEM.
AND THERE IS **ANOTHER** WAY.

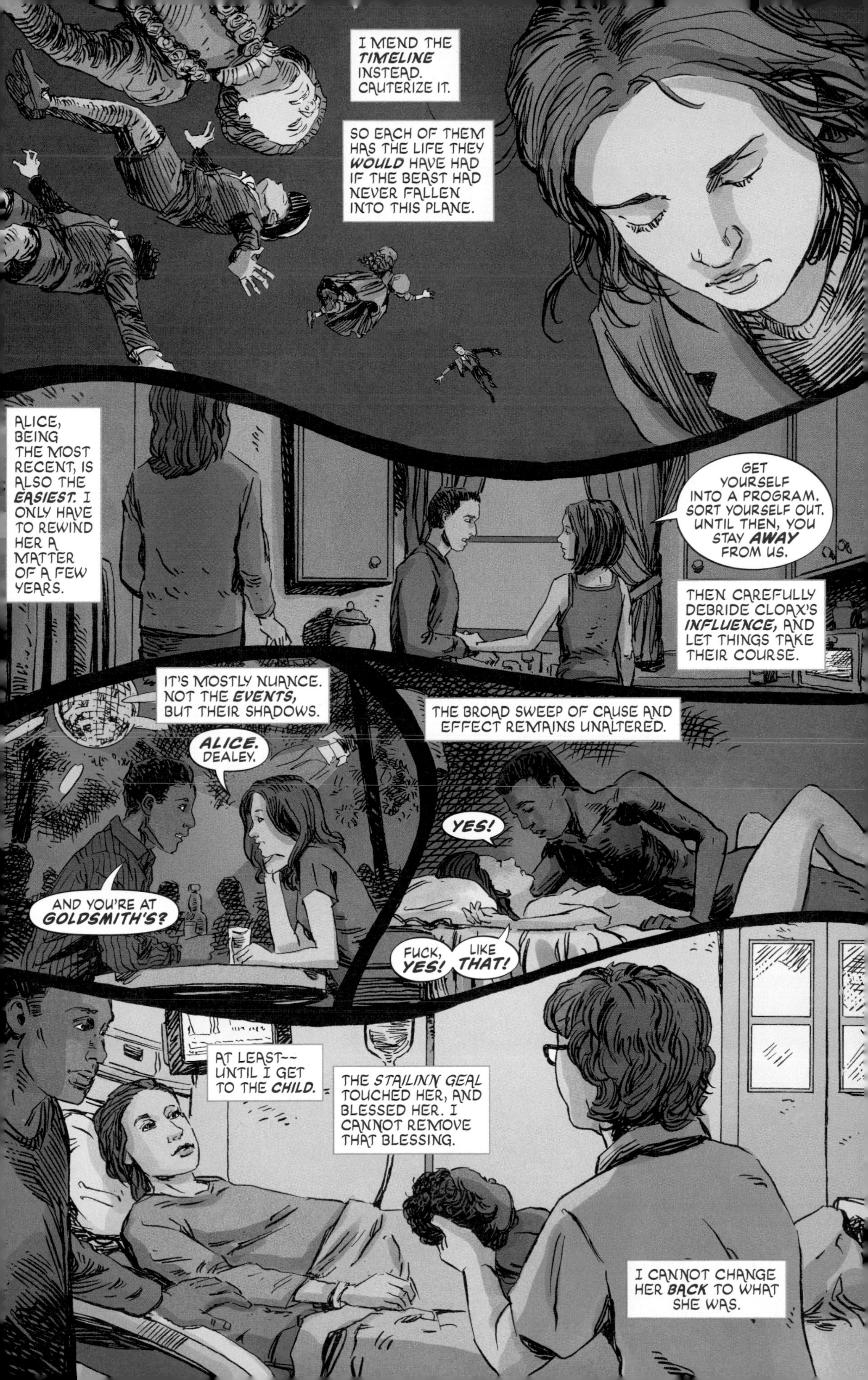
I MEND THE TIMELINE INSTEAD. CAUTERIZE IT.
SO EACH OF THEM HAS THE LIFE THEY WOULD HAVE HAD IF THE BEAST HAD NEVER FALLEN INTO THIS PLANE.
ALICE, BEING THE MOST RECENT, IS ALSO THE EASIEST. I ONLY HAVE TO REWIND HER A MATTER OF A FEW YEARS.
GET YOURSELF INTO A PROGRAM. SORT YOURSELF OUT. UNTIL THEN, YOU STAY AWAY FROM US.
THEN CAREFULLY DEBRIDE CLOAX'S INFLUENCE, AND LET THINGS TAKE THEIR COURSE.
IT'S MOSTLY NUANCE. NOT THE EVENTS, BUT THEIR SHADOWS.
ALICE. DEALEY.
AND YOU'RE AT GOLDSMITH'S?
THE BROAD SWEEP OF CAUSE AND EFFECT REMAINS UNALTERED.
YES!
FUCK, YES!
LIKE THAT!
AT LEAST-- UNTIL I GET TO THE CHILD.
THE STAILINN GEAL TOUCHED HER, AND BLESSED HER. I CANNOT REMOVE THAT BLESSING.
I CANNOT CHANGE HER BACK TO WHAT SHE WAS.

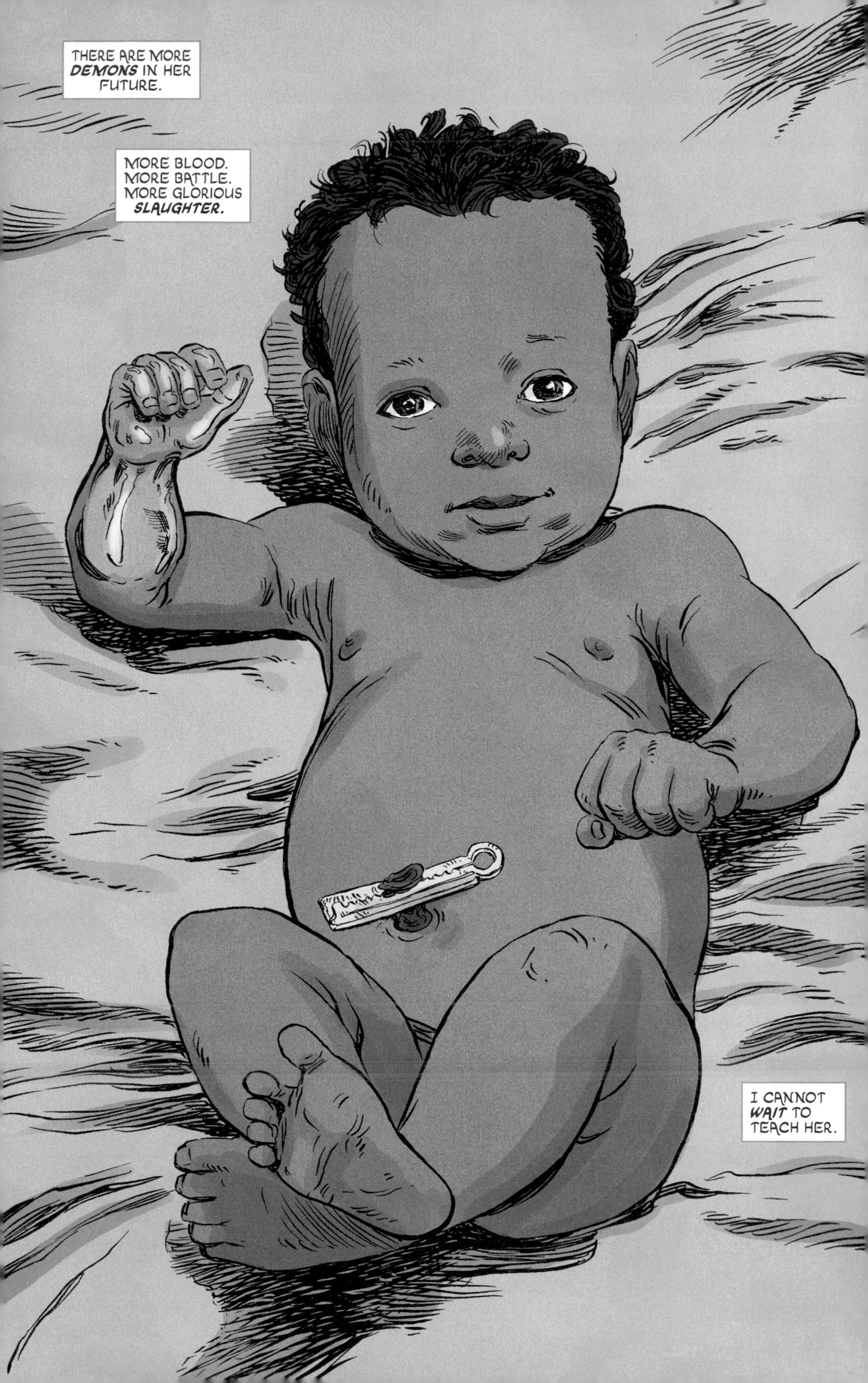
THERE ARE MORE DEMONS IN HER FUTURE.
MORE BLOOD. MORE BATTLE. MORE GLORIOUS SLAUGHTER.
I CANNOT WAIT TO TEACH HER.

VARIANT COVERS

BY **JAY ANACLETO** AND **IVAN NUNES**

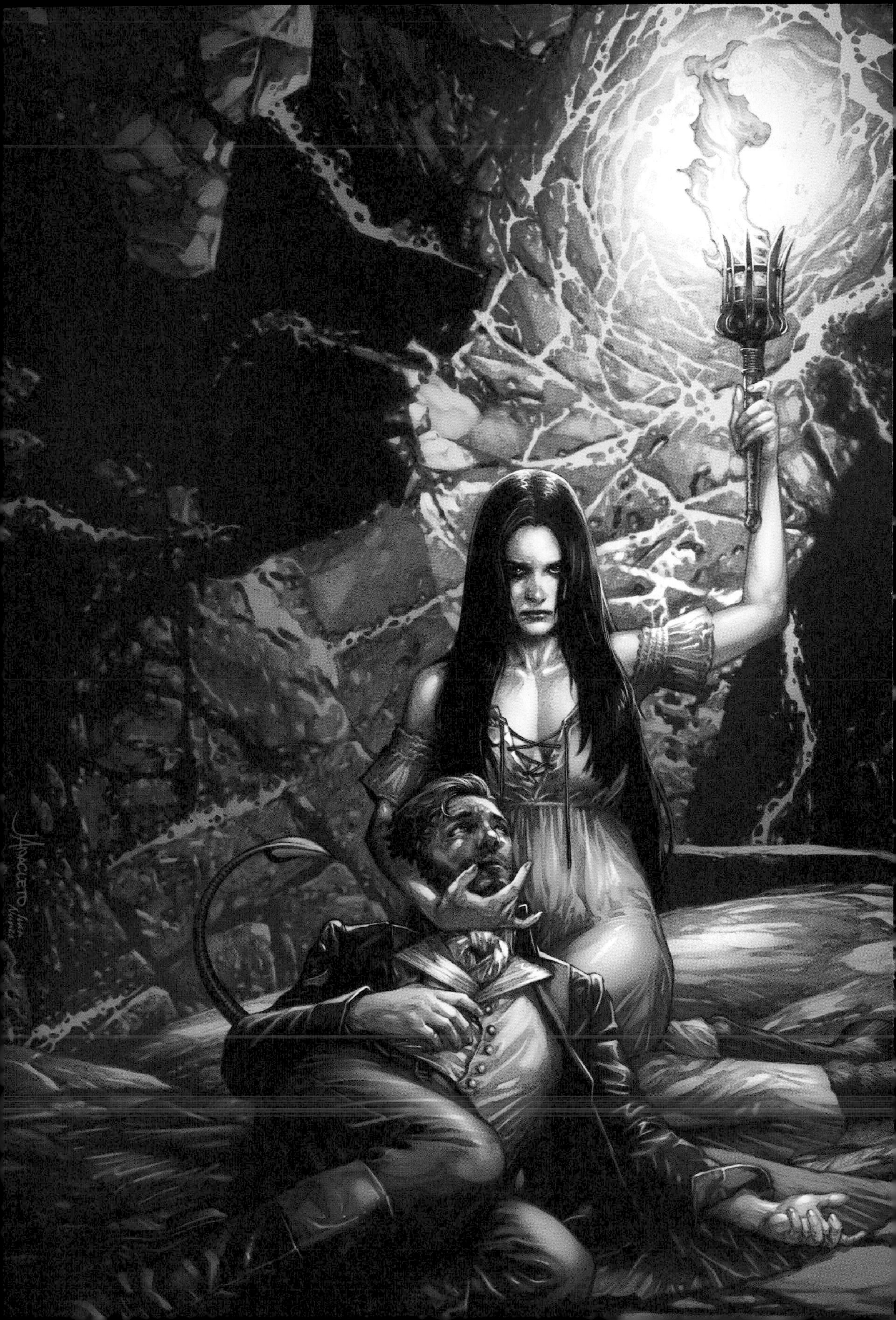

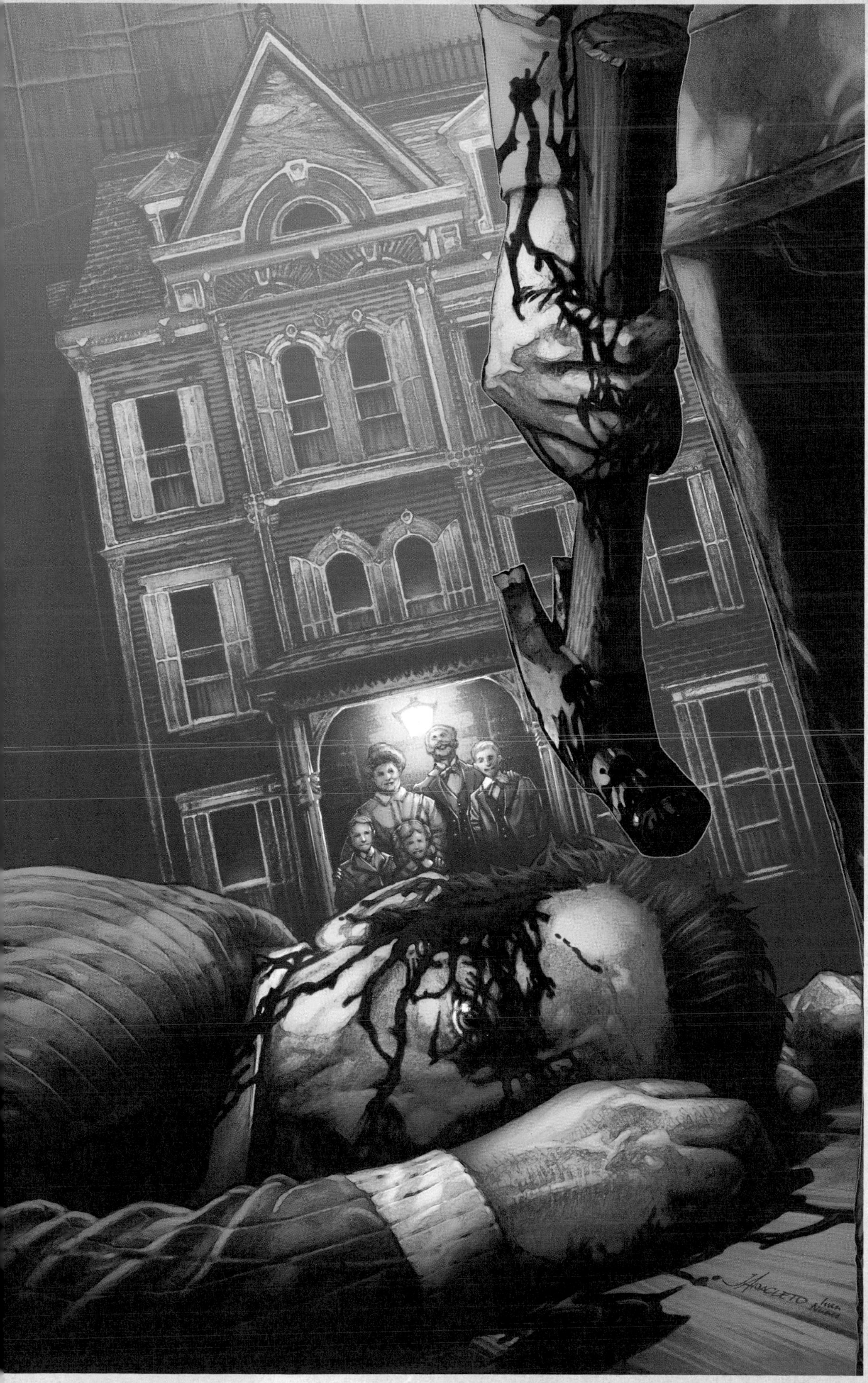

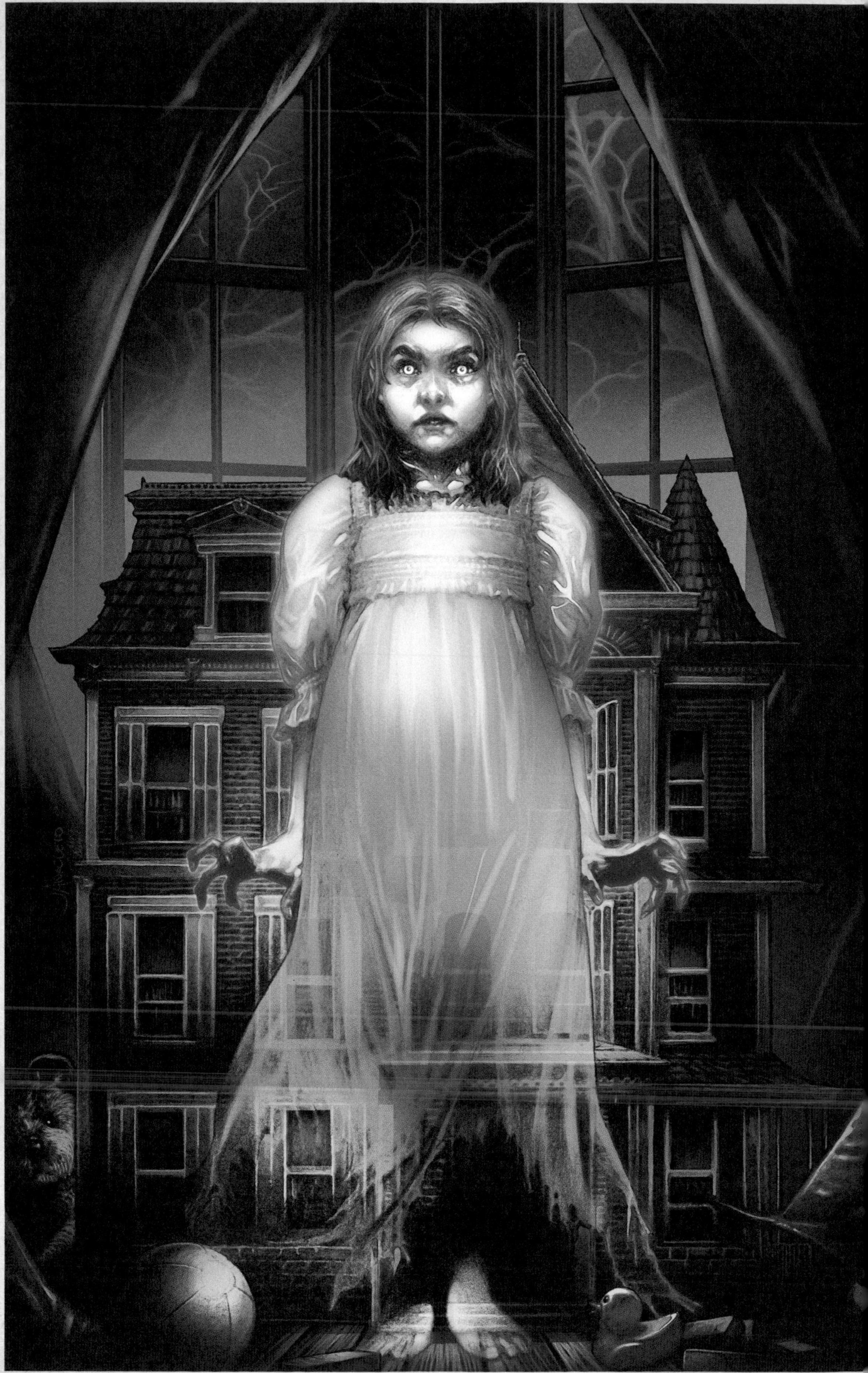

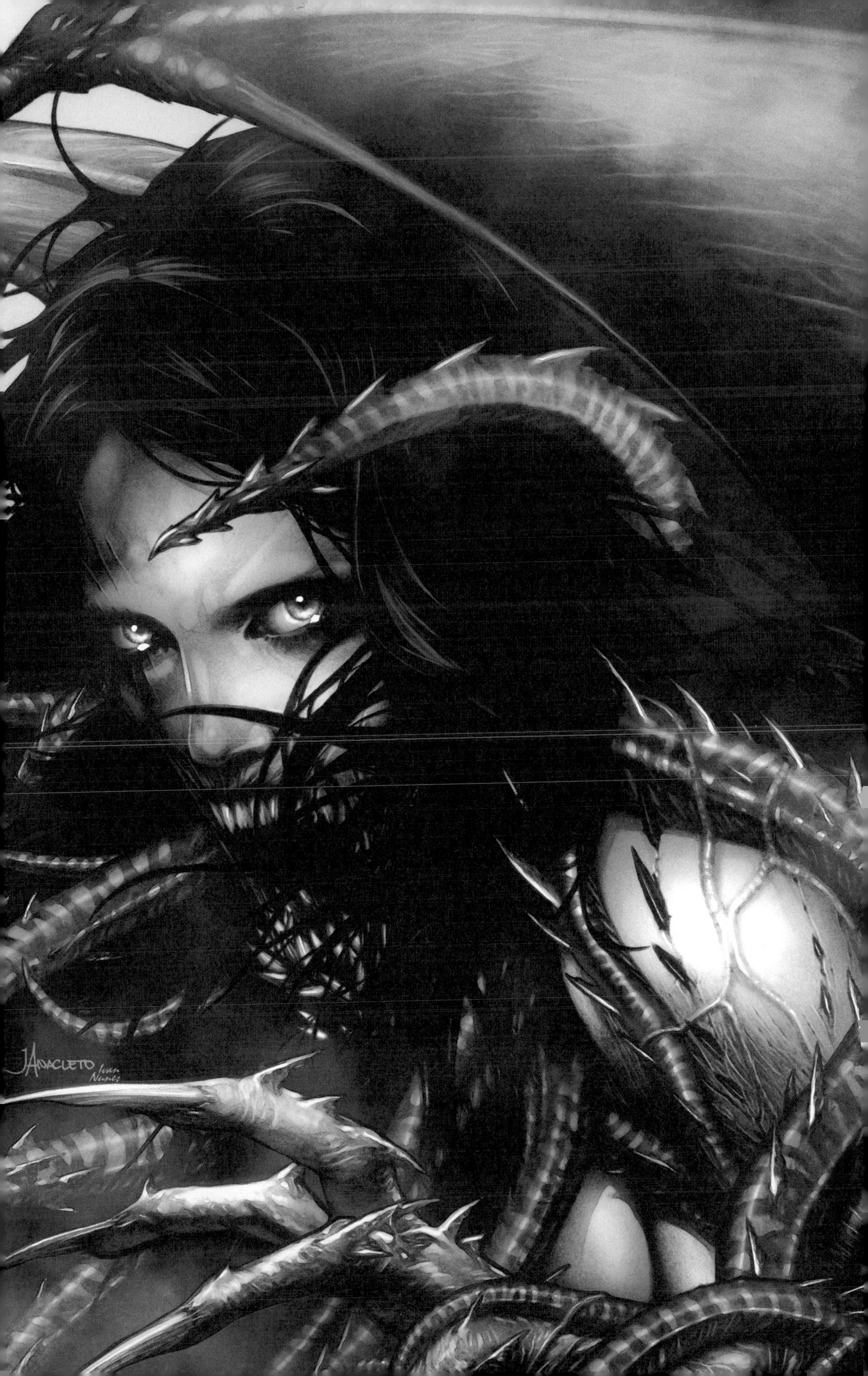
JANACLETO
Ivan Nunes

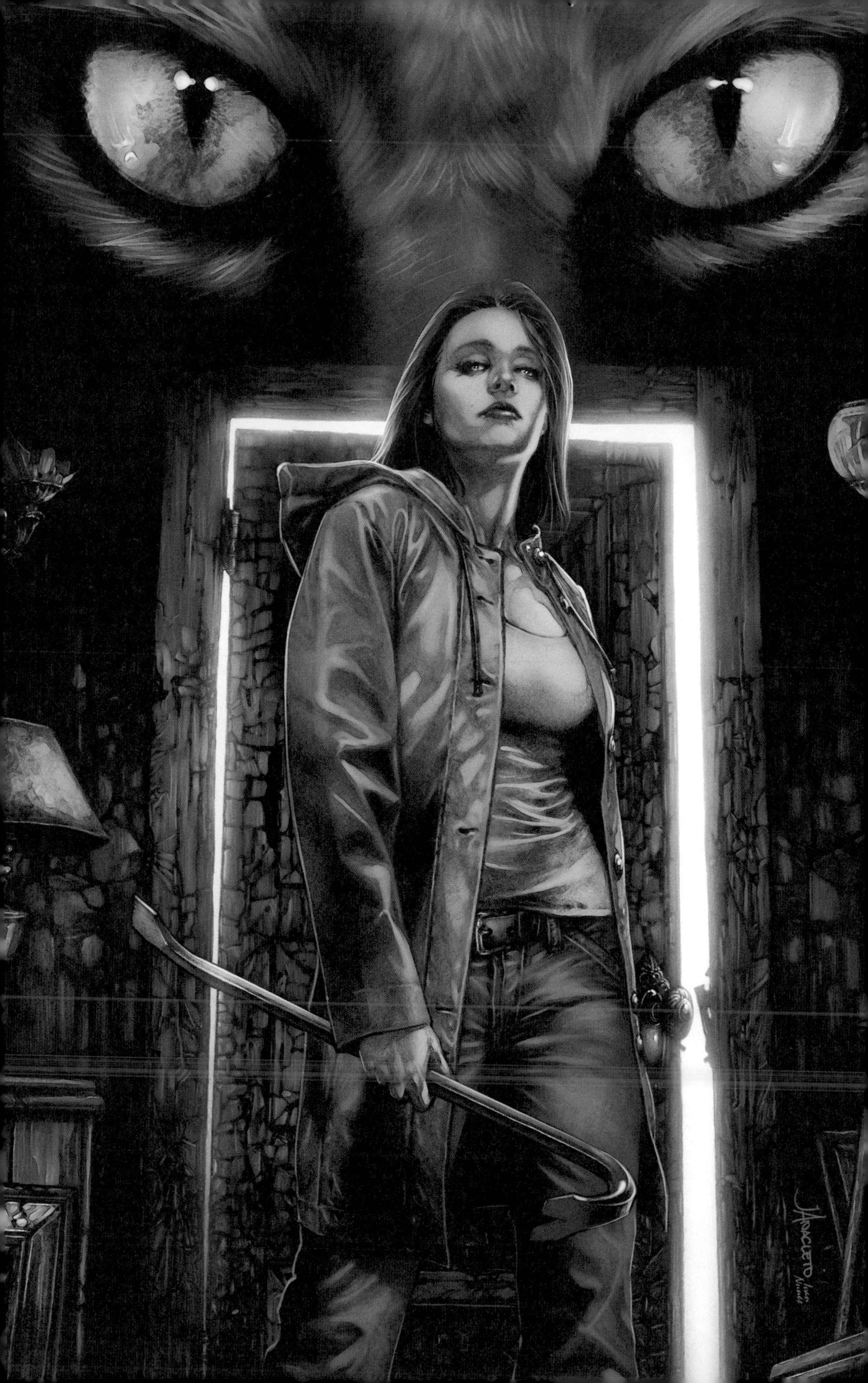

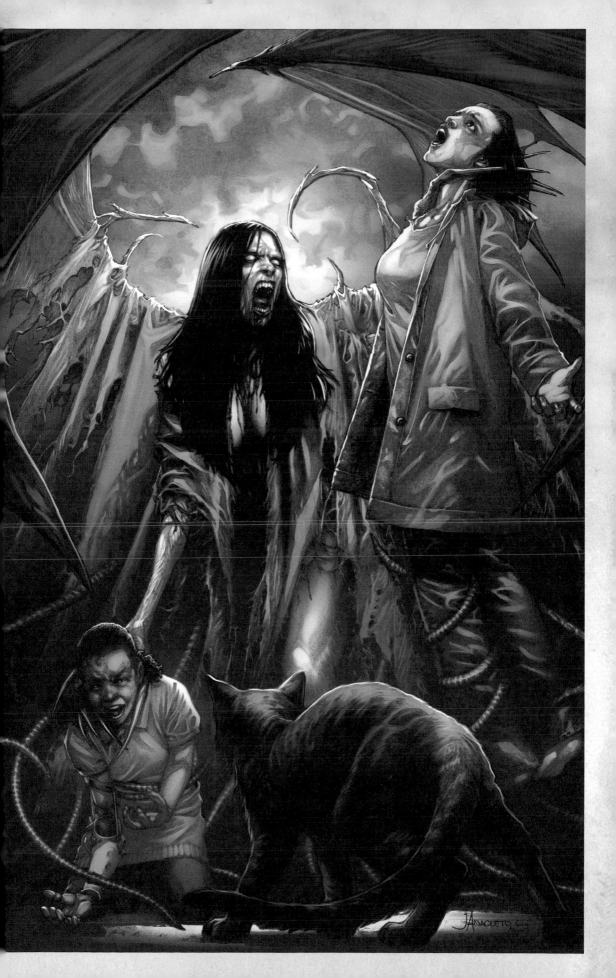

the DOLLHOUSE family

ORIGINAL PITCH BY M.R. CAREY

When Alice Dealey is six years old, a dying great aunt sends her a gift. It's a big, beautiful 19th-century dollhouse, complete with a family of antique dolls made out of cloth and ceramic. It's probably worth a fortune, but it's worth a lot more than that to Alice. She loves the dollhouse, and it becomes her favourite toy.

She's seven the first time she actually goes inside and meets the dollhouse family face-to-face.

Is it a game? A dream? A hallucination? Alice isn't even sure herself where imagination ends and reality begins. But throughout her childhood she spends a lot of time in the lovely little dollhouse, with Cordwainer and Charlotte, Aunt Elizabeth, cousin James, and a girl her own age named Peggy. Whenever she visits them, it's like she's coming for the first time: they never remember her, but always greet her arrival with joy. There's always a place at the table for her. She explores every room of the big, sprawling house, with Peggy as playmate and companion. Well, almost every room. Nobody goes into the attic, ever. There's a thing in the attic, and it's dangerous. The Dollhouse family prefer not to talk about it or acknowledge its existence.

Fast-forward a couple of decades, and a year or so on top of that. Alice is all grown-up, and that childhood make-believe is long forgotten. She's doing okay, too. She works in the veterinary unit at a zoo and runs marathons for charity. That is, until a hideous car accident leaves her with two prosthetic limbs. Alice sinks into a post-traumatic depression, gives up her job, and folds in on herself.

That's when the Dollhouse family returns, both to comfort her and to pass along an offer. The dollhouse is magic, you see. If Alice makes a wish on it, her wish will be granted. She can have her hand and leg back, be as good as new! Insane and impossible though it is, this all feels completely real. Her imaginary childhood friends have come back to be with her. They haven't aged a day. And they're offering her this crazy, wonderful gift.

Alice says no.

Somehow, she can't bring herself to embrace the close-your-eyes-and-make-a-wish logic. Better to assume the family's offer is part of her response to the psychological trauma—a test she's got to pass. She passes it, learning to live with her disabilities and refusing to let them define her.

The dollhouse goes back up into the attic. Alice meets a guy. Gets married. Gets pregnant, has a little girl, names her Margaret after her mother, yada yada. She's back on track, after that huge speed bump.

Until that little girl turns six. That's when the other shoe drops. In the middle of a conversation, something Margaret says triggers a memory in Alice, a powerful sense of déjà vu that becomes a terrifying epiphany. She's heard those words before. In the same voice, out of the same mouth. Margaret is Peggy. The six-year-old child in the dollhouse, who Alice first met thirty years before... that's her DAUGHTER!

And suddenly, Alice feels a fervent, urgent need to find out what the dollhouse is. What is this thing that grants wishes and abolishes time? And what does it mean that her own child is somehow inside there? How is that even possible, when her child is simultaneously out in the real world, being a real person? How could she have met her daughter, in the dollhouse or in visions of the dollhouse, decades before her daughter was even born?

In search of an answer, Alice digs deep into family history, and uncovers a story that starts almost two centuries earlier, during the 1824 Ordnance Survey mapping of Ireland—the most ambitious mapping project in Ireland's long and troubled history. It's a story of tragedies and atrocities across many generations, with the dollhouse as a recurring theme.

Except that it's not a dollhouse. Not really. It didn't become a dollhouse until the family arrived.

And there was always a place at the table for Alice, which she didn't take...

Told out of sequence across the seven decades of Alice's life, with glances into a historical past that continues to impact terrifyingly on the here and now, *The Dollhouse Family* aspires to stand in a tradition that includes *The Haunting of Hill House*, *Ju-On*, and *The Shining*—in the resonant sub-genre of horror that pits vulnerable, fallible human beings against unyielding, malevolent architecture.

RED INK

INTERVIEW WITH **M.R. CAREY** AND **PETER GROSS**

What kind of inherent creepiness do you see in dollhouses?

M.R. CAREY: There's a lot of talk these days about the uncanny valley. Human characters rendered through digital effects are close enough to a human template to feel real, but also just far enough away to seem strange, alienating, and frightening. Dolls have always existed in the uncanny valley. They've got human form, human features, but their immobile faces turn even the warmest of smiles into an unsettling rictus. And, you know, their eyes don't close. They're watching you while you're asleep. Whoever had the idea of turning dolls into toys clearly hadn't thought enough about their use in shamanic magic. Just saying.

PETER GROSS: How does that guy sleep at night? I'm starting to rethink this whole project because I know Mike will write creepy panel descriptions that will get under my skin. My daughter is working in my studio this summer, and while adding rough lettering into my layouts, she literally said over the course of half an hour, "That's sick...That's disgusting...Now I'm scared...Great, now I will never get that image out of my head."

CAREY: That makes me very proud.

What insights can you share about Alice, and what draws her into the world of the dollhouse?

CAREY: We meet Alice as a child, and we get to be alongside her as she grows up. She's a brave, loving, open-hearted kid whose life and personality are bent out of shape by other people's cruelty. But she doesn't ever lie down under that process. She doesn't stop being courageous, and compassionate, and also smart. She's someone who's not out of the fight until she's dead, and maybe not even then.

She receives the dollhouse as a gift, when she's around six years old. And at first, it's a huge comfort to her. Her home life is pretty awful, so she immerses herself in imaginative play in order to get away from it. She meets the dollhouse family, who are awesome. Kind, welcoming, fun. But the house has its rules—and she hasn't met all its residents yet.

The more she learns about the house, and what it's really doing, the higher the stakes get for her. She finds her own way out of the situation, as a child—but then has to go back in again as an adult, because the house is still there, and so is the trap at the heart of it.

GROSS: What can I add to that except that my daughter's name is Alice, and in the series, Alice's father is named Peter. That's creepy as hell to me—maybe not to anyone else. Is Mike sending me a message? Do I need to be worried?

Horror takes many forms—how do you describe the genre and tone of *The Dollhouse Family***?**

GROSS: Generational horror! There's a sense of time and family and history that pervades the book. You might be in the modern world, but you're also just a sideways step away from being surrounded by older things. Obviously you go into this knowing it's going to be "horror," so I think it's up to us to provide a real mood and reality to that so the reader can sink into it and experience Alice's story.

CAREY: Yeah, that real sense of place and time is crucial, I think. And not just historical time, but also deep time. The story starts in the Paleozoic era and finishes...well, let's not get into that right now.

The other thing we're offering is a kind of mystery. A lot of my favorite horror depends on a gradual unfolding of the logic of what's going on—the motivation of the monster (and we do have a monster) and the chain of cause and effect that underlies everything. I'm thinking *Ringu*, *The Orphanage*, *A Tale of Two Sisters*—or in comics, Joe's *Locke & Key*.

What does it mean to you for this series to be a part of Hill House Comics?

CAREY: Well, it wouldn't have existed without Hill House. Joe pitched me his vision for the line last year in London, at a book launch, and told me he was assembling his team of creators. I was very eager to jump on board, and I started roughing out some ideas the same week that I thought might work within the scope of what Joe was describing.

Full disclosure: I'm a huge fan of Joe's work both in comics and in prose. He's a proponent of what I think of as engaged horror. It's genuinely terrifying, but it's written with compassion and insight, so the characters and their dilemmas feel real. I've always loved that approach, and tried to use it myself.

So yeah, I'm proud to be under the Hill House umbrella. This feels like a unique opportunity.

GROSS: I love being involved in the ground floor of something that could be big. I was there at the start of Vertigo, and the launch books for Millarworld, and I hope this will have the same energy and pioneering freedom that those ventures had.

M. R. Carey is a British writer of comic books and prose fiction. He began his career at the independent comics publisher Caliber with *Inferno* and *Doctor Faustus* before making his Vertigo debut with two stories in *The Sandman Presents* series. He went on to become one of Vertigo's most prolific authors, co-creating the Eisner Award–nominated titles *Lucifer*, *Crossing Midnight*, and *The Unwritten*, along with many graphic novels and miniseries and a four-year run on *John Constantine, Hellblazer*. His novels include the Felix Castor series, *The Steel Seraglio* (written in collaboration with his wife, Linda, and their daughter, Louise), and *The Girl with All the Gifts*, for which he also wrote the BAFTA-nominated movie screenplay. His novel *The Book of Koli* was released in April 2020.

Peter Gross is the co-creator (with writer Mike Carey) of the multi-Eisner Award–nominated Vertigo series *The Unwritten* and the co-creator (with writer Mark Millar) of *American Jesus* from Image. He is also the illustrator of two of Vertigo's longest-running series: *Lucifer* and *The Books of Magic*, and he suspects that he might be the only artist/writer who had work published for Vertigo in every year of the imprint's existence. He lives in Minneapolis, Minnesota, with his wife, Jeanne McGee, their daughter, Alice, and a cat who looks suspiciously like Tommy Taylor's cat, Mingus.

Vince Locke began his comics work in 1986 illustrating *Deadworld*, a zombie horror comic that became an underground hit. Since then, he has worked on numerous comics as artist and inker, including *The Sandman*, *Witchcraft: La Terreur*, and *A History of Violence*. He has also gained notoriety by creating ultra-violent watercolor paintings used as album covers for Cannibal Corpse, and has provided illustrations for author Caitlín R. Kiernan's short story collections *Frog Toes and Tentacles* and *Tales from the Woeful Platypus*. Recent projects include *Peripheral* with Dan Schaffer and an adaptation of Lucio Fulci's *The House by the Cemetery*. He may one day write something of his own.

Cristiane or **Cris Peter** has been working as a colorist for 20 years, on almost 250 titles, and was nominated for an Eisner Award in 2012. As a writer she worked on the *CMYK* anthology for Vertigo, *Use of Color* (published only in Brazil), and her own creative projects. Cris also likes practicing painting and illustrating, and teaching about digital coloring. You can follow her @coloristdiaries on Instagram or view her online portfolio at crispeterdigitalcolors.com.

One of the industry's most versatile and accomplished letterers, **Todd Klein** has been lettering comics since 1977 and has won numerous Eisner and Harvey awards for his work. Besides being a mainstay on such Vertigo powerhouses as *Fables*, *The Invisibles*, and *The Unwritten*, he has also lettered nearly all of Neil Gaiman's DC-published titles, including *The Sandman*, *Black Orchid*, *Death: The High Cost of Living*, *Death: The Time of Your Life*, and *The Books of Magic*.